KT-166-698

Frommer's
4th Edition

San Diego

by Elizabeth Hansen

Assisted by Suzanne Osborne

Macmillan • USA

ABOUT THE AUTHOR

Long-time San Diego resident Elizabeth Hansen is also the author of *Frommer's Comprehensive Guide to Australia, Frommer's New Zealand from $45 a Day, The Woman's Travel Guide to New Zealand,* and *Bed & Breakfast New Zealand.* Elizabeth regularly writes magazine articles and gives illustrated presentations on her hometown. When not traveling, the author and her husband, Richard Adams, live in La Jolla.

MACMILLAN TRAVEL

A Simon & Schuster Macmillan Company
1633 Broadway
New York, NY 10019

ISBN 0-02-860862-3
ISSN 1047-787X

Editor: Robin Michaelson
Map Editor: Douglas Stallings
Design by Michele Laseau
Digital cartography by Jim Moore and Ortelius Design

SPECIAL SALES

Manufactured in the United States of America

Contents

List of Maps

For my mother, Katherine Nelson, with much love.

ACKNOWLEDGMENTS

I'm very grateful to Shelby Gordon of the San Diego North County Convention and Visitors Bureau and Laurie Allison of the San Diego Convention and Visitors Bureau for the assistance they provided. I'd also like to thank Janine Rojas and Ken David of Carpenter, Matthews and Walcher. And most of all I am indebted to my sister Jinny and niece Laurie who—almost three decades ago—made the cross-country trek to San Diego with me and helped me begin to find my place here.

AN INVITATION TO THE READER

In researching this book, I discovered many wonderful places—hotels, restaurants, shops, and more. I'm sure you'll find others. Please tell me about them, so I can share the information with your fellow travelers in upcoming editions. If you were disappointed with a recommendation, I want to know that, too. Please write to:

Elizabeth Hansen
Frommer's San Diego, 4th Edition
c/o Macmillan Travel
1633 Broadway
New York, NY 10019

AN ADDITIONAL NOTE

Please be advised that travel information is subject to change at any time—and this is especially true of prices. We therefore suggest that you write or call ahead for confirmation when making your travel plans. The authors, editors, and publisher cannot be held responsible for the experiences of readers while traveling. Your safety is important to us, however, so we encourage you to stay alert and be aware of your surroundings. Keep a close eye on cameras, purses, and wallets, all favorite targets of thieves and pickpockets.

WHAT THE SYMBOLS MEAN

✪ Frommer's Favorites

Hotels, restaurants, attractions, and entertainment you should not miss.

Ⓢ Super-Special Values

Hotels and restaurants that offer great value for your money.

The following abbreviations are used for credit cards:

AE	American Express	EU	Eurocard
CB	Carte Blanche	JCB	Japan Credit Bank
DC	Diners Club	MC	MasterCard
DISC	Discover	V	Visa
ER	enRoute		

Introducing San Diego

If you've never been to San Diego or your last visit was more than a few years ago, my hometown holds some surprises for you. It's grown up. San Diego is no longer just a laid-back navy town—its coming-of-age includes avant-garde architecture, sophisticated dining options, and world-class tourist facilities.

You'll notice the architecture right away. If you're driving to San Diego from the north, you'll pass the eye-catching Hyatt Regency La Jolla alongside Interstate 5. Near this striking neoclassical structure, the snow-white, multi-turreted Mormon temple seems an unlikely neighbor. If you're flying in, look out the window as you approach Lindbergh Field to note the changes, such as high-rise office towers and hotels in the downtown area adjacent to San Diego Bay. Since the flight path goes right over downtown, you may sometimes feel that you're going to land on the rooftops.

Today, approximately 1.1 million people live in San Diego, making it the sixth-largest city in the United States (after New York, Los Angeles, Chicago, Houston, and Philadelphia). While the city's population keeps increasing, I'm happy to report that San Diego hasn't completely lost its small-town ambience, and the area's Hispanic heritage and culture have been preserved.

1 Frommer's Favorite San Diego Experiences

- **Strolling Through the Gaslamp Quarter:** Victorian commercial buildings that fill a 16^1/$_2$-block area will make you think you've stepped back in time. The buildings, right in the heart of downtown, are beautifully restored and house some of the city's most popular shops, restaurants, and nightspots.
- **Shopping and Sipping Margaritas in Bazaar del Mundo:** Old Mexico is alive and well in San Diego's colorful Bazaar del Mundo. The lively strains of mariachi music add to the atmosphere.
- **Listening to Free Organ Recitals in Balboa Park on Sunday:** Even if you usually don't like organ music, you might enjoy these outdoor concerts and the crowds they draw—San Diegans with their parents, their children, their dogs. The music, enhanced

with commentary by the organist, runs the gamut from classical to contemporary. Concerts start at 2pm.

- **Relaxing with Afternoon Tea at the U.S. Grant Hotel or the Horton Grand:** A genteel tradition in San Diego, the custom of afternoon tea is at its most elegant at the U.S. Grant and quite cozy at the Horton Grand. Take your pick.

- **Taking the Ferry to Coronado:** This 15-minute ride gets you out onto San Diego Harbor and provides some of the best views of the city. The ferry runs every hour from the Broadway Pier, so you can tour Coronado on foot or by bike or trolley and return whenever you please.

- **Riding on the San Diego Trolley to Mexico:** The trip costs a mere $1.75 and only takes 40 minutes, and the clean, quick trolleys are fun in their own right.

- **Wandering Through Horton Plaza:** This place has a whimsy and an architectural appeal that blends many styles, colors, and myriad shops. It's conducive to wandering—created purposefully to keep you from getting directly from point A to point B.

- **Listening to Jazz at Croce's:** Ideally located in the center of downtown in a historic Gaslamp Quarter building, Croce's celebrates the life of musician Jim Croce and showcases the city's jazz musicians.

- **Watching the Sun Set Over the Ocean:** It's a free and memorable experience. My favorite sunset-watching spots include the Mission Beach and Pacific Beach boardwalks and the beach in Coronado in front of the Hotel del Coronado. At La Jolla's Windansea beach, it's a nightly neighborhood event where folks wander down to the water, wine glass in hand.

- **Drinking Coffee at a La Jolla Sidewalk Cafe:** San Diego offers a plethora of places to enjoy lattes, espressos, and cappuccinos, but the coffeehouses in La Jolla serve up a special panache. For my favorites, see the "Coffeehouses with Character" box in Chapter 6.

- **Enjoying Performing Arts Outdoors:** During the summer, dramas, comedies, and musicals take place on the Festival Stage at the Old Globe Theatre in Balboa Park and in the amphitheater atop Mt. Helix in La Mesa. The symphony plays a pops series on the waterfront in Embarcadero Marina Park South.

- **Walking Along the Water:** The city offers walkers several great places to stroll. One of my favorites, along the waterfront from the Convention Center to the Maritime Museum, affords views of aircraft carriers, tuna seiners, and sailboats.

- **Visiting the "Lobster Lady" in Puerto Nuevo:** South of the border, they serve lobster with rice, beans, and tortillas, and it's delicious. (See Chapter 12 for details.)

- **Purchasing Just-Picked Produce at a Farmers' Market:** On various days, markets throughout the area sell the bountiful harvest of San Diego County. For a complete schedule, see Chapter 9.

- **Floating Up, Up, and Away Over North County:** Hot air balloons carry champagne-sipping passengers over the golf courses and luxury homes north of the city. These rides are especially enjoyable at sunset.

- **Going to the Movies San Diego–Style:** Imagine sitting on the deck of the world's oldest merchant ship afloat, watching a film projected on the "screen-sail," or floating on a raft in a huge indoor pool while a movie is shown on the wall. Only in San Diego!

- **Watching the Grunion Run:** These tiny sardine-shaped fish spawn on San Diego beaches between March and August, and the locals love to be there. To know the date of the next such event, pick up a free tide chart at a surf shop or consult the daily newspaper.

- **Picnicking in a Park:** Our nearly perfect climate invites casual outdoor dining. Favorite spots include Balboa Park (I like the lawn next to the reflecting pool), Embarcadero Marina Park (near Seaport Village), and Ellen Browning Scripps Park overlooking the ocean in La Jolla.

2 The City Today

It's a real joy to live in San Diego. We've always had great weather and beaches, but now we have many "grown-up" options, too. This change resulted in part from the influx of high-tech (especially biotech) industry to San Diego. We've also become a "brainy" community, currently home to a half-dozen colleges and universities. The new arrivals contribute to the growth of the performing arts and support sophisticated dining, nightlife, and shopping.

Completion of the Convention Center, which took nearly 3 years to build, has also made a tremendous difference. The Center attracts several hundred meetings, conventions, exhibits, and trade shows per year. Its proximity to the Gaslamp Quarter contributed to the Quarter's rebirth. Now when I wander past the chic restaurants and hot nightspots along Fourth and Fifth avenues, it's hard to remember how run-down this area used to be.

Some things about San Diego, however, haven't changed. The people who live here still have an independent nature. We don't follow trends, choosing instead to "do our own thing." And we're not "rabid" fans of spectator sports. The city did take notice—big time—when the Chargers went to the Super Bowl, but didn't pay much attention to America's Cup '95. The truth is that most San Diegans are too busy in-line skating, cycling, sailing, and surfing to have time for professional sports teams.

Our enthusiasm for active pursuits goes hand-in-hand with an interest in being healthy (and a propensity toward vanity). It's not just a rumor that some of us embrace exotic herbs, holistic remedies, and nontraditional therapies at a rate unknown in other parts of the country. Large numbers also eschew red meat, and smokers are herded into smaller and smaller areas. San Diego County is home to several spas (I've described a few in Chapter 11).

I'm not alone in my affection for San Diego. The vast majority of residents love it here, which is why we call our hometown "America's Finest City." Since most people want to keep things just the way they are, it isn't hard to get "no growth" ballot issues passed. This doesn't help our economy, already weakened by cuts in defense spending, but it prevents something we all fear—"Los Angelization." Preventing Los Angelization means controlling smog and other forms of pollution and the sprawl of housing developments, which consume open space. A recent ballot issue dealt with setting aside a certain amount of open space for each residential tract so that the county won't become an endless sea of cookie-cutter houses. We're constantly debating whether or not to move Lindbergh Field, because it can't expand in its current location. Some people think there should be a binational airport just north of our border with Mexico; other groups favor converting the Miramar military airport to civilian use. Frankly, more San Diegans want to know which Northern Italian restaurant is "in" this week. The location of the airport is of secondary importance, because few of us have any intention of leaving.

3   A Look at the Past

Dateline

- **1542** San Diego Bay discovered by a Portuguese explorer, who names it San Miguel.
- **1602** Don Sebastián Vizcaíno rediscovers the bay, naming it

continues

San Diego is to the West Coast what Jamestown, Virginia, is to the East Coast. João Rodrigues Cabrilho (Juan Rodríguez Cabrillo in Spanish), a Portuguese-born explorer serving the Spanish crown, sailed into what is now San Diego Bay in 1542, 50 years after Christopher Columbus spotted land on the eastern side of the continent. Naming his discovery San Miguel, Cabrilho stayed six days, and departed. No one returned for 60 years—until 1602, when Don Sebastián Vizcaíno, a Spanish explorer, sailed into the bay and renamed it in honor of his flagship and his favorite saint, San Diego de Alcala.

Because what now is called Point Loma hid the bay from the view of passing ships, no one stumbled upon it again for another 150 years. Finally, in 1769, the Spanish took steps to settle the area. They launched expeditions by sea and land: One arrival, Fr. Junípero Serra, a 58-year-old priest, would leave his mark on San Diego forever. He said the first mass here on July 16, 1769, which is considered the birthday of San Diego, and he established the first of the mission churches—a small adobe chapel—on a hill overlooking what is now Old Town.

The chain of missions would eventually number 21, strung along the California coast 30 miles, or a day's journey, apart. A fort known as the Presidio was built on the hilltop, and a fledgling community developed around it. Despite crop failures in the arid land and attacks by neighboring Kumeyaays, San Diego survived. In 1775, the first Spanish baby was born here, and the town grew as settlers moved north from Mexico.

Spanish rule ended in California the same year it did in Mexico: 1822. By then the town had moved down the hill from the fort into the area now known as Old Town. A Mexican flag flew here until 1846, when the first American flag was raised in the plaza. California became a state in 1850.

The arrival of Alonzo Horton in 1867 started a new era of prosperity. Horton, who had profited in the California Gold Rush, was determined to turn San Diego into a great city. He recognized that the downtown area needed to be closer to the waterfront so goods could be easily shipped and received. He built a wharf (about where the Convention Center is now), bought up adjacent land (for about 27¢ an acre), sold off lots, and constructed commercial buildings. The city government moved to New Town in 1871. The arrival of the railroad in 1885 and the discovery of gold in the back country in 1869 further aided the community's growth. In 1888 San Diego's population hit 40,000; by 1890, Old Town had withered.

Two better-known entrepreneurs of this period were Elisha Babcock and H. L. Story, businessmen from the East who initially came to these parts for the curative climate and rabbit

San Diego de Alcala.

- **1769** Fr. Junipero Serra establishes first mission.
- **1822** Spanish rule ends.
- **1825–31** San Diego is the capital of California under Mexican rule.
- **1846** American flag flies for the first time; first Mormons arrive.
- **1867** Alonzo Horton founds New Town.
- **1868** 1,400 acres are set aside for Balboa Park.
- **1872** Great fire in Old Town.
- **1885** Railway arrives.
- **1888** Hotel del Coronado, equipped with "Edison electric light," opens.
- **1901** Naval military base established.
- **1915** City hosts Panama-California Exposition.
- **1916** San Diego Zoo founded.
- **1927** Charles Lindbergh tests the *Spirit of St. Louis* and plans historic transatlantic flight.
- **1935** City hosts California Pacific International Exposition;

continues

Old Globe Theatre built.

- **1941–45** Population in area doubles during WWII; military takes over Balboa Park.
- **1948** Palomar Observatory opens.
- **1969** San Diego–Coronado Bay Bridge opens; seven women invade the "gentlemen only" Grant Grill.
- **1971** San Diego becomes California's second-largest city.
- **1982** First baby condor born at San Diego Zoo.
- **1987** San Diego Yacht Club wins the America's Cup (from Australia).
- **1989** San Diego Convention Center opens, sparking a rebirth of downtown.
- **1990** Economic recession hits.
- **1992** San Diego hosts (and retains) America's Cup.
- **1995** San Diego Chargers play in the Super Bowl; San Diego hosts America's Cup; first U.S. warm-weather Olympic training center opens in Chula Vista.

continues

hunting. Once here, they decided to build a grand hotel, and in 1888, only 11 months after construction began, they opened the beautiful Hotel del Coronado, which to this day remains the largest wooden oceanside resort hotel in the world (see "A Hotel with History: Scenes from the Hotel del Coronado" in Chapter 5). Thomas Edison himself had overseen the installation of the hotel's newfangled lighting system, and each room came with the notice that it was "equipped with Edison electric light" and the admonition "Do not attempt to light with a match. The use of electricity is in no way harmful to your health." The town of Coronado was incorporated in 1890 and still remains a municipality separate from San Diego.

Another successful businessman, George Marston, came to San Diego with his family from Wisconsin in 1870 and started working in Alonzo Horton's hotel. He went on to found a successful department store, the Marston Company, which was a local landmark until it became part of the Broadway department stores in the 1960s.

Marston believed "people in this workaday world should not only have a living wage but opportunities for a great measure of health, comfort, and beauty," and he turned his enormous humanitarian and environmentalist energies, not to mention his money and clout, toward the creation of Balboa Park, Presidio Park, the Serra Museum, the San Diego Historical Society, and the Anza-Borrego Desert State Park.

In the late 1800s, San Francisco millionaire and sugar magnate John D. Spreckels became captivated by San Diego and Coronado and began investing in the area. In 1906, after the San Francisco earthquake, he made it his home. Spreckels, whose name is scattered on buildings throughout San Diego and Coronado to this day, soon owned most everything of value in both towns, including the Hotel del Coronado; two newspapers; a bank; a hotel; a railway; and the ferry, trolley, and water systems. His vast entrepreneurial skills, energy, and financial wherewithal contributed greatly to the cities' growth, beauty, and appeal over the next 20 years.

An architect who made his mark on the growing city, Irving Gill, arrived from Syracuse, New York, in 1893. Gill, influenced by the Spanish missions, built or remodeled more than 200 houses and buildings in San Diego County, and about 75 still exist; some can be seen in the Hillcrest section of San Diego and in La Jolla. At a time when ornamentation was the architectural mode, Gill set out to build houses that were "simple, plain, and substantial as a boulder," thinking it best to "leave the ornamentation to nature, who will tone it with lichens, chisel it with storms, make it gracious and friendly with vines and flower shapes as she does the stone in the meadow." He aligned himself with simplicity in an age of extravagance. Although he died in near obscurity in 1936, he is revered today.

■ **1996** San Diego hosts the Republican National Convention.

In 1868, San Diego, with a population barely topping 2,000, set aside 1,400 acres for what would become this nation's second planned city park. Work began in 1903, and in 1910 the park was named Balboa, after the explorer who was the first European to venture through the Isthmus of Panama. In 1915 the city decided to host the Panama-California Exposition, similar to a world's fair, and Bertram Goodhue from New York was called in to design the buildings for it in Balboa Park. Goodhue, quite different from Irving Gill, imagined architecture that would provide "illusion rather than reality," and he created a fantasy city that blended Old Spain and Moorish, Aztec, Mexican, and even Asian influences.

The resulting highly ornamented buildings had a magical effect that left a lasting mark on San Diego architecture. Today the buildings house many of the museums in the park, which is the nation's second-largest museum complex (after the Smithsonian Institution in Washington, D.C.).

The world-famous San Diego Zoo was founded in Balboa Park in 1916 with animals that had been imported for the Panama-California Exposition. The director of the zoo, who happened to be the city health inspector, simply quarantined the animals and wouldn't let them leave.

The zoo would also become a botanical garden, which 20 years earlier would have seemed nonsense. Southern California had been called "the most undesirable, useless land in God's realm" for its barrenness. Not one tree was native to San Diego, but Kate Sessions, a teacher from San Francisco who was also a horticulturist, set about to change the nature of things in 1892. She had come to the area with the dream of opening a plant nursery (which still exists), and in exchange for the space to do so, she promised the city she would plant 100 trees a year in Balboa Park and 300 elsewhere in San Diego. To that end, she traveled around the world looking for species that would grow in a dry climate and so created one of the country's lushest cities.

In the 1920s, San Diego became known as an aviation center, and Charles Lindbergh chose the city's Ryan Corporation to manufacture the *Spirit of St. Louis* in which he made his historic transatlantic solo flight.

In 1935 the city hosted the California Pacific International Exposition in Balboa Park. The internationally acclaimed Old Globe Theatre was built for the event, and each day shortened versions of 10 Shakespearean plays were presented. Among the exhibits, a new

Seuss on the Loose

In 1928, when he first visited San Diego, 24-year-old Theodor Seuss Geisel was working as a cartoonist in New York City. Enchanted by the balmy coastal village of La Jolla, he vowed to move there someday while he was "still young enough to enjoy it." He spent frequent summer holidays here, but it took 20 years before he and his wife built their pink Spanish-style stucco home around an old observation tower atop Mount Soledad. There, in his tile-roofed studio with sweeping coastal views from Mexico north toward Catalina Island, Geisel wrote and illustrated every Dr. Seuss book from *If I Ran the Zoo* (1950) through his last, *Oh, The Places You'll Go!* (1990).

Geisel was quite involved with the community, including Dr. Seuss art exhibits at the San Diego Museum of Art in Balboa Park and the Contemporary Art Museum on Prospect Street in La Jolla. When the San Diego Zoo's Wild Animal Park opened in the 1970s, he donated funds for a lion enclosure, which can be seen today from the Wgasa Bush Line monorail ride. However, Geisel was a shy and private man who did not want his name attached to buildings or monuments in his lifetime.

Charming Seussian memories cling to landmarks such as the Hotel del Coronado, site of the 1966 Charity Ball with a rollicking Dr. Seuss theme, and the Scripps Clinic and Research Foundation, where Geisel's multiple medical forays led to the 1984 best-seller *You're Only Old Once!* Following his death in 1991, nearly 70,000 children and their parents flocked to Balboa Park for a "Sunday in the Park with Seuss" memorial celebration.

Part of Dr. Seuss's San Diego legacy involves things you do not see. He fought against noise pollution and land destruction, an environmental concern that led to *The Lorax*. In the 1950s, he

invention called television drew a lot of attention. Another exhibit was the Zoro Gardens nudist colony, staffed mainly by young women promoting healthful natural living. That may have had something to do with the fact that many of the people who came to the exposition were young naval recruits based in the area.

Home to the U.S. Navy since 1901, San Diego today contains the largest military complex in the world, claiming more than 80 major military shore commands and more than 100 ships—that's one-third of the U.S. Pacific Fleet. As they have since the turn of the century, U.S. Navy and Marine Corps recruits come here for training. From San Diego, they ship out to the far-flung corners of the world. Many return to San Diego: Coronado claims more retired admirals than any other city in the country.

lobbied the La Jolla Town Council for a billboard ban, and wrote and illustrated a pamphlet entitled *Signs of Civilizations*. It featured two Stone Age competitors, Guss and Zaxx, who hammer out signs for their businesses until their rocky wilderness is a litter of come-ons.

> *And thus between them, with impunity*
> *They loused up the entire community*
> *And even the dinosaurs moved away*
> *From that messed-up spot in the U.S.A.*
> *Which is why our business men never shall*
> *Allow such to happen in La Jolla, Cal.*

A sign code followed and became part of a San Diego ordinance.

His favorite hangout for more than 50 years was the Whaling Bar at La Valencia Hotel, where he often sat in the second booth on the right, laughing with other writers and conspiring to commit practical jokes. His memory lives on in two old-line La Jolla bookstores: John Cole's on Prospect Street and Warwick's on Girard Avenue.

Geisel's widow, Audrey Stone Geisel, recently stunned and pleased the community by donating an undisclosed sum to the library of the University of California, San Diego. In late 1995, the library was named The Geisel Library in honor of the man behind Dr. Seuss. It houses all of Dr. Seuss's manuscripts, sketches, and personal papers. Ted Geisel's birthday—March 2—has been declared Dr. Seuss Day at UCSD, and each year students crowd the library courtyard for readings, songs, and birthday cake, while a giant balloon of the Cat and the Hat keeps watch.

—By Judith and Neil Morgan, authors of *Dr. Seuss & Mr. Geisel* (New York: Random House, 1995).

4 Famous San Diegans

Dennis Conner (b. 1943)   An accomplished yachtsman, he has won the America's Cup four times and lost it twice—to Australia in 1983 and to New Zealand in 1995.

Jenny Craig (b.1932)   The international headquarters of diet maven Jenny Craig overlooks Interstate 5 in Del Mar. Craig and her husband, **Sid,** live in San Diego and are active in the community. The San Diego Hospice, United Way, and Children's Hospital are just a few of the organizations she supports.

Joan Embery (b.1950)   As Goodwill Ambassador for the San Diego Zoo, Embery has appeared on numerous television shows with four-legged and winged friends. She lives on a ranch in Lakeside where she maintains her own collection of animals.

Françoise Gilot (b. 1921)   Born in France, Gilot has been a presence in the San Diego art community for many years. Her paintings and drawings fill *The Gods of Greece,* a collaboration with Arianna Huffington (Atlantic Monthly Press, 1993). Once the muse and model of Picasso, Gilot married Dr. Jonas Salk in 1970; he died in 1995.

Whoopi Goldberg (b. 1949)   The talented actress-comedian moved to San Diego in 1974 and was involved in the establishment of the San Diego Repertory Theater. She worked for a time at The Big Kitchen Restaurant in Golden Hill.

Janet Jackson (b. 1966)   The youngest of the musical Jackson family, she has been a performer since age seven, having won both a Grammy and an American Music Award. When she moved to Encino, California, with her family at age three, the Jacksons were one of the first African-American families in the area. She now lives in Rancho Santa Fe.

Joan Kroc (b.1929)   Her late husband, **Ray,** founded the McDonald's Restaurant chain and owned the San Diego Padres baseball team. She lives in Fairbanks Ranch and contributes generously to the community.

Frankie Laine (b. 1913)   Laine became a star in 1947 with the popular recording "That's My Desire," followed by "Mule Train," "Jezebel," and many more, including the theme to the TV western *Rawhide* (1959–66). His autobiography, the name of another hit record, is *That Lucky Old Son* (1993). He has lived in Point Loma since 1968.

Cleavon Little (1939–92)   Little was born in Oklahoma, but he spent his formative years as an actor in San Diego, where his parents still live. A 1965 San Diego State University graduate, he made early stage appearances at the La Jolla Playhouse. He is best remembered for his performance in *Blazing Saddles* (1974), his Tony Award for best actor in *Purlie* (1970), and his three years on Broadway and touring opposite Judd Hirsch in *I'm Not Rappaport* (1986–89).

Greg Louganis (b. 1960)   An Olympic gold medalist in 1984, he earned medals for both springboard and platform diving, the first Olympic athlete to do so since 1928. In his 1995 book *Breaking the Surface,* he discusses his traumatic childhood (in El Cajon), sexual orientation, and feelings about being HIV positive.

Bert Parks (1914–92)   The handsome emcee/announcer wowed 'em for 25 years with the strains of "There She Is" at Miss America pageants. He also hosted TV quiz shows, including "Break the Bank" and "Double or Nothing." Parks was born in Atlanta and made his home in La Jolla.

Gregory Peck (b. 1916)   The legendary actor was born in La Jolla, where his father owned a pharmacy on Prospect Street. He attended San Diego High School and San Diego State University. He co-founded the La Jolla Playhouse in 1947 with Dorothy McGuire and

Mel Ferrer. Peck won a 1962 Academy Award for his performance in *To Kill a Mockingbird.*

Cliff Robertson (b. 1925)   The Academy Award–winning actor (*Charley,* 1968) was born in La Jolla and graduated from La Jolla High School. He still lives here in a house on the beach and participates in various community activities, including being the grand marshal of the Christmas Parade.

Carl Rogers (1902–87)   Known as the father of humanistic psychology, he wrote *On Becoming a Person* (1961) and *A Way of Being* (1980) and founded the Center for Studies of the Person, based in La Jolla.

Dr. Jonas Salk (1914–95)   He developed the Salk polio vaccine in 1953 and founded the Salk Institute for Biological Studies in La Jolla in 1963. At the time of his death he was conducting AIDS research at his institute.

E. W. Scripps (1854–1926)   This newspaper publisher formed the Scripps-McRae League of Newspapers, which became Scripps-Howard Newspapers. He also developed United Press International (UPI). His half-sister, **Ellen Browning Scripps** (1836–1932), was a generous benefactor to Scripps Institution of Oceanography, Scripps Memorial Hospital, Scripps Clinic and Research Foundation, La Jolla Woman's Club, the Bishop's Schools, and many other causes.

2

Planning a Trip to San Diego

The Boy Scouts are right: It's a good idea to be prepared, so do your predeparture homework. It will help ensure that you will have the best possible time in San Diego.

1 Visitor Information

Before you leave home, contact the **International Visitor Information Center,** 11 Horton Plaza, San Diego, CA 92101 (☎ 619/236-1212; fax 619/232-1707). Ask for the *San Diego Official Visitors Guide*, which includes information on accommodations, dining, activities, and attractions, and has excellent maps. Also request the *Visitor Value Pack*, which is full of money-saving discount coupons, and the *Performing Arts Guide*, which contains information on upcoming theater in San Diego. The staff at the center is multilingual, and brochures are available in English, French, German, Japanese, Portuguese, and Spanish. The center is open Monday through Saturday from 8:30am to 5pm year-round and Sunday from 11am to 5pm June through August.

For information and discount tours, attractions, and theater tickets by mail, contact **Moneysaver Tickets 'N Tours** (☎ 800/721-2608). Another good source of information is the **San Diego North County Convention and Visitors Bureau.** Call to request their Visitors Guide (☎ 800/848-3336).

For cybernauts, up-to-the-minute information can be gleaned from the San Diego home page on the Internet at www.sannet.gov.

2 When to Go

San Diego is blessed with a mild climate, with low humidity, good air quality, and skies that are a welcoming blue most of the year. You probably won't find extremely hot weather here, but you will experience a temperature change of 20°F to 30°F from day to night. This means you should bring a jacket for cool evenings, even during the summer. It rains very little in San Diego; in an average year there are 9$^{1}/_{2}$ inches of rainfall. A local phenomenon you may encounter during your stay is a "Santa Ana" period of clear, dry weather brought about by winds blowing off the desert, from east to west. In the fall, this hot, dry air often contributes to brush fires.

What Things Cost in San Diego

	U.S.$
Taxi from the airport to downtown	$8.50
Bus from airport to downtown	$1.50
Local telephone call	$.20 to $.25
Double at the Marriott (expensive)	$190.00
Double at the Balboa Park Inn (moderate)	$90.00
Double at La Pensione (budget)	$50.00
Two-course lunch for one at Athens Market (moderate)	$15.00
Two-course lunch for one at Café Lulu (budget)	$8.00
Three-course dinner for one at Café Pacifica (expensive)	$32.00
Three-course dinner for one at Croce's (moderate)	$26.00
Three-course dinner for one at the Old Spaghetti Factory (budget)	$8.25
Bottle of beer	$2.25
Coca-Cola	$1.25
Cup of coffee	$1.25
Roll of ASA 100 Kodacolor film, 36 exposures	$5.20
Admission to the San Diego Zoo: Adults:	$13.00
Kids:	$6.00
Movie ticket	$7.00
Theater ticket at Old Globe	$28.00

Average Monthly Temperature

	Jan	Feb	Mar	Apr	May	June	July	Aug	Sept	Oct	Nov	Dec
High (°F)	65	66	66	68	70	71	75	77	76	74	70	66
(°C)	18	19	19	20	21	21	24	25	25	23	21	19
Low (°F)	46	47	50	54	57	60	64	66	63	58	52	47
(°C)	7	9	10	12	14	15	17	19	17	15	10	8

Average Rainfall (in.)

	Jan	Feb	Mar	Apr	May	June	July	Aug	Sept	Oct	Nov	Dec
	1.88	1.48	1.55	0.81	0.15	0.05	0.01	0.07	0.13	0.34	1.25	1.73

Impressions

What a change in weather! It was sleeting when I left St. Louis. Here, on the 23rd of February, palm leaves flutter in warm wind and sun.
—Charles Lindbergh, 1927

If you stay here for any length of time, you develop a low tolerance to change in the weather: If it's over 80 degrees, it's too hot, and if it's under 70 degrees it's too cold.   —Overheard in Horton Plaza

SAN DIEGO CALENDAR OF EVENTS

January

- **Maple Leaf Months,** which run through February, honor Canadian visitors with special discounts from merchants, hotels, restaurants, and attractions (☎ 619/236-1212).
- **Whale-watching.** The annual migration of California gray whales to the warmer waters of Baja California occurs through January and February. Visitors can watch through binoculars from the shore or go out on a boat for a closer look. For details, call 619/557-5450 or 619/236-1212.
- ✪ **Mercedes Championships.** This Professional Golfers Association (PGA) tournament, held since 1952, has been played at the La Costa Resort and Spa since 1965. It features tour winners from the past 12 months, including the British Open, the Masters, the U.S. Open, and the PGA Regular and Senior Championships. The combined purse is $1.5 million.

     Where: La Costa Resort and Spa, Carlsbad. **When:** Early January. **How:** For information, call 619/438-9111, ext. 4612, or 800/918-4653, or write La Costa Resort and Spa, Costa del Mar Rd., Carlsbad, CA 92009. Tickets go on sale in July.
- **San Diego Marathon.** The course begins at Plaza Camino Real in Carlsbad and stretches 26.2 miles, mainly along the coast. It's a gorgeous run, held the third Sunday in January. For more information, call 619/792-2900. For an entry application, send a self-addressed stamped envelope to In Motion, 511 S. Cedros, Suite B, Solana Beach, CA 92075. Spectators don't need tickets.
- **Martin Luther King Day Parade.** Held in mid-January since 1980, the parade goes along Broadway from Eighth Avenue to State Street (☎ 619/264-0542).
- **International Dance Festival.** Founded in 1993, this festival focuses on San Diego's numerous ethnic dance groups and companies. Held in mid-January, performances are at the Lyceum Theatre as well as free shows in public areas (☎ 619/239-9255).

February

- **Wildflowers in bloom.** Usually February through April at Anza-Borrego Desert State Park, the timing varies from year to year, depending on the winter rainfall. For details, call 619/767-4684 or 619/767-4205 (park information).
- ✪ **Buick Invitational of California.** In existence since 1952, this annual PGA Tour men's gold tournament draws more than 100,000 spectators each year. It features a Pro-Am Day with local and national celebrities.

     Where: Torrey Pines Golf Course, La Jolla. **When:** Early to mid-February. **How:** For information, call 619/281-4653 or 800/888-BUICK, or write Buick Invitational of California, 9449 Friars Rd., Gate P, San Diego, CA 92108.

March

- **Ocean Beach Kite Festival.** At the Ocean Beach Recreation Center, you can build and decorate kites, as well as participate in a flying contest for all ages. The festival is held the first weekend at the Ocean Beach Recreation Center, 4726 Santa Monica Ave. (☎ 619/224-0189).
- **St. Patrick's Day Parade.** A tradition here since 1980, the parade is held the Sunday before March 17. It starts at Sixth and Juniper and ends at Sixth and Laurel, and is followed by an Irish Festival. For details, call 619/299-7812.

April

- **Rosarito-Ensenada 50-Mile Fun Bicycle Ride,** Mexico. About 8,000 participants cycle from the Rosarito Beach Hotel along the two-lane free road to Ensenada and the Finish Line Fiesta, sometime in mid- to late-April. For information, call 619/583-3001.
- **San Diego Crew Classic, Crown Point Shores,** Mission Bay. Since 1973, it has drawn collegiate teams of more than 2,000 athletes from the United States and Canada. It's held the first or second weekend in April; call 619/488-0700.
- **Downtown Art Walk.** Wander between museums, studios, and galleries, rubbing elbows with artists and collectors. Food and entertainment are part of the festivities, held early to mid-April (☎ 619/232-4395).
- **Del Mar National Horse Show,** Del Mar Fairgrounds. Olympic-caliber and national championship horse and rider teams compete here, from late April to mid-May. There are also Western fashion boutiques and artists displays and demonstrations. For information, call 619/792-4288 or 619/755-1161.
- **Day at the Docks.** This sportfishing tournament and festival, held at Harbor Drive and Scott Street, Point Loma, features food, entertainment, and free boat rides. It's either the last weekend of April or first weekend in May (☎ 619/294-7912).

May

- **Cinco de Mayo Festival,** Old Town. A tradition since 1983, this fiesta on May 5 includes mariachi music and margaritas galore (☎ 619/296-3161 or 619/220-5422).
- **Wildflower Festival,** Julian Town Hall, Julian. A week-long event held since 1926, it features displays of native plants. It's held early to mid-May; for details, call 619/765-1857.
- **Balloon and Wine Festival,** Temecula. Even if you don't go up, up, and away, the sight of the balloons is spectacular (☎ 909/676-4713).
- **Mainly Mozart Festival,** held at different locations in San Diego and Tijuana from late May through mid-June (☎ 619/558-1000).

June
- **Indian Fair,** Museum of Man, Balboa Park. Native Americans from around the United States gather to demonstrate tribal dances and sell arts and crafts in mid-June (☎ 619/239-2001).
- **Twilight in the Park Concerts,** Spreckels Organ Pavilion, Balboa Park. These free concerts have been held since 1979 and run from late June through late August. For information, call 619/235-1105 or 619/226-0819.
- **Del Mar Fair.** San Diego's country fair, held from mid-June to July 4, includes exhibits of farm animals and home arts and lots of rides. Concerts by top-name entertainers are free with admission. Call 619/793-5555.
- **SummerPops Concerts.** The San Diego Symphony plays at the Embarcadero Marina Park South from late June through early September (☎ 619/699-4205 or 619/220-TIXS).

July
- ✪ **World Championship Over-the-Line Tournament.** Very much a local tradition, San Diego's original beach softball event dates from 1953 and features 1,000 three-person teams competing in an elimination tournament. (*Warning:* This event gets pretty risqué, and probably isn't appropriate for children.)

  Where: Fiesta Island, Mission Bay. **When:** Second and third weekend in July. **How:** For information, call 619/688-0817. Spectators don't need tickets.
- **U.S. Open Sandcastle Competition.** Held on the Imperial Beach Pier, this annual event attracts international competitors (☎ 619/424-6663).
- **Festival of the Bells,** Mission San Diego de Alcala. This mid-July fiesta commemorates the founding of California's first church. Music, dancing, food, and the "blessing of the animals" are included. For details call 619/281-8449.
- **22nd Annual San Diego Lesbian and Gay Pride Parade and Festival.** The parade, either the third or fourth weekend in July, begins at noon at University Avenue and Normal Street and proceeds west on University to 6th Avenue. A festival follows on Saturday from 2 to 10pm and Sunday from noon to 10pm. For information, call 619/297-7683.
- **Thoroughbred racing.** The "turf meets the surf" in Del Mar for daily races (except Tuesday), held late July through mid-September. Post time is 2pm for the nine-race program (☎ 619/792-4242 or 619/755-1141).

August
- **Hillcrest Street Fair,** Fifth Avenue, between Ivy Lane and University Avenue. Held since 1983, the street fair features arts and crafts, food booths, a beer garden, and live entertainment (☎ 619/299-3330).

- **America's Finest City Week.** More than 70 events celebrate our city in mid-August, including a Midnight Madness Bike Ride and a volleyball festival. For details, call 619/437-0369.
- **Julian Weed Show and Art Mart,** Julian. Held since 1959, this showcases the area's colorful weeds in myriad arrangements, from late August through September (☎ 619/765-1857).
- **World Body Surfing Championships.** U.S. and international body surfers compete at the Oceanside Pier (☎ 619/966-4535).
- **Miramar Air Show.** Miramar Naval Air Station, Miramar. More than 150 civilian and military flight demonstrations and the Blue Angels Navy Precision Fight Team are part of the air show, held mid- to late August (☎ 619/537-NAVY or 619/537-4117).

September
- **Cabrillo Festival,** Cabrillo National Monument. This reenactment of Cabrillo's arrival in San Diego in 1542 is staged late September or early October (☎ 619/557-5450).
- **San Diego Street Scene,** Gaslamp Quarter. California's largest, most diverse urban food and music festival occurs in early September. For tickets and information, call 619/557-8487.
- ✪ **La Jolla Rough-Water Swim.** The country's largest rough-water swimming competition began in 1916 and features masters men's and women's swims, a junior swim, and an amateur swim. All events except the junior swim are 1 mile in distance.

     Where: La Jolla Cove. **When:** First Sunday after Labor Day. **How:** To register or receive more information, call 619/456-2100. For an entry form, send a self-addressed stamped envelope to Entries Chairman, La Jolla Rough-Water Swim, P.O. Box 46, La Jolla, CA 92038. Spectators don't need tickets.
- **Apple Harvest and Back Country Arts Festival,** Julian. On weekends only from mid-September through mid-November, enjoy autumn foliage, entertainment, and apple pie. Call 619/765-1857 for details.
- **Rosarito-Ensenada 50-Mile Fun Bicycle Ride,** Mexico. See April entry for details, or call 619/583-3001.

October
- **Zoo Founders Day.** It's free for everyone to go to the zoo on the first Monday of October, and it's free for children every day of October (☎ 619/234-6541).
- **Columbus Day Parade.** Organized by the United Italian-American Association, it's been held in downtown San Diego since 1969. Call 619/727-3728.
- **Kidzartz Festival,** Balboa Park. Free performances and activities for children grades K–9 and their parents (☎ 619/239-0512).
- **Haunted Museum of Man,** Balboa Park. This local Halloween favorite runs the last 10 days of October, from 7 to 9:30pm (☎ 619/239-2001).

November

- **Veterans Day Parade,** along Pacific Highway in downtown San Diego (☎ 619/239-2300).
- **Baja 1000.** This famous off-road race for cars, trucks, and motorcycles over Baja California's most challenging terrain has been held since 1969, in early to mid-November. Viewing is free, participants pay an entry fee. For details call 818/583-8068.
- **Holiday Avenues of the Arts**. For one weekend only in mid- to late November, you'll find arts and crafts, gift items, food, and music in the Gaslamp Quarter (☎ 619/239-1143).

December

- **Coronado Christmas Celebration and Parade.** On the first Friday of December, Santa's arrival by ferry is followed by a parade along Orange Avenue (☎ 619/437-8788 or 619/435-8895).
- **Christmas on the Prado,** Balboa Park. The first weekend of December, a tradition since 1977 continues with a carol sing-a-long and food booths. Admission to all museums is free. For information, call 619/239-0512.
- **Whale-watching.** It starts in mid-December; see the January listing above.
- **Holiday Bowl Parade.** The marching bands of the two Holiday Bowl teams march with other bands through downtown San Diego (☎ 619/283-5808).
- **Mission Bay Boat Parade of Lights,** from Quivira Basin in Mission Bay. Held on a mid-December Saturday, it concludes with the lighting of a 320-foot tower of Christmas lights at Sea World (☎ 619/276-8200).
- **San Diego Harbor Parade of Lights,** from Shelter Island to Harbor Island to Seaport Village. Decorated boats of all sizes and types participate, and spectators line the shore and cheer for their favorites. Held since 1971, it's on a Sunday in mid-December. Check the local newspaper for exact day and time.
- **First Night San Diego**, San Diego Concourse, downtown. Family-oriented activities, including dancers, clowns, mimes, and rock and roll, held from approximately 4pm to midnight on December 31 (☎ 619/280-5838).

3 Tips for Special Travelers

FOR TRAVELERS WITH DISABILITIES The **Accessible San Diego hotline** (☎ 619/279-0704) helps travelers with disabilities link up with hotels, tours, attractions, and transportation accessible to them (if you call long distance and get the answering machine, leave a message and the staff will call you back collect). Or for a useful 25-page access guide that lists local social service agencies, send a $5 donation to Accessible San Diego, P.O. Box 124526, San Diego, CA 92112-4526.

In the San Diego Convention and Visitors Bureau's Dining and Accommodations guide, a wheelchair symbol designates places that are accessible to persons with disabilities.

On buses and trolleys, riders with disabilities pay a fixed fare of 75¢. Many MTS buses and all trolleys are equipped with wheelchair lifts; priority seating is available on both buses and trolleys. Bus stops served by accessible buses are marked with a wheelchair symbol. People with visual impairments benefit from the white reflecting ring that circles the bottom of the trolley door to increase its visibility.

FOR SENIORS   When making an airline reservation, ask for the senior discount of 10% offered by many airlines on most fares. Just as you would on any trip, carry proof of age with you—your driver's license, passport, Medicare card, or membership card for an organization for seniors—so you can take advantage of senior discounts offered by some hotels and restaurants and by most attractions. Transport on the San Diego bus and trolley system is 75¢ one way for people 60 or older.

A delightful way to meet older San Diegans, many of them retired, is to join a free Saturday morning stroll with Downtown Sam, a foot-loose retiree and guide with Walkabout International (see "Organized Tours" in Chapter 7).

Finally, look into **Elderhostel educational programs** in the San Diego area. There is one at the Point Loma Youth Hostel. Those qualified to attend must be 60 years of age or older; their spouse, "significant other," relative, or friend must be 50 or older. For more information, contact Elderhostel, 75 Federal St., Boston, MA 02110 (☎ 617/426-7788).

San Diego has a special senior citizens **referral and information line:** 619/560-2500.

FOR GAY AND LESBIAN TRAVELERS   Gay or lesbian travelers will particularly enjoy the Hillcrest area near Balboa Park, where there are a number of popular meeting spots (see "The Bar and Coffeehouse Scene" in Chapter 10).

The active **Lesbian and Gay Men's Community Center** is at 3916 Normal St. (☎ 619/692-2077; open Monday through Saturday from 9am to 10pm). **AIDS Foundation San Diego,** 4080 Centre St. (☎ 619/686-5000), provides information and educational programs on AIDS and social services for people with AIDS. The **Live and Let Live Alano Club,** 1730 Monroe Ave.(☎ 619/298-8008), sponsors numerous alcohol-free activities and programs. Churches that welcome gay and lesbian visitors include the **Metropolitan Community Church,** 4333 30th St. (☎ 619/280-4333), in the North Park; **St. Francis Liberal Catholic Church,** 741 Cerro Gordo Ave. (☎ 619/239-0637); and the metaphysical **Pacific Church of Religious Science,** 5333 Mission Center Rd. (☎ 619/294-9555).

The free *San Diego Gay and Lesbian Times,* published every Thursday, is often available at Quel Fromage coffeehouse and the Blue Door Bookstore, both in Hillcrest. Greg Louganis signed copies of his book *Breaking the Surface* at Obelisk, 1029 University Ave., Hillcrest (☎ 619/297-4171).

San Diego Area at a Glance

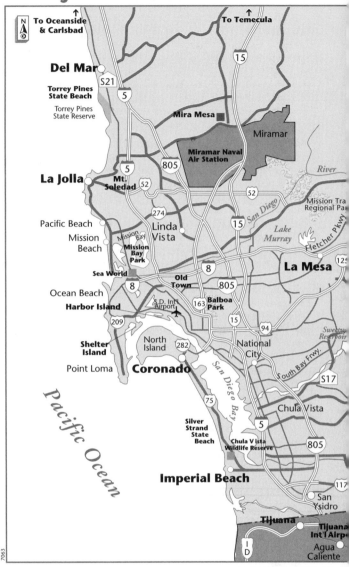

To Oceanside & Carlsbad

To Temecula

15

Del Mar

S21

5

Torrey Pines State Beach

Torrey Pines State Reserve

Mira Mesa

Miramar

Miramar Naval Air Station

River

La Jolla

Mt. Soledad

52

52

Mission Tra Regional Par

274

15

San Diego

Pacific Beach

Mission Bay

Linda Vista

Lake Murray

Fletcher Pkwy

Mission Beach

Mission Bay Park

8

La Mesa

12

Sea World

Old Town

805

Ocean Beach

8

163

Balboa Park

Harbor Island

S.D. Int'l Airport

15

94

209

North Island

282

National City

Sweetw Reservoir

Shelter Island

Coronado

San Diego Bay

South Bay Frwy.

S17

Point Loma

75

Chula Vista

Pacific Ocean

Silver Strand State Beach

5

805

Chula Vista Wildlife Reserve

Imperial Beach

117

San Ysidro

Tijuana

I D

Tijuana Int'l Airpo

Agua Caliente

7063

4   Getting There

BY PLANE

THE MAJOR AIRLINES   Incoming flights arrive at **San Diego International Airport/Lindbergh Field** (named after aviation hero Charles Lindbergh), served by many national and regional air carriers

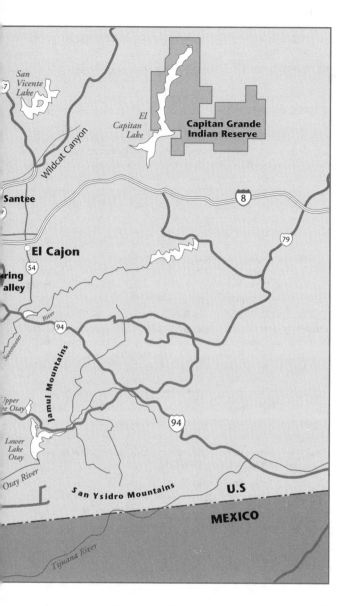

and Aeroméxico. Flights from Mexico are the only international flights landing in San Diego.

When planning your trip, consider fares available through the following airlines: Aeroméxico (☎ 800/237-6639); Alaska Airlines (☎ 800/426-0333); American Airlines (☎ 800/433-7300); America West (☎ 800/235-9292); Continental (☎ 800/525-0280); Delta Airlines (☎ 800/221-1212); Mark Air (☎ 800/627-5247); Midwest

Express (☎ 800/452-2022); Northwest Airlines (☎ 800/225-2525); Reno Air (☎ 800/736-6247); Skywest Airlines (☎ 800/453-9417); Southwest Airlines (☎ 800/435-9792); Trans World Airlines (☎ 800/221-2000); United Airlines (☎ 800/241-6522); and USAir and USAir Express (☎ 800/428-4322).

SAN DIEGO'S AIRPORT   San Diego International Airport/ Lindbergh Field is located only slightly north of downtown. The landing approach is right over the central business district, so the sight of planes threading their way through high-rise buildings on their way to the airport is quite familiar. A curfew is enforced from 11:30pm to 6:30am to cut down on noise in the surrounding residential areas. Planes may land during the curfew period, but they can't take off.

The airport has two terminals, East and West, and about nine carriers land at each one. The East Terminal has a restaurant and a cafeteria; the West Terminal, a cafeteria.

At the airport you'll also find car-rental booths, including Avis, Budget, Dollar, Hertz, and National; a counter where you may purchase traveler's insurance; two Traveler's Aid booths with plenty of brochures; and hotel information and courtesy phones for making reservations and arranging airport pickup, which some hotels offer.

GETTING INTO TOWN   By Bus   The **San Diego Transit Corporation bus stop** is at the center traffic aisle of the East Terminal and at the traffic island at the far-west end of the West Terminal. The no. 2 bus will take you to the heart of the downtown area, at Broadway and Fourth Avenue. It runs every 20 minutes from 5:30am to midnight (every 30 minutes on weekends), costs $1.50, and takes 15 minutes. The staff at the **Transit Store** (☎ 619/233-3004), one block away at Broadway and Fifth Avenue, can answer all your questions about the city's transit system (bus, trolley, and ferry) and provide free brochures, route maps, and timetables.

By Taxi   Fare into town from the airport costs approximately $8.50, including tip, and takes 5 to 10 minutes.

By Shuttle   Several airport shuttles run regularly from the airport to the downtown hotels and charge about $5. Shuttle service is also available through **Cloud 9 Shuttle** for about $5 per person (☎ 619/ 278-8877 or 800/9-SHUTTLE).

By Limo   Limousine service is available, for about $50 per hour, with 1¹/₂- or 2-hour minimum, respectively, from **Olde English Livery** (☎ 619/232-6533) and **Paul the Greek's Limo** (☎ 619/589-2299).

By Car   If you are driving the short distance into the city from the airport, follow Harbor Drive to Broadway, the main city street running east and west. Also refer to the "Getting Around" section in Chapter 4.

BY CAR

Visitors arriving in San Diego by car from Los Angeles and points north do so via coastal route I-5; from points northeast, via I-15 (link up with I-8 West and Highway 163 South or Highway 94 West); and from the east, via I-8 (link up with Highway 163 South to drive into the downtown area; Highway 163 turns into Tenth Avenue). If you arrive from the east on Highway 94, it turns into F Street. Try to avoid arriving during weekday rush hours, between 7 and 9am and 3 and 6pm. If you are heading to Coronado, take the Coronado Bridge via I-5. Stay in the far-right lanes if there's a passenger in the car with you, and you can avoid paying the toll. Maximum speed in the San Diego area is 55 miles (90km) per hour.

BY TRAIN

Trains from all points in the United States and Canada funnel through Los Angeles to get to San Diego. Seven trains make the pretty Pacific-coast–hugging trip daily, a scenic 128-mile journey that lasts just under 3 hours and costs $24 one way. You'll arrive at the striking mission-style **Santa Fe Station,** built in 1914 and centrally located at Broadway and Kettner Boulevard, 1¹/₂ blocks from the Embarcadero, a block from the YMCA and Downtown Hostel, and within walking distance of some of the city's fine downtown hotels. For price and schedule information, call 800/USA-RAIL (people with hearing impairments, call 800/523-6590).

BY BUS

Greyhound/Trailways (☎ 800/231-2222) serves San Diego; the city's bus terminal has a central downtown location on Broadway between Front Street and First Avenue, within walking distance of major hotels, the YMCA, and Downtown Hostel. Local buses and the trolley stop right outside. Lockers are available at $1 for 24 hours. If you leave belongings more than 24 hours, the charge is $3 per day. The bus station is open 24 hours a day, and security is provided from late evening to 7am.

BY SHIP

Renovated in 1985, the San Diego **Cruise Terminal,** at the B Street Pier, is awash with carnival colors inside and out. If you arrive in San Diego by sea, expect to be given a full day in port, from about 8am to 3 or 4pm. For more information about cruise ships that make San Diego their port of call, contact the port's **Cruise Liaison Office** (☎ 619/686-6200).

When a ship is in port, Traveler's Aid staffs an information booth inside the terminal; outside, tour buses are waiting to take visitors around the city. You can also tour on your own by walking up Broadway eight blocks and wandering through Horton Plaza and the Gaslamp Quarter (see Chapter 8). Local buses to Balboa Park and the San Diego Zoo leave from Broadway and Fifth Avenue and cost $1.50 in exact change (for information about other destinations, stop at the Transit Store on that corner, or call 619/233-3004).

3

For Foreign Visitors

This chapter provides specific suggestions about getting to the United States as economically and effortlessly as possible, plus some helpful information about how things are done in San Diego—from receiving mail to making a local or long-distance telephone call.

1 Preparing for Your Trip

ENTRY REQUIREMENTS

DOCUMENT REGULATIONS   Canadian nationals only need proof of Canadian residence to visit the United States. Citizens of the United Kingdom and Japan only need a current passport. Citizens of other countries, including Australia and New Zealand, usually need two documents: a valid **passport** with an expiration date at least six months later than the scheduled end of their visit to the United States and a **tourist visa** available at no charge from a U.S. embassy or consulate.

To get a tourist or business visa to enter the United States, contact the nearest American embassy or consulate in your country; if there is none, you will have to apply in person in a country where there is a U.S. embassy or consulate. Present your passport, a passport-size photo of yourself, and a completed application, which is available through the embassy or consulate. You may be asked to provide information about how you plan to finance your trip or show a letter of invitation from a friend with whom you plan to stay. Those applying for a business visa may be asked to show evidence that they will not receive a salary in the United States. Be sure to check the length of stay on your visa; usually it is six months. If you want to stay longer, you may file for an extension with the Immigration and Naturalization Service once you are in the country. If permission to stay is granted, a new visa is not required unless you leave the United States and want to reenter.

MEDICAL REQUIREMENTS   No inoculations are needed to enter the United States unless you are coming from, or have stopped over in, areas known to be suffering from epidemics, particularly cholera or yellow fever.

If you have a disease requiring treatment with medications containing narcotics or drugs requiring a syringe, carry a valid signed generic prescription from your physician to allay any suspicions that you are smuggling drugs. The prescription brands you are accustomed to buying in your country may not be available in the United States.

CUSTOMS REQUIREMENTS   Every adult visitor may bring in free of duty: 1 liter of wine or hard liquor; 200 cigarettes or 100 cigars (but no cigars from Cuba) or 3 pounds of smoking tobacco; and $100 worth of gifts. These exemptions are offered to travelers who spend at least 72 hours in the United States and who have not claimed them within the preceding six months. It is altogether forbidden to bring foodstuffs (particularly cheese, fruit, cooked meats, and canned goods) and plants (vegetables, seeds, tropical plants, and so on) into the country. Foreign tourists may bring in or take out up to $10,000 in U.S. or foreign currency with no formalities; larger sums must be declared to Customs on entering or leaving.

INSURANCE

There is no national health system in the United States. Because the cost of medical care is extremely high, we strongly advise all travelers to secure health coverage before setting out on their trip.

You may want to take out a comprehensive travel policy that covers (for a relatively low premium) sickness or injury costs (medical, surgical, and hospital); loss or theft of your baggage; trip-cancellation costs; guarantee of bail in case you are arrested; and costs of accident, repatriation, or death. Automobile clubs sell packages (for example, "Europe Assistance" in Europe) at attractive rates; they are also offered by insurance companies, travel agencies, and some airports.

MONEY

CURRENCY   The U.S. monetary system has a decimal base: One American **dollar** ($1) = 100 **cents** (100¢). Dollar **bills** commonly come in $1 (a "buck"), $5, $10, $20, $50, and $100 denominations (the last two are not welcome when paying for small purchases are not accepted in taxis or at subway ticket booths).

There are six **coin** denominations: 1¢ (one cent or "penny"); 5¢ (five cents or "nickel"); 10¢ (ten cents or "dime"); 25¢ (twenty-five cents or "quarter"); 50¢ (fifty cents or "half dollar"); and the $1 pieces (both the older, large silver dollar and the newer, small Susan B. Anthony coin).

TRAVELER'S CHECKS   Traveler's checks in U.S. dollars are accepted at most hotels, motels, restaurants, and large stores. Sometimes picture identification is required. American Express, Thomas Cook, and Barclay's Bank traveler's checks are readily accepted in the United States.

CREDIT CARDS   The most widely used method of payment is the credit card: Visa (BarclayCard in Britain), MasterCard (Euro-Card in Europe, Access in Britain, Diamond in Japan), American Express, Discover, Diners Club, enRoute, JCB, and Carte Blanche, in descending order of acceptance. You can save yourself trouble by using "plastic" rather than cash or traveler's checks in 95% of all hotels, motels, restaurants, and retail stores. A credit card can also serve as a deposit for renting a car, as proof of identity, or as a "cash card," enabling you to draw money from automatic-teller machines (ATMs) that accept them.

You can telegraph money or have it telegraphed to you very quickly using the Western Union system (☎ 800/325-6000).

SAFETY

While tourist areas are generally safe, crime is on the increase everywhere, and U.S. urban areas tend to be less safe than those in Europe or Japan. Visitors should always stay alert. This is particularly true of large U.S. cities. It is wise to ask the city's or area's tourist office if you're in doubt about which neighborhoods are safe. Avoid deserted areas, especially at night. Don't go into any city park at night unless there is an event that attracts crowds.

Remember also that hotels are open to the public, and in a large hotel, security may not be able to screen everyone entering. Always lock your room door—don't assume that once inside your hotel you are automatically safe and no longer need be aware of your surroundings.

DRIVING   Safety while driving is particularly important. Question your rental agency about personal safety, or ask for a brochure of traveler safety tips. Obtain written directions, or a map with the route marked in red, from the agency showing how to get to your destination. And, if possible, arrive and depart during daylight hours.

Recently more and more crime has involved cars and drivers. If you drive off a highway into a doubtful neighborhood, leave the area as quickly as possible. If you have an accident, even on the highway, stay in your car with the doors locked until you assess the situation or until the police arrive. If you are bumped from behind on the street or are involved in a minor accident with no injuries and the situation appears to be suspicious, motion to the other driver to follow you. Never get out of your car in such situations. Go directly to the nearest police precinct, well-lighted service station, or all-night store.

If you see someone on the road who indicates a need for help, do not stop. Take note of the location, drive on to a well-lighted area, and telephone the police by dialing **911**.

Park in well-lighted, well-traveled areas if possible. Always keep your car doors locked, whether attended or unattended. Look around you before you get out of your car, and never leave any packages or valuables in sight. If someone attempts to rob you or steal your car, do not try to resist the thief/carjacker—report the incident to the police department immediately.

2 Getting to the U.S.

Travelers from overseas can take advantage of the **APEX (advance purchase excursion) fares** that all the major U.S. and European carriers offer. Aside from these, attractive values are offered by **Virgin Atlantic**(☎ 0293/747-747 in London) to Los Angeles.

The only international flights direct to San Diego are from Mexico. Other overseas travelers bound for San Diego will need to change planes at Los Angeles International Airport (LAX) and take a short flight south. Because the Los Angeles train and bus stations are a long way from LAX it isn't convenient to use these modes of transportion to get to San Diego. However, if you're flying into LA and staying there a few days, you could get to San Diego by train or bus. Seven trains daily make the 2 hour 58 minute trip for a $24 one-way fare; the train station is located at 800 Alameda. The Los Angeles bus terminal is located at 7th and Alameda, and buses depart on the hour from 6am to 6pm daily with some later departures; check with Greyhound for current schedules. The trip takes 2 hours 45 minutes, and the one-way fare is $12.

In addition to the domestic U.S. airlines listed in Chapter 2, many international carriers serve LAX: **Aer Lingus** (☎ 01-844-4777 in Dublin), **Air Canada** (☎ 800/268-7240 in Canada), **Air New Zealand** (☎ 0800/737-000 in Auckland or 03/379-5200 in Christchurch), **British Airways** (☎ 0345/222-111 in London), **Japan Airlines** (☎ 0354/89-1111 in Tokyo), **Qantas** (☎ 1-800/062-123 in Australia), and **Swissair** (☎ 01/258-3434 in Zurich or 022/799-5999 in Geneva).

3   Getting Around the U.S.

On their transatlantic or transpacific flights, some large U.S. airlines offer special discount tickets for any of their U.S. destinations (American Airline's **Visit USA** program and Delta's **Discover America** program, for example). The tickets or coupons are not on sale in the United States and must be purchased before you leave your point of departure. This system is the best, easiest, and fastest way to see the United States at low cost. You should obtain information well in advance from your travel agent or the office of the airline concerned, since the conditions attached to these discount tickets can be changed without advance notice.

The visitor arriving by air, no matter what the port of entry, should cultivate patience and resignation before setting foot on U.S. soil. Getting through immigration control may take as long as two hours on some days, especially summer weekends, so have your guidebook or something else to read handy. Add the time it takes to clear customs and you will see you should make a very generous allowance for delay in planning connections between international and domestic flights—figure on two to three hours at least.

In contrast, for the traveler arriving by car or by rail from Canada, the border-crossing formalities have been streamlined to the vanishing point. And for the traveler by air from Canada, Bermuda, and some places in the Caribbean, you can sometimes go through Customs and Immigration at the point of departure, which is much quicker and less painful.

International visitors can also buy a **USA Railpass,** good for 15 or 30 days of unlimited travel on Amtrak. The pass is available through many foreign travel agents. Prices in 1995 for a 15-day pass are

$229 off-peak, $340 peak; a 30-day pass costs $339 off-peak, $425 peak (off peak is August 31–June 15). (With a foreign passport, you can also buy passes at some Amtrak offices in the United States including locations in San Francisco, Los Angeles, Chicago, New York, Miami, Boston, and Washington, D.C.) Reservations are generally required and should be made for each part of your trip as early as possible.

Visitors should also be aware of the limitations of long-distance rail travel in the United States. With a few notable exceptions (for instance, the Northeast Corridor line between Boston and Washington, D.C.), service is rarely up to European standards: delays are common, routes are limited and often infrequently served, and fares are rarely significantly lower than discount airfares. Thus, cross-country train travel should be approached with caution.

Although ticket prices for short bus trips between cities are often the most economical form of public transit, at this writing, bus passes are priced slightly higher than similar train passes. **Greyhound**, the nationwide bus line, offers an **Ameripass** for unlimited travel for 7 days (for $259), 15 days (for $459), and 30 days (for $559). Bus travel in the United States can be both slow and uncomfortable, so this option is not for everyone. In addition, bus stations are often located in undesirable neighborhoods. For further information specific to San Diego, see "Fast Facts: San Diego" in Chapter 4.

FAST FACTS: For the Foreign Traveler

Automobile Organizations   Auto clubs will supply maps, suggested routes, guidebooks, accident and bail-bond insurance, and emergency road service. The major auto club in the United States, with 983 offices nationwide, is the **American Automobile Association (AAA).** Members of some foreign auto clubs have reciprocal arrangements with the AAA and enjoy its services at no charge—inquire about AAA reciprocity before you leave. The AAA can provide you with an **International Driving Permit** validating your foreign license, although drivers with valid licenses from most home countries don't really need this permit. You may be able to join the AAA even if you are not a member of a reciprocal club. To inquire, call 619/233-1000 or 800/222-4357. In addition, some automobile rental agencies now provide these services, so ask when you rent your car.

Business Hours   **Banks** are open weekdays from 9am to 3pm or later and sometimes Saturday morning. The Wells Fargo Bank, on West Broadway at Front Street (☎ 619/589-5150), is open weekdays from 7:30am to 6pm and Saturday from 9am to 2pm. The **Post Office** is open weekdays from 8:30am to 5pm and Saturday from 8:30am to noon. **Shops,** especially those in shopping complexes, tend to stay open until about 9pm weekdays and until 6pm weekends.

Climate   See "When to Go" in Chapter 2.

Currency   See "Preparing for Your Trip" above.

Currency Exchange   **Thomas Cook Currency Services** (formerly Deak International) offers a wide variety of services: more than 100 currencies, commission-free traveler's checks, drafts and wire transfers, check collections, and precious metal bars and coins. Rates are competitive and service is excellent. They are located downtown at Horton Plaza (☎ 619/235-0900 or 800/287-7362), within walking distance of the train station, and at University Towne Centre near La Jolla (☎ 800/287-7362). An **American Express Travel Services office** with a currency-exchange desk is at 258 Broadway (☎ 619/234-4455), also within walking distance of the train station.

Drinking Laws   The legal age to drink alcohol in San Diego is 21. Alcohol can only be purchased between the hours of 6am and 2am, 365 days a year.

Electricity   The United States uses 110–120 volts, 60 cycles, compared to 220-240 volts, 50 cycles, as in most of Europe. Besides a 100-volt converter, small appliances of non-American manufacture, such as hairdryers or shavers, will require a plug adapter, with two flat, parallel pins. The easiest solution is to purchase dual-voltage appliances that operate on both 110 and 220 volts; then all that is required is a U.S. adapter plug.

Embassies and Consulates   All embassies are located in the national capital, Washington, D.C.; some consulates are located in major cities. Listed here are the embassies and West Coast consulates of the major English-speaking countries. Travelers from other countries can get telephone numbers for their embassies and consulates by calling "Information" in Washington, D.C. (☎ 202/555-1212).

The **Australian Embassy** is at 1601 Massachusetts Ave. NW, Washington, D.C. 20036 (☎ 202/797-3000). The **Consulate** in Los Angeles is located at 611 N. Larchmont, Los Angeles, CA 90004 (☎ 213/469-4300).

The **Canadian Embassy** is at 501 Pennsylvania Ave. NW, Washington, D.C. 20001 (☎ 202/682-1740). The **Consulate** in Los Angeles is located at 300 South Grand Ave., Suite 1000, Los Angeles, CA 90071 (☎ 213/346-2700).

The **Irish Embassy** is at 2234 Massachusetts Ave. NW, Washington, D.C. 20008 (☎ 202/462-3939). The **Consulate** in San Francisco is located at 655 Montgomery St., Suite 930, San Francisco, CA 94111 (☎ 415/392-4214).

The **New Zealand Embassy** is at 37 Observatory Circle NW, Washington, D.C. 20008 (☎ 202/328-4800). The **Consulate** in Los Angeles is located at 12400 Wilshire Blvd., Los Angeles, CA 90025 (☎ 310/207-1605).

The **U.K. Embassy** is at 3100 Massachusetts Ave. NW, Washington, D.C. 20008 (☎ 202/462-1340). The **Consulate** in Los Angeles is located at 11766 Wilshire Blvd., Suite 400, Los Angeles, CA 90025 (☎ 310/477-3322).

Emergencies Call **911** for fire, police, and ambulance. If you encounter such traveler's problems as sickness, accident, or lost or stolen baggage, call **Traveler's Aid,** an organization that specializes in helping distressed travelers. It has offices at the airport's East Terminal (☎ 619/231-7361 and West Terminal (☎ 619/231-5230) and at the Santa Fe (train) Station (☎ 619/234-5191).

The main police station is located downtown at 1401 Broadway at Fourteenth Street (☎ 619/531-2065; 619/531-2000 for hearing impaired).

U.S. hospitals have emergency rooms, with a special entrance where you will be admitted for quick attention. In Hillcrest, near downtown San Diego, there is **Mercy Hospital,** 4077 Fifth Ave. (☎ 619/260-7044); in Mission Bay, **Mission Bay Hospital,** 3030 Bunker Hill St. (☎ 619/274-7721); and in Coronado, **Coronado Hospital,** 250 Prospect Place, opposite Le Meridien Hotel (☎ 619/ 435-6251).

Gasoline (Petrol) One U.S. gallon equals 3.75 liters, while 1.2 U.S. gallons equals 1 imperial gallon. A gallon of unleaded gas (short for gasoline), which most rental cars accept, costs about $1.30 if you fill your own tank (it's called "self-serve"); 10¢ more if the station attendant does it (called "full-service").

Holidays On the following national legal holidays, banks, government offices, post offices, and many stores, restaurants, and museums are closed: January 1 (New Years Day), third Monday in January (Martin Luther King Jr. Day), third Monday in February (Presidents' Day), last Monday in May (Memorial Day), July 4 (Independence Day), first Monday in September (Labor Day), second Monday in October (Columbus Day), November 11 (Veterans Day/Armistice Day), fourth Thursday in November (Thanksgiving Day), and December 25 (Christmas Day). The Tuesday following the first Monday in November is Election Day. Presidential elections are held every four years (the next is 1996).

Mail You may receive mail c/o General Delivery, San Diego Main Post Office, 2535 Midway Dr., San Diego, CA 92138-999, USA. Pick up your mail there by taking bus no. 9, 29, 34, 34A, or 35 from downtown San Diego to Midway Drive at Barnett Avenue. Call 619/674-0000 for more information. The addressee must pick it up in person, and must produce proof of identity (driver's license, credit card, passport, and so on). Mailboxes are blue with a red-and-white logo, and carry the inscription U.S. MAIL.

Medical Emergencies See "Emergencies" above.

Newspapers/Magazines The *San Diego Union-Tribune, Los Angeles Times* and the magazines *Newsweek* and *Time* cover world news and are available at newsstands. For newspapers from Europe and elsewhere, try Seventh Near "B" Coffee and News, 1146 Seventh Ave. near B Street (☎ 619/696-7071); Horton Plaza Farmers Market,

1 Horton Plaza (☎ 619/696-7766); or Paras Newsstand and Cigar Shop, 3911 30th St. at University (☎ 619/296-2859).

Postage   Within the United States, it costs 20¢ to mail a standard-size postcard and 32¢ to send an oversize postcard (larger than 4¹/₄ by 6 inches, or 10.8 by 15.4 centimeters). Letters that weigh up to 1 ounce (that's about five 8-by-11-inch, or 20.5-by-28.2-centimeter, pages) cost 32¢, plus 23¢ for each additional ounce. A postcard to Mexico costs 40¢, a ¹/₂-ounce letter 40¢; a postcard to Canada costs 40¢, a 1-ounce letter 46¢. A postcard to Europe, Australia, New Zealand, the Far East, South America, and elsewhere costs 50¢ for the first ¹/₂ ounce and 40¢ for each additional ¹/₂ ounce; an Airgram costs 50¢.

Post Offices   See "Mail" above.

Safety   No matter what country you're in, when you're in an unfamiliar city, stay alert. Be aware of your immediate surroundings. Wear a moneybelt and don't flash expensive jewelry and cameras in public. Pay attention even in heavily touristed areas. If you're traveling in a rental car, never leave any belongings in the trunk.

San Diego is generally a safe city, but deserted areas downtown and elsewhere should be avoided at night.

Taxes   In the United States there is no VAT (value-added tax) or other indirect tax at a national level. There is a $10 Customs tax, payable on entry to the United States, and a $6 departure tax.

Sales tax in San Diego, charged on most purchases and on restaurant meals, is 7%. Tax on hotel rooms is 10.5%. Foreign visitors are subject to both these taxes, which are not refundable.

Telephone and Fax   Pay phones can be found on street corners, as well as in bars, restaurants, public buildings, stores and at service stations. Some accept 20¢, most are 25¢.

For local directory assistance ("information"), dial **411**; for long-distance information, dial 1, then the appropriate area code and **555-1212**.

For long-distance or international calls, it's most economical to charge the call to a telephone charge card or a credit card; or you can use a lot of change. The pay phone will instruct you how much to deposit and when to deposit it into the slot on the top of the telephone box.

For long-distance calls in the United States, dial 1 followed by the area code and number you want. For direct overseas calls, first dial 011, followed by the country code (Australia, 61; Republic of Ireland, 353; New Zealand, 64; United Kingdom, 44), and then by the city code (for example, 71 or 81 for London, 21 for Birmingham, 1 for Dublin) and the number of the person you wish to call.

Before calling from a hotel room, always ask the hotel phone operator if there are any telephone surcharges. There almost always are, often as much as 75¢ or $1, even for a local call. Avoid these charges by using a public phone, calling collect, or using a telephone charge card.

For reversed-charge or collect calls and for person-to-person calls, dial 0 (zero, not the letter "O") followed by the area code and number you want; an operator will then come on the line, and you should specify that you are calling collect, or person-to-person, or both. If your operator-assisted call is international, immediately ask to speak with an overseas operator.

Most hotels have fax machines available for their customers and usually charge to send or receive a facsimile. You will also see signs for public faxes in the windows of small shops.

Time   San Diego is on Pacific time, which is three hours earlier than on the U.S. East Coast. For instance, when it is noon in San Diego, it is 3pm in New York and Miami; 2pm in Chicago, in the central part of the country; and 1pm in Denver, Colorado, in the midwestern part of the country. San Diego, like the rest of the United States, observes daylight saving time during the summer; in late spring, clocks are moved ahead one hour and then are turned back again in the fall. This results in lovely long summer evenings, when the sun sets as late as 8:30 or 9pm. To verify the correct time call 619/853-1212.

Tipping   See "Fast Facts: San Diego" in Chapter 4.

Toilets   Restrooms are easy to come by in San Diego, although you won't find public facilities on street corners. Instead, expect to find them in hotel lobbies and in public places, such as Horton Plaza and Seaport Village. If there's a restroom attendant (unusual in San Diego), leave a coin—10¢ or 25¢. Restrooms in cafes and restaurants are for patrons only, but in an emergency you can just order a cup of coffee or simply ask to use the pay phone, usually conveniently positioned beside the restrooms.

4

Getting to Know San Diego

San Diego is laid out in an easy-to-decipher manner, so learning the lay of the land is neither confusing nor daunting. Add to this the fact that most San Diegans welcome visitors and are eager to answer questions and provide assistance. Chances are good that you'll feel like a local before you know it.

1 Orientation

VISITOR INFORMATION

There is a **Traveler's Aid booth** at both airport terminals, one at the train station, and (as mentioned in Chapter 3) one at the cruise-ship terminal. Volunteers can answer questions and provide helpful brochures and maps (☎ 619/231-7361, or use the courtesy phone at the airport).

In downtown San Diego, the **International Visitor Information Center** is on First Avenue at F Street, near Horton Plaza. The multilingual staff offers brochures in English, French, German, Japanese, Portuguese, and Spanish. They also provide the *San Diego Official Visitors Guide*, which includes information on accommodations, dining, activities and attractions, shopping, tours, and transportation, and also has excellent maps. You should also ask for the *Visitor Value Pack*, which is full of money-saving discount coupons. The center also sells telephone calling cards in $10, $20, and $50 denominations. These cards can be used from any telephone in the United States. The center is open Monday through Saturday from 8:30am to 5pm year-round and Sunday from 11am to 5pm June through August; it is closed Thanksgiving, Christmas, and New Year's Day. For more information, call 619/236-1212 (fax 619/232-1707).

Additional visitor information is available from **Balboa Park Visitors Center,** 1549 El Prado, San Diego, CA 92101 (☎ 619/239-0512); the **Coronado Visitor Bureau,** 1111 Orange Ave., Suite A, Coronado, CA 92118 (☎ 619/437-8788 or 800/622-8300); the **Mission Bay Visitors Information Center,** 2688 E. Mission Bay Dr., San Diego, CA 92109 (☎ 619/276-8200); **North County Convention and Visitors Bureau** (covers from La Jolla to Escondido and includes Julian and Anza-Borrego) 720 North Broadway, Escondido, CA 92025 (☎ 800/848-3336 or 619/745-4741); **Old Town Visitor Information Center,** 2461 San Diego Ave., San Diego, CA 92110

(☎ 619/291-1019); and the **La Jolla Town Council,** Box 1101, La Jolla, CA 92038 (☎ 619/454-1444). **Moneysaver Tickets 'N Tours** (☎ 800/721-2608) can provide information and discount tickets to tours, attractions, and theater by mail.

For the latest on San Diego nightlife and entertainment, pick up *the Reader,* a free newspaper which comes out on Thursday and is available at locations all over the city. Also check "Night and Day," the Thursday supplement in the *San Diego Union-Tribune.*

CITY LAYOUT

MAIN ARTERIES & STREETS   It's not hard to find your way around downtown San Diego. Most streets run one way: First through Twelfth avenues alternate running north and south (Fifth Avenue is two way in the Gaslamp Quarter only); A through K streets alternate running east and west. Broadway, the equivalent of D Street, is a two-way street, as are Market Street and Harbor Drive. East-west streets (north of A Street) bear the names of trees, in alphabetical order: Ash, Beech, Cedar, Date, etc. Harbor Drive runs past the airport and along the Embarcadero, or waterfront. The Coronado Bay Bridge leading to Coronado is accessed from I-5 south; Ash Street and Broadway are the downtown arteries that connect with Harbor Drive. I-5 north leads to Mission Bay, Old Town, La Jolla, and North County. Balboa Park, home of the San Diego Zoo, and the Hillcrest and Uptown areas lie northeast of downtown San Diego. The park and zoo are easily reached via Twelfth Avenue, which turns into Park Boulevard and leads up to their respective parking lots. Fifth Avenue leads to Hillcrest and Uptown (turn right onto University to get to the latter).

The major thoroughfares in downtown San Diego are Broadway (a major bus artery), Fourth and Fifth avenues (running south and north, respectively), C Street (the trolley line), and Harbor Drive, which hugs the waterfront and passes the Maritime Museum, Seaport Village, and the Convention Center. In the Hillcrest area near Balboa Park, the main streets are University and Washington, both two-way running east and west, and Fourth and Fifth avenues. In Mission Bay, it's Mission Boulevard, and perpendicular to it, Grand and Garnet avenues and Pacific Beach Drive; East and West Mission Bay drives and Ingraham Street enable you to zip around the periphery of the bay or bisect it. In Coronado, the main streets are Orange Avenue, where most of the hotels and restaurants are clustered, and Ocean Drive, which hugs Coronado Beach; in La Jolla, the main avenues are Prospect and Girard, which are perpendicular to one another.

FINDING AN ADDRESS   It's easy to find an address on a street running east-west when you're downtown. If the address is 411 Market St., for example, you'll find it between Fourth and Fifth avenues on Market; if it's 326 Broadway, it's between Third and Fourth avenues; if it's 1051 University, it's between Tenth and Eleventh avenues. Even numbers are located on the north or west side of streets, odd numbers are located on the south or east side of streets.

STREET MAPS   The **International Visitor Information Center,** located at First Avenue and F Street (☎ 619/236-1212), has an excellent free map that provides five easy-to-read maps: downtown San Diego and Coronado (with arrows pointing which way each street runs), Old Town, Balboa Park, La Jolla and Mission Bay, and San Diego County and vicinity.

The **Automobile Club of Southern California** (several locations including 815 Date St.; ☎ 619/233-1000) also has great maps that are free to its members and members of international auto clubs. The **Transit Store,** at the corner of Broadway and Fifth (☎ 619/233-3004), is a storehouse of bus and trolley maps, with a friendly staff on duty to answer specific questions.

Hotel receptionists can provide complimentary maps of the downtown area. You can buy maps of the city and vicinity at **Le Travel Store** at 739 Fourth Ave., the **Upstart Crow** bookstore in Seaport Village, or the **YMCA.**

If you're lucky enough to be moving to San Diego or plan to spend a long time here, I suggest you buy a copy of the *Thomas Bros. Guide,* available at bookstores, drugstores, and large supermarkets throughout San Diego. This all-encompassing book of maps deciphers San Diego for you, street by street.

NEIGHBORHOODS IN BRIEF

In this guidebook San Diego is divided into six areas, and hotel and restaurant listings are categorized under each.

Downtown   The business, shopping, dining, and entertainment heart of the city, it includes Horton Plaza, the Gaslamp Quarter, the Embarcadero (waterfront), Seaport Village, and the distinctive Convention Center. The Maritime Museum, the downtown branch of the Museum of Contemporary Art, and the Children's Museum are located here. Visitors with business to conduct in the city center would be wise to stay downtown. This is also the best area for those attending meetings at the Convention Center. The Gaslamp Quarter offers great dining and nightlife, but is surrounded by areas of questionable safety. Little Italy, a small neighborhood along India Street between Cedar and Fir at the northern edge of downtown, is the best place to find gelato, espresso, pizza, and pasta.

Hillcrest/Uptown   These two adjacent inner-city neighborhoods offer interesting dining and alternative entertainment options. Considered the city's gay area, they lie near Balboa Park, which is home to the San Diego Zoo and numerous museums, including the Museum of Art, the Museum of Photographic Arts, and the Reuben H. Fleet Space Theater and Science Center. Hillcrest and Uptown are centrally located and accommodations here are less expensive than other parts of the city.

Impressions

People in other places work hard to get somewhere, but in San Diego you're already there.

—Neil Morgan, associate editor, *San Diego Union-Tribune*

Neighborhoods at a Glance

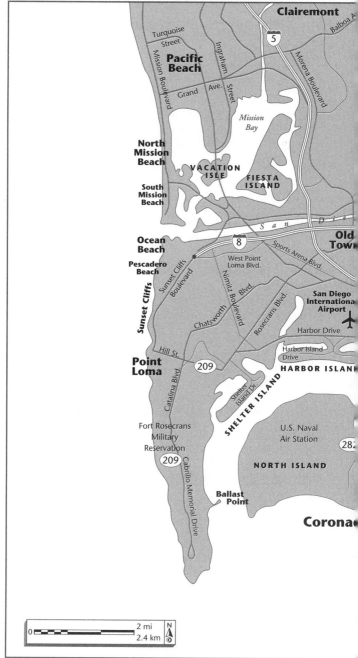

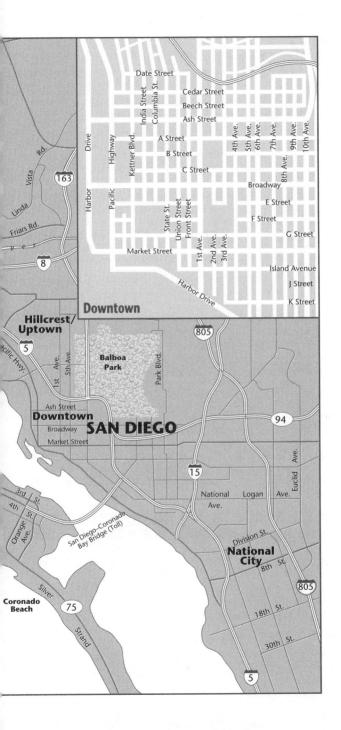

Downtown

Date Street
India Street
Columbia St.
Cedar Street
Beech Street
Ash Street
Drive
Highway
Kettner Blvd.
A Street
B Street
C Street
Harbor
Pacific
Broadway
4th Ave.
5th Ave.
6th Ave.
7th Ave.
8th Ave.
9th Ave.
10th Ave.
E Street
State St.
Union Street
Front Street
F Street
G Street
1st Ave.
2nd Ave.
3rd Ave.
Market Street
Island Avenue
Harbor Drive
J Street
K Street

Hillcrest/ Uptown

163

Vista Rd.

Linda

Friars Rd.

8

5

Pacific Hwy.

1st Ave.

5th Ave.

Balboa Park

Park Blvd.

805

Ash Street

Downtown

Broadway

SAN DIEGO

Market Street

94

15

Euclid Ave.

3rd St.

4th St.

Orange Ave.

National Ave.

Logan Ave.

San Diego-Coronado Bay Bridge (Toll)

National City

Division St.

8th St.

805

Coronado Beach

75

Silver Strand

18th St.

30th St.

5

Old Town   This area encompasses the Old Town State Historic Park, Presidio Park, Heritage Park, and numerous museums harking back to the turn of the century and the city's beginnings. There's shopping and dining here, too, all aimed at tourists. Not far from Old Town, **Hotel Circle** offers midprice and budget accommodation options on either side of I-8.

Mission Bay/Pacific Beach   Here's where they took the picture on the postcard you'll send home. Mission Bay is a watery playground perfect for water skiing, sailing, and wind surfing. The adjacent communities of Mission Beach and Pacific Beach are known for their wide stretches of sand fronting the Pacific, active nightlife, and California-casual dining. Many San Diego singles choose to live here, and once you've visited you'll understand why. The boardwalk, which runs from South Mission Beach through North Mission Beach to Pacific Beach, is a popular place for in-line skating, bike riding, and watching sunsets. This is the place to stay if you are traveling with beach-loving children or want to walk barefoot on the beach.

La Jolla   With an atmosphere that is a cross between Rodeo Drive and a Mediterranean village, this seaside community is home to an inordinate number of wealthy folks who could live anywhere, but choose to live here surrounded by the beach, the University of California San Diego, outstanding restaurants, excellent (albeit pricey) shops, and some of the world's best medical facilities. It is the wise tourist who beds down here, thereby taking advantage of the community's attributes without having to buy a piece of its high-priced real estate. The name is Spanish, as is the pronunciation—la HOY-ya—and it means "the jewel."

Coronado   Actually an incorporated city in its own right but included as a neighborhood here because of its close proximity to downtown San Diego by car and ferry, Coronado is a sedate place: home of the revered Hotel del Coronado and of more retired admirals than any other community in the country. It has a lovely duned beach (one of the area's most popular), fine restaurants, and a downtown area that reminds me of the small town in the Midwest where I grew up.

2 Getting Around

San Diego has many walkable neighborhoods, from the historic downtown area, to Hillcrest and nearby Balboa Park, to the Embarcadero, to Mission Bay Park. You get yourself there by car, bus, or trolley, and your feet will do the rest. For inspiration, turn to the city strolls in Chapter 8. Remember to cross streets at corners or in crosswalks; there's a $54 fine for jaywalking.

BY PUBLIC TRANSPORTATION

BY BUS   San Diego has an adequate, but not remarkable, bus system that will get you where you're going—eventually. Most drivers are friendly and helpful. The system, which includes 101 routes in the greater San Diego area, provides a special plus for travelers: the

Transit Store, at 449 Broadway (at Fifth Avenue). This information center can supply passes, tokens, timetables, maps, brochures, ID cards for seniors 60 and older as well as travelers with disabilities (who pay only 75¢ per ride), and lost-and-found information. Request a copy of the useful brochure *Your Open Door to San Diego,* which details the city's most popular tourist attractions and the buses that take you to them. You may also call (☎ 619/233-3004; for the hearing impaired, TTY/TDD 619/234-5005) and tell them where you are and where you want to go; Transit Store staff will tell you the nearest bus stop and what time the next couple of buses will pass by. That's service. You can call between 5:30am and 8:30pm daily except Thanksgiving and Christmas. The line is often busy, and the best times to call are noon to 3pm and on weekends. The Transit Store office is open Monday through Saturday from 8:30am to 5:30pm.

Bus stops are marked by rectangular blue signs every other block or so on local routes. More than 20 bus routes pass through the downtown area, among them nos. 2, 4, 7, 9, 29, 34, and 35. Local fare is $1.50 one way and you must have the exact change ($1 bills are accepted); express buses, whose numbers end in "0," cost $1.75.

You can get a **transfer** at no extra charge as long as you continue on a bus or trolley with an equal or lower fare (if it's higher, you simply pay the difference). Transfers must be used within an hour, and you can actually loop back to where you started as long as you use a different route on a different timetable.

A particular saving is the **Day Tripper** pass, which allows unlimited rides on the metropolitan transit system for one day for only $5 (four days for $15). Buses that go to popular tourist attractions include nos. 7, 7A, 7B, 1, 3, and 25 to Balboa Park; nos. 7, 7A, and 7B to the San Diego Zoo and Seaport Village; nos. 9 and 34 to Kemper and Midway, then no. 6A to the Cabrillo National Monument; no. 9 to Sea World and Pacific Beach; no. 2 to the Maritime Museum at the Embarcadero; and nos. 4 and 5/105 to Old Town. No. 2 goes to the airport, and no. 34 goes to Mission Beach and La Jolla. Most buses serving the downtown area pass by or close to Horton Plaza; double-check with the driver just to be sure.

BY TRAIN The **Coaster** (☎ 800/COASTER) travels between downtown and Oceanside, with stops en route at Carlsbad, Encinitas, Solana Beach, Sorrento Valley, and Old Town. Fares range from $4.75

Impressions

Of all the dilapidated, miserable-looking places I've ever seen, this was the worst . . . an altogether dreary, sunblasted point of departure for nowhere. . . .
　　　　　　—Mary Chase Walker (San Diego's first schoolteacher), 1865

A little land and a living, surely, is better than a desperate struggle and wealth, possibly.　　　　　　—William E. Smythe
　　　　　　(Utopian founder of the Little Landers Movement), 1908

to $6.20 round trip, depending how far you go; it takes 60 minutes to get to Oceanside from downtown. Trains run Monday through Friday; call for current schedule. The San Diego to Los Angeles **AMTRAK** service (☎ 800/USARAIL) stops at Solana Beach, Oceanside, and San Juan Capistrano. A round-trip ticket to Oceanside is $18 and round-trip to San Juan Capistrano is $22.

BY TROLLEY The bright-red **San Diego Trolley** is both fun to ride and an efficient form of transportation. There are two trolley lines: the east, or El Cajon, and the south, or San Ysidro. The latter is also known as the Tijuana Trolley because it takes you right to the Mexican border in only 40 minutes.

Downtown stops include the Marriott Hotel, Convention Center/ Gaslamp Quarter, Seaport Village, Santa Fe Station, Third Avenue (Civic Center), Fifth Avenue, and Twelfth Avenue (City College). Trolleys operate on a self-service fare collection system whereby, before boarding, passengers purchase tickets from machines at the trolley stops. The machines list fares for each destination and should give you your ticket and any change you require, after you push the button to specify how much you are paying. (Some machines require exact change.) Tickets are good for two hours from the time of purchase in one direction only. Fare inspectors randomly board trains and check proof of payment.

Trolleys generally run every 15 minutes and stop for less than half a minute at each stop; to board, push the lighted green button beside the doors. Stations are announced as the trolley approaches them. To exit the car, push the lighted white button beside the doors if they do not open automatically. Trolley travel within the downtown area costs $1; the fare to the border is $1.75. Senior citizens 60 and over and riders with disabilities pay a flat fee of 75¢, and children 5 and under ride free. For recorded trolley information, call 619/231-8549; to get a real person on the line, call 619/233-3004 or TTY/TDD 619/234-5005 from 5:30am to 8:30pm daily. The trolley generally operates daily from 5am to about 12:30am, although the San Ysidro line runs 24 hours on Saturday.

The **Old Town Trolley** (☎ 619/298-8687), a city tour in an open-air bus cum trolley, is actually an excellent and economical way to get around for a day of sightseeing: The trolley stops at more than a dozen locations and you can hop on and off as many times as you please during one entire loop. The tour takes 90 minutes, but keep in mind that once you've completed the circuit, you can't go around again. Major stops include Old Town, Presidio Park, Bazaar del Mundo, Balboa Park, the San Diego Zoo, the Embarcadero, Seaport Village, and the Gaslamp Quarter. The tour costs $16 for adults and $7 for kids 6 to 12, kids 5 and under ride free. The trolley operates from 9am to 5pm in summer, 9am to 4pm the rest of the year. It's a good idea to get an early start to allow time for getting on and off; a trolley passes each stop every half hour.

The economical **Coronado Shuttle,** bus no. 904, runs between Le Meridien Hotel and the ferry landing along Orange Avenue to the Hotel del Coronado and Glorietta Bay and back again. It costs only

San Diego Trolley System

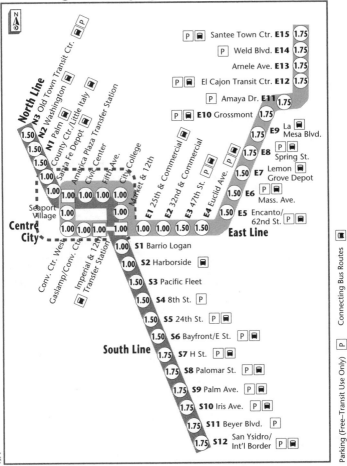

Santee Town Ctr. **E15** 1.75
Weld Blvd. **E14** 1.75
Arnele Ave. **E13** 1.75
El Cajon Transit Ctr. **E12** 1.75
Amaya Dr. **E11** 1.75
E10 Grossmont 1.75
E9 La Mesa Blvd. 1.75
E8 Spring St. 1.75
E7 Lemon Grove Depot 1.50
E6 Mass. Ave. 1.50
E5 Encanto/62nd St. 1.50

North Line
N3 Old Town Transit Ctr.
N2 Washington
N1 Palm
County Ctr./Little Italy
Santa Fe Depot
America Plaza Transfer Station
Civic Center
Fifth Ave.
City College
Market & 12th
E1 25th & Commercial
E2 32nd & Commercial
E3 47th St.
E4 Euclid Ave.

1.50
1.50
1.50
1.00
1.00 1.00 1.00 1.00
Seaport Village
1.00
1.00 1.00 1.00 1.00 1.00 1.00 1.50 1.50

Centre City

Conv. Ctr. West
Gaslamp/Conv. Ctr.
Imperial & 12th Transfer Station

East Line

1.00 **S1** Barrio Logan
1.00 **S2** Harborside
1.50 **S3** Pacific Fleet
1.50 **S4** 8th St.
1.50 **S5** 24th St.
1.50 **S6** Bayfront/E St.

South Line

1.75 **S7** H St.
1.75 **S8** Palomar St.
1.75 **S9** Palm Ave.
1.75 **S10** Iris Ave.
1.75 **S11** Beyer Blvd.
1.75 **S12** San Ysidro/Int'l Border

Connecting Bus Routes
Parking (Free-Transit Use Only)

1574

50¢ per person within Coronado. Bus no. 901 goes to Coronado from San Diego and costs $1.50 for adults or 75¢ for seniors and children (☎ 619/233-3004).

BY CAR

San Diegans complain of increasing traffic, but the city is still easy to navigate by car. Streets downtown tend to run one way, which may hamper you until you learn the lay of the land (the International Visitor Information Center map is a big help, complete with arrows). Finding a parking space can be tricky, but some reasonably priced parking lots are fairly centrally located.

RENTALS If you don't arrive by car in San Diego, you should probably rent one if your budget allows. While it's possible to get around by public transportation, having your own wheels is a big advantage.

All the major car-rental agencies have offices at the airport and in the larger hotels. **Avis,** like several other car-rental companies in San Diego, will allow its cars into Mexico as far as Ensenada. Beyond Ensenada, the roads aren't as well maintained and it's more difficult to get to the car should there be a breakdown or other problem (see "Tijuana" in Chapter 11 and "Baja California" in Chapter 12).

PARKING　The garage at Horton Plaza, at G Street and Fourth Avenue, is free to shoppers for the first three hours (the parking ticket must be validated by a merchant or you must show your cinema or theater stub from Horton Plaza), then costs $1 per half-hour afterward. A quick way to zip into Horton Plaza and avoid the ever-upward spiral until you find a parking spot is to enter the back way, via Third Avenue. The fenced-in lot adjacent to the Embarcadero, called Allright Parking, at 900 Broadway and Harbor Drive (☎ 619/298-6944), charges $3 to park between 5:30am and midnight. More convenient to downtown shopping and the Children's Museum is the open-air lot on Market Street between Front and First streets, where you can park all day weekdays for $3 and $2 for weekends. Three-hour meters line Harbor Drive opposite the ticket offices for harbor tours; even on weekends, you have to feed them.

Parking meters are plentiful in downtown San Diego; trouble is, the spaces belonging to them are usually taken. Meters take quarters, up to a two-hour limit; you have to feed them between 8am and 6pm, even on weekends.

DRIVING RULES　California has a seat belt law, so buckle up before you venture out. You may turn right at a red light after stopping unless a sign says otherwise. Likewise, you can turn left on a red light from a one-way street onto another one-way street after coming to a full stop. Most freeway exits are to the right. Keep in mind when driving in San Diego that pedestrians have the right-of-way at all times, so stop for pedestrians who have stepped off the curb.

BY TAXI

Half a dozen taxi companies serve the San Diego area, and they do not have standardized rates, except from the airport into downtown, which will cost about $8.50 with tip. Taxis don't cruise the streets here like they do in other cities, so call one of the companies for quick pickup. If you are at a hotel or restaurant, the front-desk attendant or maître d' will call for you. Among the companies are **Orange Cab** (☎ 619/291-3333)and **Yellow Cab** (☎ 619/234-6161). The **Coronado Cab Company** (☎ 619/435-6211) serves Coronado.

BY FERRY/WATER TAXI

Regularly scheduled ferry service between San Diego and Coronado (☎ 619/234-4111) provides a comfortable 15-minute ride with splendid views of the city. Take your camera. The ferry departs San Diego from Harbour Drive adjacent to the Broadway Pier on the hour from 9am to 9pm Sunday through Thursday and from 9am to 10pm Friday and Saturday; it returns from the Ferry Landing Marketplace in

Coronado to San Diego every hour on the half hour 9:30am to 9:30pm Sunday through Thursday and from 9:30am to 10:30pm Friday and Saturday. The cost is $2 one way, 50¢ extra for bikes each way. Tickets cannot be purchased on board but can be purchased from Harbor Excursions (on Harbour Drive) in San Diego and from a shop in the Ferry Landing Marketplace (look for the sign out front) in Coronado.

WATER TAXI Another option is to hire a water taxi to take you anywhere you want to go on San Diego Bay for $5 (☎ 619/235-TAXI). On Mission Bay you can catch a water taxi and go to Sea World or any of the bay-front resorts. The cost is $4 one way, $6 round trip (☎ 800/300-7447).

BY BICYCLE

San Diego is flat enough for easy exploration by bicycle and many roads have designated bike lanes. Bikes are readily rentable. Downtown, you can try **Pennyfarthing's,** 520 Fifth Ave., in the Gaslamp Quarter (☎ 619/233-7696). In Mission Bay there are **Hamel's Action Sports Center,** 704 Ventura Place, off Mission Boulevard at the roller coaster (☎ 619/488-5050); **Pacific Beach Sun and Sea,** 4539 Ocean Blvd. (☎ 619/483-6613); and **Hilton Beach and Tennis Resort,** 1775 E. Mission Bay Dr. (☎ 619/276-4010). In Coronado are **Holland's Bicycles,** 977 Orange Ave. (☎ 619/435-3153), and **Bikes and Beyond,** 1201 First St. at the Old Ferry Landing (☎ 619/435-7180). Free pickup and delivery in San Diego for a day's rental is available through **Rent A Bike,** at First Avenue and Harbor Drive (☎ 619/232-4700). Bike rentals average about $10. You can also rent by the week or month, and two-seaters for couples are available.

Any bus stops that have bike-route signs attached alert you that buses stopping here have a bike rack attached and will take your trusty two-wheeler for free. Just let the driver know you want to use it. Once you have stowed the bike on the back of the bus, board and pay your regular fare. When you get off, remind the bus driver that you need to get your bike. With this service you can bus the bike to an area you'd like to explore, do your biking there, then return by bus with your wheels in tow. Not all routes are served by buses with bike racks; call 619/233-3004 for information.

The San Diego Trolley has a **Bike-N-Ride** program that lets you bring your bike on the trolley for free during certain specified hours. You'll need to get a bike permit and display it on the bike before you board. Permits to bikers 16 and older cost $3 and are issued through **American Youth Hostels,** 500 W. Broadway (☎ 619/239-2644); it's open Monday through Friday from 9am to 4pm. Bikers must board at the back of a trolley car, which is where the bike-storage area is; cars carry only two bikes at any given time. Bikers pay the regular fare and nothing extra for their wheels. Several trolley stops connect with routes for buses that are equipped with bike tracks. For more information, call the Transit Store at 619/233-3004.

Bikes are also welcome on the ferry connecting San Diego and Coronado, which has 15 miles of dedicated bike paths.

FAST FACTS: San Diego

Airport   See "Getting There" in Chapter 2.

American Express   A full-service American Express office in downtown is at 258 Broadway (☎ 619/234-4455).

Area Code   Dial **619** to call San Diego or any town in San Diego County from anywhere outside the county.

Baby-sitters   A number of hotels will secure a bonded sitter for guests, or you can call Marion's Child, whose sitters are bonded (☎ 619/582-5029).

Business Hours   **Banks** are open weekdays from 9am to 3pm or later and sometimes Saturday morning. The Wells Fargo Bank, on West Broadway at Front Street (☎ 619/589-5150), is open weekdays from 7:30am to 6pm and Saturday from 9am to 2pm. **Shops** in shopping complexes tend to stay open until about 9pm weekdays and until 6pm weekends.

Car Rentals   See "Getting Around" earlier in this chapter.

Climate   See "When to Go" in Chapter 2.

Dentists   See "Doctors" below.

Doctors   **Doctors on Call** includes physicians, dentists, optometrists, chiropractors, and podiatrists who claim they will come to your hotel room within one hour of your call. They accept credit cards and their services are covered by most insurance (☎ 619/275-2663, 24 hours a day). Doctors speak a number of languages and will bring medications to you. In a life-threatening situation, dial 911.

Driving Rules   See "Getting Around" earlier in this chapter.

Drugstores   See "Pharmacies" below.

Embassies/Consulates   See Chapter 3, "For Foreign Visitors."

Emergencies   Call **911** for fire, police, and ambulance. The main police station is located at 1401 Broadway at Fourteenth Street (☎ 619/531-2065; 619/531-2000 for hearing impaired).

Eyeglass Repair   **Optometric Express** is in Horton Plaza, street level near the Doubletree Hotel (☎ 619/544-9000); it's open Monday through Saturday 9:30am to 6pm.

Hospitals   In Hillcrest, near downtown San Diego, there is **Mercy Hospital,** 4077 Fifth Ave. (☎ 619/260-7044); in Mission Bay, **Mission Bay Hospital,** 3030 Bunker Hill St. (☎ 619/274-7721); and in Coronado, **Coronado Hospital,** 250 Prospect Place, opposite Le Meridien Hotel (☎ 619/435-6251).

Hotlines   Adult Children of Alcoholics: 619/276-6232; AIDS Information Line: 800/922-2437 (English) or 800/922-2438 (multilingual); Alcoholics Anonymous: 619/265-8762; Debtors Anonymous: 619/525-3065; Mental Health Crisis Line: 619/236-3339; Overeaters Anonymous: 619/563-4606; Traveler's Aid Society: 619/231-7361

Information   See "Visitor Information" earlier in this chapter.

Libraries   The public library, at 820 E St. (☎ 619/236-5800), is open Monday through Thursday from 10am to 9pm, Friday and Saturday from 9:30am to 5:30pm, and Sunday from 1 to 5pm; it's closed on holidays.

Liquor Laws   The drinking age in California is 21. Beer, wine, and hard liquor are sold seven days a week from 6am to 2am, and are available in grocery stores.

Lost Property   To report a lost or found item on the trolley or bus, call 619/234-1060. Anything that has been on a bus may be retrieved the following day after 10am at the Transit Store at Broadway and Fifth Avenue. Items found on trolleys may be picked up at the Transit Store on Monday, Wednesday, or Friday after 11:30am. Lost articles are held for 30 days. The airport has a lost-and-found department, as does each airline. For items left in hotel rooms, check with housekeeping.

Luggage Storage/Lockers   The bus station, on Broadway between 1st and Front streets, has locker space available for $1 for 24 hours. Most hotels will store luggage on a short-term basis at no charge. There are no lockers at the airport, and there is only a partial storage for Amtrak passengers.

Maps   See "City Layout" earlier in this chapter.

Newspapers/Magazines   The *San Diego Union-Tribune* is published daily, and its informative entertainment section, "Night & Day," is in the Thursday edition. For the irreverent alternative press, check the *Reader*, published weekly (on Thursday) with dining and entertainment sections. *San Diego* magazine is filled with extensive entertainment and dining listings, while *San Diego Home/Garden* magazine highlights the city's homes and gardens and provides a monthly calendar of events, including garden tours and talks and family-oriented outings. Both magazines are published monthly and sold at newsstands. The free *San Diego This Week* has restaurant listings and information about shopping, attractions, nightlife, and the latest goings-on about town, as does the *Guest Quick Guide* (for coverage of San Diego, La Jolla, and North County), published quarterly by Guest Informant.

Pharmacies   Long's, Sav-On, and **Thrifty** sell pharmaceuticals and nonprescription products. Look in the phone book to find the one nearest you. If you need a pharmacy after normal business hours call **Sav-On** (800/627-2866). Local hospitals also sell prescription drugs.

Police   The downtown police station is at 1500 Broadway (☎ 619/ 525-8400 or 619/531-2000 for TDD). Call 911 in an emergency.

Post Office   The **downtown branch** of the post office, at 815 E St., between Eighth and Ninth avenues, is open Monday through Friday from 8:30am to 5pm, on Saturday from 8:30am to noon. The more centrally located **51 Horton Plaza branch,** beside the

Doubletree Hotel, is open Monday through Friday from 8am to 6pm and Saturday from 9am to 5pm.

Radio **FM** radio stations include 98.1 (KIFM) for jazz; 89.5 (KPBS-NPR) news, classical and interviews; 94.1 (KFSD), classical; 97.3 (KSON), country; 101.5 (KGB), classic rock; 103.7 (KJOY), elevator music; 105.3 (KCBQ), oldies; and 106.5 (KKLQ), Top 40. **AM** stations include 600 (KKLQ), Top 40; 760 (KFMB) and 1130 (KSDO), talk; and 1170 (KCBQ), oldies.

Restrooms Horton Plaza and Seaport Village downtown, Balboa Park, Old Town State Historic Park in Old Town, and the Ferry Landing Marketplace in Coronado all have well-marked restrooms. In general, you won't have a problem finding one.

Safety San Diego is a safe city, but parts of it tend to become deserted after 9pm, when most people have dined and are headed home. The best nights for walking in the city are Friday and Saturday, when everybody is out. It is best to avoid deserted or sparsely populated beaches after dark, even though they may appear to be romantic. In Balboa Park, stay on designated walkways and away from secluded areas. In the Gaslamp Quarter, don't go east of 5th Avenue. It's always a good idea to stay alert and aware of your surroundings when you're in any unfamiliar city, even in the most heavily touristed areas.

Taxes Sales tax in restaurants and shops is 7%. Hotel tax is 10.5%.

Taxis See "Getting Around" earlier in this chapter.

Television You can choose from San Diego and Los Angeles stations: in San Diego, channels 6 (Fox), 8 (CBS), 10 (ABC), 39 (NBC), 15 (PBS), and independent stations on channels 51 and 69; from Los Angeles, channels 2 (CBS), 4 (NBC), and 7 (ABC). Channels 12, 19, and 52 offer programming in Spanish. Many hotels have cable TV, including HBO for movies.

Time Zone San Diego, like the entire West Coast, is in the Pacific standard time zone, which is eight hours behind Greenwich mean time. Daylight saving time is observed. To find out what time it is, call 619/853-1212.

Transit Information Call 619/233-3004.

Useful Telephone Numbers For the latest San Diego arts and entertainment information, call 619/238-3810; for a beach and surf report, call 619/221-8884. For Mexico tourist information, call 619/298-4105.

Weather Call 619/289-1212.

5

San Diego Accommodations

San Diego offers a wide variety of places to stay that range from pricey high-rise hostelries to inexpensive low-rise motels and some out-of-the-ordinary B&Bs. You'll be able to sleep in historic surroundings or in rooms facing the bay or with ocean views.

With regard to rates, those given here do not include hotel tax, which is an additional 10.5%. I've noted when the price includes breakfast. Rates, of course, are subject to change. You will find that weekend rates are often less expensive at downtown hotels and higher in resort areas. Accordingly tariffs are higher from June through Labor Day—especially in the beach areas. San Diego hoteliers also sometimes raise rates during periods when the city is hosting more conventions than usual.

The hotels listed below are divided first by location, then alphabetically by price category within a given district. Price categories are arranged as follows on a double-occupancy basis: **very expensive,** $160 or more; **expensive,** $110 to $159; **moderate,** $71 to $109; **inexpensive,** under $70.

For the lowest available prices in all accommodations categories, including motels and other properties that charge $39 and up, contact **San Diego Hotel Reservations** (☎ 619/627-9300 or 800/SAVE-CASH). For information on 30 bed-and-breakfasts in the San Diego area, send $3.95 for a 20-page directory to **B&B Resources,** P.O. Box 3292, San Diego, CA 92163 (☎ 619/297-3130 or 800/619-ROOM [7666]).

For those who prefer to stay as close as possible to the airport, here are two good choices: the 1,050-room **Sheraton Harbor Island**, 1380 Harbor Island Dr. (☎ 619/291-2900 or 800/325-3535), and the 208-room **Travelodge Hotel—Harbor Island** (☎ 619/291-6700 or 800/255-3050). Both of these hotels offer guests marina views, a health club, and a pool.

Readers who want to improve their minds and/or their bodies while they are in San Diego should be sure to read the "Select Spas" box in Chapter 11. Places to stay outside of San Diego are listed in Chapters 11 and 12.

48 San Diego Accommodations

1 Best Bets

- **Best Historic Hotel:** The **Hotel del Coronado** (☎ 800/ HOTEL DEL) positively reeks of history. Built in 1888, Thomas Edison himself installed the electric lights, and later the course of history was changed when the Prince of Wales met Mrs. Simpson here at a dinner party.
- **Best for Business Travelers: The Hyatt Regency San Diego** (☎ 619/232-1234 or 800/233-1234) has a full-service business center and the other amenities that businesspeople expect. Access to downtown is also a plus.
- **Best for a Romantic Getaway:** The sense of seclusion at **Loew's Coronado Bay Resort** (☎ 619/424-4000) makes it a good choice for a tryst. The spacious well-appointed rooms, large marble bathrooms, and fine bed linens also set the stage. (For a romantic getaway farther afield, see Rancho Valencia in Chapter 11.)
- **Best for Families:** The **Hilton Beach and Tennis Resort** (☎ 619/276-4010) offers plenty of activities—enough to keep family members of all ages happy.
- **Best Moderately Priced Hotel:** The **Sommerset Suites Hotel** (☎ 619/692-5200), one of San Diego's best bargains, feels like a home away from home.
- **Best Budget Hotel:** Located in San Diego's Little Italy, **La Pensione** (☎ 800/232-4683) feels like a small European hotel and offers tidy lodgings at bargain prices.
- **Best B&B:** The **Bed and Breakfast Inn** at La Jolla (☎ 619/ 456-2066) offers attractive rooms, delicious breakfasts, and a pretty patio—all within walking distance of restaurants, shops, and the ocean.
- **Best Place to Stay on the Beach:** At **The Sea Lodge** in La Jolla (☎ 619/459-8271 or 800/237-5211), you can walk right onto the wide beach and frolic in the great waves. Lifeguards and the lack of undertow here make this a popular choice for families.
- **Best Hotel Pool:** What makes **La Valencia's** pool so special is its spectacular setting overlooking Scripps Park and the Pacific.

2 Downtown

VERY EXPENSIVE

Hyatt Regency San Diego

1 Market Place (at Harbor Drive), San Diego, CA 92101. ☎ **619/232-1234** or 800/ 233-1234. Fax 619/233-6464. 819 rms, 56 suites. A/C MINIBAR TV TEL. $159–$245 single or double; from $325 suite. Children under 12 stay free in parents' room. Numerous packages and special weekend rates. AE, CB, DC, DISC, MC, V. Self-parking, $8; valet parking, $11. Bus: 1. Trolley: Seaport Village.

The 40-story Hyatt Regency, the tallest waterfront hotel on the West Coast, offers visitors a choice of ocean, bay, or city views. The light, airy lobby with Italian limestone columns and touches of marble is embellished with two 27-foot-high paintings of country scenes by San Diegan Richard Babriel Chase; here you'll be greeted by the friendly, helpful desk staff. The quiet and restful rooms are done in a variety of fabrics, textures, and colors, each with a floral chintz bedspread, a plaid armchair, 18th-century English furniture, custom-designed lamps, and Impressionist-style paintings. Baths have ample counter space, and hallways have picture windows at either end. The Hyatt Regency, which opened in 1992, is adjacent to Seaport Village and within walking distance of the Convention Center and the Gaslamp Quarter.

Dining/Entertainment: The formal, modern Sally's restaurant is in a half-moon-shaped building beside the bay, a short stroll from the hotel. It serves lunch and dinner, featuring fresh seafood and Mediterranean and California cuisine. The more informal Lael's serves breakfast, lunch, and dinner. For pastries and light fare go to Ann-Marie's Espresso. (Sally, Lael, and Ann-Marie are the hotel owner's daughters.) All three offer al fresco dining. The library-like Worthington's lobby bar has a big-screen TV and live entertainment on weekends, while the elegant Top of the Hyatt, on the 40th floor, is a romantic bar with a spectacular view of the marina and bay bridge; both serve snacks.

Services: Concierge, 24-hour room service, dry cleaning/laundry service, twice-daily maid service, babysitting, express checkout, valet parking, airport transportation.

Facilities: In-room movies and cable TV, video rental, 75-foot outdoor pool, Jacuzzi, health club with massage rooms and aerobics classes twice a week, four outdoor tennis courts, voice-mail messages, laptop-compatible telephones, 50% nonsmoking floors, Regency Club with its own lounge and concierge, marina, boat rental, business center, meeting rooms, car-rental desk beauty salon, shops.

✪ San Diego Marriott Marina

333 W. Harbor Dr. (at Front Street), San Diego, CA 92101-7700. ☎ **619/234-1500** or 800/228-9290. Fax 619/234-8678. 1,355 rms, 50 suites. A/C MINIBAR TV TEL. $220–$225 single or double; from $330 suite. Children under 18 stay free in parents' room. AARP discount and honeymoon and other packages available. AE, CB, DC, DISC, MC, V. Self-parking $8; valet parking $11. Bus: 1. Trolley: Convention Center.

San Diego's most striking modern hotel dominates the waterfront with two graceful, curving towers and a 446-slip marina, lush grounds, and waterfall-accented outdoor pool. Many rooms have balconies with breathtaking bay-and-beyond views. The well-situated hotel is a short stroll from Seaport Village, Embarcadero Marina Park, the Convention Center, and the restaurants and nightspots of the Gaslamp Quarter.

Dining/Entertainment: There are several restaurants, as well as pleasant D. W.'s Pub and Lounge with its large-screen TV; the popular Yacht Club features casual dining and dancing on the waterfront.

Services: Concierge, 24-hour room service, on-site laundry and dry cleaning.

Facilities: No-smoking rooms, concierge floor, video rental, two outdoor pools, six lighted tennis courts, two whirlpools, fitness center, daily aerobics classes, bicycle and boat rentals, shops, hair salon, spa, business center with secretarial services, car-rental desk.

San Diego Accommodations

DOWNTOWN AREA:

Best Western
  Bayside Inn **3**
Churchill **10**
Clarion Bay View **13**
Embassy Suites **11**
Gaslamp Plaza Suites **9**
Holiday Inn on the Bay **2**
Hotel San Diego **6**
Horton Grand **12**
Hyatt Regency **14**
Hostelling International—
  San Diego **4**
La Pensione **1**
Marriott Marina **15**
Wyndham
  Emerald Plaza **5**
U.S. Grant Hotel **8**
Westgate **7**

OTHER AREAS:

Balboa Park Inn **23**
The Cottage **20**
El Cordova Hotel **26**
El Rancho Hotel **25**
Glorietta Bay Inn **28**
Hacienda Hotel **16**
Heritage Park Bed &
  Breakfast Inn **17**
Hotel del Coronado **27**
Le Meridien **24**
Loew's Coronado
  Bay Resort **29**
Park Manor Suites **22**
Sommerset Suites
  Hotel **21**
Travelodge **18**
Vacation Inn **19**

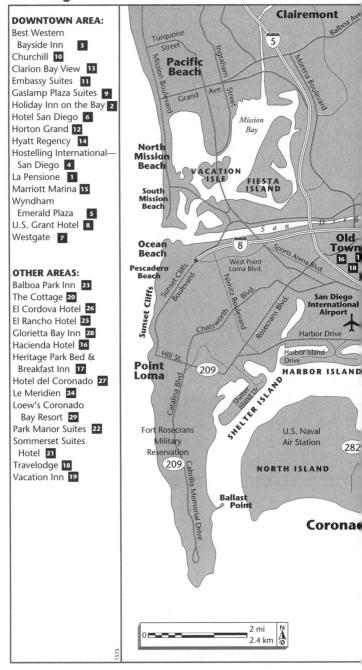

1575

1 Date Street

Cedar Street

Beech Street

Ash Street

India Street

Columbia St.

2

Drive

Highway

Kettner Blvd.

3 A Street

B Street

C Street

4th Ave.

5th Ave.

6th Ave.

7th Ave.

9th Ave.

10th Ave.

4 **5**

7 **8**

8th Ave.

10

Harbor

Pacific

6

Broadway

9 E Street

State St.

Union Street

Front Street

F Street

G Street

11

Market Street

1st Ave.

2nd Ave.

3rd Ave.

Island Avenue

12

J Street

13 K Street

Harbor Drive

Downtown

14

21

20

Hillcrest/
Uptown

22

23

805

Pacific Hwy.

5

1st. Ave.

5th Ave.

Balboa
Park

Park Blvd.

Linda Vista Rd.

163

Friars Rd.

8

Ash Street

Downtown

Broadway

Market Street

SAN DIEGO

94

Euclid Ave.

15

15

National
Ave.

Logan Ave.

3rd St.

24

4th Ave.

25

Orange Ave.

San Diego–Coronado
Bay Bridge (Toll)

Division St.

26

National
City

8th St.

27

28

805

Coronado
Beach

Silver Strand

75

18th St.

30th St.

29

5

U.S. Grant Hotel

326 Broadway (between Third and Fourth avenues), San Diego, CA 92101. ☎ **619/ 232-3121** or 800/334-6957 in California, 800/237-5029 elsewhere. 280 rms, 60 suites. A/C MINIBAR TV TEL. $165–$185 double; from $245 suite. Children under 16 stay free in parents' room. AE, CB, DC, MC, V. Parking $10. Bus: 1, 2, 3, or 25. Trolley: Civic Center (C St. and Third Ave.)

In 1910, Ulysses S. Grant Jr. opened this stately hotel, now on the National Register of Historic Places, in honor of his father. The younger Grant lived in a suite here from 1919 until his death in 1929; his wife stayed until her death in 1942. Famous guests have included Albert Einstein, Charles Lindbergh, FDR, and JFK. The elegant lobby has a luxurious, specially designed rug and, as its centerpiece, a giant floral arrangement. Rooms and baths are spacious and furnished with 18th-century reproductions and mahogany two-poster beds. Terry-cloth robes hang in the closet. The hotel is right across the street from Horton Plaza. Note: this is one of the few top-class hotels that permits pets to stay in guest rooms. Rumor has it that pooches even get their own personalized pillows.

Dining/Entertainment: The prestigious Grant Grill is a lunchtime favorite that resembles an exclusive private club. In fact, in 1969 eight determined female San Diegans defied the "gentlemen only" lunch restriction, and a plaque in the restaurant honors their successful effort. You can watch your meal being prepared in the unique rotisserie kitchen. The Grant Grill Lounge, with a working fireplace and wood-paneled walls, offers light lunches (carved sandwiches, meat and seafood pies, and salads), cocktails, and live blues and jazz, usually Thursday through Saturday nights. Afternoon tea, served in the lobby on Tuesday through Saturday, with soft piano music as a backdrop, is a highlight of a stay here.

Services: Concierge, 24-hour room service, same-day laundry/ dry cleaning (except Sunday), turn-down service, babysitting, courtesy shuttle to and from the airport and to downtown attractions, limousine service.

Facilities: In-room movies, 24-hour fitness center with panoramic view of downtown, in-room exercise bike and rowing machine rentals, access to San Diego Athletic Club, golf and tennis privileges at Singing Hills Country Club, meeting rooms, business services, safe-deposit boxes, terry-cloth robes.

Westgate

1055 Second Ave. (between Broadway and C Street), San Diego, CA 92101. ☎ **619/ 238-1818** or 800/221-3802. Fax 619/557-3604. 212 rms, 11 suites. A/C MINIBAR TV TEL. $164–$194 double; from $325 suite. Extra adult $10. Children 18 and under stay free in parents' room. Honeymoon and other packages available. AE, DC, DISC, MC, V. Underground valet parking $10. Bus: 1, 2, 3, or 25. Trolley: Civic Center (C Street and Third Avenue).

This lavish hotel, built in 1970, exemplifies European style. No two rooms are alike, and antiques have full reign. The lobby, lit with a half-dozen Baccarat crystal chandeliers, is right out of 18th-century France. Flemish and French tapestries and Persian carpets complete the picture. Not surprisingly, the Westgate is a member of the Leading Hotels of the World and is popular with foreign dignitaries. Its complimentary shuttle service to downtown appointments and attractions is an added bonus. A number of airline booking offices, among them those for Northwest, United, Delta, American, and Aeroméxico, are conveniently located in the building's base, with entrances on Broadway.

Dining/Entertainment: The Fontainebleau Room offers candlelight dining; the Westgate Room, casual dining; and the Plaza Bar, cocktails and live entertainment.

Services: Concierge; 24-hour room service; valet service; complimentary transportation to airport, downtown appointments, Sea World, zoo.

Facilities: Deli (with international foods and wines), workout room, sundeck, meeting rooms, barbershop, gift shop.

Wyndham Emerald Plaza

400 W. Broadway (between State and Columbia streets), San Diego, CA 92101-3580. ☎ **619/239-4500.** Fax 619/239-4527. 436 rms, 20 suites. A/C MINIBAR TV TEL. $180–$200 double; from $340 suite. Children under 16 stay free in parents' room. AE, CB, DC, DISC, MC, V. Underground parking $8. Bus: 2, 4, 7, 34, and many more. Trolley: America Plaza.

You can deduce that this hotel (formerly the Pan Pacific) is different from its location—the hotel/office complex that dynamically changed the skyline of San Diego as it rose in a cluster of eight hexagonal towers in 1991. Inside, you'll find a pseudo-Deco, but thoroughly modern lobby; a soaring atrium; glass elevators that glide past 26 floors; and sleek, stylish, well-lit rooms, most overlooking the city and bay. The hotel is one block from the train station and trolley stop, a short walk to the Embarcadero and Horton Plaza, and two miles from the airport. If you choose to skip the typically pricey hotel breakfast, inexpensive eateries are in the building and half a block away.

Dining/Entertainment: Romeo Cuccina specializes in northern Italian fare and is open for lunch and dinner, while The Grill serves California cuisine and is open for breakfast, lunch, and dinner. The lively Atrium lobby lounge provides cocktails, appetizers, piano music, and is popular for lunch as well.

Services: Concierge, same-day valet service, room service, express checkout, complimentary airport transportation.

Facilities: No-smoking rooms; in-room movies; outdoor heated pool; fitness center with sauna, Jacuzzi, small outdoor lap pool, exercise room, and massage, aerobics, and Jazzercise ($7 a day); meeting rooms; business center with computers, office space, fax, and secretaries; car-rental desk; currency exchange; check-cashing privileges; an ATM in the lobby.

EXPENSIVE

⑤ Clarion Hotel Bay View San Diego

660 K Street (at Sixth), San Diego, CA 92101. ☎ **619/696-0234** or 800/766-0234. Fax 619/231-8199. 312 rooms and suites. A/C TV TEL. $109–$139 double, $149–$169 suites. Children under 18 stay free in parents' room. Additional person $10. AE, DC, DISC, MC, V. Parking $7 per day. Bus: 1. Trolley: Gaslamp/Convention Center.

This relatively new entry on the San Diego hotel scene provides an economical alternative for those attending meetings at the Convention Center—it's almost as close as the Marriott and the Hyatt, but considerably less expensive. Its location near the Gaslamp Quarter makes it an excellent choice for those who plan to enjoy the nightlife and want to avoid walking far late at night. All quarters are spacious, bright, and modern, and more than half offer views of San Diego Bay and the Coronado Bridge. All rooms have sliding-glass doors that provide ample fresh air, and many have minibars. In-room safes are standard, as are tub/shower combinations; 80% of the rooms are reserved for nonsmokers. The carpeted rooftop sundeck offers a great view as well as a Jacuzzi, sauna, workout room, and video arcade.

Dining/Entertainment: Just off the marble-floored lobby is the 6th and K Cafe, serving breakfast, lunch, and dinner daily. There's a big-screen TV in the bar, and Karaoke is popular on Friday and Saturday nights.

Services: Concierge, room service 6am–10pm, dry cleaning/laundry, express checkout.

Facilities: In-room pay-per-view movies; workout room with Nautilus equipment; Jacuzzi; sauna; sundeck; video games room; coin-operated washer and dryer; in-room touch-screen TVs can be used for express checkout, ordering breakfast, and retrieving voice-mail messages.

Embassy Suites

601 Pacific Hwy. (at N. Harbor Drive), San Diego, CA 92101. ☎ **619/239-2400** or 800/EMBASSY. Fax 619/239-1520. 337 suites. A/C MINIBAR TV TEL. $140–$190 single or double (including full breakfast and afternoon cocktail). Children under 12 stay free in parents' room. AE, DC, DISC, MC, V. Indoor self-parking $7; valet $10. Bus: 2. Trolley: Seaport Village.

Built in 1988, this sand-colored building with green trim is topped with a neon design that looks like a stylized clock with the minute hand gone awry. The comfortable suites have sofa beds in the living/dining areas, and a microwave and coffeemaker. The 12-story atrium, with lush plants, bridges, waterways with giant goldfish, and a bubbling fountain, is the hotel's focal point. Glass-enclosed elevators provide a good view. The hotel is one block from Seaport Village and five blocks from downtown.

Dining/Entertainment: Barnett's Grand Café, serving Continental cuisine, looks onto the atrium; there's also patio seating. Winning Streak Sports and Games Bar, serving lunch and dinner, has a large video screen, sports memorabilia, and video interactive trivia.

Services: Complimentary breakfast and beverages, airport pickup, laundry.

Facilities: Seven no-smoking floors, microwave, coffeemaker, in-room movies, indoor pool (open long hours), sauna, weight room, Jacuzzi, sundeck, meeting rooms, gift shop.

Gaslamp Plaza Suites

520 E St. (at Fifth Avenue), San Diego, CA 92101. ☎ **619/232-9500** or 800/ 443-8012. Fax 619/238-9945. 58 suites. A/C MINIBAR TV TEL. Petite suite, $99–$119.

One-bedroom suite, $115–$140. Rates include continental breakfast. Children under 10 stay free in parents' room. AE, DC, DISC, MC, V. Valet parking $7 (with in/out privileges). Bus: 1, 3, or 25. Trolley: Civic Center (C Street and Third Avenue).

San Diego's first "skyscraper," this impressive purple-trimmed gray building was built in 1913. The lobby is set off by a striking staircase and by Corinthian marble that resembles Rorschach patterns of light and dark; marble also fills the stairways and hallways. The mirrored elevators with brass doors date from 1937. On the National Register for Historic Places, this was an important address for jewelers from the mid-1940s to the late 1970s, but it's been a hotel since 1988; the jewelers are down the street at the Jewelers Exchange Building. Suites are named for well-known writers. Corner rooms are popular because of their fine city views.

Dining/Entertainment: Breakfast is served on the rooftop terrace. There are a restaurant and nightclub on the ground level (not under hotel management); the Gaslamp Club on the rooftop terrace affords a panoramic view. Gaslamp Quarter eateries and entertainment are steps away.

Services: Concierge, room service (noon–9:30pm); complimentary transportation to and from airport and train station.

Facilities: No-smoking rooms, Jacuzzi on roof, hairdryers.

Holiday Inn on the Bay

1355 N. Harbor Dr. (at Ash Street), San Diego, CA 92101-3385. ☎ **619/232-3861** or 800/HOLIDAY. Fax 619/232-4924. 563 rms, 17 suites. A/C TV TEL. $135–$155 single or double; from $400 suite. Children under 18 stay free in parents' room. Bed-and-breakfast packages available. AE, DC, MC, V. Parking $10. Bus: 2, 9, 29, 34, 34A, or 35.

Renovated in 1992, this hotel is ideally located on the harbor, over-looking the Maritime Museum, the cruise-ship pier, and Harbor Island. It's only 1½ miles from the airport (you can watch the planes landing and taking off, as well as flight attendants and pilots checking in and out) and two blocks from the train station and trolley. The rooms, decorated in a California contemporary style, offer harbor views. The larger king rooms are a good choice for families. In general, the hotel's baths are small, but they have a separate sink with a lot of counter space.

Dining/Entertainment: The Elephant and Castle Restaurant and Ruth's Chris Steakhouse serve lunch and dinner. Shells Bar is small and intimate, while the lobby lounge is larger and has live entertainment.

Services: Room service (6am–2pm and 5:30pm–midnight); babysitting; laundry; valet.

Facilities: Cable TV and in-room movies; no-smoking rooms, out-door pool, self-service laundry; meeting rooms; minibars in some rooms; voice-mail in some rooms.

Horton Grand

311 Island Ave. (at Third Avenue), San Diego, CA 92101. ☎ **619/544-1886** or 800/542-1886. Fax 619/239-3823. 110 rms, 24 suites. TV TEL. $159 double; from $218 suite. Weekend and special packages available. Children under 16 stay free in parents' room. AE, DC, DISC, MC, V. Parking $5 day, $8 overnight guests. Bus: 1. Trolley: Convention Center.

A cross between an elegant hotel and a charming B&B, the Horton Grand combines two hotels dating from 1886—the Horton Grand and the Brooklyn Hotel, which for a time was the Kahle Saddlery Shop. Both were saved from demolition, moved to this spot, and connected by an airy atrium lobby filled with white wicker. The facade with its graceful bay windows is original.

Each room is unique and contains antiques and a gas fireplace (on a timer so you can fall asleep in front of it); even the baths, complete with WC and pedestal sink, are genteel. Rooms overlook either the city or the fig tree–filled courtyard. Each suite has a microwave, a minibar, two TVs and telephones, a sofa bed, and computer modem hookup. This is an old hotel, and sounds carry more than they might in a modern one, so if you're a light sleeper request a room with no neighbors.

Dining/Entertainment: Ida Bailey's restaurant, named for the well-loved madam whose establishment used to stand on this spot, is open for breakfast, lunch, and dinner. It opens onto the hotel's courtyard, which is used for Sunday brunch on warm days. Afternoon tea is served in the Palace Bar, Tuesday through Saturday from 2:30 to 5pm; live music is featured Thursday through Saturday evenings and Sunday afternoons.

Services: Concierge, room service (7am–10pm).

Facilities: Access to nearby pool and weight room.

MODERATE

Best Western Bayside Inn

555 W. Ash St. (at Columbia Street), San Diego, CA 92101. ☎ **619/233-7500** or 800/341-1818. Fax 619/239-8060. 122 rms. A/C TV TEL. $75–$94 double. Harbor view $10 extra. Children under 12 stay free in parents' room. Weekend rates (except in summer) and packages available. Rates include continental breakfast. AE, AM (Amoco), CB, DC, DISC, ER, MC, V. Free covered parking. Bus: 5 or 105. Trolley: C Street and Kettner.

You'll be pleased with his quiet, unassuming hotel with a friendly, accommodating staff and stunning city and harbor views. It's an easy walk to the Embarcadero (it should be called Bayview rather than Bayside), a bit farther to Horton Plaza, four blocks to the trolley stop, five blocks to the train station. The comfortable rooms, all remodeled in 1993, have balconies overlooking the bay or downtown. The lobby, glass-enclosed on the street side, is sunny and inviting.

The hotel's restaurant, the Bayside Bar and Grill, serves breakfast, lunch, and dinner; the bar has a 50-inch TV. Good restaurants and bars are nearby and meals are available from room service. Complimentary airport transportation is provided as are in-room movies, outdoor pool, and Jacuzzi.

Hotel San Diego

339 W. Broadway (between State and Union), San Diego, CA 92101. ☎ **619/234-0221,** 800/824-1244 in CA, or 800/621-5380. Fax 619/232-1305. 219 rooms. A/C TV TEL. $49–$69 low season, $79–$99 June 15–Aug; lower weekly rates. Children under 12 stay free in parents' room. AE, DC, MC, V. Bus: 2, 4, 7, 34, and many more. Trolley: America Plaza.

🏨 Family-Friendly Hotels

Hilton Beach & Tennis Resort *(see p. 63)* This bay-front property has a kids' wading pool and playground plus plenty of space for them to run around.

The Beach Cottages *(see p. 67)* Kids enjoy the informal atmosphere and the location near the beach.

Catamaran Resort Hotel *(see p. 64)* Myriad sports facilities and a safe swimming beach make this resort an ideal place for families. Accommodations are comfortable, but not so posh that Mom and Dad need to worry.

Elliott Hostel *(see p. 69)* A short drive from the beach, this hostel has four family rooms, a TV room, a big kitchen, and a patio with picnic tables.

The Sea Lodge *(see p. 72)* Right smack on the beach, kids can choose between the pool and ocean. They can even eat in their swimsuits on the patio.

Loew's Coronado Bay Resort *(see p. 77)* Its Commodore Kids Club, for children ages 4 to 12, provides year-round supervised indoor/outdoor activities during the day and some evenings, too.

If you'd like a little extra space, the Hotel San Diego might be your best bet. All rooms are oversize, and the many connecting rooms and two-room suites are ideal for families. The hotel is one of San Diego's oldest—the lobby features historical photos, antiques, and stained glass windows (and anachronistic video games tucked in the corner). The friendly management is also reminiscent of another era. Don't be afraid of the shaky elevators; they lead to nice, wide, well-lit hallways and rooms with quality furnishings and tile bathrooms. Coin-op washers and dryers are on the third and sixth floors. The hotel is close to the Amtrak and bus stations; free minivan transportation is provided, subject to the driver's schedule. The Hotel San Diego also caters to weekly and monthly residents.

INEXPENSIVE

Inexpensive motels line Pacific Highway between the airport and downtown. **Days Inn Suites,** 1919 Pacific Hwy. (☎ 619/232-1077 or 800/325-2525), and **Econo Lodge,** 1655 Pacific Hwy. (☎ 619/232-4622 or 800/446-6900), both are within walking distance of the Embarcadero, the Maritime Museum, and the Harbor Excursion.

Churchill

827 C St. (at Ninth Avenue), San Diego, CA 92101. ☎ **619/234-5186.** 92 rms, 3 suites. TV TEL. $32–$37 double without bath; $46 double with bath; from $80 suite. Lower weekly and monthly rates available. Children 6–18 stay free in parents' room. MC, V. Free parking evenings and weekends. Bus: 1, 2, 3, or 25. Trolley: C Street and Twelfth Avenue.

It takes a sense of humor to stay here. Built in 1915, the Churchill was remodeled in 1983 to depict a medieval English castle, with stone arches, weapons, a suit of armor, and a "dungeon" coffee room—which has a microwave and vending machine (your basic castle comforts). In 1989, the facade was painted to look like a castle, complete with turrets and a moat. Rooms, no less original, are decorated in numerous themes, with corresponding names on the doors—Cloud Nine, Autumn Moods, Jungle Safari, Chrome-a-Rama, and Versailles, to mention a few. Named rooms also have baths and ceiling fans. While there is a fair amount of deferred maintenance, the rooms with bathrooms are acceptable budget accommodations. I found the Music Room brighter and more pleasant than some others. You can sit in the lobby's overstuffed chairs to watch the trolleys glide by or there's a library and book swap. This kitsch castle is particularly popular with European travelers and with older people, who often stay for long periods (there's a coin-operated laundry). However, it's located in a marginal neighborhood and isn't a good choice for women traveling alone. I can't imagine staying here with children, and kidlets under 6 are not accepted. Many monthly residents are low-income senior citizens.

Hostelling International—San Diego

500 W. Broadway (between Columbia and India streets), San Diego, CA 92101. ☎ 619/525-1531. 84 beds. In dorm, $12 members, $15 nonmembers; semi-private room, $13 members, $16 nonmembers; couple's room, $14 per person members, $17 per person nonmembers. MC, V. Limited metered parking available on street. Bus: 2, 4, 7, or 29. Trolley: America Plaza.

San Diego's downtown hostel is conveniently located one block from the trolley stop, two blocks from the train station, and three blocks from the bus station. It opened in December 1993 on the second floor of the YMCA. The men's dorm has 16 beds; 3 women's dorms have 4 beds each; 4 rooms have double beds; and another 24 semiprivate rooms have 2 beds. Guests may use the TV room and the large common room with a full kitchen and plenty of books for swapping. Both the women's and the men's bathrooms are large. Vending machines are on the premises. You'll need a key to get into the elevator. Guests have 24-hour access to the hostel. Two-hour metered street parking and pay-to-park lots are nearby. You can reserve a bed or room with a credit card.

⑤ La Pensione

1700 India St. (at Date Street), San Diego, CA 92101. ☎ 619/236-8000 or 800/232-4683. Fax 619/236-8088. 80 rms. TV TEL. $44–$59 double (weekly rates available). AE, MC, V. Underground parking, free on a daily basis or $10 per week. Bus: 5/105. Trolley: County Center/Little Italy.

This place has a lot going for it: modernity, cleanliness, remarkable value, a quiet location within walking distance of the central business district, a friendly staff, and parking, which is a premium for small hotels in San Diego. La Pensione is built around a courtyard and feels like a small European hotel. The lobby is small but inviting, and the rooms, while not overly large, make the most of their space and leave you with area to move around. Each room offers a tub/shower combination, ceiling fan, wet bar, microwave, and small refrigerator. Quarters are cleaned once a week for weekly guests, daily for those who stay a shorter period. It has two restaurants: Caffè Italia, which offers sandwiches and salads, as well as Sunday brunch and jazz on Friday and Saturday, and Indigo Grill, which serves southwestern fare. The fourth floor is for nonsmoking guests. The hotel has a similarly priced sibling hotel of the same name at 1654 Columbia St. between Cedar and Date streets (☎ 619/232-3400), which is rented by the week or month only; there's no parking, however. Both properties are centrally located and within walking distance of eateries (mostly Italian) and nightspots.

3   Hillcrest/Uptown

MODERATE

Balboa Park Inn

3402 Park Blvd. (at Upas), San Diego, CA 92103. ☎ **619/298-0823.** Fax 619/294-8070. 26 suites. A/C TV TEL. $80–$120 single or double; $125–$190 for up to 6 adults; $190 honeymoon suite. Extra person $8. Children under 12 stay free in parents' room, but pay $2.50 for breakfast. All rates include continental breakfast. AE, DC, DISC, MC, V. Street parking only. Bus: 7, 7A, or 7B. Directions: From any approach to San Diego, follow the signs to the San Diego Zoo. The Inn is north of the Zoo.

This cluster of four Spanish-colonial pink buildings with a bubbling fountain outside clearly evokes a Southern California feel. It opened in 1915 to house guests for the Panama-California Exposition and has been welcoming people to San Diego ever since. Each suite is unique: Some are formal, others casual; some are spacious, others small and cozy; some have a fireplace or Jacuzzi, others a kitchen or private patio. All have refrigerators and well-lit baths. The Marianna Southwest suite sports a Southwest theme, with a lavish use of tiles. Breakfast is served on the large terrace or the courtyard. The helpful desk staff is happy to perform concierge duties. Local telephone calls are free. The Inn, only 1¹/₂ blocks north of the zoo entrance and 2 miles from downtown San Diego, is particularly popular with Europeans.

Park Manor Suites

525 Spruce St. (at Fifth Avenue), San Diego, CA 92103. ☎ **619/291-0999** or 800/874-2649. Fax 619/291-8844. 80 rms. TV TEL. $55–$95 studio for 1 or 2; $75–$125 one-bedroom unit for 1 or 2; $120–$165 two-bedroom unit for up to 4. Children under 12 stay free in parents' room. Weekly and monthly rates available. Rates include continental breakfast. AE, MC, V. Free parking. Bus: 1 or 3.

The stately Park Manor Suites is a good, convenient choice for a longer stay in the area. Built across the street from Balboa Park in 1926, it has a welcoming lobby with a hand-painted ceiling and a glittering chandelier; a young, enthusiastic staff; old-fashioned rooms (that means big, with high ceilings and ample closet space); and separate kitchen and dining areas. (A market is one block away.) Some rooms are modern, and those facing the park are quietest. Baths include tubs and showers. There's a restaurant on the ground floor, open for lunch and dinner, and many others are within walking distance. The bus stops a block away. The hotel attracts visiting actors in local productions, especially those at the nearby Old Globe Theatre. The main entrance to Balboa Park is six blocks away. Laundry and dry-cleaning services are offered. There's no air-conditioning, but you would rarely need it; there's steam heat for chilly days.

❸ Sommerset Suites Hotel

606 Washington St. (at Fifth Avenue), San Diego, CA 92103. ☎ **619/692-5200** or 800/356-1787 in California, 800/962-9665 elsewhere. Fax 619/299-6065. 80 suites. A/C TV TEL. $90 studio suite; $120–$150 bedroom suite; $180 executive suite. Children under 12 stay free in parents' room. All rates include large continental breakfast. Substantial discounts often available. AE, DC, DISC, MC, V. Free covered parking. Bus: 16 or 25. Take Washington Street exit off I-5.

This is one of San Diego's best bargains and the first choice for those who prefer a home away from home to a hotel. The staff is friendly and helpful, and in the late afternoon they serve complimentary snacks, soda, beer, and wine in the cozy guest lounge. The poolside patio, set up for barbecues, encourages impromptu gatherings and picnics among guests. Accommodations include studio, one-bedroom, and executive suites. All are tastefully furnished and have in-room safes and fully equipped modern kitchens (including dishwashers in the executive suites), large closets, and balconies. Even the studios are spacious. Services include a concierge; laundry and dry cleaning; courtesy van service (7am to 9pm) to the airport, Sea World, the zoo, and other attractions in a 5-mile radius; video rentals; and two-line phones and voice mail. Rollaway beds and cribs are available. Facilities include a small outdoor pool, a Jacuzzi, a rooftop sundeck, gas barbecue grills, a snack room, and a coin-operated laundry. No restaurants are on site, but many are within walking distance. Nonsmoking rooms are available.

INEXPENSIVE
A BED & BREAKFAST

❸ The Cottage

3829 Albatross St. (off Robinson), San Diego, CA 92103. ☎ **619/299-1564.** Fax 619/299-6213. 1 rm, 1 cottage. TV TEL. $55–$65 Garden Room for one or two; $75–$85 cottage for one or two. Third person in cottage $10. Rates include continental breakfast. AE, MC, V. Bus: 11.

The two-room cottage from the 1940s exists in a secret garden, a private hideaway tucked behind a homestead-style house, built in 1913, at the end of a residential cul-de-sac. There's an herb garden out front, birdbaths, and a flower-lined walkway to the back. Owner Carol Emerick used to have an antiques shop, and her house has inherited its treasures. The cottage has a living room with a working wood-burning stove and a queen-size sofa bed, and a charming kitchen. The bedroom features a king-size bed and a hidden TV. The Garden Room is in the main house. Both accommodations are filled with fresh flowers and antiques put to clever uses, and both feature a private entrance and bath. Carol serves guests a scrumptious breakfast, complete with the morning newspaper. Guests are welcome to use the dining room and parlor in the main house, where they sometimes light a fire and rev up the 19th-century player piano. In this haven, expect to wake up to the gentle chirping of birds. The cottage is a block from Front Street, 1¹/₂ miles from the zoo, and only 4 miles from the airport.

4 Old Town

MODERATE

Hacienda Hotel

4041 Harney St. (just east of San Diego Avenue), San Diego, CA 92110. ☎ **619/ 298-4707** or 800/888-1991. Fax 619/298-4771. 150 suites. A/C TV TEL. $109–$119 double. Children under 16 stay free in parents' room. AE, CB, DC, DISC, ER, MC, V. Free underground parking. Bus: 4 or 5/105. From I-5 take Old Town Avenue exit; turn left onto San Diego Avenue and right onto Harney Street.

Perched above Old Town, this Best Western all-suite hotel is brightly lit and creates an impressive sight at night. From the outdoor pool and patio are excellent views of Old Town. The comfortable suites have 20-foot-high ceilings, ceiling fans, refrigerators, microwave ovens, coffeemakers, VCRs, and furnishings right out of the American Southwest. The one-room units have either one or two queen-size beds. Walkways thread through courtyards with bubbling fountains, palm trees, lampposts, and bougainvillea-trimmed balconies.

Dining/Entertainment: The Acapulco restaurant (yes, it's Mexican) serves breakfast, lunch, and dinner daily from its perch atop the hotel. Guests also have signing privileges next door at the Brigantine Restaurant and down the street at Café Pacifica (see "Old Town" in Chapter 6).

Services: Concierge Monday through Friday, room service (6:30am–2pm and 4–10pm), hosted manager's social Monday through Thursday, complimentary airport/train transportation.

Facilities: Movie rentals with complimentary bag of microwave popcorn, pool, Jacuzzi, spa, fitness center, conference suites, meeting rooms, coin-operated laundry.

Vacation Inn

3900 Old Town Ave., San Diego, CA 92110. ☎ **619/299-7400** or 800/451-9846. Fax 619/299-1619. 119 rms, 6 suites. A/C TV TEL. Jan–June and Sept 11–Dec, $90–$110 double; $106–$151 suite. July–Sept 10, $98–$117 double; $116–$161 suite. Extra person $10. Children 17 and under stay free in parents' room. Rates include continental breakfast and afternoon refreshments. AE, DC, DISC, ER, MC, V. Free parking. Bus: 4 or 5/105.

It's Spanish on the outside to fit in with the Old Town architectural requirements and pure European on the inside. Rooms are beautifully appointed—even the baths have artwork in them—and practical, with a coffeemaker, microwave, and a writing table. Drapes, bedspreads, and tablecloths have a floral design. Second and third floor rooms that face the courtyard have balconies. The lobby, surrounded by five sets of French doors, features a large fireplace, several sitting areas, and a TV. Dry-cleaning and laundry services are offered; the hotel also offers an outdoor pool and Jacuzzi. The hotel entrance, on Jefferson Street, is hard to find but definitely worth the search.

A BED & BREAKFAST

Heritage Park Bed & Breakfast Inn

2470 Heritage Park Row, San Diego, CA 92110. ☎ **619/299-6832.** Fax 619/
995-2470. 9 rms (7 with bath), 1 suite. $90–$150 single or double. $205 suite.
Extra person $20. Rates include full breakfast and afternoon tea. AE, MC, V. Free
parking. Bus: 4 or 5/105. Take I-5 to Old Town Ave., turn left onto San Diego
Avenue, then turn right onto Harney Street to Heritage Park.

In this 1889 Queen Anne mansion set in a Victorian park, you can arrange for champagne or sparkling cider and chocolates on arrival, as
well as a five-course candlelight dinner for two served in your room.
Particularly winsome are the large Manor suite, with a fainting couch,
four-poster bed, and Jacuzzi bath; the Victorian Rose Room, with its
iron-and-brass bed; the sunny, secluded Turret Room in the tower of
the house; the award-winning Forget-Me-Not Room; and the small
and thoroughly Early American Country Heart Room, where an old
school desk serves as a bedside table. Any antiques that are replaceable,
as well as smaller remembrances, are for sale. Amenities include
turndown service, the services of a concierge, and a housekeeping
staff of four. In the evenings a vintage film is shown in the Victorian
parlor.

INEXPENSIVE

Room rates at properties on Hotel Circle, about 2 miles from Old
Town, are significantly less than those in Old Town itself. There you'll
find a cluster of inexpensive hotels and motels, including **Best West-
ern Seven Seas** (☎ 619/291-1300 or 800/421-6662), **Mission
Valley Center Travelodge** (☎ 619/297-2271 or 800/255-3050),
Ramada Inn (☎ 619/291-6500 or 800/532-4241), and **Vagabond
Inn** (☎ 619/297-1691 or 800/522-1555).

Travelodge

2380 Moore St., San Diego, CA 92110. ☎ **619/291-9100** or 800/292-9928. Fax
619/291-4717. 70 rms, 9 suites. A/C TV TEL. Sun–Thurs, $49–$59 double; $84–$89
suite. Fri–Sat, $59–$64 double; $89–$94 suite. Children under 18 stay free in parents'
room. Lower off-season prices. Rates include continental breakfast. AE, DC, DISC, ER,
JCB, MC, V. Free underground parking. Bus: 4 or 5/105. Follow I-5 North and take
Old Town exit; go straight at traffic light; hotel will be on right.

A friendly staff offers a warm welcome at this small, inviting
Travelodge. Rooms are comfortable and furnished in the bright colors
of the American Southwest, with coffeemakers. Suites, which are
somewhat small, have skylights, Jacuzzis, microwaves, sitting areas, refrigerators, and wet bars. About 80% of the rooms are reserved for
nonsmokers. The property is a five-minute walk from Old Town attractions. Reserve in advance for Friday and Saturday nights, when the
parents of naval graduates are likely to be in town. Movie rentals, irons,
and 24-hour coffee/tea in the lobby are available; also offered are an
outdoor pool and a Jacuzzi.

5 Mission Bay/Pacific Beach

VERY EXPENSIVE

Hilton Beach & Tennis Resort

1775 E. Mission Bay Dr., San Diego, CA 92109. ☎ **619/276-4010,** or 800/
962-6307 in California and Arizona, 800/445-8667 elsewhere. Fax 619/275-7991.
357 rms, 8 suites. A/C MINIBAR TV TEL. $175–$230 double; from $325 suite. Extra
person $20. Children under 18 stay free in parents' room. Lower off-season rates.
AE, CB, DC, DISC, MC, V. Free parking. Take I-5 to Sea World Drive exit and turn
north on E. Mission Bay Drive.

Completely renovated in 1995, this Mediterranean-style resort with
terra-cotta roofs occupies 18 acres on the east side of Mission Bay and
is a handy ¼ mile from the Visitor Information Center. All quarters
(contained in one eight-story tower or several lowrise buildings) have
ceiling fans, a balcony or terrace, a refrigerator, a coffeemaker, an iron
and ironing board, a hairdryer, and a makeup mirror. The baths are elegant, with shells surrounding the sconce-flanked mirrors. Even the
standard rooms are spacious, and many rooms interconnect. The staff
is friendly and helpful here, and the shops are fun for browsing in between lolling by the pool, biking along the bay, and taking tennis lessons. Sea World is across the bay, and the ocean is 5 miles to the west.

Dining/Entertainment: Cafe Picante, open for all meals daily,
offers casual fare and atmosphere. The Cavatappi restaurant serves
Italian cuisine nightly. You can dine and drink at Fundidos, which
overlooks Mission Bay. Cocktails are also served in the Lobby Bar and
at the poolside Banana Cabana.

Services: Concierge, room service (7am–11pm), dry cleaning/
laundry service, babysitting, supervision for children weekends and in
summer, free airport transportation.

Facilities: In-room movies, Olympic-size pool, children's wading
pool, four Jacuzzis, sauna, weight-training room, five lighted tennis courts, pro shop, water sports, scuba diving, bike and jogging
trails, putting green, arts and crafts for kids, children's playground,
business center, bike and boat rental, yacht charters, massage, game
arcade, meeting rooms, laundry facilities, hair salon, shops, voice-mail
messages.

EXPENSIVE

Blue Sea Lodge

707 Pacific Beach Dr., San Diego, CA 92109-5094. ☎ **619/488-4700** or 800/
BLUESEA. Fax 619/488-7276. 100 rms. TV TEL. Mid-Sept to mid-June, $118–$148
double; from $175 suite. Mid-June to mid-Sept, $129–$159 double; from $199 suite.
Children under 13 stay free in parents' room. AAA and AARP discounts. All rates include continental breakfast. AE, CB, DC, DISC, MC, V. Free underground and outdoor
parking. Bus: 34 or 34A. Take I-5, to Grand/Garnet exit, follow Grand Avenue to Mission Boulevard and turn left, then turn right onto Pacific Beach Drive.

The entrance here is a little strange: a stairway leads up to the lobby from an alleylike lane. Travelers with disabilities access the building from the elevator in the underground garage. Most rooms have recently been renovated, and about half have kitchens. The oceanfront accommodations have great views. The lobby offers coffee, tea, and a microwave for guests, and outside you'll find a heated pool and Jacuzzi just steps away from the beach. This is a Best Western property, within walking distance of the fun spots.

Catamaran Resort Hotel

3999 Mission Blvd., San Diego, CA 92109. ☎ **619/488-1081**, or 800/288-0770 in U.S., 800/233-8172 in Canada. Fax 619/488-1081. 160 rms, 100 studios, 50 suites. A/C TV TEL. $140–$195 single or double; from $225 suite. Children under 13 stay free in parents' room. Lower off-season rates. AE, CB, DC, DISC, MC, V. Self-parking $5; valet $7. Bus: 34 or 34A. Take Grand/Garnet exit off I-5 and go west on Grand Avenue, then south on Mission Boulevard.

Ideally situated right on Mission Bay, the Catamaran enjoys its own beach and water sport facilities. Polynesia blossoms here, with a 15-foot waterfall and full-size dugout canoe in the atrium lobby. After dark, torches blaze throughout the grounds, which burgeon with numerous varieties of bamboo and palm. Each room—located in one 13-story building and six 2-story buildings—is decorated in soft tropical colors and has a balcony or patio. Tower rooms have commanding views of the entire bay, the San Diego skyline, La Jolla, and Point Loma. The staff is among the nicest I've encountered anywhere. The hotel's bars are popular with both locals and visitors. The Catamaran is also within walking distance of many fine restaurants and nightspots and a block from the ocean. The grounds are beautifully maintained.

Dining/Entertainment: The Atoll restaurant, which offers both indoor and bay-side seating, serves light fare along with its regular dinner menu, as well as nightly specials and Sunday brunch. The large, lively Cannibal Bar hosts bands and videos. Its counterpoint, Moray's (named for the moray eels that inhabited its large aquarium until they became too aggressive), is an intimate piano bar.

Services: Concierge, room service (6:30am–11pm), dry cleaning/laundry service, babysitting, lifeguard in summer only, valet parking, pets allowed.

Facilities: Cable TV with movies, outdoor heated pool, Jacuzzi, water sports, boat rentals, jogging track, bicycle rental, meeting rooms, car-rental desk, gift shop, parking garage.

Crystal Pier Hotel

4500 Ocean Blvd. (at Garnet), San Diego, CA 92109. ☎ **619/483-6983**, or 800/748-5894, emergency 619/277-1094. 26 cottages. TV. Old cottages, 1–4 people, $140 mid-June to mid-Sept, $85–$95 rest of year; remodeled cottages, 1–4 people, $160 mid-June to mid-Sept, $105 rest of year; new cottages, 1–4 people, $165–$180 mid-June to mid-Sept, $150–$180 rest of year. Three-day minimum in summer. Weekly and monthly rates available. MC, V. Free parking. Bus: 34 or 34A. Take I-5 to Grand/Garnet exit; follow Garnet to pier.

This historic property, which dates from 1927, offers a unique opportunity to sleep over the water. Built on a pier over the Pacific Ocean,

Mission Bay Accommodations

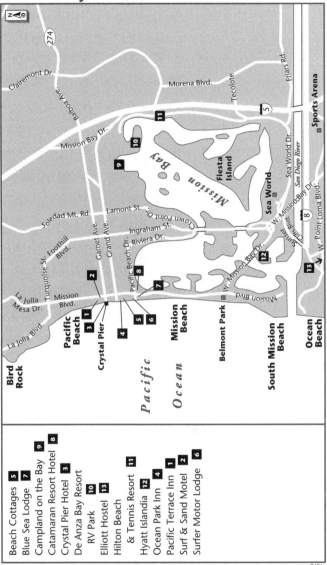

Beach Cottages **5**
Blue Sea Lodge **7**
Campland on the Bay **9**
Catamaran Resort Hotel **8**
Crystal Pier Hotel **3**
De Anza Bay Resort
RV Park **10**
Elliott Hostel **13**
Hilton Beach
& Tennis Resort **11**
Hyatt Islandia **12**
Ocean Park Inn **4**
Pacific Terrace Inn **1**
Surf & Sand Motel **2**
Surfer Motor Lodge **6**

the hotel offers self-contained cottages with breathtaking beach views. Twenty older cottages date from 1936; six newer ones from 1992. Twelve of the older cottages have been renovated. The remodeled units are really lovely, the older ones slightly down-at-the-heels. My favorite units are upstairs. Each comes with a private patio, living room, bedroom, and kitchen and has welcoming blue shutters and window boxes. The sound of waves around the clock is soothing, but the board-walk action is only a few steps (and worlds) away. If you stay here remember that the quietest quarters are the furthest out on the pier. Guests park right on the pier beside their cottage, a real boon on crowded weekends. There are vending machines and movie rentals (two for $10). Boogie boards, fishing poles, beach chairs, and umbrellas are also available. The office is open daily from 8am to 8pm. These unique accommodations book up fast. Besides being a restful place to lay your head, the pier is a great place to watch the surfers at sunset.

Hyatt Islandia

1441 Quivira Rd., San Diego, CA 92109. ☎ **619/224-1234** or 800/233-1234. Fax 619/224-0348. 346 rms, 76 marina suites. A/C TV TEL. $115–$180 single or double; from $179 suite. Children under 18 stay free in parents' room. AE, CB, DC, DISC, MC, V. Free parking. Take I-8 west to W. Mission Bay Drive.

Rising 17 stories above Mission Bay, the Hyatt Islandia is a recogniz-able landmark, providing many a room with a view. The rooms are lofty and furnished in soothing colors. Corner rooms are spacious and have canopy beds. Suites have two TVs, a queen-size sofa bed, a wet bar, a minibar, and a balcony; they're good for families. All baths have hairdryers and separate vanities; half have tubs, the rest showers. If you're a water-sports enthusiast, the Islandia, which fronts Quivira Basin marina, is a great choice; it rents speedboats, sailboats, pedal boats, Hobie Cats, canoes, and sailboards, and it provides the where-withal for waterskiing, parasailing, and sportfishing. Back on dry land, you can rent bikes, lounge by the pool, stroll through the 7 acres of beautifully landscaped grounds, or be lulled by the soft splashing of the waterfall. Kids particularly like to feed the koi fish. Sea World is a two-minute drive, and the hotel's friendly staff can provide you with a two-day pass and a 10% discount.

Dining/Entertainment: The Islandia Bar and Grill serves fresh sea-food, pasta, and meat dishes, and its lounge has live entertainment on weekends; the Baja Café offers spicy southwestern dishes.

Services: Concierge floor (Regency Club), express checkout, com-plimentary shuttle service to Nordstrom's department store.

Facilities: Nonsmoking rooms available, outdoor heated pool with large deck, Jacuzzi, access to health club and tennis courts, workout room, water sports, walking path around marina, bicycle rental, Camp Hyatt activities for kids on summer weekends; Hyatt Business Plan upgrade for $15 to a room with fax, printer, and photocopy machine, meeting rooms, shops, whale-watching expeditions available at marina.

✪ Pacific Terrace Inn

610 Diamond St., San Diego, CA 92109. ☎ **619/581-3500** or 800/344-3370. Fax 619/274-3341. 65 rms, 8 suites. A/C MINI TV TEL. $135–$175 single or double; $155–$185 single or double with kitchenette; from $205 suite. Rates about $20 higher per person in summer. Extra person $10. All rates include continental breakfast and snacks. AE, CB, DC, DISC, MC, V. Free underground-secured parking. Bus: 34 or 34A. Take I-5 to Grand/Garnet exit; turn west onto Garnet, turn right onto Mission Boulevard, left onto Diamond, and it's at end of the street on right-hand side.

My favorite hotel along the Pacific Beach boardwalk, this place is both pretty and pink. I like its upscale atmosphere and the fact that it's slightly removed from the hubbub that dominates other beachfront properties in this area. The large and comfortable bedrooms come with balconies or terraces, refrigerators stocked with soft drinks, and wall safes. Amenities include *USA Today* delivered daily, hairdryers, cotton robes, vanities with separate sinks, and voice mail. Forty rooms have kitchens. Third-story rooms have particularly nice views, and the suites have large baths with Jacuzzis. Management keeps popcorn, coffee, and lemonade in the snack room, called the Caribbean Room. There is an attractive outdoor heated pool facing the ocean, plus a Jacuzzi, valet laundry service, and a coin-operated laundry.

MODERATE

The Beach Cottages

4255 Ocean Blvd., San Diego, CA 92109-3995. ☎ **619/483-7440.** Fax 619/ 270-8819. 28 rms, 10 studios, 20 apartments, 17 cottages, 3 suites. TV TEL. Spring and fall, $70–$85 single or double, $7 extra person; $85 studio for up to 4; $115– $130 apartment for up to 6; $120–$140 cottage for up to 6; $200–$220 two-bedroom suite for up to 6. Summer, $90–$110 single or double; $115 studio; $140–$165 apartment; $145–$170 cottage; $220–$240 two-bedroom suite. Off-season, $55–$70 single or double; $75 studio; $90–$115 apartment; $95–$125 cottage; $175–$195 two-bedroom suite. Weekly rates available except in summer. AE, DISC, MC, V. Free parking. Bus: 34 or 34A. Take I-5 to Grand/Garnet exit, go west on Grand Avenue, and right on Mission Boulevard; it's a block south of Grand Avenue.

The patio courtyard with plant-covered trellises is the focal point of this beach-front cluster of motel rooms, studios, one- and two-bedroom cottages, one- and two-bedroom apartments, and two-bedroom, two-bathroom suites. It's an ideal place for families. The rustic cottages have wood floors and paneling, as well as patios with tables, chairs, and re-cliners. The rest of the facilities are more modern and all are superbly maintained by the Frost family, who have owned the property since 1948. Studios consist of one large room with a kitchen, while apartments have a separate bedroom. Guests gravitate to the courtyard to relax or grill food on the barbecue, or they stroll on the boardwalk and go to the beach, which is their front yard. There's shuffleboard, table tennis, and a laundry. Restaurants, shops, and grocery stores are within walking distance. Office hours are from 9am to 9pm.

Ocean Park Inn

710 Grand Ave., San Diego, CA 92109. ☎ **619/483-5858** or 800/231-7735. Fax 619/274-0823. A/C TV TEL. Summer $85–$150 single or double, $130–$180 suites. Extra person $10. Children under 12 stay free in parents' room. Lower off-season rates. Rates include continental breakfast. AE, DC, DISC, MC, V. Free indoor parking. Take Grand/Garnet exit off of I-5, follow Grand Avenue to ocean.

This modern oceanfront motor hotel offers attractive, spacious rooms with well-coordinated contemporary furnishings. King suites are extra large and have an additional sofa-bed and a Roman tub. Two-room suites are the most spacious. Rates vary with the view; oceanfront rooms are the most expensive. However, these high-priced digs could be noisy, so you might be wise to take a quieter pool-view room. All quarters have terraces and refrigerators. Some are set aside for nonsmokers. The Ocean Park Inn doesn't have it's own restaurant, but there are many nearby.

Surfer Motor Lodge

711 Pacific Beach Dr. (at Mission Boulevard), San Diego, CA 92109. ☎ **619/ 483-7070.** 52 units. TV TEL. Summer $89–$96 double to quadruple; $87–$105 room with kitchenette; $108 one-bedroom unit for up to 4; $110–122 family unit for up to 6. Off-season, $69–$71 double to quadruple; $69–$86 room with kitchenette; $85–$90 one-bedroom unit or family unit. Weekly rates available off-season. AE, DC, MC, V. Free parking. Bus: 34 or 34A. Take I-5 to Grand/Garnet; take Grand Avenue to Mission Boulevard; turn left, then right onto Pacific Beach Drive.

Frankly this property is a little tired, but it's still often booked solid during the summer because it offers moderately priced digs right on the boardwalk at the beach, as well as a heated pool. Most rooms in this 4-story property have balconies and views and are cooled by ocean breezes. Fans are also available. On the premises is a coin-operated laundry. A popular restaurant serving three meals a day is adjacent. The staff can arrange bike rentals and fishing or golf outings.

INEXPENSIVE

Surf & Sand Motel

4666 Mission Blvd. (at Diamond Street), San Diego, CA 92109. ☎ **619/483-7420** or 800/800-8000. Fax 619/237-9940. 25 rms. TV TEL. $55–$65 single or double during the summer. Lower off-season rates. AE, DISC, MC, V. Free off-street parking. Bus: 34 or 34A. Take I-5 to Grand/Garnet exit, go west on Garnet Avenue to Mission Boulevard and turn right.

This modest motel, a half block from the beach, has a small lobby and clean basic units with slightly worn furnishings. Rooms in the back get less noise from Mission Boulevard. Most baths have showers, but no tubs; most rooms have refrigerators, and some have kitchenettes. A small, heated pool on the property is not very appealing.

PLACES TO CAMP

Campland on the Bay

2211 Pacific Beach Dr., San Diego, CA 92109-5699. ☎ **619/581-4200,** 619/ 581-4212 (24 hours), or 800/4BAYFUN. 600 hookup sites. Summer, $26–$52 for up to 4 people. Off-season, $19–$37 for up to 4 people. Lowest-priced sites do not have hookups. Senior rates available. Weekly and monthly rates available off-season. Extra (small) charge for dogs. MC, V. Take I-5 to Grand/Garnet exit, follow Grand to Olney and turn left; turn left again onto Pacific Beach Drive.

This bay-side retreat is popular with a mixed crowd: RVers, campers (with or without van), boaters, and their children and pets. At their fingertips are parks, a beach, bird sanctuary, and dog walk. Other facilities include pools, a Jacuzzi, catamaran and windsurfer rentals and lessons, bike and boat rentals, a game room, cafe open for three meals a day, market, and laundry. Planned activities include games and crafts for children; Sea World is five minutes away.

De Anza Bay Resort RV Park

2727 De Anza Rd., San Diego, CA 92109. ☎ **619/273-3211** or 800/924-PLAY in California. 250 hookup sites. Summer, $34–$41. Off-season, $22–$30. Lower-priced sites do not have hookups. Weekly and monthly rates available off-season. MC, V. Bus: 34 or 34A. Take I-5 to the Clairemont Drive exit, go west and turn right onto E. Mission Bay Drive at the Visitor Information Center; follow E. Mission Bay Drive for about a mile to the north end of the bay.

Directly across an inlet from Campland on the Bay and under the same management, this serenely situated park caters only to RV vacationers, offering them a market, laundry, private beach, floating dock and diving platform, fishing, boating, water sports, bike rental, auto rental, free movies, potluck dinners, dancing, beach parties, and bingo. Small pets are welcome. A plus for golfers: It's adjacent to an executive 18-hole course that's open day and night.

A NEARBY HOSTEL

Hostelling International— Elliott Hostel

3790 Udall St., San Diego, CA 92107. ☎ **619/223-4778.** 62 beds. $12 dorm; $13 semiprivate (2-person room); $14 double bed; rates are per person, per night for members; nonmembers add $3. MC, V. Free parking. Bus: 35 (to Ocean Beach); catch it on Broadway (downtown) and get off at Voltaire (in front of Subway) about a 20-minute ride. Cross the street to Worden. Hostel is on the corner of Worden and Udall streets. From Los Angeles, take I-5 south to Sea World Drive exit and go west. Follow signs to Sunset Cliffs Boulevard. Turn left on Voltaire, continue for 1 mile; make a right on Worden. Hostel is on the corner of Worden and Udall. From downtown San Diego or airport, follow N. Harbor Drive; turn right on Nimitz and follow it to Chatsworth and turn right; left on Poinsettia, which merges with Udall; the hostel will be on the right.

Officially known as the Elliott (Point Loma) Hostel, these budget digs are 6 miles from downtown San Diego and 3 miles from the airport. It's a short drive, or figure 30 minutes to get there by city bus from downtown San Diego. Rooms sleep two to eight people, and there are five couples rooms (with double beds) and four family rooms. Facilities include showers, an impressive kitchen, a large common room, a TV room, and a patio with picnic tables. The hostel is a short distance to the beach and Sea World. Reception is open from 8am to 10pm every day.

6 La Jolla

I've recommended La Jolla's most centrally located places to stay. Chain hotels farther afield include a **Hyatt Regency,** at 3777 La Jolla Village Dr. (☎ 619/552-1234 or 800/233-1234), and a **Marriott Residence Inn,** at 8901 Gilman Dr. (☎ 619/587-1770 or 800/331-3131), a good choice for those who want a fully equipped kitchen and more space. The **Sheraton Grande Torrey Pines,** at 10950 N. Torrey Pines Rd. (☎ 619/558-1500 or 800/762-6160), is perched on a bluff above the Pacific Ocean adjacent to the famed Torrey Pines Golf Course. All are near the University of California San Diego.

VERY EXPENSIVE

✪ La Valencia Hotel

1132 Prospect St. (at Herschel Avenue), La Jolla, CA 92037. ☎ **619/454-0771** or 800/451-0772. Fax 619/456-3921. 100 rms, 11 suites. A/C MINIBAR TV TEL. $160–$190 single or double with village, garden, or partial ocean view; $310–$350 single or double with full ocean view; from $375 suite. Extra person $10. Children under 12 stay free in parents' room. Lower off-season rates. Check deposit required, but checkout may be paid with credit card. AE, DC, DIS, JCB, MC, V. Parking $8 a day. Take the Ardath Road exit off I-5 north; or the La Jolla Village Drive west exit off I-5 south. Take Torrey Pines Road to Prospect Place and turn right. Prospect Place becomes Prospect Street.

The La Valencia is a lovely Spanish-Colonial landmark, ensconced in an ocean-view position among the pricey boutiques on Prospect Street. Built in 1926 and expanded two years later, the hotel has eight floors, six below lobby level. Luminaries such as Greta Garbo, Charlie Chaplin, Lillian Gish, Groucho Marx, and Mary Pickford have strolled through the Mediterranean-style lounge with its hand-painted ceiling and beams. Today Barbra Streisand, Tom Cruise and Nicole Kidman, or Danny Glover are more likely to do so.

A picture window in the lounge wraps itself around the Pacific, and people pause here to savor the genteel ambience. The balcony overlooking La Jolla Cove is a fine spot to sip aged port, watch the sunset, and be served by an attentive staff. No matter how busy the hotel gets, you can always find a quiet place somewhere on the lush grounds, which are well tended by three full-time gardeners. Each hotel bedroom is attractive and distinct. The highest quality linens are combined with beautiful wallpapers and exquisite furnishings, but some rooms are on the smallish side. The two-bedroom bungalows are best for those who require more space.

Dining/Entertainment: The hotel has numerous dining areas: the Mediterranean Room, with its adjoining patio at the entrance to the hotel, for Mediterranean-style main courses; the Sky Room for French cuisine (it's a popular place to propose); and the legendary Whaling Bar (see listing in Chapter 6) with the adjoining Café La Rue and Tropical Patio for international cuisine featuring seafood and grilled meats. There is piano music in the lobby lounge Monday through Saturday evenings. Sunday brunch is served on the Mediterranean Room patio.

Services: Room service (24-hour), laundry/dry cleaning, morning newspaper, shoe shine, twice-daily maid service, babysitting, valet parking, airport transportation.

Facilities: Pool and Jacuzzi in garden setting, exercise room, sauna, shuffleboard, access to tennis courts, meeting rooms, gift shop.

EXPENSIVE

✪ Colonial Inn

910 Prospect St., La Jolla, CA 92037. ☎ **619/454-2181** or 800/826-1278. Fax 619/454-5679. 64 rms, 11 suites. TV TEL. $150 single or double with village view, $175–$210 single or double with ocean view; from $230 suite. Lower off-season rates. Children under 18 stay free in parents' room. AE, CB, DC, MC, V. Valet parking $5. Take the Ardath Road exit off I-5 north; or the La Jolla Village Drive west exit off I-5

La Jolla Accommodations

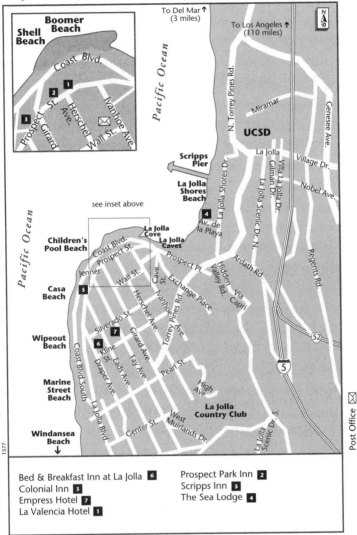

Bed & Breakfast Inn at La Jolla **6**
Colonial Inn **3**
Empress Hotel **7**
La Valencia Hotel **1**

Prospect Park Inn **2**
Scripps Inn **5**
The Sea Lodge **4**

south. Take Torrey Pines Road to Prospect Place and turn right. Prospect Place becomes Prospect Street.

The Colonial Inn is one of my favorite places in La Jolla. I like the old-world atmosphere, the tasteful decor, and the spacious room enhanced by traditional furnishings and elegant fabrics. The property was built in 1913, and its Putnam's Restaurant now occupies the site of a drugstore by the same name. The hotel is one block from the ocean and just down the street from the more expensive La Valencia. Guests who choose to stay here instead of at La Valencia will sacrifice air-conditioning for a ceiling fan in each room, but will gain elbow room (and save money). The Inn, originally an apartment hotel, has oversized closets and feels more homey. A large spray of fresh flowers is the focal point in the lounge where guests gather in front of the fireplace. The outdoor heated pool, set in a landscaped garden, is open from sunup to sundown. Walking tours of La Jolla depart from the hotel at 11am on Thursday through Saturday or other times by appointment. Airport transportation is available for $9 one way.

Dining/Entertainment: The bar in Putnam's was once a soda-fountain; today it's a popular watering hole. Drinks are also served in front of the fireplace in the lounge. The restaurant serves excellent California cuisine.

Services: Room service (24-hour), dry cleaning/laundry, turndown service on request, babysitting, valet parking, airport transportation, complimentary shoe shine.

Facilities: Heated outdoor pool, conference rooms, car rental desk, refrigerators and terry-cloth robes available upon request.

The Sea Lodge

8110 Camino del Oro, La Jolla, CA 92037. ☎ **619/459-8271** or 800/237-5211. Fax 619/456-9346. 128 rms and suites. A/C TV TEL. $155–$349 double; $399 suite. Extra person $15. Children under 12 stay free in parents' room. Lower off-season and long stay rates. AE, DC, DISC, MC, V. Free indoor parking. Take the Ardath Road exit off I-5 north; or the La Jolla Village Drive west exit off I-5 south. Take La Jolla Shores Drive; turn left onto Avenida de la Playa, turn right on Camino del Oro.

The Sea Lodge is a great location for those who want to be right on the beach as opposed to in the village near shops and restaurants. This low-rise property, with its early-California decor, has a nice pool, but my guess is that most people will prefer the Pacific. Nonsmoking rooms are available and all units offer a terrace or balcony and a refrigerator; 19 rooms come with kitchens. A nice restaurant and bar overlook the water. Babysitting and valet service are provided, and there are a car rental desk, sauna, and tennis courts on the premises.

MODERATE

✪ Empress Hotel of La Jolla

7766 Fay Ave. (at Kline), La Jolla, CA 92037. ☎ **619/454-3001** or 800/525-6552. Fax 619/454-6387. 73 rooms and suites. A/C TV TEL. $109–$135 double; $250 Jacuzzi suite. Extra person $10. Children under 18 stay free in parents' room. Rates include continental breakfast. Lower off-season and long-stay rates. AE, DC, DIS, MC, V. Valet parking $5. Take the Ardath Road exit off I-5 north; or the La Jolla Village Drive west exit off I-5 south. Take Torrey Pines Road to Girard, turn right, then left on Kline Street.

The Empress Hotel offers spacious quarters with traditional furnishings a block or two away from La Jolla's "main drag." It's definitely quieter here than at the Colonial Inn or the Prospect Park Inn. All rooms come equipped with refrigerators, hairdryers, coffeemakers, and terry-cloth robes. The four Empress Rooms have a sitting area with a full-size sofa sleeper. While these rooms have only a microwave, four suites have complete cooking facilities. Two suites come equipped with a grand piano. The top two floors in this 5-story building have partial ocean views. I like the European ambience, marble bathrooms with large mirrors, and tasteful decor. Room service comes from the award-winning Manhattan Restaurant located on the ground floor.

Prospect Park Inn

1110 Prospect St. (at Coast Boulevard), La Jolla, CA 92037. ☎ **619/454-0133** or 800/433-1609. Fax 619/454-2056. 23 rms and suites. A/C TV TEL. $95–$140 double. Lower off-season rates. Rates include continental breakfast. AE, DC, DISC, MC, V. Indoor parking off-site free of charge. Take the Ardath Road exit off I-5 north; or the La Jolla Village Drive west exit off I-5 south. Take Torrey Pines Road to Prospect Place and turn right. Prospect Place becomes Prospect Street.

This place is a real gem. It's a small property—next door to La Valencia—that offers charming rooms, some with ocean views. Built in 1947 as a boarding house for women, this spotless boutique hotel feels more European than Californian. There is no elevator in the three-story building. Fruit, cookies, and beverages are offered in the library area every afternoon and breakfast is served on the sundeck, which has a great ocean view. Prospect Park Inn enjoys essentially the same location as La Valencia and the Colonial Inn—the beach, park, shops, and myriad restaurants are within steps—at much lower prices. The Cove Suite is extra large and has an outstanding ocean view; other units have balconies or terraces. Beach towels and chairs are provided free of charge for guests to use. This is a nonsmoking establishment.

Scripps Inn

555 Coast Blvd. South (at Cuvier), La Jolla, CA 92037. ☎ **619/454-3391.** 8 rms, 5 suites. TV TEL. Summer, $110–$180 single or double. Off season, $90–$160 single or double. Extra person $10. Children under 12 stay free in parents' room. Weekly and monthly rates available off-season. Rates include continental breakfast. AE, DISC, MC, V. Free parking. Take the Ardath Road exit off I-5 north; or the La Jolla Village Drive west exit off I-5 south. Take Torrey Pines Road, turn right on Prospect Place, veer right (downhill) onto Coast Boulevard (if you miss the turn, drive through town and turn right at museum).

Only a small grassy park comes between this cozy inn and the beach, cliffs, and tide pools. All the guest rooms have ocean views and Early American furnishings; two have working fireplaces (Room 12 has a fireplace, wet bar, and a particularly fine view, rivaled only by Room 14's). The four suites have separate bedrooms and kitchenettes. The view from the second-story deck seems to hypnotize guests, who gaze out to sea indefinitely. The inn supplies beach towels, as well as wood for fireplaces. The Museum of Contemporary Art, San Diego, is next door, and Prospect Street shops and restaurants are a short walk away.

A BED & BREAKFAST

Bed & Breakfast Inn at La Jolla

7753 Draper Ave., La Jolla, CA 92037. ☎ **619/456-2066.** 16 rms. A/C. $85–$225 single or double. Children over 12 welcome. MC, V. Rate includes continental breakfast. Take the Ardath Road exit off I-5 north; or the La Jolla Village Dr. W exit off I-5 south. Take Torrey Pines Road; turn right on Prospect Place, which becomes Prospect Street; turn left at Draper; the inn is nestled between the La Jolla Women's Club and the La Jolla Presbyterian Church.

This inn is so appealing that it makes me wish I didn't live in La Jolla—then I'd have a good excuse to check in! As it is, I walk by once a week and envy the residents within. The historic house, built in 1913, was expanded and converted to its current use in 1985. The Recreation Center (tennis and basketball courts) and Museum of Contemporary Art are across the street. The Garden Room with country decor, a fireplace facing the bed, a vase of delicate flowers on the dresser, and a decanter of sherry on the writing table is a favorite room. Others include the elegant, all-white Holiday room with a king-size canopy bed. The cottage-style rooms are distinct, and the five rooms in the well-designed new wing of the house are as winsome as those in the original section. The decor of rooms varies, but each is beautiful and includes fresh flowers. It's fun to ramble from the garden to the sundeck to the sitting room, and you can enjoy complimentary wine and cheese in the afternoon from 5 to 6pm. Architect Irving Gill designed the house in his innovative "cubist" style, and local lore has it that John Philip Sousa, whose family lived in the house for seven years in the 1920s, once swung from the vines out front. The hosts feel that the property is unsuitable for children under age 12. The whole house is nonsmoking.

7   Coronado

VERY EXPENSIVE

Hotel del Coronado

1500 Orange Ave., Coronado, CA 92118. ☎ **619/435-6611,** 619/522-8000 for reservations, or 800/HOTEL DEL. Fax 619/522-8262. 692 rms (400 in the original wooden building). MINIBAR TV TEL. Original Victorian building, $169 standard; $199 deluxe; $249 ocean view; $309–$389 lanai; from $499 suite. Modern complex, from $189 rooms, $499–$599 oceanfront suite. Children under 15 stay free in parents' room. AE, DC, DISC, MC, V. Parking $10. Bus: 901. Ferry: From Broadway Pier. Driving: From I-5 take the Coronado Bridge; turn left onto Orange Avenue.

The "Hotel Del," as it is affectionately called, turned 107 years old in 1995. Built in a scant 11 months by Chinese laborers and Scandinavian wood-carvers, this National Historic Landmark is one of the world's largest wooden buildings. Its famous red roofs and turrets, white facade, rows of prim windows, and graceful verandas are instantly recognizable. Inside, the woodwork is impressive, especially in the Crown Room, where the 30-foot-high sugar-pine ceiling is put together solely with wooden pegs. The ceiling, which has never been stained, is hand-polished twice a year. The large room also has no pillar support—not surprising, since the hotel's architects had a background building railroad stations. The rooms in the original building have ceiling fans; only those in the Ocean Towers and poolside have air-conditioning. The rooms in the original building tend to be small, but the larger (preferable) ones evoke an earlier era.

A Hotel with History: Scenes from the Hotel del Coronado

Welcome to the Hotel del Coronado, romantic, unmistakable, and filled with enchanting and colorful memories.

Several familiar names helped shape the hotel. Thomas Edison personally installed the electricity in 1887; the building had its own electrical power plant, which also supplied the entire city of Coronado until 1922. Author L. Frank Baum, a frequent guest, designed the Crown Dining Room's elegant crown-shaped chandeliers. Since Baum wrote several of his beloved *Wizard of Oz* series in Coronado, many believe he modeled the Emerald City's geometric spires after the Del's conical turrets.

The hotel has hosted royalty and celebrities as well. The first visiting monarch was Kalakaua, Hawaii's last king, who spent Christmas here in the 1890s. But the best-known royal guest would be Edward, Prince of Wales (later Edward VIII and then Duke of Windsor), who came to the hotel in April 1920, the first British royal to visit California. Of the many lavish social affairs held during his stay, at least two were attended by Coronado Navy wife Wallis Warfield, 15 years before her official introduction to the prince in London. Speculation continues as to whether their love affair, which culminated in his abdication of the throne to marry her, might have begun right here.

America's own "royalty" also often visited the hotel. In 1927, San Diego's beloved son Charles Lindbergh was honored here following his historic 33¹/₂-hour solo flight across the Atlantic. Hollywood stars, including Mary Pickford, Greta Garbo, Charlie Chaplin, and Esther Williams, have flocked to the Del. Director Billy Wilder filmed *Some Like It Hot* at the hotel; long-time hotel staffers remember seeing stars Marilyn Monroe, Tony Curtis, and Jack Lemmon romping on the beach during filming. The hotel has also hosted 14 U.S. presidents. And some guests have allegedly never left: the ghost of Kate Morgan, whose body was found in 1892 where the tennis courts are today, still roams the halls.

Visitors and guests intrigued by the hotel's past should stroll through the lower level History Gallery, a mini museum of hotel memorabilia.

—by Stephanie Avnet

Dining/Entertainment: Several dining areas include the Crown Room and the smaller Coronet Room for California cuisine with a French accent; the Prince of Wales for fine dining; the Ocean Terrace for alfresco bistro fare; the Del Deli for matzoh ball soup, potato and meat knishes, and lox and bagels (24 hours); and the Palm Court in the lobby for continental breakfast. There are music and dancing nightly in the Ocean Terrace Lounge, piano music in the Palm Court bar, and Sunday buffet dinner dances in the Crown Room. The Ocean Terrace Bar has dewdrop chandeliers, a wood ceiling, and round tables that beg for a card game.

Services: Concierge, 24-hour room service, laundry/dry cleaning, valet, babysitting, beauty salon, limousine service, self-guided tour of hotel with audiocassette, $10 guided tours of the hotel, 24-hour deli, special activities for children, Airport shuttle ($9).

Facilities: Two outdoor pools, health spa, massage, six tennis courts, car rental desk, electronic games, meeting rooms, shopping arcade, lobby shop.

Le Meridien

2000 2nd St., Coronado, CA 92118. ☎ **619/435-3000** or 800/543-4300. Fax 619/435-3032. 265 rms, 7 suites, 28 oceanfront villas. A/C MINIBAR TV TEL. $165–$255 single or double; from $375 suite; from $475 waterfront villa. Children under 12 stay free in parents' room. AE, CB, DC, MC, V. Self parking $7; valet parking $9. Airport transfers ($6 each way). Bus: 901. Ferry: From Broadway Pier. Driving: From I-5 take the Coronado Bridge; turn right onto Glorietta Boulevard; take first right to hotel.

I find it confusing that they answer the phone "bonjour" here, because the French name and the restaurant cuisine are the only evidence of a Gallic connection. However, this is still one of the area's loveliest hotels, with a waterfront location, clean lines, open architecture, and an airy lobby with a rough-hewn ceiling, oversize rattan chairs, and a beige limestone floor. The rooms have thick carpeting, overstuffed chairs, pale-wood paneling and bright striped wallpaper, desks, and vanities; bathrooms with oversize bathtubs and adjustable shower heads are nicely lit and have fresh flowers, hairdryers, and terry-cloth robes. All rooms feature either balconies or patios; suites have Jacuzzis and safes. On the grounds are plenty of plants, a boardwalk to the base of the Coronado Bridge, preening pink flamingos, white and black swans, and even a walk-in aviary. From here, you feel you can almost reach across the bay and touch the San Diego Convention Center. Guests have the option of splurging and taking a one-day rejuvenator at the hotel spa: a facial, massage, herbal wrap, and spa lunch costs about $170.

Dining/Entertainment: Marius, the hotel's much-acclaimed French restaurant features French gourmet cuisine and is open for dinner only, Tuesday through Sunday. The more informal L'Escale, a brasserie restaurant, serves breakfast, lunch, and dinner daily, a Saturday jazz brunch, a Sunday champagne brunch, and provides bay views from its dining terrace; outdoor refreshments are served at La Riviera Pool. La Provence, the hotel cocktail lounge, is open daily (4pm to 1am) and features live piano music Friday and Saturday.

Services: Concierge, 24-hour room service, laundry/valet, turn-down service, twice-daily maid service, baby-sitting, bicycle rental, currency exchange, valet parking, complimentary shuttle to Horton Plaza.

Facilities: Three outdoor heated pools (including lap pool), two outdoor whirlpools, European health club and spa, yoga and exercise sessions, massage, six lighted tennis courts, tennis clinic, bicycle rental, water sports, jogging trail and bike path, private dock, business center with fax and secretarial services, meeting rooms, shopping arcade.

✪ Loew's Coronado Bay Resort

4000 Coronado Bay Rd., Coronado, CA 92118. ☎ **619/424-4000,** or 800/
23-LOEWS. Fax 619/424-4400. 403 rms, 37 suites. A/C MINIBAR TV TEL. $165–$225
single or double; from $375 suite. Extra person $20. Children under 18 stay free in
parents' room. "Romance" and tennis packages available. AE, CB, DC, DISC, MC, V.
Self-parking $8; valet parking $11. Take I-5 to the Coronado Bridge; left onto Orange
Avenue; continue 8 miles down Silver Strand Highway; left at Coronado Bay Road,
entrance to the resort.

This lovely luxury resort opened in 1991 and lounges on a secluded 15-
acre peninsula, slightly removed from both downtown Coronado and
San Diego. It's perfect for those who prefer a self-contained resort in
a get-away-from-it-all location. All quarters offer terraces that look onto
the hotel's private 80-slip marina, the Coronado Bay Bridge, and the
San Diego skyline. Each room is very well appointed with the finest
furnishings and large marble bathrooms. The resort is 30 minutes from
the airport, 3 miles from downtown Coronado, and a short drive from
Tijuana. A private pedestrian underpass leads to nearby Silver Strand
Beach. The hotel features the Commodore Kids Club, an outstanding
program for children 4 to 12, with activities daily from 9am to 4pm
and Thursday through Saturday from 6:30 to 9:30pm (additional
charge). It's available year-round, with a two-child minimum.

Dining/Entertainment: Azzura Point serves award-winning California cuisine dinners with a view, while the more casual RRR's serves
three meals a day, plus a Sunday brunch, both indoors and outdoors
with a marina view. Guests also enjoy a lounge, a poolside bar and grill,
and a gourmet market.

Services: Concierge; 24-hour room service; laundry/valet; turn-down
service; express checkout; valet parking.

Facilities: Three outdoor swimming pools; fitness center with equipment, saunas, steam room, and whirlpools; massage; large sundeck,
hydro spas; five tennis courts and pro shop; water sports; bicycle,
in-line skate, and water-sports rentals; a marina; terry-cloth robes in
rooms; in-room safes; business center; faxes in suites; meeting space;
washer and dryer; car-rental desk; beauty salon; boutiques; nonsmoking rooms.

EXPENSIVE

Glorietta Bay Inn

1630 Glorietta Blvd., Coronado, CA 92118. ☎ **619/435-3101** or 800/283-9383. Fax
619/435-6182. 98 rms (11 in original mansion). TV TEL. Mansion, $129–$139 single
or double; $165–$179 suite; $275–285 penthouse. Annex, $70–$80 economy single
or double; $99–$129 contemporary double; $129–$179 family suite. AE, CB, DC,
MC, V. Free parking. Bus: 901. Ferry: From Broadway Pier. Driving: Take I-5 to the
Coronado Bridge; turn left on Orange Avenue; after 2 miles, turn left onto Glorietta
Boulevard; it's across the street from the Hotel del Coronado.

Right across the street and somewhat in the shadow of the Hotel del
Coronado, this pretty white hotel incorporates the John D. Spreckels
mansion (1908) with the original fixtures and marble-and-brass staircase. The lobby is inviting: wicker furniture, lush hanging ferns, and
an adjoining music room and outdoor patio. Rooms in the mansion

are Victorian in style, while those in the annex are modern. They all have refrigerators. The grounds are beautifully landscaped and tended, and the hotel is within walking distance of the beach, golf, tennis, water sports, shopping, and dining.

Services: In-room movies, laundry/dry cleaning, babysitting, complimentary morning coffee, continental breakfast available for a charge.

Facilities: Kitchenettes available, heated pool and spa pool, bicycle rental, conference rooms, guest laundry.

MODERATE

El Cordova Hotel

1351 Orange Ave. (at Adella), Coronado, CA 92118. ☎ **619/435-4131** or 800/367-6467. 7 rms, 2 studios, 18 suites. TV TEL. $75–$85 single or double; $85–$105 studio with kitchen; $110–$125 one-bedroom suite; $155 two-bedroom suite. Mid-June through mid-Sept rates 10% higher. Weekly and monthly rates available off-season. Children under 12 stay free in parents' room. AE, DC, DISC, MC, V. Bus: 901. Ferry: From Broadway Pier. Driving: Take I-5 to the Coronado Bridge; turn left onto Orange Ave.

Built as a Spanish-style mansion in 1902, El Cordova became a hotel in 1930. Each room, a little different from the next, features a ceiling fan, brightly tiled bathroom, and Mexican and Native American furnishings in soothing earth tones. A suite, accommodating four to six people, has a separate living room and kitchenette. The grounds are filled with flowers and shrubs; unfortunately there's no off-street parking or air conditioning. This inviting place welcomes children and pets. It's advisable to reserve at least six months in advance, and a year ahead for the month of August. The hotel, well-located near the beach and the Hotel del Coronado, attracts a young clientele and probably isn't a good choice for those who like to go to bed early. Services include a laundry room and vending machines. Facilities include a heated pool, a patio, a barbecue area with a picnic table, an arcade with shops, and a Mexican restaurant. This venerable property is gradually being upgraded. I suggest requesting a room in the renovated section.

El Rancho Hotel

370 Orange Ave. (at 4th Street), Coronado, CA 92118. ☎ **619/435-2251.** 6 rms. A/C TV. Summer, $45–$90 single or double. Winter, $65–$75 single or double. AE, DC, DISC, JCB, MC, V. Free parking. Bus: 901. Ferry: From Broadway Pier. Driving: Take I-5 to the Coronado Bridge; turn left onto Orange Avenue.

This small, pretty, Spanish-style place is owned and lovingly tended by Cecilia Leith. The modern and clean rooms feature walk-in closets, tiled baths with Jacuzzis, sitting areas, loft-style beamed ceilings, and plush carpets. They come equipped with refrigerator, coffeemaker and microwave, and overlook a small garden filled with azaleas, roses, camellias, and flowering jasmine. The motel's reception area is tiny, but Ms. Leith can supply brochures that you can take to your room. The services include ice and soda machines, and in-room coffee, tea, and cocoa. Guests can use the table and chairs on the brick patio.

San Diego Dining

Restaurants here win kudos all the time for cuisine, service, ambience, and romantic bay and ocean views. A rich mix of ethnic restaurants exists, along with local restaurants (and restaurateurs) that are unique to San Diego.

Italian food is the current craze, and the city has some great Greek restaurants, as well as Chinese eateries. However, given our history and location, it's not surprising that Mexican fare consistently ranks as our favorite ethnic cuisine. Actually, it's more accurate to say *Americanized Mexican* food since, like Tex Mex, what you'll savor in San Diego is not what you'll be served south of the border. Some of the best Mexican restaurants are located in Old Town. The three in the Bazaar del Mundo (Casa de Pico, Rancho el Nopal, and Casa de Bandini) and the Old Town Mexican Cafe on San Diego Avenue are the most popular. Diners on the run head for Rubios, a Mexican fast-food emporium with locations throughout the city. And if you enjoy a margarita with your meal, remember that some believe the drink has local origins: a bartender at La Jolla's La Valencia Hotel supposedly first concocted the drink.

In this chapter, I've indexed restaurants by cuisine as well as by location and price category. For diners on a budget, the more expensive San Diego restaurants are very accommodating if you want to order a few appetizers instead of a main course. Dress tends to be pretty casual, even in pricey places. (Some restaurateurs post the local law—"Shoes and shirt required"—to discourage those who would be *too* laid-back.) California law mandates no smoking; however, smoking is allowed in bar areas of restaurants.

Listings are divided first by location, then alphabetically by price. I've used the following price categories, determined by the average cost of dinner main courses: **very expensive,** $20 to $40; **expensive,** $15 to $20; **moderate,** $10 to $15; **inexpensive,** $10 or less. A dollar sign by a listing denotes especially good value for money spent. A star signifies one of my particular favorites.

Note: Don't forget to look at the dining listings in Chapters 11 and 12. Many places listed as day trips or excursions further afield might make a great lunch or dinner destination.

1 Best Bets

- **Best Spot for a Business Lunch:** Dakota Grill and Spirits, at 901 Fifth Ave. (☎ 619/234-5554), has the three important ingredients of a business lunch locale: location, appropriate atmosphere, and good food (here it's great).
- **Best View:** In San Diego many restaurants overlook the ocean, but only from Brockton Villa, at 1235 Coast Blvd. (☎ 619/454-7393), can you see the La Jolla Cove. Diners with a window seat feel like they're looking out on a gigantic picture postcard.
- **Best Value:** The food at the Grand Central Cafe, located in the downtown YMCA at 500 W. Broadway (☎ 619/234-CAFE), isn't fancy, but it's very reasonably priced.
- **Best for Kids:** At the Old Spaghetti Factory, located at Fifth Avenue and K Street (☎ 619/233-4323), family dining is de rigueur—so if your kids are noisy, nobody will notice.
- **Best Chinese Cuisine:** Two words describe the fare at Mandarin House, at 2604 Fifth Ave.(☎ 619/232-1101): *Szechuan* and *delicious.* Some, but not all, dishes are spicy.
- **Best Italian Cuisine:** Tuscan food (from northern Italy) is now quite popular in San Diego, and Osterina Panevino, at 722 Fifth Ave. (☎ 619/595-7959), serves some of the best, in cozy surroundings.
- **Best Seafood:** Not only does The Fish Market/Top of the Market offer the city's best fish, at 750 N. Harbor Dr. (☎ 619/232-FISH or 619/234-4TOP), it also offers a great view out across San Diego Bay.
- **Best American International Cuisine:** Croce's menu cleverly includes dishes from a half-dozen different countries—all adapted to American tastes. The results are delicious, and can be found at 802 Fifth Ave. (☎ 619/233-4355).
- **Best Mexican Cuisine:** The women making tortillas in the front window catch the attention of passersby, but it's the great food that keeps the locals coming back to the Old Town Mexican Cafe, at 2489 San Diego Ave. (☎ 619/297-4330).
- **Best Vegetarian:** Kung Food, at 2949 Fifth Ave. (☎ 619/298-7302), offers tasty meat-free dishes from a variety of ethnic cuisines.
- **Best Pizza:** For an imaginative pizza, such as the "Greek Grilled Chicken" with marinated chicken, mozzarella, sliced tomatoes, red onion, feta cheese, and Kalamata olives, eat at D'Lish, at 7514 Girard Ave. (☎ 619/459-8118) or 4150 Mission Blvd. (☎ 619/483-4949), which also offers great salads and pasta dishes.
- **Best Desserts:** You'll forget your diet at Extraordinary Desserts, at 2929 Fifth Ave. (☎ 619/294-7001). Proprietor Karen Krasne has a Certificate de Patisserie from the Cordon Bleu in Paris, and she makes everything fresh on the premises daily.

- **Best Late-Night Dining:** Open later than any place else down-town, Cafe Lulu, at 419 F St. (☎ 619/238-0114), serves until 2am during the week, 4am on weekends.
- **Best Fast Food:** Fish tacos from Rubios, at 901 Fourth Ave. (☎ 619/231-7731) and other locations, are an institution in San Diego. Taste one and you'll know why.
- **Best Picnic Fare:** Pack a humongous sandwich from the Cheese Shop for a picnic lunch and you won't be hungry for dinner. There's one downtown at 401 G St. (☎ 619/232-2303) and an-other in La Jolla Shores at 2165 Avenida de La Playa (☎ 619/459-3921).

2 Restaurants by Cuisine

AMERICAN

Bay Beach Cafe (Moderate, Coronado)

Chart House (Very Expensive, Coronado, La Jolla)

Corvette Diner (Inexpensive, Hillcrest/Uptown)

Croce's Restaurant (Expensive, Downtown)

Dakota Grill and Spirits (Moderate, Downtown)

Firehouse Beach Cafe (Inexpensive, Mission Bay/Pacific Beach)

Galaxy Grill (Inexpensive, Downtown)

Grand Central Cafe (Inexpensive, Downtown)

Hard Rock Cafe (Inexpensive, La Jolla)

Hob Nob Hill (Moderate, Hillcrest/Uptown)

Kansas City Barbecue (Inexpensive, Downtown)

Old Columbia Brewery and Grill (Inexpensive, Downtown)

Pacific Beach Brewhouse (Inexpensive, Mission Bay/Pacific Beach)

Planet Hollywood (Moderate, Downtown)

Quel Fromage (Inexpensive, Hillcrest/Uptown)

Rhinoceros Cafe and Grill (Moderate, Coronado)

T. D. Hays (Moderate, Mission Bay/Pacific Beach)

CALIFORNIA

The Atoll (Expensive, Mission Bay/Pacific Beach)

Brockton Villa (Inexpensive, La Jolla)

Cafe Pacifica (Expensive, Old Town)

Canes California Bistro (Moderate, Hillcrest/Uptown)

George's at the Cove (Very Expensive, La Jolla)

Putnam's Restaurant and Bar (Expensive, La Jolla)

The Whaling Bar/Tropical Patio (Expensive, La Jolla)

CHINESE

Mandarin Cafe (Inexpensive, Coronado)

Mandarin House (Inexpensive, Downtown, Pacific Beach, La Jolla)

Panda Inn (Moderate, Downtown)

COFFEE SHOP

Garden House Coffee and Tea (Inexpensive, Old Town)

CONTINENTAL

Chez Loma (Expensive, Coronado)

Dobson's (Very Expensive, Downtown)

Top O' the Cove (Very Expensive, La Jolla)

DESSERTS

Extraordinary Desserts (Inexpensive, Hillcrest/ Uptown)

ENGLISH

Princess of Wales (Inexpensive, Downtown)

FRENCH

Liaison (Moderate, Hillcrest/Uptown)

GREEK

Athens Market (Moderate, Downtown)

Calliope's (Moderate, Hillcrest/Uptown)

INTERNATIONAL

Cafe Lulu (Inexpensive, Downtown)

The Green Flash (Moderate, Mission Bay/Pacific Beach)

IRISH

Hennessey's Tavern (Inexpensive, Mission Bay/ Pacific Beach)

McP's Irish Pub (Inexpensive, Coronado)

ITALIAN

Busalacchi's (Expensive, Hillcrest/Uptown)

D'Lish (Inexpensive, La Jolla, Mission Bay/Pacific Beach)

Filippi's Pizza Grotto (Inexpensive, Downtown, Mission Bay/Pacific Beach, and other locations)

Fio's (Moderate, Downtown)

Old Spaghetti Factory (Inexpensive, Downtown)

Osteria Panevino (Moderate, Downtown)

Primavera (Expensive, Coronado)

LIGHT FARE

The Cottage (Moderate, La Jolla)

Kensington Coffee Company (Inexpensive, Coronado)

Sculpture Garden Cafe (Inexpensive, Hillcrest/Uptown)

MEXICAN

Casa de Bandini (Moderate, Old Town)

Casa de Pico (Inexpensive, Old Town)

Old Town Mexican Cafe (Inexpensive, Old Town)

Rancho El Nopal (Inexpensive, Old Town)

MOROCCAN

Marakesh (Expensive, La Jolla, Downtown)

SEAFOOD

Anthony's Star of the Sea (Very Expensive, Downtown)

Bay Beach Cafe (Moderate, Coronado)

Brigatine (Expensive, Coronado)

Brigantine Seafood Grill (Expensive, Old Town)

The Fish Market/Top of the Market (Expensive, Downtown)

The Green Flash (Moderate, Mission Bay/Pacific Beach)

The Rusty Pelican (Expensive, Mission Bay/ Pacific Beach)

SOUTHWESTERN

Dakota Grill and Spirits
(Moderate, Downtown)

THAI

Celadon (Moderate,
Hillcrest/Uptown)

VEGETARIAN

Kung Food (Inexpensive,
Hillcrest/Uptown)

3 Downtown

The Gaslamp Quarter is the center of the downtown dining scene, where the city's best eating spots are housed in restored Victorian buildings. If you stroll down Fifth Avenue between E Street and K Street, you'll find your pick of places to eat. The best block is from G Street to F Street, where on the same side of the street you'll find Trattoria La Strada, Osteria Panevino, Asti Ristorante, Bella Luna, Little Joe's Pizza House, and Marakesh. Listed below are more of my favorites.

VERY EXPENSIVE

Anthony's Star of the Sea Room

Harbor Dr. and Ash St. ☎ **619/232-7408.** Reservations required one week in advance, for Sat three weeks in advance; call after 2pm. Jackets required. Main courses $16.50–$32.50. AE, CB, DC, MC, V. Daily 5:30–10:30pm. Closed major holidays. Bus: 2. Trolley: America Plaza or Seaport Village. Valet parking $4. SEAFOOD.

A San Diego dining institution since 1965, Anthony's specializes in the three S's—service, style, and seafood—all superbly delivered under the attentive eye of manager and maître d' Mario Valerio, who has been with the restaurant since it began. The "newest" waiter has worked here more than 25 years. The restaurant is set over the water on pilings (if you look, you can count more than a dozen), and its arched window wall and raised booths provide every diner a view; candlelight adds to the glow here. Popular appetizers are the clams Genovese tossed with béchamel sauce and topped with Parmesan cheese and the lobster scampi della casa. Among the seafood dishes, the baked sole à l'admiral—stuffed with lobster, shrimp, and crab—and swordfish, both prepared for two, get top billing. Portions are large.

Dobson's

956 Broadway Circle (between Broadway and Horton Plaza). ☎ **619/231-6771.** Reservations recommended. Main courses $12–$28. AE, MC,V. Mon–Wed 11:30am–10pm, Thur–Fri 11:30am–11pm, Sat 5:30pm–11pm. CONTINENTAL.

This has long been a local "in" place, especially for politicians and those who observe them. Personable owner Paul Dobson, or his wife, Carol, are likely to greet you at the door. Dobson's menu features veal, lamb, fish, duckling, quail, and venison. Popular dishes include mussel bisque; veal chops; and, for lunch, Dobson's famous hamburger or Cobb salad. Jackets aren't required here, but something about the place—beginning with the etched-glass front door and green awning—makes you want to dress up. The tables overlooking the bar are the most fun. The bar is open until midnight.

San Diego Dining

 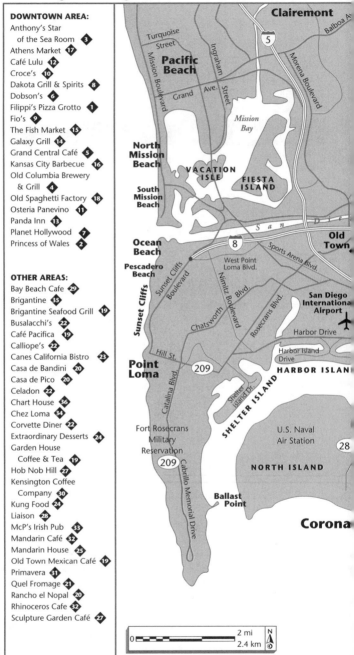
Clairemont

Balboa Av

Turquoise
Street

**Pacific
Beach**

Ingraham
Street

Morena Boulevard

5

Mission Boulevard

Grand   Ave.   Street

*Mission
Bay*

**North
Mission
Beach**

**VACATION
ISLE**

**FIESTA
ISLAND**

**South
Mission
Beach**

San Di

**Ocean
Beach**

8

**Old
Town**

Sports Arena Blvd.

**Pescadero
Beach**

West Point
Loma Blvd.

Sunset Cliffs Boulevard

Nimitz Boulevard

Rosecrans Blvd.

**San Diego
International
Airport**

Chatsworth

Harbor Drive

Sunset Cliffs

Harbor Island
Drive

Hill St.

**Point
Loma**

Catalina Blvd.

209

HARBOR ISLAN

Shelter
Island Dr.

SHELTER ISLAND

Fort Rosecrans
Military
Reservation

209

Cabrillo Memorial Drive

**U.S. Naval
Air Station**

28

NORTH ISLAND

**Ballast
Point**

Corona

0   2 mi
                     2.4 km

N

EXPENSIVE

☼ Croce's Restaurant

802 Fifth Ave. (at F Street). ☎ **619/233-4355.** Reservations suggested. Main courses $11.95–$22.95. AE, DC, DISC, MC, V. Daily 5pm–midnight. Valet parking $5. Bus: 1, 3, 25, or 945. Trolley: Gaslamp Quarter. AMERICAN/INTERNATIONAL.

Diners who choose this spot are in for a surprise if they think, as I did, that Croce's is a popular jazz and blues spot that also *happens* to serve food. NOT SO! My recent meal here, which began with a wonderful grilled lamb salad and included the salmon in puff pastry, was truly memorable. Other popular dishes are prawns wrapped in basil and proscuitto and Chef Fay Nakanishi's Alaskan halibut with sautéed prawn and spicy nasi goreng cream. The restaurant is next door to Croce's Jazz Bar and diners enjoy music with their meals. Seating is both indoors and out. Ingrid Croce has created an inviting cluster of dining and entertainment options here. In addition to Croce's Restaurant, **Ingrid's Cantina and Sidewalk Cafe** (next door) serves excellent Southwestern cuisine. **Upstairs at Croce's,** open only Friday and Saturday nights from 7pm to 2am, is a wonderful cocktail/coffee bar serving light fare. Those who dine at either of the full-service restaurants can enter the two adjacent night spots, The Jazz Bar and The Top Hat, without paying the normal cover charge. The music venues are described in Chapter 10, "San Diego After Dark."

The Fish Market/Top of the Market

750 N. Harbor Dr. ☎ **619/232-FISH** (Fish Market) or 619/234-4TOP (Top of the Market). Reservations recommended for Top of the Market. Reservations not accepted at The Fish Market. Main courses $8.65–$25 (Fish Market); $15–$31.50 (Top of the Market). AE, CB, DC, MC, V. Daily 11am–10pm. Bus: 7/7B. Trolley: Seaport Village. SEAFOOD.

The red building perched on the end of the G Street Pier at the Embarcadero houses two of San Diego's most popular seafood establishments: The Fish Market and its pricier cousin, The Top of the Market. Both offer superb fresh seafood and menus that change daily. The chalkboard out front tells you what's freshest, be it Mississippi catfish, Maine lobster, Canadian salmon, or Mexican yellowtail. At ground level, the Fish Market, a market and casual restaurant, has oyster and sushi bars and a cocktail lounge. Upstairs, the elegant Top of the Market looks like a private club, with teakwood touches, mounted fish trophies, and historic photographs. The panoramic view from here encompasses the bay, the Coronado Bay Bridge, and, sometimes, aircraft carriers (the restaurant thoughtfully provides binoculars). Besides seafood, you can get homemade pasta and choose from a wine list as extensive as the menu. This lofty place inspires some to dress up and make a reservation, but you're also welcome to drop by just for a drink and enjoy the view. Outdoor seating is directly above the water. You can spend a moderate amount downstairs here—a lot more upstairs. There is another Fish Market Restaurant in Del Mar at 640 Via de la Valle (☎ 619/755-2277).

MODERATE

Athens Market

109 W. F St. (just west of First Avenue). ☎ **619/234-1955.** Reservations recommended. Main courses $10–$20. AE, CB, DC, MC, V. Mon–Thurs 11:30am–11pm, Fri–Sat 11:30am–midnight, Sun 4pm–11pm. Bus: 1, 2, 3, 25, 34, or 34A. GREEK.

Effervescent owner Mary Pappas came to San Diego in 1961 on a student visa, and since 1974 she's been serving the tasty recipes her dad taught her. You'll quickly notice she knows most of her patrons by name and is involved in every part of the restaurant's operation, from cooking to bartending. The place itself is inviting, with soft light, and sparkling white cafe curtains and tablecloths set off by bright-blue napkins. Popular appetizers are the tiropita (pockets of phyllo pastry stuffed with three cheeses and baked) and spanakopita (spinach and cheese-stuffed phyllo). All your favorite Greek dishes are on the menu, prepared with the freshest ingredients and Pappas's creative twists (the moussaka, for instance, has a layer of zucchini). At lunch, sandwiches are available; lunch and dinner menus both offer soup-and-salad combinations, combination platters, and a vegetarian special. The lentil soup here has been such a hit they've had to send it via Federal Express back East. The restaurant is in a beautifully restored 1898 building across from Horton Plaza, and sometimes on Saturday night you may see a fire-eating belly dancer.

Dakota Grill & Spirits

901 Fifth Ave. (at E Street). ☎ **619/234-5554.** Reservations recommended. Main courses $8.50–$16.95. AE, DC, DIS, MC, V. Mon–Fri 11:30am–2:30pm, Mon–Thurs 5–10pm, Fri–Sat 5–11pm, Sun 5–9pm. Valet parking $5. Bus: 1, 3, 25, or 945. Trolley: Gaslamp Quarter. AMERICAN/SOUTHWEST.

If you like art and artifacts from the American Southwest, you'll find the interior decor of Dakota's very appealing. Dried flower arrangements in pint-size black leather cowboy boots grace every table, and a large painting of cowgirls is on the second floor. Since its opening, Dakota's has been a nonsmoking restaurant and bar. Little handguns on the menu indicate the most popular items, which include shrimp tasso (sautéed with Tasso Cajun ham and sweet peas in an ancho chile cream), spit-roasted chicken with orange chipotle glaze or Dakota barbecue sauce, and the mixed grill served with roasted garlic and grilled red potatoes. Dakota won the 1994 and 1995 Gold Medallion Award for Best American Cuisine. A pianist plays weekend nights.

Fio's

801 Fifth Ave. (at F Street). ☎ **619/234-3467.** Reservations recommended for dinner. Main courses $9.75–$17.95. AE, DC, DISC, MC, V. Mon–Thurs 11:30am–11pm; Fri–Sat 11:30am–midnight; Sun 5pm–10pm. Valet parking (from 5pm) $5. Trolley: Gaslamp Quarter. ITALIAN.

Elegant and usually filled to overflowing, this see-and-be-seen type of place features Northern Italian cuisine and is best known for its tutto mare, black linguine with seafood. For lunch, which is geared to business folk in a hurry, choose from antipasti, pizza, calzones, and panini (Italian sandwiches)—come after 1pm and get seated more quickly. The dinner menu features pasta, meat, and seafood dishes, and the bar and cocktail areas serve a full menu. All pastas may be ordered in half portions.

✪ Osteria Panevino

722 Fifth Ave. (between F and G streets). ☎ **619/595-7959.** Reservations recommended. Main courses $8.95–$19.95. AE, CB, DC, DISC, MC, V. Sun–Thurs 11:30am–10pm; Fri–Sat 11:30am–11:30pm. ITALIAN.

One of the most popular Italian restaurants in a town filled with them, Osterino Panevino deserves its loyal clientele because it offers top-notch food and wine and a decidedly unself-conscious atmosphere often lacking elsewhere. The interior is reminiscent of a Tuscan farmhouse, with ceramics and large terra-cotta tiles from Italy; old wine barrels are stacked in a rear alcove. Other nice touches include a mural of Florence opposite the bar, inviting picture windows looking onto the street, high ceilings, good lighting (you can actually see your food), and a brick oven for making pizzas. For antipasto, consider the assorted marinated vegetables with prosciutto, fresh mozzarella, and tomatoes; fried squid and parsley; or bite-size mozzarella in prosciutto, baked over sautéed spinach. More than a dozen dishes feature homemade pasta, among them egg-and-spinach noodles with radicchio and grilled chicken in a light cream sauce; spinach-and-meat ravioli tossed with butter, sage, and diced tomatoes; and angel-hair pasta with wild mushrooms and shrimp in garlic, white wine, and a touch of tomatoes. Fish and meat dishes include veal medallions topped with French string beans, smoked mozzarella, and tomato bruschetta; grilled boneless chicken with diced vegetables, crushed red pepper, and drizzled with olive oil and rosemary; and poached salmon filet with wild mushrooms, carrots, and pine nuts in white-wine sauce. Or you could opt for the risotto, lasagne, gnocchi of the day, or a simple pizza or focaccia. My favorite dish is the spinach ravioli. The atmosphere is very cozy, which might feel crowded to some people. From the time you enter Panevino, you'll feel welcome, and you're bound to leave satisfied.

Panda Inn

Horton Plaza (top floor). ☎ **619/233-7800.** Reservations recommended. Main courses $7.75–$18.25. AE, DC, DISC, MC, V. Mon–Fri 11am–10pm, Sat–Sun 11am–11pm. Bus: 1, 2, 3, 25, 34, or 34A. Trolley: America Plaza. CHINESE.

Elegant and sophisticated, this restaurant beautifully displays modern art, Chinese pottery, and Chinese art. The back dining area (one of three) looks out onto the city; a lounge offers a full bar. The varied menu features seasonal specials and Mandarin and Szechuan dishes, including sweet-and-pungent shrimp, lemon scallops, and enoki mushroom chicken. Complete dinners, a real bargain at about $10, include soup, fried rice, an egg roll, fried shrimp, a main course, tea, and cookies.

Planet Hollywood

197 Horton Plaza. ☎ **619/702-STAR(7827).** Reservations not accepted. Main courses $6.50–$13.95. AE, DC, MC, V. Daily 11am–2am. Parking Horton Plaza

---

👪 Family-Friendly Restaurants

Planet Hollywood *(see p. 88)*   Your kids can sip a "Home Alone" while they drink in the decor, which includes more than 300 pieces of movie memorabilia.

Galaxy Grill *(see p. 90)*   The waitresses make a big deal out of small fry, and the menu items, a throwback to soda fountain days, are fun.

Old Spaghetti Factory *(see p. 91)*   Kids get special attention, even their own toys. There's a special play area for them, too.

Hard Rock Cafe *(see p. 104)*   Your kids will love it here. The staff doesn't mind if they make a mess and the music is loud enough that if they scream and cry nobody will notice.

Corvette Diner *(see p. 94)*   Resembling a '50s diner, this place appeals to teens and pre-teens. They groan when their parents reminisce about *their* teen years, but enjoy the burgers and fries or other short-order fare, served in sock-hop surroundings.

Garage; 3 hours free with validation. Bus: 1, 2, 3, 25, 34, or 34A. Trolley: America Plaza. CALIFORNIA/AMERICAN.

Twenty thousand gawkers gathered here in March 1995, when this Planet Hollywood—number 19 in the chain—opened. They came to see the celebrity shareholders—Arnold Schwarzenegger, Bruce Willis, Sylvester Stallone, and Demi Moore—frolic with their celebrity friends. Today folks stand in line for a turn to eat here and ogle the myriad movie memorabilia. Glass cases contain more than 300 objects, including an animatronic owl from *Indiana Jones and The Temple of Doom,* Roddy McDowell's costume from *Planet of the Apes,* and a submachine gun from *Die Hard.* This noisy, friendly, thoroughly enjoyable place is understandably popular with families. Menu items include pizza, pasta, burgers, sandwiches, salads, and a handful of light California cuisine choices. (On a recent visit I thoroughly enjoyed grilled salmon served on a bed of trendy salad greens, atop a crisp pizza crust.) Kids can drink a "Home Alone" (an ice-cold combination of strawberry, banana, and grenadine), an "E.T." (grapefruit and orange juice topped with soda), or a "Predator" (pineapple, gingerale, and grenadine). The wait staff regularly hand out free movie posters and passes to diners. If you don't relish standing in line, be there at 11am when they open, between 2 and 5pm, or after 9pm. There's an adjacent retail outlet.

INEXPENSIVE

Cafe Lulu

419 F St. (near Fourth Avenue). ☎ **619/238-0114.** Main courses $2.50–$6. MC, V. Mon–Thurs 8am–2am, Fri 8am–4am, Sat 10am–4am, Sun 10am–2am. Trolley: Gaslamp Quarter. INTERNATIONAL.

Light fare at this sparsely decorated coffeehouse runs the gamut from Brie or pizza baguettes to bagels to croissants to quiche to lasagne. Look for the chalkboard specials and soup of the day. With regard to drinks, the emphasis is on coffees, but you can also get teas, natural sodas, Aqua Libra, sarsaparilla, and beer or wine by the glass or bottle. Also served are imported and microbrewery beers. Open quite late, Cafe Lulu is centrally located and particularly popular with students.

Filippi's Pizza Grotto

1747 India St. (between Date and Fir streets in Little Italy). ☎ **619/232-5095.** Main courses $4.60–$12.25. AE, DC, DISC, MC, V. Mon–Sat 11am–11pm, Sun 11am–10pm. Bus: 5. Trolley: America Plaza. ITALIAN.

To get to one of the half-dozen dining areas decorated with Chianti bottles, you have to walk through an Italian grocery store/deli strewn with cheeses, pastas, wines, bottles of olive oil, and salamis. You might even end up eating behind shelves of canned olives, but people have been doing that since 1950, when the place opened. Choose from more than 15 pizzas (including a vegetarian variety) and the requisite pasta dishes. Children's orders are available, and kids will feel right at home here. The original of a dozen stores, this Filippi's has free parking; other locations are in Pacific Beach, Kearny Mesa, East Mission Valley, and Escondido, among others.

Galaxy Grill

Horton Plaza (top level). ☎ **619/234-7211.** Main courses $3.50–$6.50. DISC, MC, V. Sun 11am–8pm, Mon–Thurs 11am–9pm, Fri–Sat 11am–10pm. Bus: 2, 7, 9, 29, 34, or 35. Trolley: America Plaza. AMERICAN.

The freewheeling atmosphere and waitresses make you feel most welcome. You can still get two songs for a quarter on the jukebox, and the menu is pure soda fountain. Remember the last time you had a cherry Coke or a malted? Fare includes burgers, supersonic chili, grilled-cheese sandwiches, tuna melts, shakes, and sundaes. Coffee comes leaded or unleaded, and they serve beer.

Grand Central Cafe

500 W. Broadway (in YMCA building). ☎ **619/234-CAFE.** Main courses $5.50–$6.95. AE, DISC, MC, V. Daily 7am–9pm. Closed Thanksgiving, Christmas. Bus: 2, 7, 9, 29, 34, or 35. AMERICAN.

You can get basic fare, such as eggs, home fries, soup-and-sandwich combos, and meat loaf, as well as daily breakfast, lunch, and dinner specials. The cafe has added vegetarian and "heart healthy" dishes to the menu. It also serves American wines and beers. The dining room is sunny and cheerful, with high ceilings and tall arched windows looking onto Broadway. It's an inviting spot to read the paper or write home, and they'll prepare a picnic lunch for the train for you. This cafe is popular with families because portions are large and prices low. When it gets busy, especially at lunch, service can slow down.

Kansas City Barbecue

610 W. Market St. ☎ **619/231-9680.** Main courses $8.95–$16. MC, V. Daily 11am–1am. Trolley: Seaport Village. AMERICAN.

Part of Kansas City Barbecue's honky-tonk mystique derives from the fact that the bar scene in the movie *Top Gun* was filmed here. The walls are covered with county fair memorabilia, old car tags from Kansas,

Top Gun posters, and a photograph of official bar wench Carry Nation. The top culinary draw is the barbecue, slow-cooked over an open fire and served with sliced white bread and your choice of coleslaw, beans, fries, onion rings, potato salad, or corn on the cob. The food is okay, but the atmosphere is the real draw. Dress casually, or you'll feel foolish. It's catercorner to the Hyatt Regency Hotel.

ⓢ Mandarin House

2604 Fifth Ave. (at Maple). ☎ **619/232-1101.** Most main courses $6.50–$9.95. AE, DC, MC, V. Mon–Thurs 11am–10pm; Fri 11am–11pm; Sat noon–11pm; Sun 2–10pm. CHINESE.

San Diego's most popular Chinese restaurant, Mandarin House has won many awards. My favorite dish is the kung pao chicken; not spicy, but just as delicious, is the mo-shu pork. If you expect the usual Chinese-red decor, you'll be surprised by the pleasant sea foam and peach color scheme. Mandarin House also has locations in La Jolla and Pacific Beach.

Old Columbia Brewery & Grill

1157 Columbia St. (between B and C streets). ☎ **619/234-BREW.** Main courses $7–$13. MC, V. Mon–Wed 11:30am–10pm (beer until midnight), Thurs–Sat 11:30am–midnight (beer until 1am), Sun 11:30–10pm. Bus: 5. Trolley: America Plaza. AMERICAN.

This is an actual brewery where you can see the stainless-steel vats from your seat at the bar and taste some of the outstanding beers, lagers, and ales made on the premises. (They're best known for the amber.) Five-ounce samplers are 85¢ each, and eight to nine choices are available on any given day. There's also nonalcoholic beer, as well as $1 samplers of 10- and 20-year-old port and sherry. The menu befits the beer emphasis—dishes like chili with black beans and sausage, baby-back ribs, beer-battered fish and chips, and hot pastrami sandwiches. There are burgers and salads, too—and wines by the glass. Beer-related memorabilia and brewery tours are available.

ⓢ Old Spaghetti Factory

Fifth Avenue and K Street. ☎ **619/233-4323.** Main courses $4.25–$8.10. DISC, MC, V. Mon–Thurs 11:30am–10pm; Fri 11:30am–10pm; Sat–Sun noon–10pm. Bus: 1. Trolley: Gaslamp Quarter. ITALIAN.

Lively is the best word to describe this place, followed quickly by economical. For the price of a main course, you also get salad, sourdough bread, ice cream, and coffee or tea with refills. Wine is available by the glass or decanter. No wonder folks are always waiting on the over-stuffed divans inside or the benches outside for their names to be called. The restaurant, housed in what used to be a printing company, has creative seating; some people even dine inside a 1917 trolley car. The decor is lavish early bordello, and the service is cordial. There's a small play area for kids.

Princess of Wales

1675 India St. (at Date Street). ☎ **619/238-1266.** Main courses $7.50. AE, DISC, MC, V. Sun–Tues, 10:30am–midnight, Wed–Sat 10:30am–1am. Bus: 5. Trolley: Santa Fe Depot. ENGLISH.

This local haunt is great for Anglophiles and others hungry for a ploughman's plate, Cornish pasty, steak-and-kidney pie, fish and chips, and bangers in hefty portions. Photos and commemorative plates of Princess Diana hang everywhere, along with flags from the motherland, a well-worn dart board, and a photo of the Queen Mother downing a pint; you can usually find a copy of the *Union Jack*, too. Among 10 English beers available are Guinness, Bass, and Watney's. They have hard Devon cider, too. Friday nights are particularly busy, and on Saturday British and Commonwealth expatriates living in San Diego filter in. There's take-out during the day.

4 Hillcrest/Uptown

Hillcrest and Uptown are filled with reasonably priced ethnic restaurants and inexpensive mom-and-pop eateries offering down-home cooking. The Sculpture Garden Café at the Museum of Art is within adjacent Balboa Park. The other restaurants listed here are within walking distance of the park (and also a quick bus or cab ride away if you don't want to walk).

EXPENSIVE

Busalacchi's

3683 Fifth Ave. (between Pennsylvania and Upas). ☎ **619/298-0119.** Main courses $9.25–$25. AE, CB, DC, MC, V. Mon–Thurs 11:30am–9:45pm; Fri 11:30am–10:45pm; Sat 5pm–10:45pm; Sun 5pm–11pm. Bus: 1 or 3. ITALIAN.

Traditional Sicilian cooking comes out of this 100-plus-year-old house, where the atmosphere is relaxed and inviting. There are several small dining rooms with fireplaces and an enclosed patio in which to feast on filling dishes, among them saltimbocca; veal marsala or piccata; seafood pasta with calamari, clams, and mussels; and shrimp in red sauce with garlic.

MODERATE

Calliope's

3958 Fifth Ave. ☎ **619/291-5588.** Main courses $10.95–$16.95. AE, DC, MC, V. Mon 11:30am–9pm; Tues–Thurs and Sun 11:30am–10pm; Fri–Sat 11:30am–11pm. Bus: 16 or 25. GREEK.

The sparkling white walls graced with framed needlework, and the flowers at Calliope's (pronounced cal-ee-O-pees) are most welcoming. The menu features egg-lemon-rice soup, calamari salad, spanakopita, moussaka, lamb souvlaki, fettuccine Aegean, and roast leg of lamb. At lunch you can choose from four pita sandwiches.

Canes California Bistro

Vermont Street, (1¹/₂ blocks north of University Avenue). ☎ **619/299-3551.** Main courses $8.50–$16.75. AE, DC, DISC, MC, V. Mon–Thurs 11:30am–10pm, Fri 11:30am–midnight, Sat–Sun 10am–10pm. Directions: Fifth Ave. to University; turn right and proceed 5 lights; then left on Vermont. CALIFORNIA.

A popular place for Sunday brunch and dinner, Canes also offers interesting lunches, from a shrimp BLT on grilled sourdough bread and a California Slider (their version of a burger) to pizza to pasta prepared with gourmet flourishes. The brunch buffet, served on Sunday from 10am to 3pm, is enormous—unlimited champagne is an extra $7—but you can get lighter, less expensive fare, including pancakes and egg dishes (Canes's eggs, poached with artichoke hearts and topped with cream cheese and spinach, are particularly popular). The dinner menu features spicy grilled Thai shrimp and coq au vin, along with barbecue items and nightly specials, including fresh seafood. The friendly owners are George and Piret Munger; the walking canes displayed everywhere—from which the place takes its name—belong to George. Can you spot the fishing pole cane, complete with hook, line, and sinker? This is a nice place to linger, with indoor and outdoor seating; snappily clad, attentive waiters and waitresses; and a good wine list.

Celadon

3628 Fifth Ave. (between Brooks and Pennsylvania). ☎ **619/295-8800.** Reservations recommended on weekends. Main courses $8.50–$14.50. AE, MC, V. Mon–Fri 11:30am–10pm; Fri 11:30am–10pm; Sat 5–10pm. Bus: 1 or 3. THAI.

A modern place with ample use of pink and rose hues and glass blocks, Celadon serves such specialties as shrimp in spicy, creamy coconut sauce; sautéed scallops in "burnt" sauce with a touch of garlic; a pineapple boat filled with rice, chicken, pineapple, and Chinese sausage; and Bua Sawan, shrimp, chicken, and cashews served in lotus-shape leaves. Popular appetizers include Poo Ja, deep-fried pork and crabmeat; Goong Sarong, shrimp wrapped in noodles and deep-fried; and satay. Statues and pots from Thailand are displayed throughout the restaurant. The gold, red, and green outfit displayed in the entrance is the costume of a Thai classical dancer. Service is friendly, and there are plenty of eating nooks from which to choose.

Liaison

2202 Fourth Ave. (at Ivy). ☎ **619/234-5540.** Fixed-price dinner $13.50–$18.50. AE, CB, DC, DISC, MC, V. Tues–Fri 11:30am–10:30pm, Sat–Sun 5pm–10:30pm. Bus: 1 or 3. FRENCH.

The cuisine and the decor hark back to the French countryside in this cozy little cafe with stone walls, blue-and-white tablecloths, candles on the tables, and copper pots hanging from the rafters. The fixed-price dinner is a particular savings, since the meal includes pâté, salad or soup, a main course, and dessert. The lunch menu features salads, including warm duck salad with balsamic vinaigrette and shrimp-and-avocado salad; pastas (a bow to the popularity of Italian food in San Diego) like homemade crab ravioli in lobster sauce; and three fresh fish dishes daily. At dinner you can choose from lamb curry, medallions of pork or beef, coquilles St. Jacques, roast duckling à l'orange, salmon with crayfish butter, and more. The house specialty dessert costs extra: a Grand Marnier chocolate or Amaretto soufflé for two, at $5 per person. Ooh la la!

Hob Nob Hill

2271 First Ave. (at Juniper). ☎ **619/239-8176.** Breakfast and lunch $3.25–$8.25; dinner $8–$14. AE, DISC, MC, V. Daily 7am–9pm. Bus: 1 or 3. AMERICAN.

Consider this your kitchen away from home, as do many professional and retired San Diegans. It's been serving up home-style cooking since 1946, and some of the waitresses have been greeting patrons here for 30 years. Everything is made from scratch, and the rolls are tops. The large breakfast menu includes eggs (from fried to Florentine), pancakes, waffles, and heartier fare like beef hash; there's even champagne by the glass (pretty fancy for a mom-and-pop place). Lunch features sandwiches, salads, and meat or fish meals; dinner, old-fashioned chicken and dumplings, roast turkey, prime rib, turkey croquettes, and a vegetarian plate. A children's menu is available.

INEXPENSIVE

Corvette Diner

3946 Fifth Ave. (between Washington and University). ☎ **619/542-1001.** Reservations not accepted. Main courses $4.50–$9.95. AE, DC, DISC, MC, V. Sun–Thurs 11am–11pm, Fri–Sat 11am–midnight. Bus: 1 or 3. AMERICAN.

The slightly faded facade lets you know you're in for something a little unusual: a trompe l'oeil painting of a cafe with a giant female strolling across the roof. Inside, the decor is Art Deco; the centerpiece is a sleek Corvette. Portraits of popular singers by local artist Gina Falk—from the Beatles to Connie Francis—fill the walls. Do pay your respects to Norma Jean. The menu features burgers, sandwiches, and other diner fare. Besides the old-fashioned soda fountain, there's a full bar. At night, a DJ plays your requests; on Tuesday and Wednesday evenings, a magician performs, an eight-year tradition. This is a fun place with a young crowd, and it's great for kids; expect a line on weekends.

Extraordinary Desserts

2929 Fifth Ave. (between Palm and Quince). ☎ **619/294-7001.** Desserts $1.75–$4.95. MC, V. Mon–Thurs 8:30am–11pm; Fri 8:30am–midnight; Sat 11am–midnight, Sun 2pm–11pm. DESSERTS.

This cute place is one of the only dessert shops in town. Fresh flowers top small wooden tables, set on a painted concrete floor. More tables are outside on the patio. Owner and chef Karen Krasne earned a Certificate de Patisserie from the Cordon Bleu School in Paris. Everything is made fresh on the premises daily. Tahitian cheesecake, brownies, macaroons, macadamia-nut triangles, and chocolate-macadamia torte are especially popular.

Kung Food

2949 Fifth Ave. (between Palm and Quince). ☎ **619/298-7302** (deli/take-out 619/298-9232). Main courses $6–$9.55. Mon–Thur 11:30am–9pm, Fri 11:30am–10pm, Sat 8:30–10pm, Sun 8:30–9pm; deli, daily 10am–10pm. MC, V. Bus: 34 or 34A. VEGETARIAN.

Around since 1975, San Diego's top vegetarian eatery offers an extensive menu, from stuffed grape leaves and tofu dishes to quesadillas and garden burgers. Drinks include iced sun tea, fruit smoothies, and wine by the glass. On Saturdays and Sundays, brunch is served until 1pm. There is indoor and outdoor seating, and the deli next door provides take-out service. This peaceful place is filled with plants and soothing music. Parking is available.

Quel Fromage

523 University Ave. ☎ **619/295-1600.** Menu items $1.25–$5. No credit cards. Sun–Thurs 7:30am–11pm, Fri–Sat 7:30am–midnight. Bus: 1 or 3. AMERICAN.

This no-smoking coffeehouse, with monthly exhibits by local artists, is strewn with newspapers and people at leisure. Coffee is always on tap, even iced cappuccino, along with muffins, English scones, and desserts. They also sell lasagne, quiche, curry rolls, and cheeses. There's a cozy upstairs seating area. Note the subtle door decor.

Sculpture Garden Cafe

1450 El Prado (at the Museum of Art), Balboa Park. ☎ **619/232-7931.** Menu items $1–$8. AE, MC, V. Tues–Fri 10am–3pm, Sat–Sun 9am–5pm. Bus: 7/7B, 16, or 25. LIGHT FARE.

To get to the Museum of Art sculpture garden, you have to walk through this open-air cafe, which displays a half-dozen sculptures, including works by Auguste Rodin. A favorite is *Accelerated Point*, a playful, celebratory pool and sculpture by Claire Falkenstein that you'll pass as you leave the cafe to enter the sculpture garden. While service is friendly and fast, the atmosphere is unhurried. Drop by before 2pm for the free Sunday organ concert in the park. The cafe serves wine and beer.

5   Old Town

EXPENSIVE

Brigantine Seafood Grill

2444 San Diego Ave. ☎ **619/298-9840.** Reservations recommended on weekends. Main courses $7.95–29.95. AE, CB, DC, MC, V. Mon–Fri 11:30am–10:30pm; Sat 11:30am–11pm; Sun 10:30am–11pm. Bus: 4 or 5/105. SEAFOOD.

The Brigantine is best known for its oyster-bar happy hour from 4 to 7pm (until 9:30pm on Mondays), when beer, margaritas, and food are heavily discounted and you can expect standing room only. On Sunday through Thursday, early bird specials are offered from 5 to 7pm; the dinners include seafood, steak, or chicken served with several side dishes and baked bread. Inside, the decor is upscale and nautical; outside, there's a pleasant patio with a fireplace to take the chill off the night air. At lunch, you can get everything from crab cakes or fish and chips to fresh fish or pasta. Lunch specials come with sourdough bread and two side dishes.

Cafe Pacifica

2414 San Diego Ave. ☎ **619/291-6666.** Reservations recommended. Main courses, $15–$26. AE, DC, MC, V. Lunch Mon–Fri 11:30am–2pm; dinner Mon–Sat 5:30–10pm, Sun 5:30–9:30pm. Bus: 4 or 5/105. CALIFORNIA.

The framework of an old house provides a unique backdrop here; the walls and rafters are painted white and the beams accented with tiny white lights. Mirrors add more twinkle, and latticework and candles on the tables add to the charm. Among the temptations on the menu are grilled shrimp cocktail with spicy Chinese mustard; oysters on the half shell; and Dungeness crab salad with papaya, avocado, and endive—

and these are just for starters. Main courses include saffron linguine with rock shrimp, clams, mussels, and calamari; herb-crusted sea bass; and lamb chops with tomatoes, sweet garlic, and mint pesto. The signature dish is Hawaiian ahi with shiitake mushrooms and ginger butter. Patrons tend to dress up, though it's not required. To avoid the crowds, arrive in the early evening. A "Prix" Theater Dinner is served between 5:30 and 6:45pm and costs $14 to $17. *Note*: I've never experienced it myself, but some readers recently wrote to report poor service. Should you have a problem here, please let me know.

MODERATE

Casa de Bandini

Opposite Old Town Plaza, Old Town. ☎ **619/297-8211.** Reservations not accepted. Main courses $6.50–$14. AE, CB, DC, MC, V. Sun 10am–9:30pm, Mon–Thurs 11am–9:30pm, Fri–Sat 11am–10pm. Bus: 4 or 5/105. MEXICAN.

As much an Old Town tradition as the mariachi music that's played here on weekends, this lively restaurant—with its appealing balcony and courtyard—fills the nooks and crannies of an adobe hacienda. The house was built in 1823 for Juan Bandini, once a merchant and politician in these parts; later, with a second floor added, it became a hotel. Today it's the scene of many a happy repast over dishes like crab enchiladas, chicken-and-avocado salad, crab brochette with mild green chiles, and jumbo cod filet with sautéed vegetables. Some of the dishes are gourmet Mexican, others simple south-of-the-border fare; you'll never run short of refried beans, guacamole, or jumbo margaritas. It's the house itself that makes the restaurant extra special.

INEXPENSIVE

Casa de Pico

Bazaar del Mundo, Old Town. ☎ **619/296-3267.** Reservations not accepted. Main courses $5–$14. AE, CB, DC, MC, V. Sun–Thurs 10am–9:30pm, Fri–Sat 10am–10pm. Bus: 4 or 5/105. MEXICAN.

The heartbeat (or, more aptly, the salsa beat) of Bazaar del Mundo, Casa de Pico has a carnival atmosphere and a colorful courtyard complete with fountain, flags and umbrellas, and mariachis and guitarists who will serenade your table on request. The restaurant sits on the original site of the home of General Pío Pico, the last governor of Mexican California. Flowers and birds are stenciled in primary colors on the white walls, and ceiling beams are bright yellow and orange. The extensive and daunting menu includes a diagrammed explanation of the Mexican dishes. A popular selection is the Mexican sampler, called La Especial de Juan, with chimichangas, enchiladas, and fajitas. You can also get some health-conscious choices like chicken fajita salad or black-bean burritos. The guacamole is good, but the chips can be greasy. Breakfast is served all day. To avoid standing in line for a table, try coming here before 5pm or after 8pm Sunday through Thursday.

Garden House Coffee & Tea

2480 San Diego Ave. ☎ **619/220-0723.** Menu items $1–$3. No credit cards. Mon–Thur 7am–6pm, Fri 7am–7pm, Sat 8am–7pm, Sun 8am–5:30pm. Bus: 4 or 5/105. COFFEE SHOP.

Set off San Diego Avenue along a brick walkway beside the Whaley House, this gourmet coffee and tea shop in an old wooden house is always good for a cup of fresh-brewed coffee (any variation or size). You get 10¢ off if you bring your own cup the way the locals do; refills are half price. Muffins and pastries are also available. While it's mostly a take-out place, there are a few chairs on the porch and some benches nearby. This is a great place to rest in the shade of the wizened pepper trees. It's next to the Old Town Drug Store Museum.

Old Town Mexican Cafe

2489 San Diego Ave. ☎ **619/297-4330.** Reservations accepted for groups of 10 or more. Main courses $5–$11. AE, DISC, MC, V. Daily 7am–11pm for dining, bar service until 2am. Bus: 4 or 5/105. MEXICAN.

This place is so popular it's almost an Old Town tourist attraction in its own right. Most folks are lured by the sight of tortillas being hand made and whole chickens roasting right in the window. Inside are a maze of booths and tables, as well as a patio and banquet room. There are two bars, one inside and one on the patio. The most popular dishes are carnitas, the house specialty, and rotisserie chicken, but you'll also find all your Mexican favorites. Patrons usually wait a half hour to be seated at lunch and up to an hour at dinner, but nobody seems to mind.

Rancho el Nopal

Bazaar del Mundo, Old Town. ☎ **619/295-0584.** Main courses $5–$9. AE, CB, DC, DISC, MC, V. Daily 11am–9:30pm. Bus: 4 or 5/105. MEXICAN.

This place is saturated with color—from the swirling skirts of the waitresses to the bar, where tiny lights are sprinkled throughout hanging ivy. A glass of iced tea is big enough to serve the whole family, and you get chips and salsa with every meal. Of the many Mexican dishes to choose from, the chicken fajita salad is popular. The decor is pure south of the border, with indoor and outdoor dining. There's also a kids' menu. "We're here to catch the spillover from Pico," my waitress told me. And spill over they do. It's next door to park headquarters.

6 Mission Bay/Pacific Beach

Additional locations of several restaurants described elsewhere in this chapter are in the Mission Bay/Pacific Beach area: **D'Lish,** at 4150 Mission Blvd., in the Promenade Shopping Center (☎ 619/483-4949); **Mandarin House,** at 1820 Garnet St., in Pacific Plaza (☎ 619/273-2288); and **Fillippi's Pizza Grotto,** at 962 Garnet St. (☎ 619/483-6222).

EXPENSIVE

⑤ The Atoll

3999 Mission Blvd. (in the Catamaran Resort Hotel) ☎ **619/488-1081.** Main courses $8–$20; Sun brunch $20.50. AE, CB, DC, DISC, MC, V. Sun–Thurs 6:30am–10pm, Fri–Sat 6:30am–11pm. Bus: 34 or 34A. CALIFORNIA.

While the food is gourmet, you can get a burger or sandwich if that's all you want. Among the appetizers are spicy crab cakes with lime and ginger-butter sauce; lamb ravioli on ratatouille or spinach salad; and vine-ripened tomatoes with mozzarella, olive oil, and basil. Main courses include grilled sea bass, salmon, tenderloin, veal chop, and broiled lamb chops or swordfish. To add to the restaurant's pleasant yet casual ambience, fresh flowers grace the linen tablecloths. There are nightly specials, and the wine list features selections from France, Italy, Germany, and California. Sunday brunch, served from 10am to 2pm, comes with unlimited champagne. The service is friendly. You can dine on the bay-front patio (weather permitting).

The Rusty Pelican

4325 Ocean Blvd. (at Thomas Street). ☎ **619/274-3474.** Reservations recommended on weekends. Main courses $16–$19. AE, DISC, MC, V. Mon–Thurs 11:30am–10pm, Fri 11:30am–11pm, Sat 10am–11pm, Sun 9am–10pm (brunch to 2:30pm). Bus: 34 or 34A. SEAFOOD.

The Rusty Pelican is popular mainly because it offers a great ocean view. The dining room, lush with hanging ivy, has paneled walls, a beamed ceiling, lamps suspended from lampposts, and an expansive window overlooking the sea. Appetizers include calamari fritti, spicy sautéed shrimp, and ichiban (marinated charbroiled fish and shrimp). Among the dinner main courses are Creole carbonara, stuffed trout, blackened catfish, and the popular ruby-rare ahi (pseudo sushi); daily specials feature fresh fish. If you aren't hungry for seafood, consider prime rib or filet mignon. Come early and enjoy the congenial bar and the reasonable sunset dinner specials. There's a children's menu.

MODERATE

The Green Flash

701 Thomas Ave. (at Mission Boulevard). ☎ **619/270-7715.** Main courses $10–25. AE, DC, DISC, MC, V. Mon–Thur 8am–9:30pm, Fri 8am–10pm, Sat 7:30am–10pm, Sun 7:30am–9:30pm. Bus: 34 or 34A. SEAFOOD/INTERNATIONAL.

You can spend as much or as little as you choose in this place; the menu matches a variety of budgets and hankerings. It's known for its fresh fish, but you may also order steaks and prime rib, steak-and-seafood combos, chicken dishes, or burgers. Or simply make a meal of appetizers: fresh oysters, steamed clams, shrimp cocktail, and ceviche. Salads and sandwiches are available at lunch, and there are $9.95 sunset dinner specials Sunday through Thursday from 5 to 7pm. The outdoor tables here are prime real estate, especially when the sky begins to blush. The ambience couldn't be livelier. Ask your waitperson to explain how the restaurant got its name.

Mission Bay Dining

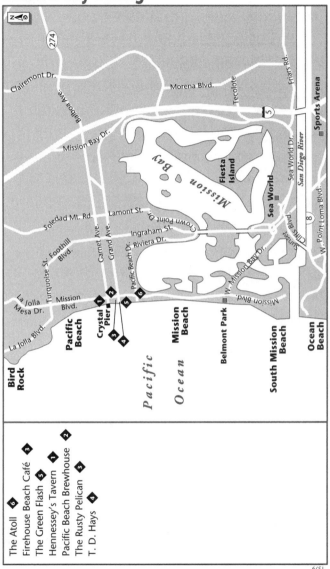

The Atoll **6**
Firehouse Beach Café **3**
The Green Flash **5**
Hennessey's Tavern **1**
Pacific Beach Brewhouse **2**
The Rusty Pelican **3**
T. D. Hays **4**

1579

T. D. Hays

4315 Ocean Blvd. (at Grand Avenue), second floor. ☎ **619/270-6850.** Reservations recommended on weekends. Main courses $10–$20. AE, DISC, MC, V. Dinner only, Mon–Thurs 5–10pm, Fri–Sat 4:30–10pm, Sun 4–9pm. Bus: 34 or 34A. AMERICAN.

    T. D. Hays is popular among locals for its prime rib and picture windows overlooking the sea. Start off with potato skins, sautéed mushrooms, or shrimp cocktail, and your main course—the prime rib, mesquite-broiled steaks and chicken, and many shrimp dishes—comes with bread and rice or a baked potato. You can also get a whole lobster. Bender's, next door, is their bar.

INEXPENSIVE

✪ Firehouse Beach Cafe

722 Grand Ave. ☎ **619/272-1999.** Reservations recommended on weekends. Main courses $8–$12. AE, DISC, MC, V. Sun–Thurs 7am–9pm, Fri–Sat 7am–10pm. Bus: 34 or 34A. AMERICAN.

Ceiling fans stir the air in this cheerful, comfortably crowded place, and there's pleasant rooftop dining with an ocean view if you're lucky enough to snag a seat. Specialties are black-bean burritos, fish and chips, and lasagne. You can make a meal of appetizers, which are served all day long. A children's menu is available.

Hennessey's Tavern

4650 Mission Blvd. (at Emerald). ☎ **619/483-8847.** Menu items $5–$8. AE, MC, V. Daily 7am–2am. Bus: 34 or 34A. IRISH.

Look for the bright-green and brick facade of this neighborhood pub that's been around since 1976. It's Irish through and through, even serving corned beef hash and eggs for breakfast. For lunch, try the hamburgers, steaks, and deli sandwiches; nightly specials include corned beef and cabbage, a homemade turkey dinner, and fish and chicken entrees.

Pacific Beach Brewhouse

4475 Mission Blvd. (at Garnet). ☎ **619/274-2537.** Menu items $2–$7. MC, V. Daily 11:30am–2am. Bus: 34 or 34A. AMERICAN.

Whether you're after a hearty meal, a leisurely game of darts, a dose of large-screen TV, a free brewery tour, or just a beer or two, head for the Brewhouse with its relaxed atmosphere and college crowd. Burgers are big, the french fries spicy and curly. You can also get pizza, fish tacos, sandwiches, salads, and fish and chips. The fare complements the brews made on the premises, which are priced at $1.25 for a $5^{1}/_{2}$-ounce taster, $5 for a set of five, or $2.75 for a pint; the Sunset and Red is the most popular. Happy hour is Monday through Friday from 3 to 7pm, and on Thursday the 10-ounce brews cost only $1.

7 La Jolla

Most of La Jolla's top restaurants are clustered along Prospect Street and Pearl Street in the village. However, a great Greek restaurant, **Aesop's Tables,** is located in the Costa Verde shopping center on Genesee Avenue near La Jolla Village Drive (☎ 619/455-1535). "Sisters" of dining places described elsewhere in this chapter include **Mandarin House,** at 6765 La Jolla Blvd. (☎ 619/454-2555) and the **Chart House,** at 1270 Prospect (☎ 619/459-8201). La Jolla also has a McDonald's, so small that it's named McSnack, on Prospect Street in the heart of town.

VERY EXPENSIVE

✪ George's at the Cove

1250 Prospect St. ☎ **619/454-4244.** Reservations recommended. Main courses $16.50–$30. AE, DC, DISC, MC, V. Mon–Thurs 11:30am–10pm, Fri–Sat 11:30am–11pm; Sun 11am–10pm. CALIFORNIA.

This popular local restaurant gets raves for its seafood dishes, creative pastas, ocean view, and great sunsets in summer. There are several seating areas in this lively place; the Garden Room and Wine Room are the quietest choices. For lunch, you can go light with a soup and salad or have one of the many seafood dishes. For dinner, start with steamed mussels or pâté de foie gras and proceed to the rack of lamb; sautéed venison chops with yam cakes; or mixed grill of shrimp, king salmon, and swordfish with three sauces. Owner George Hauer, whom you might meet Tuesday through Saturday, started out as a waiter in Pacific Beach and became a legend in San Diego's restaurant business. Upstairs, the more casual Café Bar and George's Ocean Terrace have indoor and outdoor seating overlooking La Jolla Cove and offer light fare and lower prices. Valet parking is available for $3 during the day, $4 at night.

Top O' the Cove

1216 Prospect St. ☎ **619/454-7779.** Reservations recommended. Jackets suggested for men at dinner. Main courses $25–$29. AE, CB, DC, MC, V. Mon–Sat 11:30am–10:30pm, Sun 10:30am–10:30pm. CONTINENTAL.

San Diego magazine has voted this restaurant "the most romantic" for the past nine years; Table 6, the most frequently requested table, is booked through the year 2000 for New Year's Eve. Any other time, call two to three weeks in advance to reserve it. If it's not available, don't worry, as plenty of other tables have created their own share of magic in this restaurant, which opened in 1955. One of the prettiest restaurants anywhere, in a historic cottage with fig trees out front, it has fireplaces glowing on chilly evenings, an elegant circular bar upstairs, and a gazebo and patio for dining on balmy days—perfect, in fact, for Sunday champagne brunch. Lunch is on the light side—creative salads, pasta dishes, or a burger or club sandwich—while dinner is more lavish, with fish, duck, veal, lamb, and venison prepared and served quite elegantly. The house coffee is laced with Grand Marnier, crème de cacao, and Amaretto; complement it with the dessert specialty, a bittersweet chocolate box filled with cream and fruit in a raspberry sauce. A computerized wine list keeps track of the 10,000 bottles in the cellar. Proprietor and community dynamo Ron Zappardino heads a stellar staff.

EXPENSIVE

Ⓢ Marakesh

634 Pearl St. (at Draper). ☎ **619/231-8353.** Main courses $15–16.95; five-course "feasts" $16.50–$23. AE, DC, DISC, MC, V. Sun–Thur 5–10pm; Fri–Sat 5–11pm. MOROCCAN.

Diners get more than a meal here—they get a total experience. It starts when you're seated on cushions around a low table and continues when your server washes your hands in traditional Moroccan style. The decor consists of colorful North African fabrics and objet d'art. I recommend ordering one of the feasts, a multicourse meal that starts with soup, salad, and bastilla (a wonderful pastry), and includes a choice of lemon chicken, lamb in honey sauce, or—my favorite—lamb couscous, the national Moroccan dish. Your feast concludes with fruit, pastry, and mint tea poured from a height of three feet. If you aren't up for all that, you can order a dinner, accompanied only by soup or salad and bastilla. Did I mention that Moroccan meals are eaten with fingers, not knives and forks? Marakesh also has a location downtown at 756 Fifth Ave. (☎ 619/231-8353), but it isn't as traditional, and therefore, not as much fun.

✪ Putnam's Restaurant & Bar

910 Prospect St. (in the Colonial Inn). ☎ **619/454-2181.** Reservations suggested. Main courses (dinner) $12–$21. AE, DC, MC, V. Mon–Fri 7–10am and 11am–2:30pm, Sat–Sun 7am–2:30pm; Sun–Thur 5–10pm, Fri–Sat 5–11pm. Valet parking $5. CALIFORNIA.

When the Colonial Inn was completed in 1928 it housed a drug store named Putnam's, known in La Jolla as "Putty's." Gregory Peck's father was the pharmacist, and locals flocked there to buy their sundries and enjoy a soda. Today, that corner of the hotel is the site of Putnam's Restaurant, which retains an elegant, old-world atmosphere, complete with polished terrazzo floors, gleaming woodwork, brass fixtures, crisp white tablecloths, and fresh flowers. The dinner menu changes seasonally, but often contains grilled farm-raised chicken with honey-onion marmalade, grilled marinated duck breast with golden tomato curry sauce, grilled Atlantic salmon filet, and roasted rack of lamb with mustard herb crust. This is also a popular spot for breakfast and weekend brunch.

The Whaling Bar/Tropical Patio

In La Valencia Hotel, 1132 Prospect St. (at Herschel Ave.). ☎ **619/454-0771.** Reservations recommended. Main courses $10–$15 at lunch, $11–$25 at dinner. AE, CB, DC, MC, V. Lunch daily 11:30am–5pm; dinner daily 6–10:30pm. CALIFORNIA/MEDITERRANEAN

In 1947, 21 years after the founding of La Valencia Hotel, the Whaling Bar became a permanent fixture here. For several decades it was the haunt of movie stars such as Ginger Rogers and Charlton Heston, who came down from Los Angeles to perform at the La Jolla Playhouse. The bar feels like a club, filled with authentic New Bedford harpoons and lanterns, pewter candle holders, wooden shutters, scrimshaw displays, and whale murals by artist Wing Howard. The barrel clock behind the bar and the full-rigged sailing ship model were gifts from hotel devotees. At lunchtime, the Tropical Patio, at the hotel's entrance, is popular. The Mandarin chicken salad, duck quesadilla, and carne asada are old standbys, and you can expect generous portions, whatever you order.

MODERATE

✪ The Cottage

7702 Fay Ave. (at Kline). ☎ **619/454-8409.** Reservations accepted for dinner only. Main courses $6.95–$11.95. MC, V. Mon–Fri 7:30am–3pm; Sat–Sun 8am–3pm; open for dinner during summer only. LIGHT FARE.

La Jolla Dining

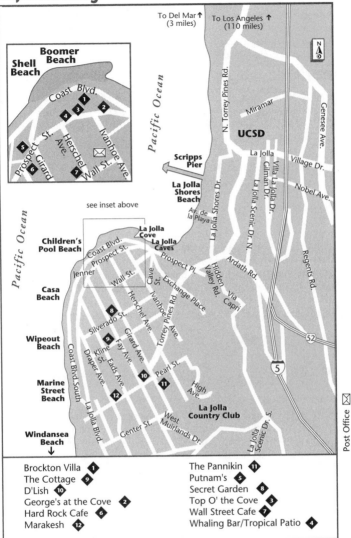

Brockton Villa	**1**	The Pannikin	**11**
The Cottage	**9**	Putnam's	**5**
D'Lish	**10**	Secret Garden	**8**
George's at the Cove	**2**	Top O' the Cove	**3**
Hard Rock Cafe	**6**	Wall Street Cafe	**7**
Marakesh	**12**	Whaling Bar/Tropical Patio	**4**

The turn-of-the-century Cottage, on a sunny corner in downtown La Jolla, is light and airy inside—with booths and tables under a skylight and a welcoming white fence, trellis, and large brick patio outside. You can get farm-fresh eggs most any style, granola and fresh fruit, oatmeal pancakes, Belgian waffles, or vegetable frittata, or a filling continental breakfast for $4.25. For lunch, my favorite soup is the Mexican chicken and rice, served with baked tortilla chips and grated cheddar cheese and the hot tuna is my favorite sandwich. For dinner, I like the chicken Jerusalem, tender chicken breast sauteed in a light cream sauce with garlic white wine, artichoke hearts, and fresh mushrooms, served on a bed of steamed and wild rice. The Cottage bakery makes the *wonderful* desserts, pastries, and bread (with the exception of foccacia). There's no smoking inside or out.

INEXPENSIVE

Brockton Villa

1235 Coast Blvd. (across from La Jolla Cove). ☎ **619/454-7393.** Lunch main courses $6.25–$9.95. AE, DISC, MC, V. Daily 8am–8pm (later in summer). CALIFORNIA.

Located in beach cottage that dates from 1894, Brockton Villa offers good food, a great view of the La Jolla Cove, and charming historic surroundings. The blue and white bungalow has a wooden floor that's appropriately worn and perhaps not entirely level. Diners can sit inside, outside on the patio, or on a semienclosed porch. My favorite lunch choice is Shari's turkey meat loaf sandwich on toasted sourdough bread with spicy tomato mint chutney. Favorite breakfast items include homemade granola, "coast toast" (French toast that resembles a soufflé), and Greek steamers (three eggs steam scrambled using the espresso machine and mixed with feta, tomato, and basil). You can also just enjoy one of their many coffee drinks, with or without a baked goody. Here's a tip: If you're thinking of having dessert, ask them to take it out of the refrigerator case ahead of time. I've eaten some chilly sweets that would have been more enjoyable at room temperature. There's no alcohol served here, no smoking allowed, and no access for people with disabilities.

Ⓢ D'Lish

7514 Girard Ave. (at Pearl Street). ☎ **619/459-8118.** Main courses $5.95–$8.99. AE, DC, DISC, MC, V. Sun–Thur 11:30am–10pm, Fri–Sat 11:30am–11pm. Bus: 34 or 34A. Free underground parking. ITALIAN.

I confess to having a weakness for pizza, not the traditional style, but the trendy wood-fired kind with toppings you wouldn't have imagined a decade ago. So it's not surprising that I've checked out all the places in La Jolla that serve such fare and, while there are two other candidates within a few blocks, D'Lish definitely gets my vote. My favorite is the Greek grilled chicken (described in "Best Bets"), but I also like the pizza with shrimp, mozzarella, Roma tomatoes, Kalamata olives, sun-dried tomatoes, pesto sauce, and pine nuts. Their salads make it painless to feel virtuous when ordering. My husband loves the pasta dishes, especially the shrimp-scallop angel hair, one of many heart-healthy choices. Here's a hot tip: Don't sit upstairs when the weather's warm. There's another D'Lish in Pacific Beach.

Ⓢ Hard Rock Cafe

909 Prospect St. (at Fay Avenue). ☎ **619/454-5101.** Reservations not accepted. Main courses $5.50–$13.95. AE, DC, MC, V. Sun–Thurs 11:30am–11pm, Fri–Sat 11:30am–11:30pm. Bus: 34, 34A. AMERICAN.

San Diego's branch of "the Smithsonian of rock 'n' roll," as Andy Warhol described the Hard Rock Cafe, is a great spot for families. In fact, pre-teens, teens, and tourists seem to comprise the majority of

Coffeehouses with Character: Choices in La Jolla

While cafes specializing in espresso, latte, and cappuccino have sprung up all over San Diego, no other area in the city offers java hounds the variety of settings and styles. Here are descriptions of a few La Jolla coffeehouses that serve up caffeine as well as charm (they are plotted on the "La Jolla Dining" map).

My personal favorite is the **Wall Street Cafe,** at 1044 Wall St., between Girard and Herschel avenues (☎ 619/551-1044). I used to bank here, before the Security Pacific turned into a coffeehouse. Today the old vault contains the restrooms, so patrons who use the facilities pass through the huge door that once secured much of La Jolla's money. I like this cafe for its visual appeal, friendly staff, and really good fare. Local businesspeople pop in for cups to go or for lunch; the midmorning and afternoon crowd has time to read the newspaper. Live entertainment, such as light jazz or a mellow guitar, makes this a particularly popular place on Friday and Saturday night between 8 and 11pm.

When it opened in 1968, **The Pannikin,** at 7467 Girard Ave., near Pearl (☎ 619/454-5453), was La Jolla's first coffeehouse, and, in some ways, it still is 1968 here. Long-haired men ponder chess moves on the porch, and the notice board tells of the next meditation seminar. While the crowd may appear a bit scruffy, this is a favored hangout of UCSD students and faculty. Inside the old house, the fireplace and communal seating are conducive to impromptu intellectual discussions. Some customers wander next door to D. G. Wills bookstore. The Pannikin's retail store across the street draws loyal locals.

At **The Secret Garden,** at 928 Silverado Ave., between Fay and Girard avenues (☎ 619/551-0928), the weekday customers are almost all "regulars." Many work or work out nearby and, whether they're wearing ties or tights, the staff knows their names and their preferred drinks—it's like the *Cheers* of the local coffeehouse scene. This is a good choice for early risers: The official opening time is 7am, but locals know that they can get a fresh hot cup anytime after 6:15am. Shoppers who want to take a break comprise most of the weekend crowd. (Stairs into the cottage may hinder access for travelers with disabilities.)

No matter where you enjoy your java, mind the time limit for your parking spot. La Jolla doesn't have meters, but street parking in the village is restricted to either one or two hours, and zealous parking enforcement officers dole out tickets with great regularity.

their customers. It isn't *just* the huge inventory of music memorabilia on display—the Hard Rock also serves generous portions of really good food, with most main courses costing about $6.95. Burgers are the house specialty; salads and sandwiches are also served. The service isn't swift, but there's plenty to listen to and look at in the interim, such as Madonna's bustier from the "Who's That Girl" tour, a vintage Cher doll, and one of John Lennon's band leader coats from the Sgt. Pepper era. If the line is long and you're really starving, see if there's a place at the counter. You can also eat in the bar—the only place where smoking is allowed. A small retail-sales shop is at the entrance.

8   Coronado

Coronado has some wonderful hotels and each presents a variety of dining options. You may wish to consider **Marius** in Le Meridien, **Azzura Point** in Loew's Coronado Bay Resort, and the **Crown Room, Prince of Wales Grill,** and others at the Hotel del Coronado.

VERY EXPENSIVE

Chart House

1701 Strand Way. ☎ **619/435-0155.** Reservations recommended. Main courses $15.95–$39.95. AE, CB, DC, DISC, MC, V. Sun–Thurs 5–10pm, Fri 5–10:30pm, Sat 5–11pm. AMERICAN.

Perched at the edge of Glorietta Bay and looking like a cupola that escaped from the Hotel del Coronado up the hill, this restaurant has been here in the Del's former boathouse since 1968. Inside, you'll find 38 antique tables and the largest collection of Tiffany lamps in Southern California (about 20 at last count). Enjoy dinner on the deck in summer or in the upstairs lounge; the mahogany, teak, and stained-glass bar came from Atlanta and dates from 1880. The fare here is straightforward—seafood, steaks, or prime rib, with plenty of fresh fish specials daily. The view from the restaurant encompasses Glorietta Bay, the Coronado Yacht Club, and the Coronado Bay Bridge.

EXPENSIVE

Brigantine

1333 Orange Ave. ☎ **619/435-4166.** Reservations required. Main courses $7.95–$42.50. AE, DC, MC, V. Mon–Thurs 11:30am–10:30pm; Fri 11:30am–11:30pm; Sat 5pm–11:30pm; Sun 5–10:30pm. SEAFOOD.

Intimate booths, wood paneling, and a lively bar—all inside a tidy white house with blue awnings—make this an inviting place. At lunch try an albacore or calamari sandwich or chowder or a spinach salad. Seafood dishes are popular, with fresh fish specials for lunch and dinner. Oysters are half price at happy hour on Monday through Friday from 3 to 6pm.

Chez Loma

1132 Loma (off Orange Ave.). ☎ **619/435-0661.** Reservations recommended. Main courses $14–$20. Daily 5:30–10pm; Sun 10am–2pm. AE, DC, MC, V. CONTINENTAL.

In a house dating from 1889, Chez Loma has been welcoming diners since 1975. Plenty of windows, ceiling fans, and soft lighting complement Victorian decor. The upstairs salon, reminiscent of a Victorian

parlor, is a cozy spot for sipping wine or coffee and nibbling on appetizers or dessert. Among the creative entrées are salmon with smoked-
tomato vinaigrette and duck with cherry-and-lingonberry sauce. The
duck, which is tender and not at all oily, has been on the menu since
the restaurant opened. All main courses are served with soup or salad,
rice or potatoes, and fresh vegetables. California wines and American
microbrewery beers are available. Follow dinner with a creamy crème
caramel or Kahlúa crème brûlée. Chez Loma's service is attentive, and
the herb rolls are absolutely habit forming.

✪ Primavera

932 Orange Ave. ☎ **619/435-0454.** Reservations recommended. Main courses
$10.95–$19.95. AE, DC, DISC, MC, V. Mon–Fri 11am–10:30pm. ITALIAN.

Primavera serves tasty Northern Italian dishes and pays remarkable attention to detail. The bar is as pretty as the long, narrow dining room;
an elevated seating area is set off by wood panels with etched glass.
Besides pasta, meat, and fish dishes at lunch, you can order different
filling Italian salads and sandwiches. At dinner, popular appetizers are
bagna caoda primavera (grilled eggplant, roasted red peppers, sun-dried
tomatoes, Montrachet, and Parmesan cheese, with bagna caoda sauce)
and the Caesar salad for two; main courses include angel-hair pasta
with mushrooms, garlic, prosciutto, capers, anchovies, and herbs; filet
mignon in Cognac sauce with fresh mushrooms; and chicken breast
with eggplant, mozzarella cheese, mushrooms, and wine sauce. The
menu always includes fish, veal, and lamb specials.

MODERATE

Bay Beach Cafe

1201 1st St. (in the Ferry Landing Marketplace). ☎ **619/435-4900.** Dinner main
courses $10.95–$16.05. Pub menu $7.95. AE, DISC, MC, V. Daily 7am–10pm.
AMERICAN/SEAFOOD.

The setting here is positively wonderful. Diners gaze across San Diego
Bay to the city skyline, which is pretty by day and even better at
night. The ferry docks at a wooden pier, discharging passengers into
the Ferry Landing Marketplace where shops and eateries await. There's
a congenial bar for drinks, and meals are served indoors and alfresco.
Several fresh fish specials are offered daily; rack of lamb, vegetarian
pasta, and roasted free-range chicken with wild mushroom sauce are
other popular dinner items. The pub menu consists of sandwiches and
burgers.

Rhinoceros Cafe & Grill

1166 Orange Ave. (between 10th and 11th). ☎ **619/435-2121.** Main courses
$8.95–$17.95. AE, MC, V. Sun 8am–12:30pm; Mon–Sat 11am–3pm; Fri–Sat 5–10pm;
Sun–Thurs 5–9pm. AMERICAN.

Owner Scott Hanlon won't explain to the wait staff why he named this
place as he did, so they made up a story. If they tell you it refers to the
large portions served here, they're pulling your leg. This light, bright
bistro is a good place for people watching, as large windows face the
sidewalk outside. Inside, white walls, hung with large, colorful abstract
paintings, reach up to the very high ceiling. Lunch possibilities include

salads, burgers, sandwiches, and pasta. Favorite dinner specials are char-broiled swordfish with citrus glaze, halibut with cucumber dill sauce, and live Maine lobster. There's a good wine list, or you might decide to try Rhino Chaser's American Ale. This is a good choice for a pre-theater dinner, as Lamb's Players Theatre is next door.

INEXPENSIVE

Kensington Coffee Company

1106 1st St. ☎ **619/437-8506.** Menu items $1.50–$4.50. AE, DISC, MC, V. Daily 6am–11pm. LIGHT FARE.

Dropping by here is a great way to start or end the day—or take a break during it. Choose an international coffee from one of five giant thermoses; top it with a little cinnamon or chocolate; then complement it with a bagel, croissant, filled pastry, muffin, or scone—or if it's dessert time, with cheesecake, gelato, brownies, or chocolate truffles. The creamy cappuccinos and double mochas can substitute for dessert. Light fare, such as burritos and salad, is served at lunchtime. You can buy the *Coronado Journal*, the *San Diego Union-Tribune*, the *Los Angeles Times*, and postcards here. Indoor and outdoor seating is available.

Mandarin Cafe

1330 Orange Ave. (in Coronado Plaza, second floor). ☎ **619/435-2771.** Main courses $5.75–$12.50. AE, MC, V. Mon–Thurs 11:30am–10pm, Fri 11:30am–11pm, Sat 3–11pm, Sun 1–10pm. CHINESE.

Specializing in Mandarin and Szechuan cuisine, this modern-looking restaurant serves early bird combination dinners until 6:30pm; gourmet dinners are available for two or more. House favorites are the honey shrimp and the sizzling seafood noodles. Conscientious waiters bring sherbet and cookies at the end of the meal, and the kitchen will hold the MSG, sugar, and salt on request. Despite its address, the restaurant is actually on Churchill Street, within steps of the beach.

McP's Irish Pub

1107 Orange Ave. ☎ **619/435-5280.** Main courses $5–$18. AE, DC, MC, V. Daily 11am–9pm; brunch Sun 10am–2pm. IRISH.

This *Cheers* of Coronado is authentic down to the aroma of stale beer. You'll assume most customers have been darkening its door for years to socialize and enjoy the hearty fare that includes mulligan stew, corned beef and cabbage, and fish and chips. The varied menu also features homemade soups, deli-style sandwiches, burgers, and daily specials. The nightly live entertainment, jazz or rock 'n' roll, draws a large blue jeans–clad crowd, especially on Thursdays.

9 Only in San Diego

Southern Californians have a reputation for living in their cars, and while this is more true of Los Angelenos, I have to admit that the automotive culture is alive and well in San Diego, too. So is "car cuisine," aka fast food. How can we live in our vehicles if we can't eat there? A local favorite is **Rubios,** home of the fish taco, mahimahi burrito, and other Cali-Mex specialties. You'll find these emporia scattered around the city. Some convenient locations are 901 Fourth Ave., at E Street (☎ 619/231-7731); in Pacific Beach at 910 Grand Ave. (☎ 619/270-4800); and at 3555 Rosecrans St., near Midway Drive (☎ 619/223-2631).

You might also try **In-N-Out Burgers.** Some of my most highbrow friends admit to a private passion for these thin meat patties, doused in secret sauce, and served with fresh lettuce and tomato on toasted buns. Even my husband sneaks a meal here now and then because I find the wrappers in the car! There is an In-N-Out just off I-5 in Pacific Beach at 2910 Damon Ave., near E. Mission Bay Drive (no phone).

Because San Diego's benign climate lends itself to al fresco dining, portable meals can, and often do, take the form of picnics. My favorite spot to pick up sandwiches is **The Cheese Shop,** downtown at 401 G St. (☎ 619/232-2303), or in La Jolla at 2165 Avenida de La Playa (☎ 619/459-3921). Other places to buy picnic fare include **D. Z. Akins Deli** at 6930 Alvarado Rd. (☎ 619/265-0218); **Boudin Sourdough Bakery and Cafe** and **The Farmer's Market,** both in Horton Plaza); and **Old Town Liquor and Deli,** at 2304 San Diego Ave. (☎ 619/291-4888). Another spot that's very popular with San Diegans is **Point Loma Seafoods,** located on the water's edge in front of the Municipal Sportfishing Pier, at 2805 Emerson, near Scott Street, south of Rosecrans and west of Harbor Drive (☎ 619/223-1109). There's a fish market here, and they sell seafood sandwiches and salads to go.

San Diegans also are reputed to consume large amounts of sushi. If you like it, you'll love **Cafe Japengo,** adjacent to the Hyatt Regency La Jolla at 8960 University Center Lane, just off La Jolla Village Drive (☎ 619/450-3355).

7

What to See & Do

You won't run out of things to see and do in San Diego. I've lived here most of my life and continue to find activities I want to try and picturesque places I want to explore. The San Diego Zoo, Sea World, and the Wild Animal Park are our top three drawing cards, but many other activities—a substantial number free—also await. And with San Diego's near-perfect climate, chances are good that the sun will shine while you're here, making everything you do just that much more fun. Some attractions offer free admission on certain days; see "Free of Charge and Full of Fun" below for details.

SUGGESTED ITINERARIES

If You Have 1 Day

Visit the zoo in the morning and have lunch at Albert's in the Treehouse in Gorilla Tropics. In the afternoon, walk along the Embarcadero, stopping to tour the vessels that comprise the Maritime Museum, or shop until you drop in Horton Plaza. Either way, finish off the day with a meal in the Gaslamp Quarter.

If You Have 2 Days

Day 1   Spend the day as outlined above.
Day 2   Visit Sea World during the day. In the evening, enjoy a play at one of San Diego's outstanding theaters or hear the San Diego Symphony.

If You Have 3 Days

Days 1–2   Spend these days as outlined above.
Day 3   Visit the Wild Animal Park during the day. When you return to the city, ferry over to Coronado for a look at the Hotel del Coronado and dinner. A walk on the beach would be lovely before or after dinner.

If You Have 5 Days or More

Days 1–3   Spend these days as suggested above.
Day 4   Plan a visit to the Cabrillo National Monument in the morning and spend the rest of the day in La Jolla or Del Mar.

What's Special About San Diego

Beaches
- Windansea Beach, a picturesque patch of coastline in La Jolla that's great for surfing.
- Pacific Beach to Mission Beach, a 3-mile stretch of sand that's wonderful for walking, especially at low tide.

Monuments
- The Cabrillo National Monument on windswept Point Loma, always a good place to view San Diego and beyond.

Buildings
- The Gaslamp Quarter, a National Historic District full of restored Victorian structures.
- Mission San Diego de Alcala, symbol of the city's Hispanic past.

Museums
- The Aerospace Museum in Balboa Park, a monument to San Diego's aviation history.
- The Maritime Museum, comprised of three historic vessels that contain informative exhibits.

Parks
- Balboa Park, where the majority of the city's museums are located, making it the best retreat on a rainy day.
- Embarcadero Marina Park, on the water's edge behind the Convention Center, with the best view of the bay and bridge.

Events
- The Del Mar Fair, from mid-June to July 4th, a Southern California–style county fair.
- The World Championship Over-the-Line Tournament, a raunchy summertime softball happening.

Holiday Highlights
- Christmas on the Prado, a community sing-along in the Organ Pavilion that's good family fun.
- San Diego Harbor Parade of Lights, where boats are festooned with lights and Santa's sleigh has a mainsail.

Attractions
- The San Diego Zoo, slated to be the home of the only pair of pandas in North America.
- Sea World, a theme park with a marine focus that's home to Shamu and the Mission Bermuda Triangle.

Outdoor Activities
- Hiking, biking, and cycling, all more enjoyable in sunny weather.
- Hot-air ballooning over North County, for a bird's-eye view of mansions and golf courses.

Day 5   For ventures farther afield, consider Temecula, Julian, the Anza-Borrego Desert, or Tijuana (see Chapter 12).

1 Ménagerie à Trois: The Zoo, Wild Animal Park & Sea World

Looking for wild times? San Diego supplies them like no other city can. Our world-famous Zoo is home to more than 4,000 animals, many of them rare and exotic. A sister attraction, the San Diego Wild Animal Park, offers another 2,500 creatures of 275 species in an au natural setting. And Shamu and his friends form a veritable chorus line at Sea World—waving their flippers, waddling across an ersatz Antarctica, and blowing killer-whale kisses—in more than a dozen shows a day.

✪ San Diego Zoo

Park Boulevard and Zoo Place, Balboa Park. ☎ **619/234-3153**. Admission $13 adult, $6 children 3–11, military in uniform free. Admission plus bus tour, $17 adults, $15.30 seniors 60 and over, $9 children. Daily 9am–4pm; grounds close at 5pm; with extended summer hours. Bus: 7/7B.

This world-famous zoo, home to 4,000 birds and beasts, is set in 100 subtropical acres and is also a botanical garden. It was the brainchild of a local physician, Dr. Harry Wegeforth, who, while driving down Sixth Avenue in 1916, happened to hear the roar of the caged lions at the Panama-California International Exposition in Balboa Park. "I turned to my brother, Paul, who was riding with me, and half jokingly, half wishfully, said, 'wouldn't it be splendid if San Diego had a zoo! You know . . . I think I'll start one.'"

"Dr. Harry" did start a zoo, and if he could see it now—eighty years later—he would no doubt be very pleased. His vision of a zoological garden where animals would be integrated with plants and contained without bars or cages has become a reality. Wegeforth also used his medical knowledge to care for the four-legged and winged occupants to a degree previously unknown at zoos, and this tradition continues. In 1994, Dr. Stuart Jamieson, the internationally renowned head of cardiothoracic surgery at UCSD Medical Center, performed open-heart surgery on Karen, a two-year-old Sumatran orangutan. During the historic seven-hour procedure and in the following weeks, more than 100 local medical professionals volunteered their time to attend to the little primate. The result: Karen got a new lease on life (and get-well cards from all over the world), and the intensive care unit set up by the volunteers—the only one of its kind—benefited not only Karen, but also an okapi with meningitis and a monkey with cardiac arrest.

Double-decker bus tours, which last 40 minutes, provide close-up glimpses of the animals and lively commentary by a staff member. You're still 15 to 20 feet from the animals, so photographers will need long lenses; sit on the left-hand side for the best views. In general, it's better to take the tour in the early morning or the late afternoon, when the animals are more active. The last tour starts an hour before closing; it's not as crowded as the others, but you won't see the elephants because it's their feeding time. There is no extra charge for animal shows and aerial tram rides (which let you see things from a bird's-eye view). Lines for the tram tend to be longest at the western end, so you may want to board it at the eastern end near the zoo entrance and stroll back through some of the exhibits. Stroller and wheelchair rentals are available.

The zoo, by the way, is one of a few outside Australia to have koalas. Don't miss the Children's Zoo, Gorilla Tropics, Tiger River, or Hippo Beach. You'll find several above-average eating options in the Treehouse Complex; next to the exit is an excellent shop.

Wild Animal Park

15500 San Pasqual Valley Rd., Escondido. ☎ **619/747-8702**. Admission $18.95 adults, $11.75 children 3–11, free for children 2 and under. Daily 9am–4pm; extended summer hours. Take I-15 to Via Rancho Pkwy; follow signs from here for about 3 miles.

Just 30 miles north of San Diego in the San Pasqual Valley, you leave California behind and enter the African plains and other landscapes where 3,000 animals, many of them endangered species, roam freely over 2,200 acres, while humans are enclosed. This living arrangement encourages breeding colonies, so it's not surprising that more than 75 white rhinoceroses have been born here. Several species of rare animals that had vanished from the wild have been reintroduced to their natural habitats from stocks bred by the zoo.

The best way to see the animals is by riding the 5-mile monorail (included in the price of admission); for the best views sit on the right-hand side. During the 50-minute ride, as you pass through areas resembling Africa and Asia, you'll learn interesting tidbits—did you know that rhinos are susceptible to sunburn and mosquito bites? Trains leave every 20 minutes; you can watch informative videos while you wait in the stations. On the 1³/₄-mile Kilimanjaro hiking trail, you'll see tigers, elephants, and cheetahs close up, as well as the Australian rain forest and views of East Africa. Approximately 650 baby animals are born every year in the park, which also is a botanical preserve with more than 2 million plants, including 300 endangered species. Photo tours take place May through September on Wednesday, Thursday, Saturday, and Sunday, and they cost $60 or $85 depending on the tour. Stroller and wheelchair rentals are available. Take a jacket along; it can get cold in the open-air monorail. Local public transportation will get you here, but it takes three buses and 3¹/₂ hours; Gray Line offers a 7-hour tour for about $40 for adults and $25 for kids, including admission and shows (for more information, call 619/491-0011).

Sea World

1720 S. Shores Rd., Mission Bay. ☎ **619/226-3901** or 714/939-6212 in Los Angeles; TDD for the deaf 619/226-3907. Admission $28.95 adults, $24.60 seniors 55 and older; $20.95 children 3–11. Guided 90-minute behind-the-scenes tours, $5 adults, $4 children. Ticket sales stop 1¹/₂ hours before closing. Daily 9am–dusk; extended hours in summer and on holidays. Bus: 9 or 81. By car, exit I-5 west onto Sea World Drive or from I-8 onto W. Mission Bay Drive to Sea World Drive East.

This 150-acre marine-life theme park provides a whale of a good time and show, especially in the 5,000-seat Shamu Stadium, where you'll see

4-ton black-and-white killer whales glide through the air, sometimes with a person perched on their nose. Penguins, dolphins, sea lions, and otters steal a few shows as well, and there are four aquariums. Don't miss Rocky Point Preserve, where visitors get to touch and sometimes feed friendly bottlenose dolphins, many of them born at Sea World, and view otters rescued from the 1989 Alaskan oil spill. At Shark Encounter, if you got any closer to the sharks, you'd be wet—or worse. Mission Bermuda Triangle is a unique theater experience taking people on an underwater adventure that is moving in more ways than one. Shamu's Happy Harbor is an adventure land where kids of all ages can run, jump, play, and get wet. The newest attraction is Baywatch at Sea World, a water-ski show named for the popular TV show featuring "spills, stunts, and beach-front antics."

Although Sea World is best known as Shamu's home, the facility also plays an important role in rescuing and rehabilitating animals found beached along the San Diego coast—more than 300 seals, sea lions, marine birds, and dolphins in a recent year. Sea World also helps out with injured marine species in other parts of the world, such as the oil-soaked victims of the *Exxon Valdez* disaster.

2 San Diego's Beaches

San Diego County is blessed with 70 miles of sandy coastline and more than 30 beaches that attract surfers, snorkelers, swimmers, and sunbathers. In summer, the beaches teem with locals and visitors alike. The rest of the year they are popular places to walk and jog, and surfers don wetsuits to pursue their passion.

Here I've listed some of San Diego's most accessible beaches, each with its own personality and devotees. If you are interested in others, *The California Coastal Access Handbook,* published by the California Coastal Commission, is helpful; it's available locally at Bookstar for $16, or you can order it through your local bookseller. All California beaches are public to the mean high-tide line, and this publication tells you how to get to each one. If you plan to poke around in tide pools, get a tide chart, available free or for a nominal charge from many surf and diving shops, including Emerald City Surf Shop, at 118 Orange Ave., Coronado, and San Diego Divers Supply, at 5701 La Jolla Blvd., La Jolla.

Ocean Beach   Near the pier off I-8 and Sunset Cliffs Boulevard, this is surfers' and sunset-lovers' heaven and the stuff Beach Boys songs are made of. Not far away are **Dog Beach,** where four-legged beach lovers roam unleashed, and **Garbage Beach,** another surfing spot (it doesn't live up to its name).

Mission Bay Park   In this 4,600-acre aquatic playground, you'll discover 27 miles of bay front, 17 miles of oceanfront beaches, picnic areas, children's playgrounds, and paths for biking, roller-skating, and jogging. The bay lends itself to windsurfing, sailing, jet skiing, waterskiing, and fishing. There are dozens of access points; one of the most popular is off I-5 at Clairemont Drive, where there's a visitor information center.

San Diego Beaches

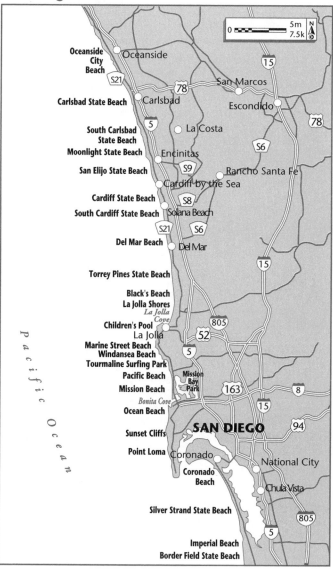

Oceanside City Beach — Oceanside

S21

Carlsbad State Beach — Carlsbad

San Marcos

15

Escondido

78

5

South Carlsbad State Beach

La Costa

Moonlight State Beach — Encinitas

S6

San Elijo State Beach

S9

Rancho Santa Fe

Cardiff by the Sea

Cardiff State Beach

S8

South Cardiff State Beach — Solana Beach

S21

S6

Del Mar Beach — Del Mar

15

Torrey Pines State Beach

Black's Beach

La Jolla Shores

La Jolla Cove

805

Children's Pool — La Jolla

52

Marine Street Beach

5

Windansea Beach

Tourmaline Surfing Park

Pacific Beach — Mission Bay Park

163

8

Mission Beach

15

Bonita Cove

Ocean Beach

SAN DIEGO

94

Sunset Cliffs

Point Loma — Coronado

National City

Coronado Beach

Chula Vista

Silver Strand State Beach

805

5

Imperial Beach

Border Field State Beach

Pacific Ocean

5m
7.5k
N

7070

Pacific Beach   Here you'll find a popular beach and boardwalk for meeting friends, grabbing a bite to eat, jogging, biking, or in-line skating. It runs along Ocean Boulevard (just west of Mission Boulevard), north of Pacific Beach Drive.

Mission Beach   Surfing is popular year-round here. The long beach and boardwalk extend from Pacific Beach Drive south to Belmont Park and beyond to the jetty.

Bonita Cove/Mariner's Point and Mission Point   Facing Mission Bay in South Mission Beach, these spots are perfect for families, with calm waters, grassy areas for picnicking, and playground equipment.

Windansea   One of California's finest surfing beaches, this area along Neptune Street in La Jolla achieved cult status in 1968, when the serious surfers who rode its waves were the subject of Tom Wolfe's book *The Pumphouse Gang*. Hang around for the usually memorable sunset.

✪ La Jolla Cove   The protected, calm waters—praised as the clearest along the California coast—attract swimmers, snorkelers, scuba divers, and families on outings. There's a small sandy beach and on the cliffs above, the Ellen Browning Scripps Park. The Cove's "look but don't touch" policy protects the colorful Garibaldi, California's state fish, plus other marine life, including abalone, octopus, and lobster. The unique Underwater Park stretches from here to the northern end of Torrey Pines State Reserve and incorporates kelp forests, artificial reefs, two deep submarine canyons, and tidal pools.

La Jolla Shores Beach   A mile-long flat stretch of beach, it's popular for jogging, swimming, and body and board surfing for beginners. Families often come here, where lifeguards are on duty year-round.

Black's Beach   The area's unofficial nude beach, it lies between La Jolla Shores Beach and Torrey Pines State Beach. Located below some steep cliffs, it is out of the way and not easy to reach. To get here, take North Torrey Pines Road, park at the Glider Port, and walk from there. Note: Although the water is shallow and pleasant for wading, this area is known for its rip currents.

Del Mar   After a visit to the famous fairgrounds that host the Del Mar Thoroughbred Club, you may want to make tracks for the beach, a long stretch of sand backed by grassy cliffs and a playground area. Del Mar is about 15 miles from downtown San Diego (see Chapter 11).

Northern San Diego County   Those inclined to venture even farther north in San Diego County won't be disappointed. Pacific Coast Highway leads to some inviting beaches, such as these in Encinitas: peaceful **Boneyards Beach, Swami's Beach** for surfing, and **Moonlight Beach,** popular with families and volleyball buffs. Farthest north in this beach-blessed county is **Oceanside,** which has one of the West Coast's longest wooden piers, wide sandy beaches, and several popular surfing areas.

Coronado Beach   Lovely, wide, and sparkling white, this beach is conducive to strolling and lingering, especially in the late afternoon. It fronts Ocean Boulevard and is especially pretty in front of the Hotel

Impressions

Let Coronado wear her crown
As Empress of the Sea;
Nor need she fear her earthly peer
Will e'er discovered be.   —L. Frank Baum, 1905

del Coronado. The islands visible from here, but 18 miles away, are named "Los Coronados," and they belong to Mexico. It's an ideal spot for a marriage proposal.

South of San Diego   Half an hour south of San Diego by car or trol-ley, and only a few minutes from the Mexican border lies **Imperial Beach.** Besides being popular with surfers, it hosts the annual U.S. Open Sandcastle Competition in July, with world-class sand creations ranging from sea scenes to dragons to dinosaurs.

3 Attractions in Balboa Park

Balboa Park's 1,174 acres encompass walkways, gardens, historical buildings, a few restaurants, an ornate pavilion with the world's larg-est outdoor organ, a high-spouting fountain, an Omnimax theater, a nationally acclaimed theater, and a world-famous zoo. The park's most distinctive feature is the architectural beauty of the Spanish-Moorish buildings lining El Prado, its main street, and the group of outstand-ing and diverse museums contained within it. Free tram transportation within the park is provided Monday through Friday from 8am to 5pm and Saturday and Sunday from 11am to 4pm. Ask at the Visitor Center about free walking and museum tours. I've also mapped out a stroll—Walking Tour no. 5—in Chapter 8. Many Balboa Park attractions are free on certain days; refer to "Free of Charge and Full of Fun" below for specifics.

✪ San Diego Aerospace Museum

Pan-American Plaza, Balboa Park. ☎ **619/234-8291.** Admission $5 adults, $1 chil-dren 6–17, free for active military with ID. Daily 10am–4:30pm. Bus: 7/7B, 16, or 25.

The Aerospace Museum, with its International Aerospace Hall of Fame, provides an overview of our nation's air and space history, from the days of hot-air balloons to the space age. There is special empha-sis on local aviation history, including the construction here of the *Spirit of St. Louis.* The museum is housed in the cylindrically shaped Ford Building, built by the Ford Motor Company for the California Pacific International Exposition of 1935. Behind-the-scenes restoration tours are available.

Museum of Art

1450 El Prado, Balboa Park. ☎ **619/232-7931.** Admission $5 adults, $4 seniors 65 and over, $3 military with ID, $2 children 6–17 and students any age. Tue–Sun 10am–4:30pm. Bus: 7/7B, 16, or 25.

The museum has outstanding collections of Italian Renaissance and Dutch and Spanish Baroque art, along with contemporary paintings and sculptures. In the Grant-Munger Gallery on the ground floor are works by Monet, Toulouse-Lautrec, Renoir, Pissarro, van Gogh, and Dufy. Bouguereau's arresting *Young Shepherdess* commands Gallery 9. Upstairs in the Fitch Gallery is El Greco's *Penitent St. Peter,* and in the Gluck Gallery, Modigliani's *Boy with Blue Eyes* and Braque's *Coquelicots.* The museum has a shop, sculpture garden, and cafe with out-door seating. Its rotunda features a striking Spanish-style tile staircase.

Museum of Photographic Arts

1649 El Prado, Balboa Park. ☎ **619/239-5262.** Admission $3 adults, free for children 12 and under with adult. Daily 10am–5pm. Bus: 7/7B, 16 or 25.

One of the country's finest photography museums exhibits the works of master international photographers. Historical and contemporary works are featured.

Natural History Museum

1788 El Prado, Balboa Park. ☎ **619/232-3821.** Admission $5 adults, $4 seniors and military, $2 students 6–17. Fri–Wed 9:30am–4:30pm, Thur 9:30am–6:30pm. Bus: 7/7B, 16, or 25.

The museum focuses on the flora, fauna, and mineralogy of the Southwest. Kids marvel at the animals they find here and enjoy exploring the Desert Lab downstairs, home to live snakes and tarantulas.

Reuben H. Fleet Space Theater and Science Center

1875 El Prado, Balboa Park. ☎ **619/238-1233.** Space Theater, for IMAX/OMNIMAX shows, $6 adults, $3.50 children 5–15, $4.50 seniors 65 and over; for laser light shows, $7.50 adults, $5 children, $6 seniors. Science Center $2.50 adults and seniors, $1.25 children. Mon–Tues 9:30am–9pm, Wed–Thurs 9:30am–10pm, Fri–Sat 9:30am–11pm, Sun 9:30am–10pm, shorter hours in winter. Bus: 7/7B, 16, or 25.

The Reuben H. Fleet Space Theater and Science Center houses the world's first OMNIMAX theater, a 76-foot tilted-dome screen that shows not only IMAX/OMNIMAX films but also three-dimensional laser light shows. The Science Center features more than 50 hands-on exhibits. It's possible to buy tickets in advance to circumvent waiting in line, especially on weekends, which tend to be busy.

Museum of Man

1350 El Prado, Balboa Park. ☎ **619/239-2001.** Admission $4 adults, $2 students 13–18, $1 children 6–12. Daily 10am–4:30pm. Bus: 16 or 25.

In a landmark building in the park, just inside the entrance at the Cabrillo Bridge, this museum is devoted to the progress, diversity, and achievements of the peoples of North and South America. Favorite exhibits include the life-size replicas of a dozen varieties of Homo sapiens, from Cro-Magnon and Neanderthal to Peking Man, along with Lucy, a 3$^{1}/_{2}$-million-year-old skeleton discovered in Ethiopia in 1974. Don't overlook the annex across the street, which houses more exhibits.

The San Diego Automotive Museum

2080 Pan American Plaza, Balboa Park. ☎ **619/231-2886.** Admission $5 adults, $4 seniors and military, $2 children 6–17, children under 6 free. Daily 10am–4:30pm. Bus: 7/7B, 16, or 25.

Classic, antique, and exotic cars and motorcycles are on view here in changing shows. The museum has an extensive automotive-related gift shop and a full automotive research library. On your visit you might see a 1927 Bentley; a 1931 Duesenberg Model J; a 1931 Rolls-Royce Phaeton; the late actor Steve McQueen's Allard, made in 1953; as well as the ill-fated 1948 Tucker and 1981 DeLorean.

Balboa Park

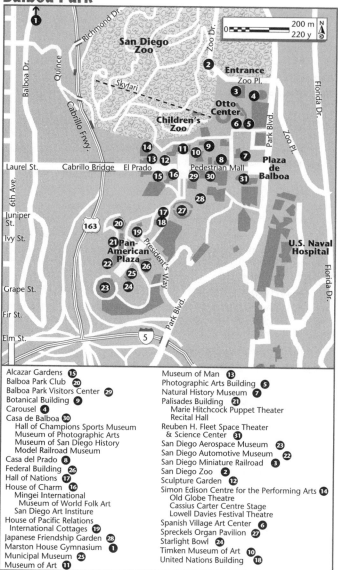

Botanical Building and Lily Pond

El Prado. ☎ **619/235-1100.** Admission Free. Fri–Wed 10am–4pm. Bus: 7/7B, 16, or 25.

Within a serene park, ivy, ferns, orchids, impatiens, begonias, and other plants—about 1,200 tropical and flowering varieties—are sheltered beneath the domed lath house. The building, part of the 1915 Panama-California Exposition, measures 250 feet long by 75 feet wide by 60 feet high and is one of the world's largest lath structures. The lily pond out front attracts sun worshipers and street entertainers.

Hall of Champions

1649 El Prado, Balboa Park. ☎ **619/234-2544.** Admission $3 adults, $2 seniors 65 and older and military, $1 children 6–17. Daily 10am–4:30pm. Bus: 7/7B, 16, or 25.

A favorite of sports fans since 1961, it highlights more than 40 different professional and amateur sports, as one of the country's few multisport museums. More than 25 exhibits surround a centerpiece statue, the Discus Thrower. An excellent exhibit is devoted to athletes with disabilities. Tour in a counterclockwise direction.

House of Pacific Relations International Cottages

Balboa Park. ☎ **619/234-0739.** Admission free or donation. Sun 12:30–4:30pm and fourth Tues of month 11:30am–3pm. Bus: 7/7B, 16, or 25.

This cluster of one- and two-room cottages disseminates information about the culture, traditions, and history of 31 countries. Light refreshments are served, and outdoor lawn programs are presented March through October.

Japanese Friendship Garden

Balboa Park. ☎ **619/232-2780.** Admission $2 adults, $1 seniors 65 and older and children 7–17, $5 family pass, free for children under 7. Tues and Fri–Sun 10am–4pm. Bus: 7/7B, 16, or 25.

Of the 11½ acres designated for the garden, only an acre—a beautiful, peaceful one—has been developed, but inside the garden's information center a model shows that the garden, named San-Kei-En (Three-Scenery Garden), will eventually include a shallow lake with a shoreline of Japanese irises; a pastoral scene, such as a meadow abloom with springtime trees; and a rushing mountain waterfall and a stream filled with colorful koi. A self-guided tour is available at the main gate. From the gate, a crooked path (to confound evil spirits, which move only in a straight line) threads its way to the information center in a Zen-style house; here you can view the most ancient kind of garden, the sekitei, made only of sand and stone. Refreshments are served on a Japanese-style deck to the left of the entrance. Japanese holidays are celebrated here, and the public is invited.

Marston House Museum

Northwest corner of Balboa Park (at Balboa Drive and Upas Street). ☎ **619/232-6203.** Admission $3, $5 in combination with Villa Montezuma, free for children under 13. Sat–Sun 10am–4pm. Bus: 1, 3, 16, or 25.

Designed in 1905 by noted San Diego architect Irving Gill for local businessman/philanthropist George Marston and his wife, Anne, this house is a classic example of Craftsman-style architecture, reminiscent of Frank Lloyd Wright's work. Opened to the public in 1991, it contains few original pieces, but does exhibit Roycroft, Stickley, and Lampert furniture and is slowly being furnished with Craftsman-era pieces or copies as funds come in. The San Diego Historical Society manages the house, with its wide hallways, brick fireplaces, and redwood paneling; enter at the left side. There's a small bookstore and gift shop.

✪ Model Railroad Museum

Casa de Balboa Building, El Prado, Balboa Park. ☎ **619/696-0199.** Admission $3 adults, discounts for seniors, students, and military with ID, free for children under 15. Tues–Fri 11am–4pm, Sat–Sun 11am–5pm. Bus: 7/7B, 16, or 25.

Four permanent scale-model railroads depict Southern California's transportation history and terrain, including San Diego County's "Grand Canyon," the Carriso Gorge. Children enjoy the hands-on Lionel trains, and train buffs of all ages like the interactive multimedia exhibits. The gift shop sells rail-related items, including toys, mugs, signs, and kids' overalls and shirts.

Museum of San Diego History

1649 El Prado, Balboa Park. ☎ **619/232-6203.** Admission $4 adults, $3 seniors and military with ID, $3 for groups of 10 or more, $1.50 for children 5–12, children under 5 free. Wed–Sun 10am–4:30pm, second Tues of every month 10am–4:30pm. Bus: 7/7B, 16, or 25.

A good place to start if you are a newcomer to San Diego, the recently remodeled museum offers changing exhibits from the San Diego Historical Society collections and from national and international traveling shows. Many of the museum's photographs depict Balboa Park and the growth of the city. The gift shop sells history books about San Diego.

Spreckels Organ Pavilion

Balboa Park. ☎ **619/226-0819.** Free 1-hour Sunday concerts year-round and free Summer Festival concerts in July and August, 8pm Mon and 6:15pm Tues, Wed, and Thurs. Seating for 2,400. Bus: 7/7B, 16, or 25.

Given to San Diego citizens in 1914 by brothers John D. and Adolph Spreckels, the ornate, curved pavilion houses a magnificent organ with 4,445 individual pipes, ranging in length from less than a half-inch to more than 32 feet. With only brief interruptions, the organ has been in continuous use in the park, and today visitors may enjoy free hourlong concerts on Sunday at 2pm.

Timken Museum of Art

1500 El Prado, Balboa Park. ☎ **619/239-5548.** Admission free. Tues–Sat 10am–4:30pm, Sun 1:30–4:30pm. Closed during September. Bus: 7/7B, 16, or 25.

Called the "Jewel of the Park," it houses the Putnam Foundation's collection of European old masters, 19th-century American paintings, and an outstanding collection of Russian icons.

4 More Attractions

DOWNTOWN AND BEYOND

In downtown San Diego, you can wander in the **Gaslamp Quarter** (see Walking Tour 2 in Chapter 8) or **Horton Plaza,** where you can shop for hours, stroll, snack or dine, enjoy free entertainment, see a

San Diego Attractions

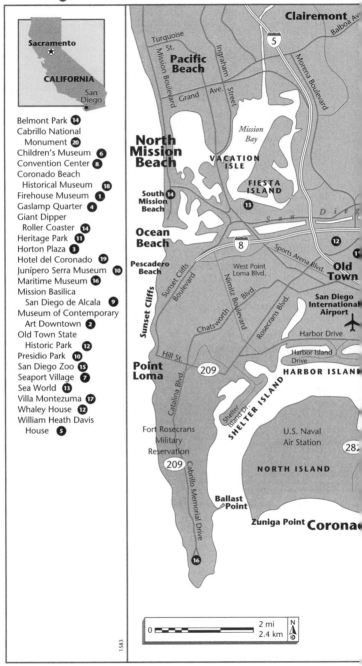

Belmont Park ⑭
Cabrillo National
  Monument ⑳
Children's Museum ⑥
Convention Center ⑧
Coronado Beach
  Historical Museum ⑱
Firehouse Museum ①
Gaslamp Quarter ④
Giant Dipper
  Roller Coaster ⑭
Heritage Park ⑪
Horton Plaza ③
Hotel del Coronado ⑲
Junípero Serra Museum ⑩
Maritime Museum ⑯
Mission Basilica
  San Diego de Alcala ⑨
Museum of Contemporary
  Art Downtown ②
Old Town State
  Historic Park ⑫
Presidio Park ⑩
San Diego Zoo ⑮
Seaport Village ⑦
Sea World ⑬
Villa Montezuma ⑰
Whaley House ⑫
William Heath Davis
  House ⑤

Downtown

Date Street
Cedar Street
Beech Street
Ash Street
A Street
B Street
C Street
Broadway
E Street
F Street
G Street
Island Avenue
J Street
K Street

Drive
Highway
Harbor
Pacific
Kettner Blvd.
State Street
Union Street
Front Street
Market Street
1st Ave.
2nd Ave.
3rd Ave.
4th Ave.
5th Ave.
6th Ave.
7th Ave.
8th Ave.
9th Ave.
10th Ave.
11th Ave.

Vista Rd.
Linda
Friars Rd.

Gaslamp Quarter

Harbor Dr.

Hillcrest/ Uptown

Pacific Hwy.
1st Ave.
5th Ave.
Ash Street
Broadway

Balboa Park
Park Blvd.

SAN DIEGO

National Ave.
Logan Ave.
Euclid Ave.

3rd St.
4th St.
Orange Ave.
San Diego-Coronado Bay Bridge (Toll)

Division St.

National City
8th St.

Coronado Beach
Silver Strand

18th St.

30th St.

movie, and people-watch—all within a unique and colorful architectural framework. The **Convention Center,** which opened in 1989, is a dramatic addition to the city's skyline.

✪ Cabrillo National Monument

Point Loma. ☎ **619/557-5450.** Admission $4 per vehicle, $2 for walk-ins, free for American citizens age 62 and older, who have a National Parks Service Golden Age Passport, and children 16 and younger. Daily 9am–5:15pm. Bus: 6. Directions: Take I-5 to Rosecrans Street west, which leads to Point Loma, and then take Catalina Boulevard to the monument.

Breathtaking views mingle with the early history of San Diego, which began when Juan Rodríguez Cabrillo arrived in 1542. His statue dominates the tip of Point Loma, which is also a vantage point for watching migrating gray whales en route from the Arctic Ocean to Baja California from December through March. The restored lighthouse (1855) allows a glimpse of what life was like here in the past century. It's worth the ride out here or taking the tour. The road into the monument passes Fort Rosecrans National Cemetery, with row after row of white markers. National Park Service rangers lead walks at the monument, and there are tide pools that beg for exploration. Films on Cabrillo, tide pools, and California gray whales are shown daily from 10am to 4pm, on the hour. Cabrillo National Monument welcomes almost 1.2 million visitors annually, making it one of the country's most visited national monuments.

Children's Museum of San Diego

200 W. Island Ave. ☎ **619/233-8792.** Admission $5 for adults and children over 2 and $2.50 for seniors; children under 2 are free. Tues–Sat 10am–4:30pm, Sun noon–4:30pm. Trolley: Convention Center stop; the museum is a block away.

This interactive "museum," which encourages participation, is a home away from home for kids. It provides ongoing supervised activities, as well as a monthly special celebration, such as earth awareness or African-American history, with changing exhibits every five or six months. A big draw for kids ages 2 to 10 is the indoor and outdoor art studio. There is also a theater with costumes for budding actors to don, plus an observation walk above the exhibits that kids climb up on and exit via a spiral slide. The museum shop is filled with toys, games, crafts, and books. School groups come in the morning. There's all-day parking across the street for about $3.

Firehouse Museum

1572 Columbia St. (at Cedar). ☎ **619/232-FIRE.** Admission $2 adults, $1 seniors and military in uniform, $1 juniors (13–17), firefighters and children 12 and under free. Wed–Fri 10am–2pm, Sat–Sun 10am–4pm. Bus: 5, 16, or 105.

Appropriately housed in San Diego's oldest firehouse, the museum features shiny fire engines, including hand-drawn and horse-drawn models, a 1903 steam pumper, and memorabilia such as antique alarms, fire hats, and foundry molds for fire hydrants. There's also a small gift shop.

Maritime Museum

1306 N. Harbor Dr. ☎ **619/234-9153.** Admission $12 families, $6 adults, $4 seniors over 62 and teens 13–17, $4 children 5–12, free for children under 5. Daily 9am–8pm. Bus: 2. Trolley: America Plaza.

This unique museum consists of a fine trio of ships: the full-rigged merchant ship *Star of India* (1863), whose impressive masts are an integral part of the San Diego cityscape; the gleaming white San Francisco–Oakland steam-powered ferryboat *Berkeley* (1898), which worked round the clock to carry people to safety following the 1906 San Francisco earthquake; and the sleek steam yacht *Medea* (1904), one of the world's few remaining large steam yachts. You can board and explore each vessel, and from April through October, you can watch movies on deck (see Chapter 10, "San Diego After Dark," for details).

Museum of Contemporary Art, Downtown (MCA)

1001 Kettner Blvd. (at Broadway). ☎ 619/234-1001. Admission $3 adults, $1 students and seniors, 50¢ children 5–12; free Friday 5:30pm–8pm. Tues–Sun 10:30am–5:30pm; Friday 10:30am–8pm. Trolley: America Plaza.

MCA Downtown is the second location of the Museum of Contemporary Art, San Diego. The downtown space, comprised of two large galleries and two smaller ones, presents changing exhibitions of nationally and internationally distinguished contemporary artists. Lectures and tours for adults and children are offered. There's a gift shop/bookstore on the premises. Situated in the One America Plaza office/retail complex, MCA Downtown is conveniently located in the city center's transportation hub.

Villa Montezuma

1925 K St. (at 20th Avenue). ☎ 619/239-2211. Admission $3 adults, $5 in combination with Marston House, free for children 12 and under. Sat–Sun noon–4:30pm. Bus: 3, 3A, 4, 5, 16, or 105 to Market and Imperial streets. Drive along K Street to the house.

Just east of downtown, this stunning mansion was built in 1887 for internationally acclaimed musician and author Jesse Shepard. Lush with Victoriana, it features more stained glass than most churches have; windows depict Mozart, Beethoven, Sappho, Rubens, St. Cecilia (patron saint of musicians), and other notables. The striking ceilings are of pressed canvas coated with linseed oil (called Lincrusta Walton), a forerunner of linoleum, which never looked this good. Shepard lived in the house with his life companion, Lawrence Tonner, for only two years and died in obscurity in Los Angeles in 1927. The San Diego Historical Society painstakingly restored the house, on the National Register of Historic Places, and furnished it with period pieces. Unfortunately, the neighborhood is not as fashionable as the house, but it's safe to park your car here in the daytime. If you love Victorian houses, don't miss this one for its quirkiness.

William Heath Davis House Museum and Information Center

410 Island Ave. (at Fourth Avenue). ☎ 619/233-4692 or hotline 619/233-4691. Admission $1. Call for museum hours and tour information. Bus: 1, 3, or 3A. Trolley: Gaslamp Quarter/Convention Center.

Built in 1850, this is the oldest house in the Gaslamp Quarter. The ground floor is open to the public, as is the small park adjacent to the house. The top floor houses the Gaslamp Quarter Foundation, which sponsors walking tours of the quarter on Saturday at 11am for $5 (see "Organized Tours" later in this chapter).

OLD TOWN AND BEYOND

The birthplace of San Diego—indeed, of California—Old Town brings back to life Mexican California, which existed here until the mid-1800s. In Chapter 8, Walking Tour no. 4 goes through Old Town. In addition, free walking tours leave daily at 2pm from the **Old Town State Historic Park's** visitors center (☎ 619/220-5422), located at the head of the pedestrian walkway that is the continuation of San Diego Avenue. Admission to the center, open daily from 10am to 5pm, is free. The park has seven original buildings; the rest are reconstructed. Two museums charge admission: The Estudillo House, which depicts the living conditions of a wealthy family in 1872; and Seeley Stables, named after A. L. Seeley, who ran the stagecoach and mail service in these parts from 1867 to 1871. The stables have two floors of wagons, carriages, stagecoaches, and other memorabilia, including washboards, slot machines, and hand-worked saddles, as well as a 17-minute slide show. On weekdays during the school year, Old Town buzzes with fourth graders; it's an enormous classroom.

Heritage Park

2455 Heritage Park Row (corner of Juan and Harney streets), Old Town. ☎ **619/ 694-3049.** Admission free. Daily 9:30am–3pm. Bus: 4 or 5/105.

This small 7.8-acre county park is filled with seven original 19th-century houses moved here from other places and given new uses, among them a bed-and-breakfast inn, a doll shop, and a gift shop. The most recent addition is the small synagogue, placed near the park's entrance in 1989. A glorious coral tree crowns the top of the hill.

Junipero Serra Museum

2727 Presidio Dr., Presidio Park, Old Town. ☎ **619/297-3258.** Admission $3 adults, free for children 12 and under. Tues–Sat 10am–4:30pm, Sun noon–4:30pm. Directions: Take Interstate 8 to the Taylor Street exit. Turn right on Taylor, then left on Presidio Drive.

Perched on a hill above Old Town, the stately mission-style building overlooks the hillside where California began. Here in 1769, the first mission and first non-Indian settlement on the west coast of the United States and Canada were founded. Inside, the museum's exhibits introduce visitors to California's origins, and to the Native American, Spanish, and Mexican people who first called this place home. On display are their belongings, from cannons to cookware, a Spanish furniture collection, and one of the first paintings brought to California, which survived being damaged in an Indian attack. The mission remained San Diego's only settlement until the 1820s, when families began to move down the hill into what is now known as Old Town. Watch an ongoing archaeological dig uncover more of the items used by early settlers. From the 70-foot tower, visitors can compare the spectacular view with historic photos to see how this land has changed over time.

The museum is located in **Presidio Park**, called the "Plymouth Rock of the Pacific." The large cross in the park was made from floor tile from the Presidio ruins. Sculptor Arthur Puntnam made the statues of Father Serra, founder of the missions in California, and the Native American. Climb up to Inspiration Point, as many have done for marriage ceremonies, for a sweeping view of the area.

Mission Basilica San Diego de Alcala

10818 San Diego Mission Rd., Mission Valley. ☎ **619/281-8449.** Admission $2 adults, $1 seniors and students; 50¢ children 12 and under. Daily 9am–5pm; mass daily 7am and 5:30pm. Bus: 6, 16, 25, 43, or 81. Take I-8 to Mission Gorge Road to Twain Avenue.

Established in 1769, this was the first link in a chain of 21 missions founded by Spanish missionary Junípero Serra. In 1774, the mission was moved to its present site for agricultural reasons and to separate Native American converts from a fortress that included the original building. A few bricks belonging to the original mission can be seen in Presidio Park in Old Town. Mass is held regularly in this still-active Catholic parish.

Whaley House

2482 San Diego Ave. ☎ **619/298-2482.** Admission $5 adults, $4 seniors over 65, $2.50 children 12–16, $1.50 children 5–11. Daily 10am–5pm.

In 1856, this striking two-story house (the first one in these parts) just outside Old Town State Historic Park was built for Thomas Whaley and his family. Whaley was a New Yorker who arrived here via San Francisco, where he had been lured by the Gold Rush. The house is one of only two authenticated haunted houses in California, and 10,000 schoolchildren come here each year to see for themselves. Exhibits include a life mask of Abraham Lincoln, one of only six made; the spinet piano used in the movie *Gone with the Wind;* and the concert piano that accompanied Swedish soprano Jenny Lind on her final U.S. tour in 1852. Director June Reading will make you feel at home, in spite of the ghost.

MISSION BAY/PACIFIC BEACH

Giant Dipper Roller Coaster

3146 Mission Blvd. ☎ **619/488-1549.** Admission $2.50. Sun–Thur 11am–10pm, Fri–Sat 11am–11pm. Take I-5 to the Sea World exit, and follow W. Mission Bay Park to Belmont Park.

A local landmark for 70 years, the Giant Dipper is one of two surviving fixtures from the original Belmont Amusement Park (the other is the Plunge swimming pool). After sitting dormant for 15 years, this vintage wooden roller coaster, with more than 2,600 feet of track and 13 hills, underwent an extensive restoration and reopened in 1991. The minimum height requirement to ride the roller coaster is 50 inches. You can also ride on the Giant Dipper's neighbor, the Liberty Carousel ($1).

LA JOLLA

My favorite place in my hometown is the **La Jolla Cove** and **Ellen Browning Scripps Park** on the cliff above it. Here, swimming, sunning, picnicking, barbecuing, reading, and strolling along the oceanfront walkway are ongoing activities. The unique 6,000-acre **San Diego–La Jolla Underwater Park,** established in 1970, stretches from La Jolla Cove to the northern end of Torrey Pines State Reserve.

For a scenic drive, follow La Jolla Boulevard to Nautilus Street and turn east to get to **Mount Soledad** and a 360-degree view of the area. The cross on top, erected in 1954, is 43 feet high and 12 feet wide. In town, **Mary Star of the Sea,** a beautiful Roman Catholic church, stands at 7727 Girard (at Kline), and the **La Valencia Hotel** at 1132 Prospect St. is another pretty Spanish Colonial structure. The **La Jolla Woman's Club,** located at 7791 Draper Ave.; and the adjacent **Museum of Contemporary Art**, San Diego; **La Jolla Recreation Center;** and **The Bishop's School** are examples of village buildings designed by architect Irving Gill.

At La Jolla's north end, you'll find the 1,200-acre, 15,000-student **University of California at San Diego** (UCSD), established in 1960. On campus are the Stuart Collection of public sculpture and the Scripps Institution of Oceanography with its aquarium-museum (see individual listings, below). Louis Kahn designed the **Salk Institute for Biological Studies,** at 10010 North Torrey Pines Rd.

Mingei International Museum of World Folk Art

University Towne Centre, 4405 La Jolla Village Dr., Building I-7. ☎ **619/453-5300.** Admission $3 adults, $1 children (5–12) and students with ID Tues–Sat 11am–5pm, Sun 2–5pm. Take I-5 to La Jolla Village Dr. East; continue to University Towne Centre shopping center; museum is on upper level across from Nordstrom.

The museum, whose name means "art of the people" in Japanese (pronounced "min-gay"), lives up to its moniker. Changing exhibitions celebrate human creativity manifested in textiles, costumes, jewelry, toys, pottery, paintings, and sculpture—all using natural materials from countries all over the world. Calling All Angels, the museum's annual holiday exhibit in December and January, showcases ornamental angels. Martha Longenecker, a potter and professor of art emeritus at San Diego State University, founded the Mingei in 1977; she still is director. As one of only two major U.S. museums devoted to crafts on a worldwide scale (the other is in Santa Fe), the 6,000-object collection contains Indian art, Japanese folk art, and toys and dolls. The outstanding museum shop, called the Collector's Gallery, has unique ethnic gifts at reasonable prices, along with museum-quality pottery. The Mingei is scheduled to move to the House of Charm in Balboa Park in 1996.

Museum of Contemporary Art, San Diego

700 Prospect St. ☎ **619/454-3541.** Admission $3 adults, $1 students and seniors, 50¢ children 5–12; free Friday 5:30pm–8pm. Take the Ardath Road exit off I-5 north; or the La Jolla Village Drive west exit off I-5 south. Take Torrey Pines Road to Prospect Place and turn right. Prospect Place becomes Prospect Street.

Focusing primarily on work produced since 1950, the museum is known internationally for its permanent collection and thought-provoking exhibitions. The ocean views from the galleries are gorgeous. However, it should be reopening after renovations by spring 1996.

La Jolla Attractions

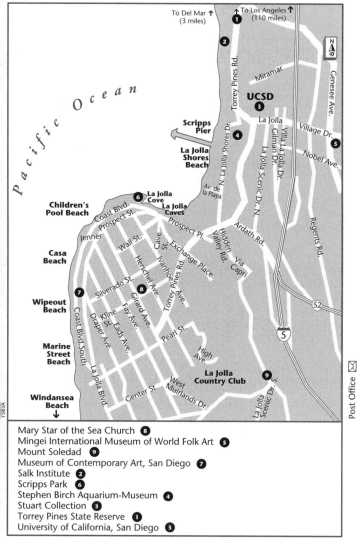

To Del Mar (3 miles)

To Los Angeles (110 miles)

Pacific Ocean

Miramar

Torrey Pines Rd.

UCSD

La Jolla

Scripps Pier

Scripps Pier
La Jolla Shores Beach

La Jolla Shores Dr. N.

Villa La Jolla Dr.
Gilman Dr.

Village Dr.

Genesee Ave.

Nobel Ave.

La Jolla Scenic Dr. N.

Av. de la Playa

Children's Pool Beach

La Jolla Cove

La Jolla Caves

Coast Blvd.
Prospect St.
Jenner

Prospect Pl.

Hidden Valley Rd.

Ardath Rd.

Via Capri

Regents Rd.

Casa Beach

Wall St.

Cave St.
Exchange Place

Herschel Ave.
Ivanhoe Ave.

Silverado St.

Wipeout Beach

Girard Ave.
Kline St.
Fay Ave.

Torrey Pines Rd.

Coast Blvd. South

Draper Ave.
Eads Ave.

Pearl St.

52

5

Marine Street Beach

La Jolla Blvd.

High Ave.

La Jolla Country Club

La Jolla Scenic Dr. S.

Windansea Beach

Genter St.

West Muirlands Dr.

Post Office ⊠

Mary Star of the Sea Church ⑧
Mingei International Museum of World Folk Art ⑤
Mount Soledad ⑨
Museum of Contemporary Art, San Diego ⑦
Salk Institute ②
Scripps Park ⑥
Stephen Birch Aquarium-Museum ④
Stuart Collection ③
Torrey Pines State Reserve ①
University of California, San Diego ③

Stephen Birch Aquarium-Museum

Scripps Institution of Oceanography. ☎ **619/534-FISH.** Admission $6.50 adults, $5.50 seniors, $4.50 students and teenagers 13–17, $3.50 children 3–12; $2.50 parking lot fee. Daily 9am–5pm. Take I-5 to La Jolla Village Drive exit, go west one mile, and turn left at Expedition Way.

Part of the Scripps Institution of Oceanography, a branch of the University of California at San Diego, it offers close-up views of the Pacific Northwest, the California coast, Mexico's Sea of Cortez, and the tropical seas in 33 marine life tanks. The giant kelp forest is particularly impressive (keep an eye out for a tiger shark or an eel floating through it), and the demonstration tide pool shows visitors marine coastal life.

The museum has numerous interpretive exhibits on the current and historic research done at the Scripps Institution, which was established in 1903 and became part of the university in 1912. In the museum, you'll learn what fog is and why salt melts snow, be astounded at the number of supermarket products that come from the sea (toothpaste, ice cream, and matches, to name a few), feel what an earthquake is like, and experience a 12-minute simulated submarine ride. This beautiful new facility opened in 1992; the aquarium is to the right of the entrance, the museum to the left. The bookstore is well stocked with textbooks, science books, educational toys, gifts, and T-shirts.

Stuart Collection

University of California, San Diego (UCSD). ☎ **619/534-2117.** Admission free. From La Jolla, take Torrey Pines Road to La Jolla Village Drive, turn right, go two blocks to Gilman Drive and turn left into the campus; in about a block the information booth will be visible on the right.

Consider the Stuart Collection a work in progress on a large scale. Through an agreement between the Stuart Foundation and UCSD back in 1982, the still-growing collection consists of site-related sculptures by leading contemporary artists throughout the 1,200 acres of the UCSD campus. Among the 12 diverse sculptures on view are Niki de Saint-Phalle's *Sun God,* a jubilant 14-foot-high fiberglass bird on a 15-foot concrete base, nicknamed "Big Bird" and made an unofficial mascot by the students, who make it the centerpiece of their annual celebration, the Sun God Festival. Also in the collection are Alexis Smith's *Snake Path,* a 560-foot-long slate tile pathway that winds up the hill from the Engineering Mall to the east terrace of the University Library; and Terry Allen's *Trees,* three eucalyptus trees encased in lead, one of them emitting songs and another poems and stories, while the third stands silent in a grove of trees the students call "The Enchanted Forest." Pick up a brochure and map with marked sculpture locations from the information booth at the Northview Drive or Gilman Drive entrance to the campus. Guides, parking permits, and general information are available.

CORONADO

It's hard to miss one of Coronado's most famous landmarks: the **Coronado Bay Bridge.** Completed in 1969, the four-lanes-wide bridge spans 2 miles across the bay, linking San Diego and Coronado; it's the only officially dedicated scenic highway in the United States. When built, it put the commuter ferries out of business, although in 1986, ferry service restarted and today is used by tourists. Crossing the bridge by car or bus is an undeniable thrill because you can see Mexico, the San Diego skyline, Coronado, the naval station, and San Diego Bay. The bridge's middle section floats, so that if it's destroyed in wartime, naval ships would still have access to the harbor and sea beyond.

Traveling from San Diego to Coronado, a toll of $1 for one-person ve-
hicles is charged; however, there's no charge if two or more people are
in the car or if you're traveling from Coronado to San Diego.

Coronado Beach Historical Museum

1126 Loma Ave., Coronado. ☎ **619/435-7242.** Admission free. Wed–Sun 10am–
4pm. Follow Orange Avenue to Loma Avenue and turn right; it's on the left side
beside Chez Loma restaurant.

In the Thomson House (ca. 1898), this little museum goes back to the
Coronado of yesteryear, with photographs of the Hotel Del in its
infancy; the old ferries; and Tent City, the seaside campground for
middle-income folks from 1900 to 1939. Other memorabilia includes
army uniforms, old postcards, and even recorded music. You'll
learn about the island's military aviation history during World Wars
I and II.

✪ Hotel del Coronado

1500 Orange Ave., Coronado. ☎ **619/435-6611.** Admission free. Bus: no. 901.
Ferry: Broadway Pier, then ¹/₂-hour walk, or take a bus or trolley or rent a bike.

Built in 1888, this turreted Victorian seaside resort in Coronado
remains an enduring, endearing national treasure. Whether you stay
here, dine here, dance here, or simply wander through on a tour of its
grounds and photo gallery, prepare to be enchanted. See Chapter 5 for
more details.

5 Free of Charge and Full of Fun

It's easy to get charged up on a vacation—$10 here, $5 there and pretty
soon your credit card statement looks like the National Debt. To keep
that from happening, I've compiled a list of free San Diego activities.
In addition, scan the list of "Spectator Sports" and "Special Interest
Sightseeing" below, and the "San Diego Calendar of Events" in
Chapter 2. Many events listed in these sections, such as the **NAS
Miramar Naval Air Show,** are free of charge. San Diego also has
numerous **parades,** such as the Holiday Bowl Parade and the Parade
of Lights both in December.

DOWNTOWN & BEYOND

It doesn't cost a penny to stroll around the **Gaslamp Quarter,** along
the **Embarcadero,** and around **Seaport Village** or **Horton Plaza.** And
don't forget **Walkabout International** offers free guided walking tours
as described below. If you'd rather drive around, ask for the map of the
52-mile **San Diego Scenic Drive** when you're at the International
Visitor Information Center. The downtown branch of the **Museum
of Contemporary Art, San Diego,** is free Fridays from 5:30 to 8pm.
Another fun activity is the **Sunset Cinema** discussed under "Movies"
below. And you can **fish** free of charge off any municipal pier.

BALBOA PARK

The **San Diego Zoo** is free to all on the first Monday of October,
Founders Day, and children ages 11 and under get in free every day
during October.

All the museums in Balboa Park are open to the public without charge one day a month. Here's a list of the free days:

> First Tuesday of month: **Natural History Museum, Reuben H. Fleet Science Center,** and **Model Railroad Museum.**
> Second Tuesday of month: **Museum of Photographic Arts, Hall of Champions,** and **Museum of San Diego History.**
> Third Tuesday of month: **Museum of Art, Museum of Man,** and **Japanese Friendship Garden**.
> Fourth Tuesday of month: **Aerospace Museum** and **San Diego Automotive Museum.**

These Balboa Park attractions are always free: The **Botanical Building and Lily Pond, House of Pacific Relations International Cottages,** and **Timken Museum of Art**.

Free one-hour Sunday concerts and free Summer Festival concerts are given at the **Spreckels Organ Pavilion.**

OLD TOWN & BEYOND

Explore **Heritage Park**, **Presidio Park**, or **Old Town State Historic Park,** and there's free entertainment (mariachis and folk dancers) at the **Bazaar del Mundo** on Saturday and Sunday. There's also no admission charge to **Mission Trails Regional Park,** with hiking trails and an interpretive center.

MISSION BAY/PACIFIC BEACH

Walk along the beach or around the bay—it's free, fun, and good for you.

LA JOLLA

Enjoy the ✪ **free outdoor concerts** at Scripps Park on Sundays from 2 to 4pm, mid-June through mid-September (☎ 619/525-3160). Anytime is a good time to walk around the **La Jolla Cove, Ellen Browning Scripps Park,** and **Torrey Pines State Reserve.** If you're a diver check out the 6,000-acre **San Diego–La Jolla Underwater Park,** which stretches from La Jolla Cove to the northern end of Torrey Pines State Reserve. If you like arts and crafts, you'll love the **La Jolla Arts Festival,** held every September. It's also fun to meander around the campus of University of California at San Diego (UCSD), and view the **Stuart Collection of Outdoor Sculpture.** The La Jolla branch of the **Museum of Contemporary Art, San Diego,** is free Friday from 5:30 to 8pm. For the best vista, follow the "Scenic Drive" signs to **Mount Soledad** and a 360-degree view of the area.

CORONADO

Drive across the **Coronado Bay Bridge** (free for two or more people in car) and take a self-guided tour of the **Hotel del Coronado's** grounds and photo gallery. Take a walk on the beach and continue on to the **Coronado Beach Historical Museum.**

6 Especially for Kids

If you didn't know better you would think that San Diego is a destination designed by parents planning for a long summer vacation. Activities abound for toddlers to teens. Dozens of public parks, 70 miles
of beaches, and myriad museums are just part of what awaits kids of
all ages. For up-to-the-minute information about activities for children,
pick up a free copy of the monthly *San Diego Family Press;* its calendar of events is geared toward family activities and kids' interests. The
International Visitor Information Center, at First Avenue and
F Street (☎ 619/236-1212), is always a great resource. *Frommer's California with Kids,* by Carey Simon and Charlene Marmer Solomon
(Macmillan Travel, 1995), is also quite helpful.

THE TOP ATTRACTIONS

Balboa Park *(see p. 117)* has street entertainers and clowns that always
rate high with kids. They can usually be found around El Prado on
weekends. The **Natural History Museum** and the **Reuben H. Fleet
Theater and Science Center,** with its hands-on exhibits and IMAX/
OMNIMAX theater, draw kids like magnets.

San Diego Zoo *(see p. 112)* is appealing to children of all ages, and the
double-decker bus tours bring all the animals into easy view of even the
smallest, shortest visitors.

Sea World *(see p. 113),* on Mission Bay, entertains everyone with killer
whales, pettable dolphins, and the park's penguin exhibit, home to
more penguins than all other zoos combined. Try out the new
family adventure land "Shamu's Happy Harbor," where everyone is
encouraged to explore, crawl, climb, jump, and get wet in more
than 20 interactive areas; or take a one-way ride on "Mission Bermuda
Triangle."

The **Wild Animal Park** *(see p. 113)* brings geography classes to life
when kids find themselves gliding through the wilds of Africa and Asia
in a monorail.

OTHER ATTRACTIONS

The **Children's Museum of San Diego** *(see p. 124)* is a wonderful
interactive, imagination-probing experience.

Seaport Village *(see p. 185)* has an old fashioned carousel.

Old Town State Historic Park *(see p. 126)* has a one-room schoolhouse that rates high with kids. They also love the haunted Whaley
House, just outside the park.

The **Stephen Birch Aquarium-Museum** *(see p. 129),* in La Jolla, lets
kids explore the realms of the deep and learn about life in the sea.

La Jolla Cove *(see p. 116)* is where kids enjoy splashing in tranquil
waters that are bathtub smooth.

Belmont Park, in Mission Beach, lures kids with bumper cars; a carousel; a games arcade; the Plunge, an enormous indoor swimming pool; and the Giant Dipper, a restored wooden roller coaster with 2,600 feet of tracks.

ENTERTAINMENT

San Diego Junior Theater is located in Balboa Park's Casa del Prado. The theatrical productions here are acted and managed by kids 6 to 18. Sunday afternoon is a great time for kids in Balboa Park, because they can visit the outdoor **Spreckels Organ Pavilion** *(see p. 00)* for a free concert (the mix of music isn't too highbrow for a young audience) and the **House of Pacific Relations** *(see p. 00)* to watch folk dancing on the lawn and experience food from many nations. Or get a taste of Punch and Judy at **Marie Hitchcock Puppet Theatre** (☎ 619/235-1100), in Balboa Park's Palisades Building. Shows run on Fridays at 10:30am and weekends at 11am, 1, and 2:30pm.

7 Special-Interest Sightseeing

FOR THE ARCHITECTURE ENTHUSIAST   Lovers of period houses will enjoy walking through the Victorian **Villa Montezuma** and the Craftsman-style **Marston House Museum** (described earlier in this chapter). The Gaslamp Quarter walking tour (outlined as Walking Tour 2 in Chapter 8) will lead you past the area's **restored Victorian commercial buildings.** Downtown high-rises of particular interest include the **Hyatt Regency San Diego**, the **Emerald-Shapery Center,** at 400 W. Broadway, and **One America Plaza** at 600 W. Broadway. This last building is 498 feet high, which is 24 inches under the maximum height allowed by the FAA. Some people say San Diego's new skyline resembles the contents of a toolbox: a straight screwdriver, a Phillips screwdriver, and a cluster of Allen wrenches. Take a look and see what you think. While you're in the central business district, the 12-by-12-foot scale model of the city at the Center City Development Corporation Downtown Information Center, at 225 Broadway, might be of interest.

Students of architecture will also want to see the Louis Kahn–designed **Salk Institute** and the **classic buildings created by Irving Gill** (see "La Jolla" earlier in this chapter). Every year the local chapter of the AIA gives Orchid and Onion Awards to the best and worst of the city's new and restored buildings. La Jolla's **Wall Street Cafe** and **Brockton Villa** (both described in Chapter 6, "Dining") have received Orchids. The **Hyatt Regency San Diego** was bestowed a Major Raw Onion in 1993—the same year the Salk Institute was lambasted for adding an extension that completely compromised Louis Kahn's design. Not far from the Salk Institute, the Michael Graves–designed **Hyatt Regency La Jolla** has also garnered an Onion. In 1994 my two favorite Orchid Award winners were the ✪ **Jacob Weinberger Courthouse,** on F Street between State and Union streets, and the ✪ **Treehouse restaurant complex at the San Diego Zoo.** For further information, phone the AIA (619/232-0109).

FOR GARDENERS   San Diego is a gardener's paradise, thanks in part to the efforts and inspiration of Kate Sessions. In Balboa Park, visit the **Japanese Friendship Garden,** the **Botanical Building and Lily Pond,** and the **rose and desert gardens** (across the road from Plaza de Balboa). And when you're at the **San Diego Zoo** and **Wild Animal Park,** you'll notice that these are both outstanding botanical gardens. Many visitors, who admire the landscaping at the zoo, don't realize that the plantings have been carefully developed over the years. The 100 acres here were once scrub-covered hillsides with few trees. Today towering eucalyptus and graceful palms, birds-of-paradise, and hibiscus are just a few of the 6,500 botanical species from all over the world that flourish here, providing a beautiful garden setting as well as dinner for some animals. If you'd like to take plants home with you, visit some of the area's nurseries, including the one run by Kate Sessions, **Mission Hills Nursery,** 1525 Fort Stockton Dr., San Diego (☎ 619/ 295-2808), established in 1910; and **Weidners,** 695 Normandy Rd., Leucadia (☎ 619/436-2194). For more information, contact the **San Diego Floral Association** in the Casa del Prado in Balboa Park (☎ 619/232-5762).

FOR MILITARY BUFFS   At the Broadway Pier, near the intersection of Broadway and Harbor Drive, a Navy ship is in port and open for free tours most Saturdays and Sundays from 1 to 4pm (☎ 619/ 532-1430, ext. 9). There is usually a marine corps recruit parade at the Marine Corps Recruit Depot (MCRD) off Pacific Coast Highway on Friday mornings (☎ 619/225-3141); and a Navy recruit review at the Naval Training Center off Rosecrans in Point Loma most Friday afternoons at 1:15, featuring a marching band, drum-and-bugle corps, flag teams, and color guards (☎ 619/225-5311). Old Town Trolley Tours (☎ 619/298-TOUR) is the only company allowed on San Diego military bases. Their passengers view the ships at Naval Station San Diego, ride alongside an aircraft carrier at North Island Naval Air Station, watch F-14s take off from Miramar Naval Air Station, or see recruits undergoing training at MCRD. Military buffs may want to time their visit to include the **NAS Miramar Air Show,** held in late August. This aviation expo features the Blue Angels. For information call 619/537-NAVY.

FOR TRAVELERS INTERESTED IN WINE   Visit **Thomas Jaegar Winery/Orfila Vineyards** (☎ 619/738-6500) near the Wild Animal Park in Escondido. Italian-born wine-maker Leon Santoro is a veteran of the Napa Valley (Louis Martini and Stag's Leap). In addition to producing excellent Chardonnay and Merlot, the winery also makes several Rhone and Italian varietals, including Viognier, Syrah, and Sangiovese. Tours and tastings are offered daily from 10am to 6pm. The property includes a ✪ parklike picnic area and a shop.

If you have time to go farther afield, the wineries along Rancho California Road in Temecula, just across the San Diego County line, are open for tours and tastings. For further details, see Chapter 12.

8 Organized Tours

I'm a firm believer in starting out a visit to a new city—or one I haven't visited in a long time—with a tour. That way, I get an idea of the lay of the land and, most important, a sense about what I'd like to see in depth on my own. In San Diego, I'd start with a bus or trolley tour, complemented by a downtown walking tour or a bay excursion.

ORIENTATION TOURS
BAY EXCURSIONS

Bahia Belle
998 W. Mission Bay Dr. ☎ **619/488-0551.** Operates 7:30pm–12:30am Fri–Sat nights Sept–June except December, Wed–Sun nights July–Labor Day. Tickets $5 adults, $3 children under 12. Children allowed with parent until 9:30pm. After 9:30 must be 21 with valid ID.

Cruise Mission Bay aboard this festive stern-wheeler, which picks up passengers at the dock of the Bahia Hotel on the half-hour from 7:30pm to 12:30am, and at the Catamaran Resort Hotels on the hour from 8pm to midnight.

Hornblower Invader Cruises
1066 N. Harbor Dr. ☎ **619/234-8687.** Tickets $41 for dinner cruise; $30.80 brunch cruise; children are half price.

This company offers daily tours of San Diego Bay on the *Invader*, an antique schooner built in 1905. Nightly dinner cruises with music and dancing are available aboard the 145-foot-long yacht, the *Entertainer*, as well as weekend brunch cruises from 11am to 1pm and, in winter, whale-watching trips.

San Diego Harbor Excursion
1050 N. Harbor Dr. (foot of Broadway). ☎ **619/234-4111** or 800/442-7847. Tickets $12 one-hour excursion; $17 two-hour excursion; half price for children.

The company offers daily one- and two-hour narrated tours of the bay, plus dinner cruises and in winter, whale-watching excursions. Narrators have been with the company for at least five years. Times and frequency vary seasonally.

BUS TOURS

San Diego Mini Tours (☎ 619/477-8687) offers city sightseeing tours, including a "Grand Tour" that includes San Diego, Tijuana, and a one-hour harbor cruise. They also offer trips to the Zoo, Sea World, Disneyland, Universal Studios, Tijuana, Rosarito Beach, and Ensenada. Prices range from $26 to $62 for adults, $14 to $44 for children under 12, and include admissions. Multiple tours can be combined for discounts.

Gray Line Tours (☎ 619/491-0011) offers city sightseeing, including Cabrillo National Monument and La Jolla, along with trips that take you farther afield to Sea World, Wild Animal Park, wine country, and Tijuana and Ensenada, Mexico. Prices range from $24 to $50 for adults and $10 to $33 for children.

Centre City Development Corporation's Downtown Informa-tion Center (☎ 619/235-2222) offers free trolley tours of the down-town area on the first and third Saturdays of the month from 10am to noon. Downtown residential walking tours for five or more people are offered from 1pm to 3pm. The tours require reservations and start at 225 Broadway, Suite 160. Go inside to see models of the Gaslamp Quarter and the downtown area. The office is open Monday through Saturday from 9am to 5pm.

TROLLEY TOURS

In San Diego, it's a good idea to invest an hour and a half in a narrated ✪ **Old Town Trolley** tour (☎ 619/298-TOUR). The 30-mile route has more than a dozen stops, and you can get off at any of them, explore at leisure, and reboard when you please (a bus-cum-trolley passes each stop every half hour). Stops include the Embarcadero, downtown area, Horton Plaza, Gaslamp Quarter, Coronado, San Diego Zoo, Balboa Park, Heritage Park, and Presidio Park (Cabrillo National Monument is not included). The tour costs $16 for adults, $7 for children 6 to 12, free for children under 5, for one complete loop, no matter how many times you hop on or off the trolley. One entire tour is 90 minutes long. It's a good idea to start early in the day. Old Town Trolley Tours offers military base tours Monday through Friday from 9am to noon on a reservation-only basis. These bases are open for tours: the Marine Corps Recruit Depot, the Naval Air Station Miramar, the Naval Air Station North Island, and the Naval Submarine Base and Naval Station San Diego. Tour participants will see giant aircraft carriers, nuclear-powered submarines, surface warfare ships, and navy fighter aircraft.

SPECIALTY TOURS
WHALE WATCHING

It's fun to be in San Diego from December through March when the California gray whales migrate to the warmer waters of Baja California to mate. Many local tour operators provide special excur-sions this time of year to help you catch a glimpse of the mighty ani-mals; two are **Invader Cruises** and **San Diego Harbor Excursion** (see "Bay Excursions," above). The **Stephen Birch Aquarium-Museum** (☎ 619/534-FISH) offers expeditions out of Mission Bay, with a naturalist on board to talk with passengers and answer questions.

WALKING TOURS

Established in 1977, **Walkabout International** (☎ 619/231-7463) sponsors 150 free walking tours every month, led by volunteers in the San Diego area. A lively guide known as Downtown Sam, who retired from the Air Force in 1972, leads downtown tours, which are par-ticularly popular with retired San Diegans eager for exercise and cama-raderie. He's easy to spot, in walking shorts and a cap with a button proclaiming "No thanks, I'd rather walk." Sam's Saturday morning tours draw 20 to 40 people, and they end with a stop for coffee or a meal. Sam also leads a $1^1/_2$-hour downtown theme tour at 11am on

Tuesday, focusing on bookstores, shopping, pubs, thrift shops, bank lobbies—you name it.

On Saturday from 1 to 3pm, the **Centre City Development Corporation (CCDC),** 225 Broadway, Suite 160 (☎ 619/235-2222), offers free walking tours that focus on downtown area development. Reservations are required.

Coronado Touring (☎ 619/435-5993 or 619/435-5444) provides upbeat, informative 90-minute walking tours of Coronado, including the Hotel del Coronado. Enthusiastic guides Nancy Cobb and Gerry MacCartee have been doing this since 1980, so they know their subject well. Tours leave at 11am on Tuesday, Thursday, and Saturday from the Glorietta Bay Inn. The price is $5.

At the **Cabrillo National Monument** on the tip of Point Loma, rangers often lead free walking tours (see "Other Top Attractions" earlier in this chapter). The **Gaslamp Quarter Association** offers tours of the Gaslamp Quarter on Saturday at 11am for a $5 donation. Tours leave from William Heath Davis House at 410 Island Ave. (☎ 619/233-5227).

You can peruse **La Jolla** on walking and/or shopping tours led by local tour guide Ann Wilson Jones (☎ 619/453-8219). Volunteers from the **Natural History Museum** (☎ 619/232-3821, ext. 203) lead nature walks throughout San Diego County.

9 Outdoor Activities

BALLOONING

For a balloon's-eye glimpse of the area at sunrise or sunset, followed by champagne and hors d'oeuvres, contact **A Skysurfer Balloon Company** (☎ 619/481-6800), **Pacific Horizon Balloon Tours** (☎ 800/244-1790), or—my favorite—✪ **California Dreamin** (☎ 800/748-5959). The balloon rides provide sweeping vistas of the Southern California coast, rambling estates, and golf courses. You may also be interested in the **Temecula Balloon and Wine Festival** held in late April. Call 909/676-4713 for information.

BIKING

The Mission Bay and Coronado areas, in particular, are good for leisurely bike rides. The boardwalk in Pacific Beach and Mission Beach can get very crowded, especially on weekends. Most major thoroughfares offer a bike lane. Just remember to wear a helmet; it's the law. For information on bike rentals, see "Getting Around" in Chapter 4.

For a downhill thrill of a lifetime, take the **Palomar Plunge.** From the top of Palomar Mountain to its base, you'll experience, courtesy of gravity, a 5,000-foot vertical drop stretched out over 16 miles. Or try the **Desert Descent,** a 12-mile, 3,700-foot descent down the Montezuma Valley Grade to the desert floor, followed by a tour of the Visitor Center and a delicious lunch. **Gravity Activated Sports** (☎ 619/742-2294 or 800/985-4427) supplies the mountain bike, helmet, gloves, souvenir photo, and T-shirt.

Outdoor Activities in the San Diego Area

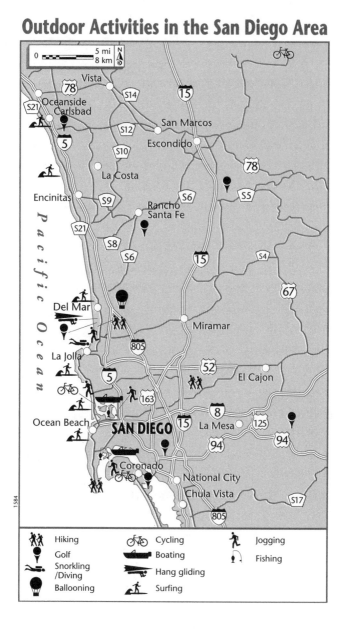

Adventurous cyclists might also like to participate in the **Rosarito-Ensenada 50 Mile Fun Bicycle Ride,** held every April and September. This event attracts over 8,000 riders of all ages and abilities. It starts at the Rosarito Beach Hotel and finishes in Ensenada. For information call Bicycling West (☎ 619/583-3001).

BOATING

Club Nautico, a concession at the San Diego Marriott Marina, 333 W. Harbor Dr. (☎ 619/233-9311), provides guests and nonguests an exhilarating way to see the bay by the hour, half day, or full day in 20- to 27-foot offshore power boats. Rentals start at $89 per hour. They allow their boats to be taken into the ocean and also provide diving, waterskiing, and fishing packages.

Seaforth Boat Rental, 1641 Quivira Rd., Mission Bay (☎ 619/223-1681), has a wide variety of fishing boats for bay and ocean, 15hp to 90hp powerboats for $40 to $80 per hour, and 14- to 27-foot sailboats for $20 to $45 per hour; with half-day and full-day rates. Canoes, pedal boats, and rowboats are available for those who prefer a slower pace. **Mission Bay Sportcenter,** 1010 Santa Clara Place (☎ 619/488-1004), rents sailboats, catamarans, sailboards, kayaks, jet skis, and motorboats, with prices starting at $10 per hour, $30 for 4 hours, and $40 for a full day. Instruction is available.

Coronado Boat Rental (owned by the Seaforth folks), 1715 Strand Way, in Coronado (☎ 619/437-1514), has powerboats with 90hp and 110hp motors renting from $60 to $90 per hour, with half- and full-day rates; 14- to 27-foot sailboats from $30 to $45 per hour; and jet skis, ski boats, canoes, pedal boats, fishing skiffs, and charter boats.

Sail USA, P.O. Box 6431, San Diego 92166-0431, (☎ 619/298-6822), offers custom-tailored skippered cruises on a 34-foot Catalina sloop. A half-day bay cruise costs $295 for six passengers. Full-day and overnight trips are also available, as are trips up the coast and to Catalina.

FISHING

Public fishing piers are at Shelter Island (where there's a statue dedicated to anglers), Ocean Beach, and Imperial Beach. Anglers of any age can fish free of charge without a license off any municipal pier in California. Fishing charters depart from Harbor and Shelter islands, Point Loma, the Imperial Beach pier, and Quivira Basin in Mission Bay (near the Hyatt Islandia Hotel). Participants in these trips over the age of 16 need a California fishing license.

For **sportfishing,** you can go out on a large boat for about $25 for half a day or $35 to $85 for three-quarters to a full day. To charter a boat for up to six people, the rates run about $550 for half a day and $850 for an entire day, more in summer. Call around and compare prices. Summer and fall are excellent times for excursions. Locally, the waters around Point Loma are filled with bass, bonita, and barracuda; the Coronado Islands, which belong to Mexico but are only about 18 miles from San Diego, are popular for abalone, yellowtail, yellow fin, and big-eyed tuna. Some outfitters will take you farther into Baja California waters.

The following outfitters offer short or extended outings with daily departures: **H&M Landing** (☎ 619/222-1144), **Islandia Sportfishing** (☎ 619/222-1164), **Lee Palm Sportfishers** (☎ 619/224-3857), **Point Loma Sportfishing** (☎ 619/223-1627), and **Seaforth Boat Rentals** (☎ 619/233-1681).

For **freshwater fishing,** San Diego's lakes and rivers provide catches of bass, channel and bullhead catfish, bluegill, trout, crappie, and sunfish. Most lakes have rental facilities for boats, tackle, and bait, and they also provide picnic and (usually) camping areas.

Lake Cuyamaca, 45 minutes from San Diego near Julian, is 5,000 feet above sea level, set in the midst of pines and cedars, and filled with trout year-round. It's open daily from sunrise to sunset; there are motorboat and rowboat rentals and a small charge for fishing (☎ 619/447-8123).

For more information on fishing in California, contact the **California Department of Fish and Game** (☎ 619/467-4201). For fishing in Mexican waters, including off the Coronado Islands, angling permits are required. Contact the **Mexican Department of Fisheries,** 2550 Fifth Ave., Suite 101, San Diego, CA 92103-6622 (☎ 619/233-6956).

GOLF

With nearly 80 courses, 50 of them open to the public, San Diego County, home of pro golfers Billy Casper and Craig Stadler, has much to offer the golf enthusiast. Courses are diverse, some with vistas of the Pacific, others with views of country hillsides or of desert. **M&M Tee Times** (☎ 619/456-8366) can arrange tee times for you at most golf courses. **Greenlink** (☎ 619/I-LOVE-GOLF [456-8346]) is also a valuable source of information about golf courses, schools, and equipment.

And where else but San Diego can you practice your golf swing in the middle of the central business district? The **Harborside Golf Center,** on Broadway at Pacific Highway (☎619/239-GOLF), is open from 6am to 10pm daily. Here you will find 80 tees, 40 with automatic pop-up; a USGA putting and chipping area; night lighting; a pro shop; golf school; and golf simulators. Club rental is available at $1 each; a large bucket of balls costs $6; a small bucket, $3.

Aviara Golf Club

7447 Batiquitos Drive, Carlsbad. ☎ **619/929-0077.**

Opened in July 1991, this spot has a reputation as one of the area's most memorable courses. The 18 holes (each with 4 tees) spread out over 500 acres overlooking the Pacific Ocean and the Batiquitos Lagoon, California's largest lagoon and home to more than 130 species of birds. The 7,007-yard, par-72 course is open to the public, and greens fees ($95 Monday through Thursday; $115 Friday through Sunday; $70 after 3pm) include golf cart and the use of the clubhouse, which has lockers, saunas, and showers. The Argyle restaurant and lounge is on the premises.

Coronado Municipal Golf Course

2000 Visalia Row, Coronado. ☎ **619/435-3121.**

This is the first sight that welcomes you as you cross the Coronado Bay Bridge (the course is off to the left). The 18-hole, par-72 course overlooks Glorietta Bay, and there's a coffee shop, pro shop, and driving range. Two-day prior reservations are strongly recommended; call anytime after 7am. Greens fees are $20 for 18 holes.

Morgan Run

5690 Cancha de Golf, Rancho Santa Fe. ☎ **619/756-3255.**

Formerly Whispering Palms, these three nine-hole courses (one par 35; two par 36) are part of a resort, but you don't have to stay there to play. Course architect Jay Morrish redesigned one of the courses in 1995. There's also a driving range. Greens fees are $50 during the week and $60 on weekends, including a cart.

Mt. Woodson Country Club

16422 North Woodson Drive, Ramona. ☎ **619/788-3555.**

One of San Diego County's dramatic golf courses, Mt. Woodson is a par-70, 6,180-yard course on 150 beautiful acres. The award-winning 18-hole course, which opened in 1991, meanders up and down hills, across bridges, and around granite boulders. Elevated tees provide striking views of Ramona and Mount Palomar, and on a clear day you can see for almost 100 miles. It's easy to combine a game of golf with a weekend getaway to Julian (see Chapter 11). Greens fees here for 18 holes are $42 Monday through Thursday, $50 Friday, and $58 on Saturday and Sunday. Lower twilight rates are also available. Mt. Woodson is about 40 minutes north of San Diego. To get there, exit I-5 at Poway Road; at the end of Poway Road turn left (north) onto Route 67 and drive 3³/₄ miles to Archie Moore Road; turn left. The golf course entrance is on the left.

Rancho Bernardo Inn

17550 Bernardo Oaks Dr., Rancho Bernardo. ☎ **619/487-1611** or 800/542-6096.

Home to Ken Blanchard's Golf University of San Diego since 1992, Rancho Bernardo's attributes include a mature 18-hole, 72-par championship course with terrains, water hazards, sand traps, lakes, and waterfalls; and three 9-hole, 30-par executive courses. Lessons or 1-hour clinics with a pro, 2- to 4-day schools through the Golf University with meals and lodging included, and a standard golf package are available. Greens fees are $58 during the week and $75 Friday through Sunday, including a cart.

Singing Hills

3007 Dehesa Rd., El Cajon. ☎ **619/442-3425** or 800/457-5568.

The only resort in Southern California offering 54 holes of golf (two championship courses and a par-54 executive course), Singing Hills has taken advantage of the area's natural terrain, using mountains, natural rock outcroppings, and aged oaks and sycamores to add character to individual holes. The golf courses are part of the Singing Hills Country Club, a lovely resort, but nonstaying guests can play. Greens fees are $29 during the week and $35 on weekends for the two par-72 courses and $12 on the shorter course. Cart rental costs an additional $20. The resort offers a variety of good-value packages.

Temecula Creek Inn

44501 Rainbow Canyon Rd., Temecula. ☎ **800/96-CREEK.**

The resort is one hour north of San Diego in a country setting. The 27-hole, 10,014-yard championship golf course is a par 36 per nine holes and features rolling hills and fairways lined with 100-year-old live oaks. Pheasants and bobcats put in occasional appearances. The stone house on one of the nines is one of Temecula's oldest buildings (see Chapter 11). Lessons and golf package available. Greens fees for 18 holes are $44 Monday through Thursday, $50 on Friday, and $60 on Saturday and Sunday, including a cart.

✪ Torrey Pines Golf Course

11480 Torrey Pines Rd., La Jolla. ☎ **619/552-1784** for information; 619/570-1234 to book a tee time.

Two gorgeous 18-hole championship courses are located on the coast between La Jolla and Del Mar, only 15 minutes from downtown San Diego. Home of the Buick Invitational Tournament, these municipal courses are very popular. Both overlook the ocean; the north course is more picturesque, the south course more challenging. Tee times are taken by computer starting at 5am up to seven days in advance by telephone only. Confirmation numbers are issued, and you must have the number and photo identification with you when you check in with the starter 15 minutes ahead of time. If you're late, your time may be forfeited. Golf professionals are available for lessons, and the pro shop rents clubs, if you left yours at home. Greens fees for out-of-towners are $42 during the week and $49.50 Saturday and Sunday for 18 holes; $21 for nine holes.

HANG GLIDING

If you have a U.S. Hang Gliding Association rating card to prove your proficiency, you can soar above the cliffs and coast at Torrey Pines State Reserve, about 4 miles north of La Jolla. For information about lessons or gear, contact the **Hang Gliding Center** (☎ 619/450-9008).

HIKING

The **Sierra Club** sponsors regular hikes in the San Diego area, and nonmembers are welcome to participate. There's always a Wednesday mountain hike, usually in the Cuyamaca Mountains, though sometimes in the Lagunas; there are evening and day hikes as well. Most are free. For a recorded message of upcoming hikes, call 619/299-1744, or call the office Monday through Friday from noon to 5pm and on Saturday from 10am to 4pm (☎ 619/299-1743).

  Torrey Pines State Reserve in La Jolla (☎ 619/755-2063) offers hiking trails with wonderful ocean views and a chance to see the rare torrey pine. Access is via N. Torrey Pines Road. The trails are free of charge, parking costs $4 per car, $3 for seniors. The Bayside Trail near **Cabrillo National Monument** is also popular because hikers can stop and look in the tide pools. Drive to the monument and follow signs to trail. ✪ **Mission Trails Regional Park,** 8 miles northeast of downtown, offers a glimpse of what San Diego looked like before development. Located between Highway 52 and I-8 and east of I-15, rugged hills, valleys, and open areas provide a quick escape from urban hustle-bustle. A visitor and interpretive center (☎ 619/668-3275) is open daily from 9am to 5pm. Access is via Mission Gorge Road.

HORSEBACK RIDING

Hosts Earl and Liz Hammond at ✪ **Holidays on Horseback,** located 40 miles east of San Diego in Descanso, offer half- and full-day outings, as well as overnight camping trips, through Cuyamaca Rancho State Park. Riders pass through beautiful scenery that includes native chaparral, live oak, and manzanita. The Hammonds have 14 horses, almost all Missouri fox trotters. A 4-hour ride with a picnic lunch on the trail costs $55. If you're interested, write to P.O. Box 474, Descanso, CA 91916 (☎ 619/445-3997).

JOGGING/RUNNING

One of my favorite places to jog is the sidewalk that follows the east side of **Mission Bay**. Start at the Visitor Information Center and head south past the Hilton to Fiesta Island. A good spot for a short run is **La Jolla Shores Beach,** because there's hard-pack sand to run on even when it isn't low tide. The beach at **Coronado** is also a good place for jogging, as is the shore at **Pacific Beach** and **Mission Beach**—just watch your tide chart to make sure you won't be there at high tide. If you'd like to watch others run, see "Marathons" below.

You shouldn't run after dark or run in secluded areas of Balboa Park even in broad daylight. It's also not a good idea to leave valuables in your car while you're out for a jog.

RACQUETBALL

Aficionados may play for free in San Diego at San Diego City College, 1313 Twelfth Ave. (☎ 619/230-2486), Monday through Friday from 1 to 5pm, Saturday noon to 6pm, and Sunday 9am to 6pm.

SKATING—IN-LINE OR ICE

Gliding around San Diego, especially the Mission Bay area, on in-line skates is as much a Southern California experience as sailing or surfing. In Mission Beach, rent a pair of regular or in-line skates from **Skates Plus,** 3830 Mission Blvd. (☎ 619/488-PLUS), or **Hamel's Action Sports Center,** 704 Ventura Place, off Mission Boulevard at the roller coaster (☎ 619/488-5050); and in Pacific Beach, at **Pacific Beach Sun and Sea,** 4539 Ocean Blvd. (☎ 619/483-6613). In Coronado, go to **Mike's Bikes,** at 1343 Orange Ave. (☎ 619/435-7744); or **Bikes and Beyond,** 1201 First St. and at the Ferry Landing (☎ 619/435-7180). Be sure to ask for protective gear.

If you'd rather ice skate, try the **Ice Capades Chalet** at University Towne Center, La Jolla Village Drive at Genesee Street (☎ 619/452-9110).

SCUBA DIVING & SNORKELING

The **San Diego–La Jolla Underwater Park,** especially the La Jolla Cove, is the best spot for scuba and snorkeling. For more information see "San Diego's Beaches" earlier in this chapter. The **Underwater Pumpkin Carving Contest,** held at Halloween, is a fun local event. For information phone 619/565-6054.

SPAS

San Diego County hosts some of the best spas in the country. For details see "Select Spas" in Chapter 11.

SWIMMING

San Diego's resort hotels and the Pan Pacific and Embassy Suites downtown have pools, as does the **YMCA,** located at 500 W. Broadway, between Columbia and India streets (☎ 619/232-7451). The charge for use of the Y's pool and other health facilities, including a sauna, Jacuzzi, free weights, aerobics classes, and a gym with running track, is $10 a day, $7 for ages 18 to 22, free for members of a Y outside San Diego County; it's open Monday through Friday from 6am to 9pm and on Saturday from 8am to 5pm (towels are supplied but bathing suits and locks are not). In Mission Bay, you'll find a famous and well-maintained pool called **The Plunge,** part of **Belmont Park** since 1925. Pool capacity is 525 and there are 10 lap lanes and a viewing area inside. It's open Monday through Friday from 6am to 8am, noon to 1pm, and 3:30 to 8pm and Saturday and Sunday from 8am to 4pm. Admission is $2.50 for adults and $2.00 for children.

Swimmers may want to compete in one of the rough water swims held in the area. These include the **Oceanside Rough Water Swim** (☎ 619/966-4530) and the **La Jolla Rough Water Swim** (☎ 619/456-2100).

TENNIS

There are 1,200 public and private tennis courts in San Diego. Public courts are located throughout the city, including the **La Jolla Recreation Center** and **Morley Field** in Balboa Park. **River Valley Sports Center,** at 2440 Hotel Circle N. (☎ 619/297-3391), has six lighted courts, which may be rented for $5 per court per hour for singles, $8 for doubles. It's only a few minutes from Old Town. Many resort hotels, including the ones listed below, offer tennis courts to their guests and others.

Hilton Beach & Tennis Resort

1775 E. Mission Bay Dr. ☎ **619/276-4010.**

There are five lighted courts and a practice half-court with a ball machine; tennis packages are available. Only the half-court and ball machine are available to nonguests.

La Costa Resort and Spa

Costa del Mar Road, Carlsbad. ☎ **619/438-9111.**

The 23 courts here provide play on three different surfaces: two Wimbledon-quality grass courts, four clay courts, and 15 hard courts. Eight courts are lighted for evening play, and six professional practice lanes are available. The courts are available to spa guests and members only; professional coaching and video assessment are available.

Rancho Bernardo Inn

17550 Bernardo Oaks Dr., Rancho Bernardo. ☎ **619/487-1611** or 800/542-6096.

Combine a visit to San Diego with some work on your backhand by enrolling in the Rancho Bernardo Tennis College, which has improved more than 35,000 games since 1971 and is open to nonhotel guests. Programs include a Tennis Holiday package with a two-night minimum and daily court time but no instruction, a two-day Stroke and Strategy package for all levels, a two-day Drill and Play package for experienced players, a comprehensive five-day "Set" program, and a two-day doubles clinic. Rancho Bernardo has 12 courts, four lighted for night play.

Sheraton Harbor Island
1380 Harbor Island Dr. ☎ **619/291-2900.**

Right across the street from the airport, the hotel has four lit tennis courts where nonguests are welcome. There's a pro shop.

10 Spectator Sports

AUTO RACING

The **Score Baja 500,** held in June, is an annual off-road car, motorcycle, and truck loop race that starts and ends in Ensenada. The **Score Baja 1,000** is held in November. For information call 818/583-8068.

BASEBALL

The National League **San Diego Padres** play April through September at San Diego Jack Murphy Stadium, 9449 Friars Rd., in Mission Valley (☎ 619/283-4494 for schedules and information; 619/29-PADRES for tickets). The Padres Express bus costs $5 round trip and picks up fans at several locations throughout the city, beginning two hours before the game (☎ 619/233-3004 for bus information). The bus operates only for home games on Friday, Saturday, and Sunday. Tickets are readily available.

BOATING

San Diego has probably hosted the America's Cup for the last time, but several other boating events of interest are held here. These include the **America's Schooner Cup,** held every March or April (☎ 619/223-3138), and the **Annual San Diego Crew Classic,** held on Mission Bay every April (☎ 619/488-0700). The Crew Classic rowing competition draws teams from throughout the United States and Canada. The **Wooden Boat Festival** is held on Shelter Island every May (☎ 619/574-8020). Approximately 90 boats participate in the festival, which features nautical displays, food, music, and crafts.

FISHING

Fishing enthusiasts will want to attend the **Day at the Docks** event held at the San Diego Sportfishing Landing, Harbor Drive and Scott Street, in Point Loma, every April. For information call 619/294-7912.

FOOTBALL

San Diego's professional football team, the **San Diego Chargers,** played in the 1995 Super Bowl, losing to the San Francisco 49ers. And in 1998, San Diego will host the Super Bowl. The Chargers play their home games at San Diego Jack Murphy Stadium, 9449 Friars Rd., Mission Valley (☎ 619/280-2121). The season runs from August through December. The Chargers Express bus costs $5 round trip and picks up passengers at several locations throughout the city, beginning 2 hours before the game (☎ 619/233-3004 for bus information). The bus operates for all home games.

San Diego hosts the collegiate **Holiday Bowl** every December. This event, held at San Diego Jack Murphy Stadium, pits the Western Athletic Conference Champion against a team from the Big 10. For information call 619/283-5808.

GOLF

San Diego hosts some of the country's most important golf tournaments, including the **Mercedes Championships,** held at La Costa Resort in Carlsbad in early January (tel 800/918-4653 for tickets; 619/438-9111 ext. 4612 for information). Another popular event is the **Buick Invitational of California,** held every February at Torrey Pines Golf Course in La Jolla (☎ 619/281-4653 or 800/888-BUICK). The **HGH Pro-Am Golf Classic** is held at Singing Hills Golf and Country Club every September (☎ 619/448-3700).

GREYHOUND RACING

At the Caliente Racetrack, Boulevard Agua Caliente, Tijuana, Mexico (☎ 619/231-1910 in San Diego, 81-78-11 in Tijuana), racing takes place Wednesday through Monday at 7:45pm; there's also Monday and Friday matinees at 2pm. Admission is free, and minimum bets are $2.

HORSE RACING

Live thoroughbred racing takes place at the **Del Mar Racetrack** from late July through mid-September every year. Post time is 2pm for the nine-race program; there is no racing on Tuesdays. Last season there was a 4pm post time on Friday, which may continue. Seating is in the members-only Turf Club, the Clubhouse ($6), or the Grandstand ($3). For information call 619/755-1141; the ticket office number is 619/792-4242. Bing Crosby and Pat O'Brien founded the track in 1937, and it has been frequented by stars such as Lucille Ball and Desi Arnaz, Dorothy Lamour, Red Skelton, Paulette Goddard, Jimmy Durante, and Ava Gardner. Del Mar's 1993 season marked the opening of a new $80-million grandstand, built in the Spanish mission style of the original structure. The new grandstand features more seats, better race viewing, and a centrally located scenic paddock. (See also Chapter 11.)

HORSE SHOWS

The **Del Mar National Horse Show** takes place at the Del Mar Fair Grounds from late April to mid-May. Olympic-caliber and national championship riders participate. For information call 619/792-4288 or 619/755-1161.

ICE HOCKEY

The **San Diego Gulls** ice hockey team of the International Hockey League skate their games at the San Diego Sports Arena. For schedules, tickets, and information call 619/688-1800.

JAI ALAI

Experience the excitement of this fast-action game at the **Jai Alai Palace,** Calle 7 and Revolución (☎ 619/260-0454 in San Diego, 85-36-87 in Tijuana), in the heart of downtown Tijuana. Admission ranges from $3 to $5. Doors open Friday through Wednesday at 7pm, play starts at 8pm. It's closed 2 weeks during the Christmas/New Year period.

MARATHONS/TRIATHLONS

San Diego is a wonderful place to run or watch a marathon because the weather is usually mild. The **San Diego Marathon** takes place in January; it actually starts in Carlsbad, 35 miles north of San Diego, and stretches mostly along the coastline. For more information, contact the San Diego Track Club (☎ 619/452-7382) or In Motion (☎ 619/792-2900). Another popular event is the **La Jolla Half Marathon,** held every April. It begins at the Del Mar Fair Grounds and finishes at the La Jolla Cove. For information call 619/454-1262. The **America's Finest City Half Marathon** is held in August every year. The race begins at Cabrillo National Monument, winds through downtown, and ends in Balboa Park. For information call 619/297-3901.

The **San Diego International Triathlon** includes a 1,000-meter swim, 30-kilometer bike ride, and 10K run. It starts at Spanish Landing on Harbor Island. For information call 619/627-9111 or 619/687-1000.

POLO

The public is invited to watch polo matches on Sundays from June through October at the Rancho Santa Fe Polo Club, 14555 El Camino Real, Rancho Santa Fe (☎ 619/481-9217). Admission is $5.

RODEOS

Not downtown, but in the outlying areas of the county you can watch bull riding, bronco busting, and calf roping several times a year. In April there's **Lakeside Western Days,** which features seven major rodeo events as well as food and entertainment. For information call 619/561-1031 or 619/561-4331. The **Ramona Rodeo,** held in May, is one of the country's top 50 rodeos. For information call 619/789-1311. The **KSON Country Fest Rodeo,** held in Lakeside every June, features bands, music and a full scale rodeo. For information call 619/561-6070.

SANDCASTLE COMPETITIONS

For sandcastle enthusiasts there is the two-day **Annual U.S. Open Sandcastle Competition** at the pier in Imperial Beach in July. Saturday there is a parade and children's castle contest at 2pm, Sunday is the main event. For information call 619/424-6663. A similar event is held in October: the ✪ **Ocean Beach Sandcastle Event and Family Fun Carnival.** For information call 619/222-2683.

SOCCER

The **San Diego Sockers,** 10-time champions of the Major Indoor Soccer League, have joined the new Continental Indoor Soccer League. They play from June through October at the San Diego Sports Arena, 3500 Sports Arena Blvd. (☎ 619/224-GOAL). Admission costs from $5 to $12.50.

SOFTBALL

The highlight of many San Diegans' summer is the World Championship Over-the-Line Tournament, held on Fiesta Island in Mission Bay on the second and third weekends of July. For more information see the "San Diego Calendar of Events" in Chapter 2.

TENNIS

San Diego hosts some major tennis tournaments, including the **Toshiba Tennis Classic,** held at the La Costa Resort and Spa in Carlsbad. In 1996, this professional women's tennis tournament is being held August 19 to 25. For tickets call 619/438-LOVE; for information 619/436-3551.

8

City Strolls

San Diego lends itself to strolling, and the following five walking tours will give you a sense of the city as well as a look at some of its most appealing sights and structures. There is no better way to get to know a place than by walking. Wandering a city's streets and parks gives you insights that are hard to come by any other way—and the exercise can't be beat, especially under the warm (but usually not unbearably hot) Southern California sun.

WALKING TOUR 1
Downtown

Start: First Avenue and F Street.
Finish: Horton Plaza, at Broadway and Fourth Avenue.
Time: Allow approximately 2 hours, not including shopping or dining.
Best Times: Mornings or afternoons during the week.
Worst Times: Lunch hour on weekdays, when the streets are filled with office workers on break, and weekends, when office buildings and some stores are closed.

Downtown San Diego is an exhilarating place, with an ever-changing skyline, interesting architecture, and generous use of public sculpture. Since the mid-1980s, the city core has experienced a resurgence and growth; this positive energy is readily apparent.

Start at the:

1. **International Visitor Information Center,** on First Avenue at F Street. You won't find "Information Anderson" here (Adolph H. Anderson manned the information booth at the original Horton Plaza from 1915 to 1948 and answered an estimated 22 million questions on all aspects of San Diego), but you will find friendly staff to answer your questions. You can also stock up on maps and brochures before starting out on your walk. From here, follow F Street to Union Street. In front of you to the left on F Street is the:

2. **Jacob Weinberger Courthouse.** This historic building was the city's first post office and now serves as the bankruptcy court. Across F Street is a single tall brown building. This is the:

3. **Metropolitan Corrections Center,** which has played host to Timothy Leary and Patty Hearst, among others. A holding facility only, it has phones on each floor and a volleyball court for detainees. The guards here don't carry guns.

Go north on Front Street and walk a half block. The large red building is the:

4. **Federal Building,** which houses FBI offices on the top floor and INS on the ground floor. Outside is a black pyramidlike sculpture called:

5. *Ex-caliber.* Internationally known sculptor Beverly Pepper built this 32-by-40-by-60-foot structure in 1976. From one vantage point some say it reminds them of a sleek seal with its nose in the air. The fence was put around it to discourage daredevil skateboarders.

☕ **TAKE A BREAK**   The **cafeteria** on the Federal Building's second floor—little known to visitors or many San Diegans—is popular with judges and juries. It's open for breakfast and lunch. Enter through the door beside the sculpture and take the escalator up to it.

Walk up Front Street and through the small landscaped plaza with the kinetic sculpture called:

6. *Light, Water, and Rock* by Charles Ross.

The plaza fronts the modern:

7. **Wells Fargo Bank Building,** with an entrance at Broadway and First Avenue. Inside the lobby stands a bright-red 1868 Concord stagecoach, an engineering marvel of its day that Mark Twain praised as "a cradle on wheels." Six horses pulled the Concord coaches that carried nine passengers and eagerly awaited mail. In 1852, Henry Wells and William Fargo founded the Wells Fargo Company in San Francisco. Wells, an advocate for women's education, also founded Wells College for women in Aurora, New York, in 1868; Fargo, who had been a mail carrier on horseback at the age of 13, was mayor of Buffalo, New York, during the Civil War, and the city of Fargo, North Dakota, was named for him.

Continue on Broadway toward Second Avenue, where on your right you will see the:

8. **Spreckels Building,** which dates from 1912 and houses the neo-baroque Spreckels Theater. When built, it was thought to be California's largest reinforced concrete building. The large exits on either side of the stage made it easy to use live horses in productions. Al Jolson and Will Rogers played here when the theater was a vaudeville house. When John Barrymore performed here, he supposedly retired to the bar around the corner (now Dobson's) for a quick one between acts. If the theater is open, go inside and admire the marble lobby; the guard may let you look in the auditorium.

Turn left on Second Avenue. You'll pass the:

9. **Westgate Hotel** on your right, a member of Leading Hotels of the World. If you venture into the lobby, you'll feel you've suddenly stepped into a hall at the palace at Versailles. Afternoon tea is served here Monday through Saturday. Continue on Second Avenue to C Street; this intersection is a:

10. **Trolley stop.** In 1981 when the bright-red San Diego Trolley was unveiled, many San Diegans felt this "modern" mode of transportation was an answer to the mounting challenges of parking, pollution, and traffic. Most didn't realize that San Diego had an electric streetcar system from 1892 to 1949 that was retired due to the popularity of the automobile. In fact, the trolley follows many of the old streetcar routes.

Cross C Street and go through the glass doors of the:

11. **City Administration Building** at 202 C St. City offices mainly fill this tall crenellated building; the San Diego Opera administrative offices are also housed here.

Proceed through the concourse; on your right will be the curving facade of the:

12. **Civic Center.** Straight ahead (follow the splashing sounds) is a public sculpture called:

13. *The Bow Waves,* by Malcolm Leland, resembling the prow of a ship cutting its way through the sea.

From here, go east to B Street and walk along the street's right side. At B Street between Fourth and Fifth avenues, on your right, is the:

14. **First Interstate Plaza.** The male and female figures atop the fountain appear to be discussing the events of the day; the work, by Sergio Benvenuti, is called:

15. *The Fountain of Two Oceans.* Proceed to:

16. **The corner of Sixth Avenue and B Street;** from here if you turn and look northeast to the corner of Seventh Avenue and Ash Street, you can see the **El Cortez Center,** once a fine downtown hotel. When the El Cortez Hotel opened in 1956, it was featured in *Time, Life,* and *Business Week* because it had the world's first outside glass hydraulic elevator. As many as 16 passengers could ride up to the 15th floor and get a panoramic view of the city. In 1978 Rev. Morris Cerullo bought the hotel, and it was used as an international ministry school until 1981. Today a white elephant, the building's fate remains undecided.

Cross Sixth Avenue and look to the north; the white building with blue trim and awnings is the:

17. **World Trade Center San Diego,** donated to the city by Harcourt Brace and Company in 1993. For many years, the 13-story building served as headquarters for the publishing company Harcourt Brace and Jovanovich; now it houses city offices and trade-related businesses.

Walking Tour—Downtown

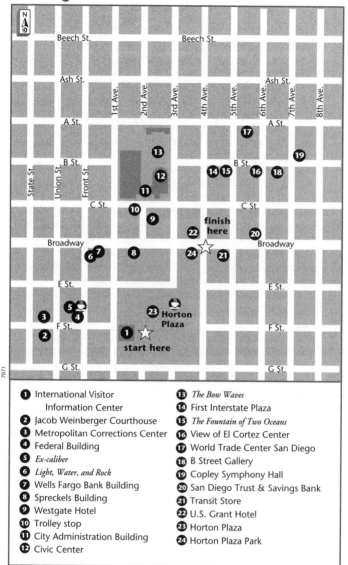

Map legend:

1. International Visitor Information Center
2. Jacob Weinberger Courthouse
3. Metropolitan Corrections Center
4. Federal Building
5. *Ex-caliber*
6. *Light, Water, and Rock*
7. Wells Fargo Bank Building
8. Spreckels Building
9. Westgate Hotel
10. Trolley stop
11. City Administration Building
12. Civic Center
13. *The Bow Waves*
14. First Interstate Plaza
15. *The Fountain of Two Oceans*
16. View of El Cortez Center
17. World Trade Center San Diego
18. B Street Gallery
19. Copley Symphony Hall
20. San Diego Trust & Savings Bank
21. Transit Store
22. U.S. Grant Hotel
23. Horton Plaza
24. Horton Plaza Park

Continue down B Street. At 641 B St., just before you reach Seventh Avenue, is the:

18. B Street Gallery, which exhibits the work of many local artists. The contemporary gallery has focused on abstract impressionism since 1989. The works are mainly originals, with some lithographs and serigraphs.

Across the street, the San Diego Symphony performs at:

19. Copley Symphony Hall. Once known as the Fox Theatre, this lavish Rococo-style theater opened November 8, 1929, and was the third-largest theater in the West. Originally designed for vaudeville and movies, the theater still has its original Robert Morton organ, which has been restored. Its 2,478 pipes make it the largest pipe organ in a California theater. In 1985 the theater was restored and reopened as Symphony Hall, and is now topped by the soaring Symphony Towers. Peek inside at the 80-foot-long mural by Denver artist James Jackson. The work, which captures the mood and movements of an orchestra at work, is oil on canvas that has been adhered to the wall.

From here, walk down Seventh Avenue to C Street and turn right; proceed to Sixth Avenue and turn left. The building with the pagoda-shape tower (its familiar outline is lit at night) is the:

20. Former home of **San Diego Trust and Savings Bank**, built in 1928 and once San Diego's tallest building. A tall Romanesque archway decorated with three bands of carved sandstone surrounds a large revolving door (downtown's only one) between two hinged doors. The roof was home to the first aviation beacon and a shooting gallery, installed during the original construction. The lights, in a cupola 240 feet above the sidewalk, were visible for a radius of more than 25 miles. Bank employees used the shooting gallery for recreation and to discourage bank robbers. The bank supplied the ammunition for rifles and revolvers. The FBI also made use of this 75-foot-deep, soundproof range. It was converted to offices in the 1950s when the FBI relocated.

You are standing in the heart of the city's business district. Continue walking west one block to Fifth Avenue. This major city intersection has a bus stop on every corner and the everhelpful:

21. Transit Store at no. 449. Walk along Broadway to Fourth Avenue and the:

22. U.S. Grant Hotel, built by Ulysses S. Grant Jr. as a memorial to his father. Grant Jr. had come to San Diego in 1893 for his wife's health. The $1.95 million hotel opened in 1910 after many delays. The hotel featured a marble staircase, 426 rooms, a roof garden, two indoor plunges, and Turkish baths. Take a look at the lobby before crossing Broadway to explore:

23. Horton Plaza, a colorful conglomeration of shops, eateries, and architecture—and a tourist attraction in its own right. Ernest W. Hahn, selected to plan and implement the redevelopment and

Impressions

In the arts of landscaping and architecture, the spirit of a city can be perpetuated for the ages. —George Marston, (philanthropist), 1929

revitalization of downtown San Diego, built the plaza in 1985. This core project, which covers 11.5 acres and 6.5 city blocks in the very heart of downtown, represents the successful integration of public and private funding.

The ground floor at Horton Plaza is home to the 1906 Jessop Street Clock. This timepiece has 20 dials, 12 of which tell the time in places throughout the world. Designed by Joseph Jessop Sr. and built primarily by Claude D. Ledger, the clock stood outside Jessop's Jewelry Store on Fifth Avenue from 1927 until they moved to Horton Plaza in 1985. In 1935, when Mr. Ledger died, the clock stopped; it was restarted, but it stopped again three days later—the day of his funeral. In front of Horton Plaza is:

24. Horton Plaza Park. Its centerpiece is a fountain designed by well-known local architect Irving Gill and modeled after the choragic monument of Lysicrates in Athens. Dedicated October 15, 1910, it was the first successful attempt to combine colored lights with flowing water. On the fountain's base are bronze medallions of Juan Rodríguez Cabrillo, Father Junipero Serra, and Alonzo Horton, three men important to San Diego's development.

☕ **WINDING DOWN**   The **Grant Grill,** in the U.S. Grant Hotel, one of San Diego's finest restaurants, is steeped in tradition, boasts a talented French chef, and is open for lunch and dinner and afternoon tea Tuesday through Sunday. At **Horton Plaza** you can choose from many kinds of cuisine, from California to Chinese along with good old American fast food.

WALKING TOUR 2
Gaslamp Quarter

Start: Fourth Avenue and E Street, at Horton Plaza.
Finish: Fourth Avenue and F Street.
Time: Allow approximately 1¹/₂ hours, not including shopping and dining.
Best Times: During the day.
Worst Times: Evenings, when the area's popular restaurants and night spots attract big crowds.

A National Historic District covering 16¹/₂ city blocks, the Gaslamp Quarter contains many Victorian-style commercial buildings built between the Civil War and World War II. The quarter—set off by the electric version of the old gaslamps—is bounded by Fourth Avenue to the west, Sixth Avenue to the east, Broadway to the north, and L Street and the waterfront to the south. The blocks are noticeably short; developer Alonzo Horton knew corner lots were more desirable to buyers, so he created more of them. This tour hits some highlights of buildings along Fourth and Fifth avenues. If it whets your appetite for more, the Gaslamp Quarter Foundation offers a 2-hour walking tour on Saturdays at 11am. The foundation is located at 410 Island Ave. (☎ 619/233-4692 or hotline 619/233-4691). Other tours are also available (see "Organized Tours" in Chapter 7), and the book *San Diego's Historic Gaslamp Quarter: Then and Now* by Susan H. Carrico and Kathleen Flanagan, with photos, illustrations, and a map, makes an excellent, lightweight walking companion.

The tour begins at the:

1. Balboa Theatre, at the southwest corner of Fourth Avenue and E Street. Constructed in 1924, the building is Spanish Renaissance style, with a distinctive tile dome, striking tile work in the entry, and two 20-foot-high ornamental waterfalls inside. In the past the waterfalls would run at full power during intermission; however, when turned off they would drip and irritate the audience. The ship mosaic at Fourth and E depicts Balboa discovering the Pacific Ocean in 1513. In its heyday, plays and vaudeville took top billing.

Cross Fourth Avenue and proceed along E Street to Fifth Avenue. The tall, striking building to your left is the:

2. Watts-Robinson Building, built in 1913. One of San Diego's first skyscrapers, it was a favorite of jewelers, once housing 70 of them. Currently a hotel, the building is gradually being converted into time-share units. Take a minute to look inside at the marble wainscoting, tile floors, ornate ceiling, and brass ornamentation.

Return to the southwest corner of Fifth Avenue. To your right, at 837 Fifth Ave., is the unmistakable "grand old lady of the Gaslamp," the twin-towered baroque revival:

3. Louis Bank of Commerce. (You can admire the next few buildings from the west side of the street and then continue south from here.) Built in 1888, the proud building, San Diego's first to be made of granite, once housed a 24-hour ice-cream parlor for which streetcars made unscheduled stops; an oyster bar frequented by Wyatt Earp; and upstairs, a number of rooms inhabited by ladies of the night. After a fire in 1903, the original towers of the building, with eagles perched atop them, were removed.

Next door, at 831 Fifth Ave., is the Romanesque revival:

4. Nesmith-Greely Building, also built in 1888, with its 12-foot-wide entry. Clara Shortridge Foltz, the first woman admitted to the California State Bar and the founder of the Woman's Bar Association of California, once had an office in this building, as did Daniel Cleveland, a lawyer who founded the city's public library. The face of this building, with the exception of the fire escapes, retains its original appearance.

On the corner, at 809 Fifth Ave., stands the two-story:

5. Marston Building. This Italianate Victorian style building dates from 1881, and housed humanitarian George W. Marston's department store for 15 years. In 1885, San Diego Federal

Walking Tour—Gaslamp Quarter

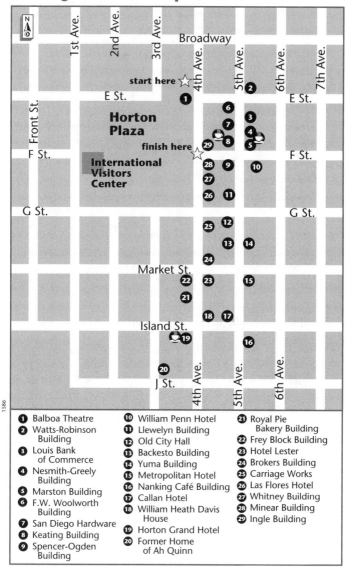

- ❶ Balboa Theatre
- ❷ Watts-Robinson Building
- ❸ Louis Bank of Commerce
- ❹ Nesmith-Greely Building
- ❺ Marston Building
- ❻ F.W. Woolworth Building
- ❼ San Diego Hardware
- ❽ Keating Building
- ❾ Spencer-Ogden Building
- ❿ William Penn Hotel
- ⓫ Llewelyn Building
- ⓬ Old City Hall
- ⓭ Backesto Building
- ⓮ Yuma Building
- ⓯ Metropolitan Hotel
- ⓰ Nanking Café Building
- ⓱ Callan Hotel
- ⓲ William Heath Davis House
- ⓳ Horton Grand Hotel
- ⓴ Former Home of Ah Quinn
- ㉑ Royal Pie Bakery Building
- ㉒ Frey Block Building
- ㉓ Hotel Lester
- ㉔ Brokers Building
- ㉕ Carriage Works
- ㉖ Las Flores Hotel
- ㉗ Whitney Building
- ㉘ Minear Building
- ㉙ Ingle Building

Saving's first office was located here, and the Prohibition Temperance Union held its meetings here in the late 1880s. After a fire in 1903, the building was remodeled extensively.

On the west side of Fifth Avenue, at no. 840, near E Street, you'll find the:

6. F. W. Woolworth Building, built in 1910. It has housed:

7. **San Diego Hardware** since 1922; the original tin ceiling, wooden floors, and storefront windows remain, and the store, which also has an entrance on Fourth Avenue, deserves a quick browse. The red-brick Romanesque revival:

8. **Keating Building,** on the northwest corner of Fifth Avenue and F Street, is a San Diego landmark dating from 1890. Mrs. Keating built it as a tribute to her late husband George, whose name can still be seen in the top cornice. Originally heralded as one of the city's most prestigious office buildings, it featured conveniences such as steam heat and a wire-cage elevator. Note the architecturally distinctive rounded corner and windows.

☕ **TAKE A BREAK**   Housed in the Keating Building, **Croce's** cluster of dining and entertainment possibilities serves up generous portions of good food and drink, live jazz, national acts, and inviting ambience. Owner Ingrid Croce has created a memorial to the life and music of her late husband, musician Jim Croce, with photos, guitars, and other memorabilia. Across the street is the perennially popular **Fio's** Italian restaurant.

Continuing south on Fifth Avenue, cross F Street and stand in front of the:

9. **Spencer-Ogden Building,** on the southwest corner at 429 F St. Built in 1874, it was purchased by business partners Spencer and Ogden in 1881, and has been owned by the same families ever since. In *San Diego's Historic Gaslamp Quarter: Then and Now,* it is noted that a number of druggists leased space in the building over the years, including the notorious one "who tried to make firecrackers on the second floor [and] ended up blowing away part of the building." Other tenants included realtors, an import business, a home furnishing business, and dentists, one who called himself "Painless Parker." Directly across the street stands the:

10. **William Penn Hotel,** built in 1913. In the building's former, more elegant life as the Oxford Hotel, it touted itself as "no rooming house but an up-to-the-minute, first-class, downtown hotel"; a double room with private bath and toilet cost $1.50. It reopened in 1992 as a mostly all-suites hotel at substantially higher prices.

On the west side of the street, at 722–728 Fifth Ave., you'll find the:

11. **Llewelyn Building,** built in 1887 by William Llewelyn; the family shoe store was located here until 1906. Over the years it has been home to hotels of various names with unsavory reputations. Of architectural note are its arched windows, molding, and cornices. On the southwest corner of Fifth Avenue and G Street is the:

12. **Old City Hall,** dating from 1874, when it actually was a bank. This Florentine Italianate building features 16-foot ceilings, 12-foot

windows framed with brick arches, antique columns, and a wrought-iron cage elevator. Notice that the windows on each floor are different (the top two stories were added in 1887, when it became the city's public library). The entire city government filled this building in 1900, with the police department on the first floor and the council chambers on the fourth.

Continue down Fifth Avenue toward Market, and you'll notice the three-story:

13. **Backesto Building** (1873), which fills most of the block. Originally a one-story structure on the corner, the classical revival/Victorian-style building expanded to its present size and height over its first 15 years. Across the street in the middle of the block, at 631–633 Fifth Ave., is the:

14. **Yuma Building,** built in 1882 and later expanded upward two floors to feature inviting bay windows. It was one of the first brick buildings downtown. Across Market Street, on the east side of the street, is the former:

15. **Metropolitan Hotel,** with an arresting trompe l'oeil by artists Nonni McKinnoon and Kitty Anderson. The building had actual bay windows when it was built in 1886.

The center of the city used to be at Fifth Avenue and Market Street, but as San Diego expanded and gradually moved north, the hub became Fifth and Broadway. When Horton Plaza was completed in 1985, it moved a block west to Broadway and Fourth Avenue. Back in its heyday, however, when Fifth Avenue was the main drag, it was the scene of many a parade, and Buffalo Bill Cody and John Philip Sousa numbered among those who marched up it.

Proceed to Island Avenue. On the southeast corner, the unassuming:

16. **Nanking Café Building** illustrates the Chinese influence in the area. At the turn of the century, Chinatown was located nearby. The building currently houses Royal Thai Cuisine Restaurant. Turn right on Island. The mural-covered building on the corner is the:

17. **Callan Hotel** (1904). The artwork, by Heidi Hardin, depicts a turn-of-the-century park scene with faces of contemporary San Diego citizens who contributed to the Gaslamp Quarter's rebirth. The saltbox house next to the hotel is the:

18. **William Heath Davis House.** This 140-year-old New England prefabricated lumber home was shipped to San Diego around Cape Horn in 1850 and is the oldest surviving structure in Alonzo Horton's "New Town." Horton lived here in 1867. The first floor and the small park next to it are open to the public; the Gaslamp Quarter Association and Gaslamp Quarter Foundation have their headquarters on the second floor. Saturday morning walking tours of the Gaslamp Quarter leave from here.

At the southwest corner of Island and Fourth avenues stands a bay window-clad building sure to steal your heart, the:

19. Horton Grand Hotel. It actually is two 1886 hotels that were moved here—very gently—from other sites, then renovated and connected by an atrium; the original Horton Grand is to your left, the Brooklyn Hotel to your right. The life-size papier-mâché horse (Sunshine) in the lobby near the reception area used to stand in front of the Brooklyn Hotel when it was a saddlery shop. The reception desk is a recycled pew from a choir loft, and old post office boxes now hold guests' keys. By the concierge desk, to your right, is an old photo of the original Horton Grand hotel, much less elegant in olden days. In its small museum hangs a portrait of Ida Bailey, a local madam whose establishment, the Canary Cottage, once stood on this spot. Artist Pamela Russ had been asked to retouch the somewhat austere face of her subject, but Russ's husband murdered her before she could get around to it.

Around the corner from the Horton Grand, at 429–431 Third Ave., stands the:

20. Former Home of Ah Quinn, the first Chinese resident of San Diego, who arrived in 1879 at the age of 27 and became known as the "Mayor of Chinatown," an area bounded by Island, J, 3rd, and 4th. Ah Quinn helped hundreds of Chinese immigrants to find work on the railroad and owned a successful general merchandise store on Fifth Avenue. He was a respected father (of 12 children), leader, and spokesperson for the city's Chinese population. When he died in 1914—he was hit by a motorcycle—his amassed wealth included farmland, a mine, and other real estate. The modest house is not open to the public.

🍵 **TAKE A BREAK** The **Palace Bar** in the Horton Grand Hotel is the perfect place to find yourself at teatime or in the evening, when live music, piano or jazz, adds to the already inviting atmosphere. The bar is part of the same choir-loft pew that has been turned into the reception desk.

When you leave the Horton Grand, head north on Fourth Avenue; in the middle of the block on the west side you will come to the:

21. Royal Pie Bakery Building, erected in 1911. This particular bakery, preceded by others, has been here since 1920; the second floor used to house the Anchor Hotel, run by "Madam Cora."

At the southwest corner of Fourth Avenue and Market Street, at the:

22. Frey Block building (1911), a plaque reads "Home of the Crossroads, the oldest live jazz club in San Diego." Across the street on the southeast corner, at 401–417 Market St., is the:

23. Hotel Lester, which dates from 1906. It used to house a saloon, pool hall, and a hotel of ill repute when this was a red light district.

On the northeast corner of Fourth Avenue and Market Street (at 402 Market St.) stands the:

24. Brokers Building, constructed in 1889; it has 16-foot-high wood-beam ceilings and cast-iron columns. At the north end of this block, the:

25. Carriage Works, established in 1890, now houses the Cheese Shop; instead of wagons and carriages, you get sandwiches and pastries. Cross G Street and walk to the middle of the block.

26. The Las Flores Hotel, the gray building with blue-and-red trim at 725–733 Fourth Ave., was built in 1912 and is the only Gaslamp Quarter structure completely designed by architect Irving Gill, whose work can be seen throughout San Diego and in La Jolla. Next door, at 739–745 Fourth Ave., is the:

27. Whitney Building, dating from 1906, with striking arched windows on the second floor. While you're studying details, take a look at the trim on the top of the:

28. Minear Building (1910), at the end of the block, on the southeast corner of Fourth Avenue and F Street. Across the street is the:

29. Ingle Building, dating from 1907. The mural on the F Street side of the building depicts a group of men toasting inside the original Golden Lion Tavern, which served 'em up from 1907 to 1932. Original stained-glass windows front Fourth Avenue. Inside, the restaurant's stained-glass ceiling was taken from the Elks Club in Stockton, California, and much of the floor is original.

☕ WINDING DOWN   Walk to **Cafe Lulu,** 419 F St., near Fourth Avenue, for casual coffeehouse atmosphere and fare, or walk to **Fio's** in the Marston Building for a drink, some pizza, or an Italian meal. They serve meals at the bar, if you're lucky enough to snag a seat.

WALKING TOUR 3
Embarcadero

Start: The Maritime Museum, at Harbor Drive and Ash Street.
Finish: The Convention Center, at Harbor Drive and Fifth Avenue.
Time: Allow 1 1/2 hours, not including museum and shopping stops.
Best Times: Weekday mornings.
Worst Times: Weekends, especially in the afternoon, when Maritime Museum and Seaport Village are crowded; also when cruise ships are in port (days vary).

San Diego's colorful Embarcadero, or waterfront, cradles a bevy of seagoing vessels—frigates, ferries, paddle-wheelers, yachts, cruise ships, and even a multimasted merchant vessel. You'll also find the equally colorful Seaport Village, a vital aspect of the city's life.

Start at the:

1. Maritime Museum on Harbor Drive at Ash Street. Making up part of the floating museum is the magnificent *Star of India,* the world's oldest merchant ship still afloat, built in 1863 as the *Euterpe.* The ship, whose billowing sails are a familiar sight along Harbor Drive, once carried cargo to India and immigrants to New Zealand, and it braved the arctic ice in Alaska to work in the salmon industry. Another member of the Maritime Museum is the ferry *Berkeley,* built in 1898 to operate between San Francisco and Oakland. In service through 1958, it carried survivors to safety 24 hours a day for four days after the 1906 San Francisco earthquake. The *Medea,* the third and smallest member of the floating museum, is a private steam yacht. (One ticket gets you onto all three boats.)

From this vantage point you get a fine view of the:

2. County Administration Center, built in 1936 with funds from the Works Progress Administration and dedicated in 1938 by President Franklin D. Roosevelt. The 23-foot-high granite sculpture in front, completed by Donal Hord in 1939 and called *Guardian of Water,* represents a pioneer woman shouldering a water jug. The building is even more impressive from the other side because of the carefully tended gardens; it's well worth the effort and extra few minutes to walk around to Pacific Highway for a look. On weekdays the building is open from 8am to 5pm; there are restrooms and a cafeteria inside.

🍵 **TAKE A BREAK**   The **cafeteria** on the fourth floor of the County Administration Center has lovely harbor views; it's open weekdays until 3:35pm. If you can't pass up the chance to have some seafood, return to the waterfront to **Anthony's Fishette,** the simplest entity in the Anthony's group of seafood houses, which provides short orders al fresco.

Next door is **Anthony's Star of the Sea Room,** one of the city's finest seafood restaurants, where reservations and a coat for men are a must; it's open for dinner only.

Continue south along the Embarcadero. The large carnival-colored building on your right is the:

3. San Diego Cruise Ship Terminal on the B Street Pier, with a large nautical clock at the entrance. Totally renovated in 1985, the terminal is light and airy inside, with flags for decor.

4. Harbor Cruises depart from this location from sunup to sundown on their tours of San Diego harbor; ticket booths are right on the water. A little farther south, near the Broadway Pier, the:

5. Coronado Ferry makes hourly trips between San Diego and Coronado; the trip takes only 15 minutes. Ferries leave San Diego on the hour and return from Coronado on the half hour. Buy the inexpensive tickets from the Harbor Excursion booth. To your left as you look up Broadway, you'll see the two gold mission-style towers of the:

Walking Tour—Embarcadero

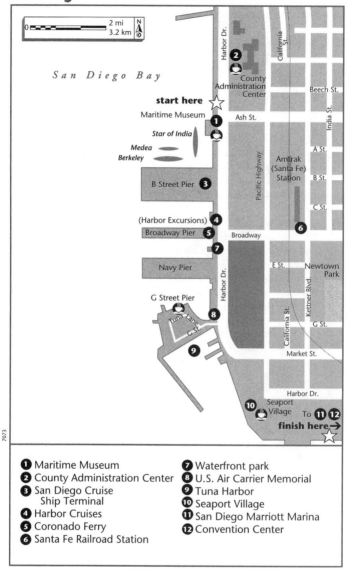

0   2 mi
    3.2 km
N

San Diego Bay

start here
Maritime Museum ❶

Star of India

Medea
Berkeley

B Street Pier ❸

(Harbor Excursions) ❹
Broadway Pier ❺
❼

Navy Pier

G Street Pier
❽
Tuna Lane
G St.
❾

❿ Seaport
Village
To ⓫ ⓬
finish here→

Harbor Dr.
❷
County
Administration
Center
Beech St.

Ash St.

A St.
Amtrak
(Santa Fe)
Station
B St.

C St.
❻

Broadway

E St.
Newtown
Park

Harbor Dr.

G St.

Market St.

Harbor Dr.

California St.
India St.
Pacific Highway
Kettner Blvd.
California St.

7073

❶ Maritime Museum
❷ County Administration Center
❸ San Diego Cruise
   Ship Terminal
❹ Harbor Cruises
❺ Coronado Ferry
❻ Santa Fe Railroad Station
❼ Waterfront park
❽ U.S. Air Carrier Memorial
❾ Tuna Harbor
❿ Seaport Village
⓫ San Diego Marriott Marina
⓬ Convention Center

6. Santa Fe Railroad Station, built in 1915. It's only 1½ blocks
away, so stroll up and look inside at the vaulted ceiling, wooden
benches, and walls covered in striking green and gold tiles.

   Continuing south on Harbor Drive, you'll stroll through a
small tree- and bench-lined:

7. Waterfront park. Then at Pier 11, there is the:

8. **U.S. Air Carrier Memorial,** a compact black-granite obelisk that honors the nation's carriers and crews. Erected in 1993, it stands on the site of the old Navy fleet landing, where thousands of servicemen boarded ships over the years.

Continue along the walkway to:

9. **Tuna Harbor,** where the commercial fishing boats congregate. San Diego's tuna fleet, at about 100 boats, is one of the world's largest.

🍵 **TAKE A BREAK** The red building off to your right houses the **Fish Market,** a market and casual restaurant and its elegant upstairs counterpart, **Top of the Market.** Be assured a meal here is fresh off the boat. Both serve lunch and dinner, and the Fish Market has a children's menu, as well as an oyster and sushi bar. It's acceptable to drop in just for a drink and to savor the view, which is mighty. Prices here are moderate to expensive, but if you prefer something quick and cheap, save yourself a walk and stop in at casual **Anthony's Fishette** (a cousin to the one you passed earlier), just outside Seaport Village. For desserts or coffee, go inside Seaport Village to **Upstart Crow,** actually a bookstore/coffeehouse, and sip cappuccino in the company of your favorite authors.

Meander along the winding pathways of:

10. **Seaport Village** with its myriad shops and restaurants. The Broadway Flying Horses Carousel is pure nostalgia. Charles Looff, of Coney Island, carved the animals out of poplar in 1890. The merry-go-round was originally installed at Coney Island and later moved to Salisbury, Massachusetts. Seaport Village purchased it in the 1970s and spent more than two years restoring it to its original splendor—the horses even have real horsehair tails. If you decide to take a twirl, pick your mount from the 40 horses, three goats, and three St. Bernard dogs. This carousel comes complete with the ever-elusive brass ring.

As you stroll further, you will no doubt notice the official symbol of Seaport Village. This 45-foot high detailed replica of the famous turn-of-the-century Mukilteo Lighthouse of Everett, Washington, towers above the other buildings. From Seaport Village, continue your waterfront walk south to the:

11. **San Diego Marriott Marina,** snugged in by Embarcadero Marina Park, which is well used by San Diegans for strolling and jogging; the southern arm of the park is the scene for outdoor San Diego Summer Pops concerts in summer. A concession at the marina office rents boats by the hour at reasonable rates and arranges diving, skiing, and fishing outings. The impressive hotel resembles an ocean liner at berth. The boardwalk continues to the:

12. **Convention Center,** another striking piece of architecture on the city's waterfront. Completed in late 1989, it also has a seafaring

theme, and its presence on the waterfront has contributed to the revitalization of downtown San Diego.

☕ **WINDING DOWN**   The waterfront bar at the Marriott, called the **Yacht Club,** looks out onto the marina and the bay beyond and is a choice spot for watching the sunset (you're in luck if the end of your walking tour coincides with it). You can get drinks, appetizers, and short orders here, and if you linger into the evening, there's likely to be live music and dancing. Across from the Convention Center at the water's edge, the **Chart House,** housed in the historic San Diego Rowing Club built in 1899, is a more upscale candidate for a drink or a bite to eat.

WALKING TOUR 4
Old Town

Start: Old Town State Historic Park Visitor Information Center.
Finish: Heritage Park.
Time: Allow approximately 2 hours, not including shopping or dining.
Best Times: Weekends (except the first one in May) and any day before 2pm or after 3pm (so you can take the free park tour from 2 to 3pm if you wish).
Worst Times: Weekdays, when numerous school groups are touring (although it's fun to watch on-site education in action), and Cinco de Mayo weekend, the first weekend in May, when Old Town is a madhouse in celebration of Mexico's defeat of the French on May 5, 1862, in the Battle of Puebla.

Old Town is the Williamsburg of the West. When you visit, you go back to a time of one-room schoolhouses and village greens, when many of the people who lived, worked, and played here spoke Spanish. Even today, life moves more slowly in this part of the city, where the buildings are either old or built to look that way. The stillness is palpable, especially at night when you stroll the streets and look up at the stars. You don't have to look hard or very far to see yesterday. Begin at the Visitor Information Center, at the eastern end of the park—not so much a park in the sense of having grass and trees, but a historic district that preserves the essence of the small Mexican and fledgling American community that existed here from 1821 to 1872. The center of Old Town is a 6-block area with no vehicular traffic.

Start at the Visitor Information Center in Old Town State Historic Park. The center is in the:

1. **Robinson-Rose House,** built in 1853 as a family home; it has also served as a newspaper and railroad office. Here you will see a large model of Old Town the way it looked in 1872, the year a large fire broke out (or was set), destroying much of the town and initiating the exodus of the local citizenry to New Town, now downtown San Diego. Old Town State Historic Park contains

seven original buildings, including the Robinson-Rose House, and a growing number of reconstructions of buildings that once existed here.

From the Visitor Information Center turn left and stroll into the colorful world of Mexican California called:

2. **Bazaar del Mundo,** where international shops and restaurants spill into a flower-filled courtyard. Designer Diane Powers created the unique setting from the dilapidated Casa de Pico motel, constructed here in 1936. On Saturday and Sunday afternoons, Mexican dancers perform for free at the bazaar. While you're here, be sure to visit the Guatemala Shop, the Design Center, and Libros Bookstore.

☕ **TAKE A BREAK**   You can't leave San Diego without sampling the Mexican food in Bazaar del Mundo. Try **Rancho El Nopal, Casa de Pico,** or, a block away, **Casa de Bandini.** You can also enjoy Italian food at **Lino's.** All offer indoor and outdoor dining and lively ambience. Historic Casa de Bandini, completed in 1829, was the home of Peruvian-born Juan Bandini, who became a Mexican citizen; in 1869 the building, with a second story added, became the Cosmopolitan Hotel. Within the park, restaurants are open from 10am to 9pm and stores from 10am to 8pm (9pm in Bazaar del Mundo).

From Bazaar del Mundo, stroll into the grassy plaza, where you'll see a:

3. **Large Rock Monument,** which commemorates the first U.S. flag flown in Southern California (on July 29, 1846). In the plaza's center stands a flagpole that resembles a ship's mast. There's a reason: the original flag hung from the mast of an abandoned ship. Straight ahead, at the plaza's western edge, is the:

4. **Estudillo House.** An original adobe building dating from 1827, it has covered walkways and an open central patio. The patio covering of the U-shaped house is made of corraza cane, the seeds for which were brought by Father Serra in 1769. The walls are 3 to 5 feet thick, holding up the heavy beams and tiles, and they work as terrific insulators against summer heat. In those days, the thicker the walls the wealthier the family. The furnishings in the "upper-class" house are representative of the 19th century (don't overlook the beautiful four-poster beds); the original furniture came from the East Coast and from as far away as Asia. The Estudillo family, which then numbered 12, lived in the house until 1887; today family members still live in San Diego. Admission is $2 for adults and $1 for children 6 to 17.

After you exit the Estudillo House, turn left. In front of you is the reconstruction of the three-story:

5. **Colorado House,** built in 1851 and destroyed by fire in 1872, as were most buildings on this side of the park. Today it's the

Walking Tour—Old Town

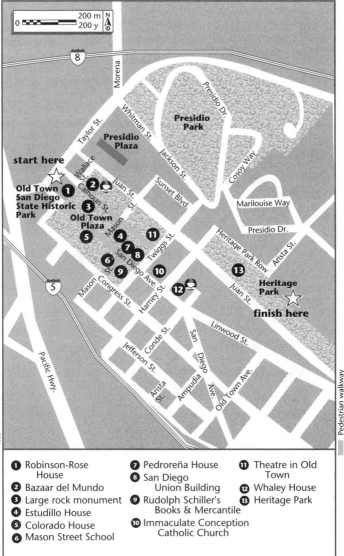

| 0 | 200 m |
| | 200 y |
N

start here

Old Town San Diego State Historic Park

Presidio Plaza

Presidio Park

Old Town Plaza

Presidio Dr.

Morena

Taylor St.

Wallace St.

Calhoun St.

Juan St.

Whitman St.

Jackson St.

Sunset Blvd

Cosoy Way

Marilouise Way

Presidio Dr.

Mason St.

Twiggs St.

San Diego Ave.

Harney St.

Arista St.

Heritage Park Row

Heritage Park

finish here

Juan St.

Mason St.

Congress St.

Conde St.

Jefferson St.

Linwood St.

San Diego Ave.

Ampudia

Arista St.

Old Town Ave.

Pacific Hwy.

Pedestrian walkway

1588

- ❶ Robinson-Rose House
- ❷ Bazaar del Mundo
- ❸ Large rock monument
- ❹ Estudillo House
- ❺ Colorado House
- ❻ Mason Street School
- ❼ Pedroreña House
- ❽ San Diego Union Building
- ❾ Rudolph Schiller's Books & Mercantile
- ❿ Immaculate Conception Catholic Church
- ⓫ Theatre in Old Town
- ⓬ Whaley House
- ⓭ Heritage Park

home of the Wells Fargo Historical Museum, but the original housed San Diego's first two-story hotel, with the "best food and drink this side of San Francisco." Next door to the Wells Fargo museum, and catercorner to the Estudillo House, is the small red-brick San Diego Court House and City Hall. (A reconstruction of the three-story Franklin House is planned to the right of the

Colorado House.) From here, continue along the pedestrian walkway one short block, turn right, and walk another short block to the one-room:

6. **Mason Street School** (a reddish-brown building to your right), an original building dating from 1865. It was commissioned by Joshua Bean, uncle to hanging judge Roy Bean; Joshua Bean was also San Diego's first mayor and the state of California's first governor. If you look inside you'll notice that the boards that make up the walls don't match; they were leftovers from the construction of San Diego homes. Mary Chase Walker, the first teacher, ventured here from the East when she was 38 years old. She enjoyed the larger salary but hated the fleas, mosquitoes, and truancy; after a year, she resigned to marry the president of the school board.

When you leave the schoolhouse, retrace your steps to the walkway (which is the extension of San Diego Avenue), and turn right. On your left, you will see two buildings with brown-shingle roofs. The first, the:

7. **Pedroreña House** (no. 2616), is an original Old Town house built in 1869, with stained glass over the doorway. The owner, Miguel Pedroreña, also owned the house next door, which would become the:

8. **San Diego Union Building.** The paper was first published in 1868. This house arrived in Old Town after being prefabricated in Maine in 1851 and shipped around the Horn. Inside you'll see the original hand press used to print the paper, which merged with the *San Diego Tribune* in 1992. The offices are now located in Mission Valley, about 3 miles from here.

Across the street is:

9. **Rudolph Schiller's Books and Mercantile,** which sells books that celebrate people and places at the turn of the century; it also has a wonderful paper-doll collection and coloring books, and just inside the door to your left, a wall-size photo of Old Town in 1896 taken by photographer Schiller.

At the end of the pedestrian part of San Diego Avenue stands a railing; beyond it is Twiggs Street, dividing the historic park from the rest of Old Town, which is more commercial in comparison. In this part of town you'll find interesting shops and galleries and outstanding restaurants.

At the corner of Twiggs Street and San Diego Avenue stands the Spanish mission–style:

10. **Immaculate Conception Catholic Church.** The cornerstone was laid in 1868, but with the movement of the community to New Town in 1872, it lost its parishioners and was not dedicated until 1919. Today the church serves about 300 families in the Old Town area. (Visitors sometimes see the little church and on a romantic whim decide to get married here, but arrangements have to be made nine months in advance.) Halfway up the hill

from the church, on the opposite side of Twiggs Street, is the:

11. Theatre in Old Town, at 4040 Twiggs St., where there's usually a comedy or musical in production. This is also an Old Town Trolley stop.

Return to San Diego Avenue and continue along it one block to Harney Street. On your left is the restored:

12. Whaley House, the first two-story brick structure in Southern California, built from 1855 to 1857. The house, which is haunted by the ghost of a man who was hanged out back, is beautifully furnished in period pieces and features the life mask of Abraham Lincoln, the spinet piano used in the film *Gone with the Wind,* and the concert piano that accompanied Swedish soprano Jenny Lind on her final U.S. concert tour in 1852. The house's north room served as the county courthouse for a few years, and the courtroom looks now as it did then.

From the Whaley House, walk uphill 1 1/2 blocks along Harney Street to a Victorian jewel called:

13. Heritage Park. The seven buildings on this grassy knoll were moved here from other parts of the city and are now used in a variety of ways; among them are a winsome bed-and-breakfast inn (in the Queen Anne shingle-style Christian House, built in 1889), a down-memory-lane–style doll shop, an antique store, and offices. Toward the bottom of the hill is the Classic Revival Temple Beth Israel, dating from 1889. On Sunday, local art is often exhibited in the park. If you've brought picnic supplies, enjoy them under the sheltering coral tree at the top of the hill.

☕ **WINDING DOWN** At the end of your walk, wend your way back down Harney Street, turn left at San Diego Avenue, and take a left just beyond the Whaley House. The brick walkway will lead you to **Garden House Coffee and Tea,** a small coffee shop in a turn-of-the-century house that's so small, in fact, that you have to take your fresh brew and sip it on the front porch or in the yard under the gnarled old pepper trees. This is a quiet, secluded spot.

WALKING TOUR 5
Balboa Park

Start: Cabrillo Bridge, entry at Laurel Street and Sixth Avenue.
Finish: San Diego Zoo.
Time: Allow 2 hours, not including museum or zoo stops. If you get tired at any point, hop on the free park tram, which will get you around effortlessly.
Best Times: Anytime, but if you want to get good photographs, come in the afternoon. Most museums are open until 4:30pm. The zoo closes at 5pm in the summer, 4pm other times of the year.

Worst Times: Some say weekends, when more people (especially families) visit the park, but I love it then—particularly on Sunday afternoons, when at 2pm there is a free organ concert at the outdoor Spreckels Organ Pavilion.

Balboa Park is the second-oldest city park in the United States, after New York's Central Park. Its striking architecture, much of which was the product of the Panama-California Exposition in 1915–16 and the California Pacific International Exposition in 1935–36, now houses outstanding museums and contributes to the park's uniqueness and beauty. The park, previously called "City Park," was named in 1910 when Mrs. Harriet Phillips won a name contest; she submitted "Balboa Park" in honor of the Spanish explorer who was the first European to see the Pacific Ocean in 1513.

Take bus no. 1 or 3 via Fifth Avenue or bus no. 25 via Sixth Avenue to Laurel Street, which leads into Balboa Park via its most dramatic entrance, the:

1. Cabrillo Bridge, with its striking views of downtown San Diego and scenic sycamore-lined Highway 163. Built in 1915 for the Panama-California Exposition and patterned after a bridge in Ronda, Spain, this cantilever-style bridge, with seven pseudo-arches, makes a dramatic entrance to Balboa Park. As you cross the bridge, to your left you'll see the yellow cars of the zoo Skyfari and, directly ahead, the distinctive California Tower of the Museum of Man. The delightful sounds of the 100-bell Symphonic Carillon can be heard every quarter hour. Sitting atop this San Diego landmark is a shaped weather vane similar to the ship that Cabrillo sailed to California in 1542. The city skyline lies to your right. Once you've crossed the bridge, go through the:

2. Arch (the two figures represent the Atlantic and Pacific oceans) and into the park itself, a treasure of nature and culture. For now, just view the museums from the outside (read more about them in Chapter 7). You have entered the park's major thoroughfare, called El Prado, and to your left is the:

3. Museum of Man, an anthropological museum focusing on the peoples of North and South America. Architect Bertram Goodhue designed this building, originally known as the California Building, in 1915. Goodhue, considered the world's foremost authority on Spanish-Colonial architecture, was the master architect for the 1915-1916 exposition. Just beyond it and up the steps to the left is the nationally acclaimed:

4. Old Globe Theatre, part of the Simon Edison Centre for the Performing Arts. The "Globe," as the locals refer to it, was built for the 1935 Exposition. This replica of Shakespeare's Old Globe Theatre was meant to be demolished after the exposition but was not, and it has survived to be California's oldest professional theater. In 1978, an arsonist destroyed the theater, which was subsequently rebuilt into what it is today. If you have the opportunity to go inside, you can see the bronze bust of Shakespeare

Walking Tour—Balboa Park

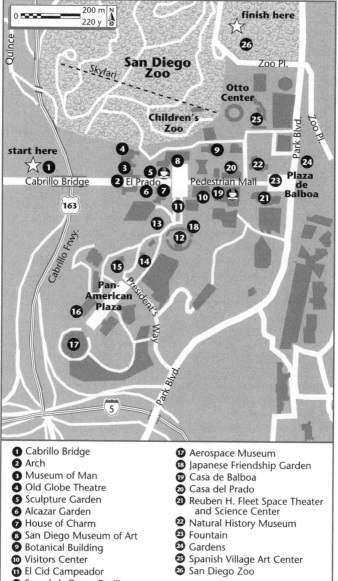

1 Cabrillo Bridge
2 Arch
3 Museum of Man
4 Old Globe Theatre
5 Sculpture Garden
6 Alcazar Garden
7 House of Charm
8 San Diego Museum of Art
9 Botanical Building
10 Visitors Center
11 El Cid Campeador
12 Spreckels Organ Pavilion
13 Palm Arboretum
14 UN International Gift Shop
15 House of Pacific Relations
   International Cottages
16 San Diego Automotive Museum

17 Aerospace Museum
18 Japanese Friendship Garden
19 Casa de Balboa
20 Casa del Prado
21 Reuben H. Fleet Space Theater
   and Science Center
22 Natural History Museum
23 Fountain
24 Gardens
25 Spanish Village Art Center
26 San Diego Zoo

that miraculously survived the fire with minor damage. Beside the theater is the:

5. **Sculpture Garden** of the Museum of Art. Across the street, to your right as you stroll along the Prado, is the:

6. **Alcazar Garden,** designed in 1935 by Richard Requa, who patterned it after the gardens surrounding the Alcazar Castle in Seville, Spain. The garden is formally laid out and trimmed with low clipped hedges; in the center walkway are two star-shaped yellow-and-blue tile fountains.

Exit to your left at the opposite end of the garden and you'll be back on El Prado. Proceed to the corner; on your right is the site of the:

7. **House of Charm,** the site of the **San Diego Art Institute Gallery,** a nonprofit gallery that primarily exhibits works of local artists. The **Mingei International Museum of World Folk Art,** which offers changing exhibitions celebrating human creativity manifested in textiles, costumes, jewelry, toys, pottery, paintings, and sculpture, is also located here. (At press time, the House of Charm was undergoing reconstruction, scheduled to be completed by the end of 1995. These occupants are scheduled to be open by mid-1996.)

To your left is the imposing:

8. **Museum of Art,** a must for anyone who fancies fine art. The latticework building you see beyond it is the:

9. **Botanical Building,** where colorful flowers and plants are shaded within. Directly in front of you are the newly renovated House of Hospitality and the park's:

10. **Visitors Center,** where you can pick up maps and a discount ticket to some of the museums. Turn right toward the statue of the mounted:

11. **El Cid Campeador,** created by Anna Hyatt Huntington and dedicated in 1930. This sculpture of the 11th-century Spanish hero was made from a mold of the original statue in the court of the Museum of Hispanic Society in New York. A third one is in Seville, Spain. Walk down the hill to the ornate:

12. **Spreckels Organ Pavilion,** donated to San Diego by brothers John D. and Adolph B. Spreckels. Famed contralto Madame Ernestine Schumann-Heink sang at the December 31, 1914, dedication; a brass plaque honors her charity and patriotism. Free, lively recitals featuring the largest outdoor organ in the world (its vast structure contains 4,428 pipes) are given Sunday at 2pm. Exit to your right, cross the two-lane road, and follow the sidewalk down the hill. The pathway leading into the ravine to your right is the:

13. **Palm Arboretum,** which goes to the Alcazar Garden and requires some climbing. More secluded, it may not always be as safe as the main roads, but you can get a good sense of its beauty by venturing only a short distance along it. As you walk down the hill, you'll see the Hall of Nations on your left, and beside it, the:

Impressions

This is the most beautiful highway I've ever seen.
   —John F. Kennedy (Speaking about Highway 163, which winds through Balboa Park), 1963

---

14. United Nations International Gift Shop, no. 2171, a favorite shop for its diverse merchandise, much of it hand-made by peoples from around the world. You'll recognize the shop by the U.S. and U.N. flags out front. Check the bulletin board, or ask inside, for the park's calendar of events. If you need to rest, there's a pleasant spot with a few benches opposite the gift shop.

   You will notice a cluster of small houses with red tile roofs. They are the:

15. House of Pacific Relations International Cottages, which promote ethnic and cultural awareness and are open to the public on Sunday afternoons year-round. March through October lawn programs are presented with folk dancing. Take a quick peek into some of the cottages, then continue following the road to the bottom of the hill to see more of the park's museums, most notably the:

16. San Diego Automotive Museum to your right, filled with exquisite and exotic cars, and the round:

17. Aerospace Museum straight ahead. The museums in this part of the park are housed in structures built for the 1935 exposition.

   It is not necessary to walk all the way to the bottom of the hill, unless you plan to tour one or two of the museums now. Instead, cross the road and go back up the hill past a parking lot and the Organ Pavilion. Take a short cut through the pavilion, exit directly opposite the stage, and follow the sidewalk to your right, leading back to El Prado. Almost immediately, you come to the:

18. Japanese Friendship Garden of San Diego, an 11¹/₂-acre canyon in the first stage of development. Its information center is inside a teahouse with shoji screens, and the small garden beside it inspires meditation.

   ☕ **TAKE A BREAK**   Now's your chance to have a bite to eat, sip a cool drink, and review the tourist literature you picked up at the Visitors Center. For light fare in an outdoor setting, cross El Prado and go to the Museum of Art's **Sculpture Garden Café.** The garden features sculptures by Zuñiga and Rodin, among others.

   Back on El Prado, which is strictly a pedestrian mall from this point, set your sights on the fountain at the end of the street and head toward it. En route, you'll probably pass street musicians, artists, and clowns. One of their favorite haunts is in front of the Botanical Building; it takes only a minute to wander through and is a delightful little detour. Stroll in the middle of the street to get the full benefit of the lovely buildings on either side of you. On your right, in the:

19. **Casa de Balboa Building,** you'll find the **Hall of Champions Sports Museum,** the **Museum of Photographic Arts,** the **Model Railroad Museum,** and the **Museum of San Diego History,** with engaging exhibits that interpret past events in the city and relate them to the present. Be sure to take a look at the realistic-looking female figures atop the Casa de Balboa. On the other side of El Prado, on your left, note the ornate work on the:

20. **Casa del Prado.**

At the end of El Prado are two museums particularly popular with children, the:

21. **Reuben H. Fleet Space Theater and Science Center** to your right. To the left is the:

22. **Natural History Museum,** where kids are likely to be climbing atop the whale statue outside. Look for the sundial that is inscribed "Presented by Joseph Jessop; December 1908; I stand amid ye sommere flowers To tell ye passage of ye houres." This sundial, which is accurate to the second, was originally presented to the San Diego Public Library and relocated in front of the museum in the mid-1950s when the library moved. In the center of the Plaza de Balboa is a high-spouting:

23. **Fountain.** This seemingly ordinary fountain, built in 1972, holds 25,000 gallons of water and spouts 50 to 60 feet into the air. The unique feature is actually on top of the Natural History Museum where a wind-regulator is located. As the wind increases, the fountain's water pressure is lowered so that the water doesn't spray out over the edges. The fountain fascinates children, who giggle when it sprays them and marvel at the rainbows it creates. From here, cross the road via the small bridge to visit the near-secret:

24. **Gardens** tucked away on the other side of the highway: to your left, a garden for cacti and other plants at home in an arid land-scape; to your right, formal rose gardens. After you've enjoyed the flowers and plants, return to El Prado.

☕ **TAKE A BREAK** Tucked in the Casa de Balboa building, there's a tiny **snack bar,** with seating, that has outstanding sandwiches; you can order only half a sandwich, along with muffins, cookies, coffee, juice, or milk. A block from El Prado on Village Place (the street is on your left as you stand on El Prado and face the fountain) is **another snack bar** with picnic tables. You can get almost anything: sodas, iced tea, lemonade, milkshakes, pizza, burritos, sandwiches, nachos, chili, and hot dogs. In this lovely spot, towering eucalyptus trees flank the Casa del Prado Theatre. The voluptuous Moreton Bay Fig tree, which is fenced off across the street, was planted in 1915 for the exposition; now it's more than 62 feet tall, with a canopy 100 feet in diameter.

Impressions

Wouldn't it be splendid if San Diego had a zoo!
    —Dr. Harry Wegeforth, (San Diego Zoo founder), 1916

Across Village Place from the snack bar is the sleepy:

25. Spanish Village Art Center, where artists are at work daily from 10am to 4pm, creating jewelry, paintings, and sculptures in tile-roof studios around a courtyard. (There are restrooms here.)

Exit at the back of the Spanish Village Art Center and take the paved, palm-lined sidewalk to the left. Then turn right onto the palm-lined path that will take you to the world-famous:

26. San Diego Zoo (or retrace your steps and visit some of those tempting museums you've just passed and save the Zoo for another day). From here, you can also walk out to Park Boulevard through the zoo parking lot to the bus stop, on your right, where the no. 7 bus will take you back to downtown San Diego. You'll pass, on the right, the **San Diego Miniature Railroad**. The Miniature Train Company of Rensaeler, Indiana, made this $1/5$-scale, 16-inch-gauge train that has been a fixture here since 1948. The railroad is open every day that public schools are closed and the $1/2$-mile ride through "San Diego's back country" takes about 4 minutes (☎ 619/239-4748). Just before you reach Park Boulevard you will see The **Balboa Park Carousel** (☎ 619/460-9000). The historic carousel was made in North Tonawanda, New York, in 1910 and was temporarily located in Luna Park (Los Angeles) and Tent City (Coronado). The carousel and its menagerie of original European hand-carved animals (except for two pairs of miniature horses) permanently settled in Balboa Park in 1922. The bus stop is a brown-shingled kiosk.

9

Shopping

Whether you're looking for a souvenir, a gift, or a quick replacement for an item inadvertently left at home, you'll find no shortage of stores in San Diego. This is, after all, Southern California, where looking good is a high priority and shopping is a way of life.

1 The Shopping Scene

The best buys in San Diego are often unusual or one-of-a-kind gift items. Many galleries sell wearable art, and you can still find art by up-and-coming local artists priced within your budget. The city has outstanding galleries, and while some work has high prices, it's not unusual to find something you fancy for $25 or $50. And don't forget that Mexico is only half an hour away; *tiendas* in Tijuana, Rosarito Beach, and Ensenada are stocked with colorful crafts.

Shops here tend to stay open late. Expect to find the welcome mat out until 9pm on weeknights, 8pm on Saturdays, and 6pm and sometimes 8pm on Sundays, particularly in shopping clusters (much more creative than malls) such as The Paladion, Horton Plaza, Seaport Village, and Bazaar del Mundo. Exploring them is fun because the stores are part of an environment that is architecturally interesting and incorporates shopping, strolling, snacking, dining, and lolling.

Department store names you'll recognize after only a brief stay in San Diego are Nordstrom and The Broadway, both at Horton Plaza (and elsewhere). In Old Town, shops are strung along San Diego Avenue and within Old Town State Historic Park. In Coronado, Orange Avenue is a magnet for shoppers, and in La Jolla, the most elegant stores and galleries line Prospect Street and Girard Avenue.

Purchases in San Diego come with a 7% sales tax. If your hotel room has a copy of *Guest Informant,* look inside for more information on shops and shopping in San Diego.

SHOPPING CLUSTERS

Bazaar del Mundo

2754 Calhoun St., Old Town State Historic Park. ☎ **619/296-3161.** Bus: 4 or 5/105.

Take a stroll down Mexico way and points south through the arched passageways of this colorful corner of Old Town. Always festive, its central courtyard vibrates with folkloric music, mariachis, and a splashing fountain. Shops feature one-of-a-kind folk art, home furnishings, clothing, and textiles from Mexico and South America, and you'll find a top-notch bookstore called Libros, with a large kids' selection. Don't miss the Design Center and the Guatemala Store. Open daily from 10am to 9pm.

The Ferry Landing Marketplace

1201 1st St. (at B Avenue), Coronado. ☎ **619/435-8895.** Bus: 901. Ferry: From Broadway Pier. Driving: Take I-5 to Coronado Bay Bridge, to B Avenue, and turn right.

The entrance is impressive—turreted red rooftops with jaunty blue flags that draw closer as the ferry to Coronado pulls into the slip. Then a stroll up the pier and you're in the midst of shops filled with gifts, imported and designer fashions, jewelry, and crafts. You can get a quick bite to eat or have a leisurely dinner with a view, wander along landscaped walkways, or laze on a friendly beach or grassy bank. Open daily from 10am to 9pm.

Horton Plaza

324 Horton Plaza. ☎ **619/238-1596.** Bus: 2, 7, 9, 29, 34, or 35. Trolley: City Center.

The Disneyland of shopping malls, it is right in the heart of San Diego; in fact, it *is* the heart of the revitalized city center, bounded by Broadway, First and Fourth avenues, and G Street. Covering 6¹/₂ city blocks, this multilevel shopping center has 140 specialty shops, including art galleries, clothing and shoe stores, several fun shops for kids, bookstores, a seven-screen cinema, three major department stores, and a variety of restaurants and short-order eateries. It's almost as much a San Diego attraction as Sea World or the San Diego Zoo, partly for its unusual eclectic designs and colors. The plaza is purposefully designed for meandering, so expect to take some wrong turns and make some delightful discoveries (or stay close to the escalator, which you can pick up at the front of the plaza beside Long's Pharmacy, or take the elevator beside Nordstrom). Among the favorite shops here are the Nature Company; Horton Toy and Doll, for inexpensive toys for kids and great gag gifts for adults; and Eddie Bauer for travel supplies and outdoor gear. Horton Plaza usually has free entertainment daily from noon to 2pm. Parking is free the first three hours with validation, $1 per half-hour thereafter; parking levels are confusing, and temporarily losing your car is part of the Horton Plaza experience. Open Monday through Friday from 10am to 9pm, Saturday from 10am to 6pm, Sunday from 11am to 6pm (extended summer and holiday hours).

The Paladion

777 Front St. (opposite Horton Plaza between 1st and G streets). ☎ **619/232-1627.** Bus: 2, 7, 9, 29, 34, or 35. Trolley: Civic Center.

The posh Paladion brought world-class shopping to downtown San Diego when it opened early in 1992, with tony tenants like Alfred Dunhill, Cartier, Tiffany, Gianni Versace, and Salvatore Ferragamo. Equally alluring is the Ivy Court, on the ground level, a lovely spot for coffee, a light lunch, or cocktails—all with piano music as a back-drop. There is also a rooftop Italian restaurant called Bice, a French-Caribbean restaurant called Alizé, and even free valet parking and concierge service. Open Monday through Saturday 10am to 6pm, Sunday noon to 5pm.

Seaport Village

849 W. Harbor Dr. (at Kettner Boulevard). ☎ **619/235-4014** or 619/235-4013 for events information. Bus: 7. Trolley: Seaport Village.

This 14-acre ersatz village snuggled alongside San Diego Bay was built to resemble a small Cape Cod community, but the 75 shops are very much the Southern California cutesy variety. Favorites include the Tile Shop; the Seasick Giraffe for resort-wear; and the Upstart Crow bookshop/coffeehouse with the Crow's Nest children's bookstore inside. Be sure to see the 1890 carousel imported from Coney Island, New York. Open September to May, daily from 10am to 9pm; June to August, daily from 10am to 10pm.

DEPARTMENT STORES

The Broadway

Horton Plaza. ☎ **619/231-4747.** Bus: 2, 7, 9, 29, 34, or 35.

Many San Diegans frequent this comprehensive store, where you'll find clothing for women, men, and children, as well as housewares, electronics, and luggage. It's well known for handbags and cosmetics. Open Monday through Friday from 10am to 9pm, Saturday 10am to 8pm, Sunday from 11am to 7pm.

Nordstrom

Horton Plaza. ☎ **619/239-1700.** Bus: 2, 7, 9, 29, 34, or 35.

An all-time San Diego favorite and best known for its outstanding customer service and fine selection of shoes, Nordstrom features a variety of stylish fashions and accessories for women, men, and children. Tailoring is done on the premises. There's a full-service restaurant on the top floor where coffee and tea cost only 25¢. Open Monday through Friday from 10am to 9:30pm, Saturday from 10am to 7pm, Sunday from 11am to 6pm.

MALLS

Fashion Valley

352 Fashion Valley Rd. ☎ **619/297-3381.** Bus: 6, 16, 25, 43, or 81. Driving: Highway 163 to Friars Road west.

My favorite place to shop, this outdoor mall is about 1 1/2 miles west of Mission Valley Center. Department stores here include Neiman-Marcus, Nordstrom, Saks Fifth Avenue, Robinsons-May, The Broadway, and J. C. Penney, plus 140 specialty shops and a quadriplex movie theater. Open Monday through Friday from 10am to 9pm, Saturday from 10am to 6pm, Sunday from 11am to 6pm. (Nordstrom has slightly longer hours.)

Mission Valley Center

1640 Camino del Rio North. ☎ **619/296-6375.** Bus: 6, 16, 25, 43, or 81. Driving: Take I-8 to Mission Center Road.

About 5 miles from downtown San Diego and just over 2 miles east of Old Town on I-8, you'll find San Diego's largest outdoor shopping center. Among the stores here are Bullocks, Montgomery Ward, and Robinsons-May, plus more than 150 specialty shops and eateries. Open Monday through Friday from 10am to 9pm, Saturday from 10am to 6pm, Sunday from 11am to 6pm.

University Towne Center (UTC)

4545 La Jolla Village Dr., San Diego. ☎ **619/546-8858.** Bus: 50 express, 34, or 34A. Driving: Take I-5 to La Jolla Village Drive and go east to UTC or from I-805 take La Jolla Village Drive and go west.

This outdoor shopping complex has a landscaped plaza and 160 stores, including some big ones like Nordstrom, Sears, and The Broadway. It is also home to a year-round ice-skating rink; the popular Hops Bistro and Brewery; cinemas; and the outstanding Mingei International Museum of Folk Art. (The latter is scheduled to move to Balboa Park sometime during 1996.) Open Monday through Friday from 10am to 9pm, Saturday from 10am to 7pm, Sunday from 11am to 6pm.

MARKET & DISCOUNT SHOPPING

Kobey's Swap Meet

Sports Arena Parking Lot (west end), 3500 Sports Arena Blvd. ☎ **619/226-0650** (24-hour information). Admission Thursday and Friday 50¢, Saturday and Sunday $1; children under 12 free. Driving: Take I-8 to Sports Arena Boulevard turnoff; or I-5 to Rosecrans Street, turn right on Sports Arena Boulevard.

Since 1980, this gigantic open-air market has been a bargain hunter's dream come true. Approximately 3,000 vendors fill row after row with new and used clothing, jewelry, electronics, hardware, appliances, furniture, collectibles, crafts, antiques, auto accessories, toys, and books. There's produce, too, along with food stalls and restrooms. Open Thursday through Sunday from 7am to 3pm.

San Diego Factory Outlet Center

4498 Camino de la Plaza, San Ysidro. ☎ **619/690-2999.** Trolley: Take the southbound trolley to the San Ysidro (last) stop, walk back (north) one block, and turn left on Camino de la Plaza; it's a half-mile walk or a very short taxi ride. Driving: Take I-5 or I-805 south to Camino de la Plaza exit (last U.S. exit before Mexico); turn right and continue one block—center is on right.

This strip of 35 factory outlets saves you money because you buy directly from the manufacturers. Some familiar names represented include Mikasa, Levi's, Eddie Bauer, Guess?, Maidenform, Van Heusen, Bass, Nike, Carter's, Osh Kosh B'Gosh, Panasonic, Ray-Ban, and Jockey. Open Monday through Friday from 10am to 8pm, Saturday from 10am to 7pm, Sunday from 10am to 6pm.

2 Shopping A to Z

ANTIQUES

Olde Cracker Factory Antiques Shopping Center

448 W. Market St. (at Columbia Street). ☎ **619/233-1669.** Bus: 7. Trolley: Seaport Village. It's across the street from the Hyatt Regency San Diego.

Prepare to spend some time here exploring three floors of individually owned and operated shops filled with antiques and collectibles. It's a

San Diego Shopping

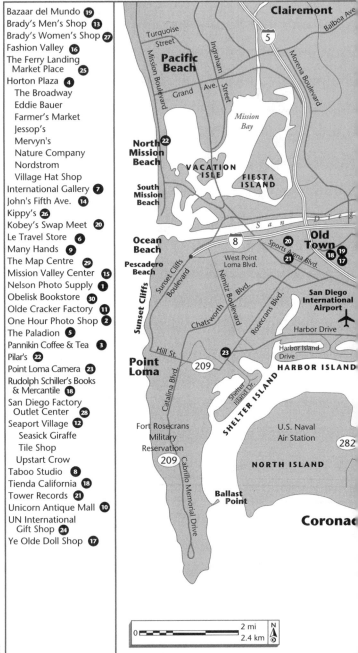

Downtown

Hillcrest/Uptown

SAN DIEGO

National City

Coronado Beach

Date Street
Cedar Street
Beech Street
Ash Street
A Street
B Street
C Street
Broadway
E Street
F Street
G Street
Market Street
Island Avenue
J Street
K Street

India Street
Columbia St.
Kettner Blvd.
Highway
Drive
4th Ave.
5th Ave.
6th Ave.
7th Ave.
8th Ave.
9th Ave.
10th Ave.
State St.
Union Street
Front Street
1st Ave.
2nd Ave.
3rd Ave.
Harbor
Pacific
Harbor Drive

Vista Rd.
Linda
Friars Rd.
Pacific Hwy.
1st Ave.
5th Ave.
Balboa Park
Park Blvd.
Ash Street
Broadway
Market Street
National Ave.
Logan Ave.
Euclid Ave.
Division St.
8th St.
18th St.
30th St.
3rd St.
4th St.
Orange Ave.
San Diego-Coronado Bay Bridge (Toll)
Silver Strand

163
8
5
805
94
15
805
75

block north of Seaport Village. Open Tuesday through Sunday from 11am to 5pm.

Unicorn Antique Mall

704 J St. (at Seventh Avenue). ☎ **619/232-1696.**

Antiques and collectibles fill three floors of this 30,000-square-foot building, presenting a wide selection of American oak and European furniture. Free off-street parking is available. Open Monday through Saturday from 10am to 5:30pm, Sunday from noon to 5:30pm.

ART

San Diego boasts some outstanding art galleries, tops among them **The Artist's Gallery,** 7420 Girard Ave., La Jolla (☎ 619/459-5844), featuring 20 regional artists in a variety of media including paintings, sculpture, and three-dimensional paper wall sculptures; **B St. Gallery,** 641 B St. (☎ 619/239-5882), focusing on original contemporary work, particularly abstract impressionism; **Brushworks,** 425 Market St. (☎ 619/238-4381), with changing exhibits of contemporary work; **Galeria Dos Damas,** 415 Market St. (☎ 619/231-3030), specializing in art from Mexico and the Californias; the **International Gallery,** 643 G St. (☎ 619/235-8255), offering authentic African and Melanesian primitive art, including ritual masks and sculpture, as well as contemporary American crafts in ceramics, glass, jewelry, and wood; the **Pratt Gallery,** 2161 India St. (☎ 619/236-0211), displaying original paintings including landscapes and cityscapes by Southern California artists; and the **David Zapf Gallery,** 2400 Kettner Blvd. just south of Laurel (☎ 619/232-5004), specializing in the works of San Diego–area artists. San Diego also has numerous fairs where arts and crafts can be purchased, such as the **La Jolla Arts Festival,** held every September (☎ 619/454-5718).

BOOKS

John Cole's Book Shop

780 Prospect St., La Jolla. ☎ **619/454-4766.**

Cole's, a favorite of many locals, is housed in a turn-of-the-century wisteria-covered cottage, the former guest house of philanthropist Ellen Browning Scripps. John and Barbara Cole founded the shop in 1946 and moved it into the cottage 20 years later. Today Barbara and her children continue to run it. Visitors will find cookbooks in the old kitchen and paperbacks in a former classroom. The children's book section fairly bulges, and there are plenty of books about La Jolla and San Diego. Sitting and reading in the patio garden is acceptable, even encouraged. Open Monday through Saturday from 9:30am to 5:30pm.

Obelisk Bookstore

1029 University Ave., Hillcrest. ☎ **619/297-4171.**

This bookstore, which caters to gay men and lesbians, is where Greg Louganis signed copies of his book *Breaking the Surface.* Open Monday through Saturday from 10am to 11pm, Sunday noon to 8pm.

Traveler's Depot

1655 Garnet Ave., Pacific Beach. (☎ **619/483-1421**).

This bookstore offers an extensive selection of travel books and maps, plus travel gear and accessories, with discounted prices for backpacks and luggage. The well-traveled owners, Ward and Lisl Hampton, are happy to give advice about favorite restaurants in a given city while pointing you to the right shelf for the appropriate book or map. Open Monday to Friday 10am to 6pm (until 8pm in summer), Saturday 10am to 5pm, Sunday noon to 5pm.

Upstart Crow

835 Harbor Dr., Seaport Village. ☎ **619/232-4855**. Bus: 7. Trolley: Seaport Village.

This wonderful place combines a well-stocked bookstore and a coffeehouse with tables and chairs nestled amid the volumes. It smells heavenly—of new books and fresh-brewed coffee—and refills are only 25¢. Open Sunday through Thursday from 9am to 10pm, Friday and Saturday from 9am to 11pm (until 11pm every night in summer).

Warwick's Books

7812 Girard Ave., La Jolla. ☎ **619/454-0347**.

This popular family-run bookstore is a browser's delight, with more than 40,000 titles to choose from, including a large travel section, not to mention gifts, cards, and stationery. The well-read Warwick family has been in the book and stationery business for almost 100 years, and the current owners are the third generation involved with the store. Open Monday through Saturday from 9am to 5:30pm, Sunday from 11am to 4pm.

COFFEE & TEA

Pannikin Coffee & Tea

675 G St. ☎ **619/239-7891**. Bus: 3, 5/105, or 16.

Coffees, teas, herbs, and spices are the order of the day here, and you can buy a pound or half-pound, from aged Java to Sumatra Mandheling. Decaffeinated beans and a large assortment of teas, from Lapsang Souchong to English Breakfast, are also available, plus all sorts of kitchen paraphernalia. Open Monday through Friday from 9am to 5:30pm, Saturday and Sunday from 10am to 5pm. Pannikin has many locations throughout San Diego.

CRAFTS

Many Hands

302 Island Ave. ☎ **619/557-8303**. Bus: 1, 4, 16, or 5/105. Trolley: Gaslamp Quarter.

This cooperative gallery, in existence since 1972, has 35 members who engage in a variety of crafts, including toys, jewelry, posters, pottery, baskets, and wearable art. Open Sunday through Thursday and Saturday from 11am to 6pm, Friday from 11am to 9pm.

DOLLS

Ye Olde Doll Shoppe

2454 Heritage Park Row, Old Town. ☎ **619/291-1979.** Bus: 4 or 5/105.

Doll lovers small and large will find treasures in this five-room Victorian house—mostly American-made black, white, Asian, and Latin porcelain dolls along with some wax ones, priced from $25 to $3,600. There are also black figurines and nativity sets, as well as international miniatures and collectibles. Owner Arlys Rapp also sells cases for dolls, dollhouse kits (from $20 to $400), trains, and music boxes (you choose the music to go in it), baseball cards, and baseball player dolls. Mail order is available. Open daily from 10:30am to 5:30pm.

FASHIONS FOR CHILDREN

Mervyn's

120 Horton Plaza. ☎ **619/231-8800.**

This department store, not as flashy as others in San Diego, is known for its large children's department, with reasonably priced clothing for infants to teens. Mervyn's has many locations in San Diego; this one is open Monday through Friday from 10am to 9pm, Saturday from 9:30am to 9pm, Sunday from 10am to 7pm.

City Kids

7756 Fay Ave., La Jolla. ☎ **619/459-4877.**

This is the place to go for really cute garb for newborns to preteens at reasonable prices. Open Monday through Saturday from 9:30 to 5:30, Sunday from 10am to 4pm. City Kids also has a store in Del Mar.

FASHIONS FOR MEN

Nordstrom department store also has a large men's clothing section.

Brady's Men's Shop

In the Hyatt Regency San Diego. ☎ **619/236-0123.**

Owner Rick Brady has a good eye for fashion, particularly when it comes to sports coats, sweaters, and ties. Some suits are made specially for the store. Check out the suits made of the wrinkle-resistant Micro-Touch fiber that feels like suede and is perfect for traveling. Brady's features American designers, including the striking, architecture-inspired sweaters, shirts, and socks of Jhane Barnes. Open Monday through Saturday from 9am to 10pm, Sunday from 9am to 6pm. There is also a Brady's Men's Shop in the Hotel del Coronado.

FASHIONS FOR WOMEN

For upscale shopping try Girard Street in La Jolla, San Diego's answer to Rodeo Drive, where both sides of the street are lined with boutiques such as **Armani Exchange, Polo Ralph Lauren, Ports International,** and **Sigi's Boutique.**

Brady's Women's Shop

Hotel del Coronado, Coronado. ☎ **619/435-6766.** Bus: 901.

This shop is filled with stylish day and leisure wear and splashy pool-side fashions. And if you're staying at the "Hotel Del," you're in the perfect place to wear them. Open Monday from 9am to 9pm, Tuesday through Thursday from 9am to 10pm, Friday and Saturday from 9am to 11pm, Sunday from 9am to 7pm.

Kippy's

1114 Orange Ave., Coronado. ☎ **619/435-6218.** Bus: 901.

A Coronado tradition, this family owned store has stylish and playful clothing and prices that range from reasonable to rarefied. An unusual feature of Kippy's: clothes rotate from the ceiling on a dry-cleaning device. Look for the sale rack inside. Kippy's designs and manufactures its own collection of belts, leather goods, and embellished clothing. Open Monday through Saturday from 10am to 5:30pm, Sunday from 11am to 4pm.

Pilar's

3745 Mission Blvd., Pacific Beach. ☎ **619/488-3056.**

If you forgot to bring your suit or have decided that you need something new, Pilar's is the place to go for Southern California's largest selection of swimwear and cruisewear. Open Monday through Saturday from 9am to 8pm, Sunday from 9am to 6pm.

GIFTS & SOUVENIRS

Rudolph Schiller's Books & Mercantile

Old Town State Historic Park. ☎ **619/298-0108.** Bus: 4 or 5/105.

This old-timey shop is filled with postcard books, coloring books, cut-out-and-assemble books, songbooks, cookbooks, seasonings and sauces for Southwest cooking, and children's classics. It also sells patterns for clothes worn in the 1800s and has an extensive paper-doll collection, including a Civil War family, Shirley Temple, famous American women, John Wayne, and great African-American entertainers. There's always music playing in the store, from classical to New Age to Broadway show tunes. And don't overlook the wall-size photo of Old Town in 1896, taken by Schiller himself. Open daily from 10am to 6pm.

United Nations International Gift Shop

Balboa Park. ☎ **619/233-5044.** Bus: 16 or 25.

You'll find inexpensive, imaginative offerings from around the world: origami from Japan, hand-carved boxes from Poland, necklaces from Africa, Russian nesting dolls, Christmas decorations (year-round) from all over the world, and jackets, bags, and pillow covers decorated with distinctive needlework by Laotians living in San Diego. UNICEF cards are a given. Look for the U.S. and U.N. flags out front. Open Monday through Friday from 10am to 5pm, Saturday and Sunday from 11am to 5pm (shorter hours in winter).

HATS

Village Hat Shop

Horton Plaza. ☎ **619/232-4997.** Bus: 2, 7, 9, 29, 34, or 35. Trolley: Civic Center.

Entering the portal is like going into a costume shop. Trying on is quite acceptable, and from hat to hat you can become a pilot, a cowpoke, the Mad Hatter, or Davy Crockett. Prices range from $3 to $200 and there's something for men, women, and kids of all tastes. Open daily from 10am to 9pm. There's a second shop at Seaport Village.

JEWELRY

International Gallery

643 G St. ☎ **619/235-8255.**

Besides its outstanding folk and primitive art and quality ceramics, the International Gallery sells contemporary and costume jewelry by American artists. Much of it is silver, but there are some gold pieces.

Jessop's

149 Horton Plaza. ☎ **619/239-9311.** Bus: 2, 7, 9, 29, 34, or 35. Trolley: Civic Center.

Jessop's is well entrenched in San Diego, having sold jewelry and watches to the folks here since 1893. Most everything that glitters here is gold, ornamented with diamonds, rubies, and sapphires if you prefer. You can also find the finest watches and pearls, as well as Mont Blanc pens, Lalique crystal, and Lladro porcelain figurines. The giant clock that stands in front of the store has 21 dials. Open Monday through Friday from 10am to 9pm, Saturday from 10am to 6pm (8pm in summer), Sunday from 11am to 6pm.

Taboo Studio

542 Fifth Ave. (at Market). ☎ **619/696-0055.**

This impressive shop exhibits and sells the work of jewelry designers from throughout the United States. The jewelry is made of silver, gold, and inlaid stones, in one-of-a-kind pieces, limited editions, or custom work. The gallery represents 45 artists. Open Tuesday through Saturday from 11am to 6pm.

LUGGAGE

John's Fifth Avenue Luggage

3833 Fourth Ave. ☎ **619/298-0993** or 619/298-0995.

This San Diego institution carries just about everything you can imagine in the way of luggage, travel accessories, business cases, pens, and giftware. On the premises is a luggage repair center, which is an authorized airline repair facility. Open Monday through Friday from 9am to 5:30pm, Saturday from 9:30am to 4pm. There is also a store in Fashion Valley.

MAPS

The Map Centre

2611 University Ave. ☎ **619/291-3830.** Fax 619/291/3840.

This shop, three blocks east of Texas Street, may be tiny but it's got the whole world covered—in maps, that is. If you plan to spend some serious time in San Diego or move here, buy the *Thomas Guide;* it's $15.95 but indispensable. The Map Centre is easily recognizable by its bright yellow awning. Open Tuesday through Friday from 10am to 5:30pm, Saturday from 10am to 5pm.

MARKETS

Farmers' Markets throughout San Diego County sell fresh local fruits, vegetables, and flowers, as well as specialty items such as raw apple cider (in the fall), macadamia nuts, and rhubarb pies. The best place to see and sample San Diego County produce, these open-air events are very popular with locals who can be seen pushing strollers, in-line skating, and walking the family dog while procuring just-picked fruits and vegetables for their tables. Friendly farmers happily provide information, advice, and sometimes even free samples.

Here's a daily schedule:

- Sunday, **Uptown San Diego**   "The Boulevard," El Cajon at Marlborough (3 blocks east of 40th Street), from 10am to 2pm.
- Tuesday**, Coronado**   Corner of First and B streets (Ferry Landing Marketplace), from 2:30 to 6pm; and **Escondido,** Grand Avenue and Broadway, from 3 to 7pm.
- Wednesday**, Escondido**   North County Market, 3660 Sunset Drive (across from North County Fair), from 9am to noon; **Ocean Beach,** 4900 block of Newport Avenue (west of Sunset Cliffs Boulevard), from 4 to 8pm; and **Carlsbad**, Roosevelt Street between Grand Avenue and Carlsbad Village Drive, from 3 to 6pm.
- Thursday, **Oceanside**   Downtown, corner of Coast Highway and 3rd Street, from 9am to 12:30pm; **Mission Valley,** Hazard Center, Friars Road at Highway 163, from 3 to 6:30pm; and **Chula Vista,** Third Avenue and E Street, from 3 to 6pm.
- Friday, **Rancho Bernardo**   Bernardo Winery, 13330 Paseo del Verano Norte, from 9am to noon; and **La Mesa,** 8500 Allison St. (east of Spring Street), from 3 to 6pm.
- Saturday, **Pacific Beach**   Promenade Mall, Mission Boulevard between Reed and Pacific Beach Drive, from 8am to noon; **Vista,** corner of Eucalyptus and Escondido Avenue (City Hall parking lot), from 8 to 11am; **Poway** (Old Poway Park), corner of Midland and Temple, from 8 to 11am; **Del Mar** (City Hall Parking Lot), corner of El Camino Del Mar and 10th Street, from 1 to 4pm; and **Carlsbad,** parking lot north of Andersen's Pea Soup, from 2 to 5pm.

MUSIC

Tower Records

3601 Sports Arena Blvd. ☎ **619/224-3333.**

Whatever your taste in music, you are sure to find it here. Tower Records has the area's most complete music selection and a knowledge-able staff. Chances are if you can hum a tune their resident music expert will be able to tell you the recording artist and on which album, tape, or CD it can be found. Open daily from 9am to midnight.

PHOTOGRAPHY

Nelson Photo Supply

1909 India St. (at Fir Street). ☎ **619/234-6621.** Bus: 5/105. Trolley: America Plaza.

All you need in the way of camera accessories, film, and one-hour pro-cessing is here. Open Monday through Friday from 8:30am to 5:30pm, Saturday from 8:30am to 5pm.

One Hour Photo Stop

419 C St. ☎ **619/232-8291.** Bus: 2, 7, 9, 29, 34, or 35. Trolley: Civic Center or Fifth Avenue.

Conveniently located in the heart of downtown between Fourth and Fifth avenues, the store can process your film in an hour. Just drop it off, have lunch or do a little shopping, then pick it up. They also sell film and batteries. Open Monday through Friday from 8am to 5:30pm.

Bob Davis' Camera Shop

7720 Fay St., La Jolla. ☎ **619/459-7355.**

If your camera starts acting strange while you're in La Jolla, this is the best place to go for advice. It's also a good choice for picking up extra film or batteries. Open Monday through Saturday from 9am to 5:30pm.

Point Loma Camera Store

1310 Rosecrans St. ☎ **619/224-2719.**

This is a good source for photography supplies and film processing. They also have an excellent selection of frames and similar accessories. Open Monday through Saturday from 9am to 5:30pm, Sunday lab hours are from 11am to 6pm.

SPECIALTY FOODS

Farmer's Market

Horton Plaza (bottom level). ☎ **619/696-7766.** Bus: 2, 7, 9, 29, 34, or 35. Trolley: Civic Center.

The specialty food section in this large deli/market carries an abundant supply of foods, produce, and wines. The staff can prepare food baskets with fruit (and/or dried fruit), crackers, cheese, pâtés, caviar, wine, and much more. Open Monday through Friday from 8am to 9pm, Saturday from 8am to 8pm, Sunday from 10am to 7pm (in win-ter the market opens at 9am Monday through Saturday; Sunday hours remain the same).

Trader Joe's

8657 Villa La Jolla Dr., La Jolla. ☎ **619/546-8629.**

A local institution, Trader Joe's sells specialty food items, as well as basic grocery supplies. Most items are packaged under their house label and sold for less than they would be as a name brand. Look for

---

Homegrown San Diego

Few visitors realize that San Diego County produces a billion (no, that isn't a typo) dollars worth of fruit, vegetables, flowers, and nuts every year.

Avocados, known locally as "green gold," are our most profitable crop and have been grown here for more than 100 years. A common variety is called *fuerte* (Spanish for strong and vigorous), because only this type survived the freeze of 1913 that killed every other tree that had been imported from Mexico. The bright green trees grow from 20 to 60 feet tall; an average-sized tree bears up to 300 avocados.

Avocado Trivia

1. What has been a long-standing nickname for the avocado?
2. In which U.S. city are the most avocados eaten?
3. What is the best way to ripen an avocado?

Oranges, lemons, and grapefruit also have been grown here since the turn of the century. Oddly enough, the Atchison, Topeka and Santa Fe Railway popularized citrus production here. In 1906, the railway bought a large tract of land, now known as the community of Rancho Santa Fe, where they planted and grew eucalyptus trees. They planned to make railroad ties from the wood, but when it proved unsuitable, they found themselves holding the bag, or the acreage in this case. In order to sell their turf, they promoted the area as ideal for large-scale, commercial citrus groves, which it was. Growers from Orange County joined in, after a land boom there resulted in their orchards being paved over.

Flowers are San Diego's third most important crop (after avocados and citrus). Ranunculus bulbs from here are sent all over the world, as are our famous Ecke poinsettias. And proteas like our Mediterranean climate, even though they're native to South Africa. Macadamias, which are native to Australia, also flourish here; rumor has it that macadamia growing became popular after World War II because some retired admirals wanted business reasons to travel down under.

Answers to Avocado Trivia: 1. alligator pear; 2. Los Angeles; 3. place it in an ordinary paper bag and store at room temperature; including an apple in the bag will accelerate the process.

great deals on wine, a wide selection of imported beers, and wonderful treats from the bakery (try the cheese scones). This is the place to get the ingredients for your picnic at the beach. Trader Joe can also be found in Pacific Beach and La Mesa.

THRIFT SHOPS

A large **Goodwill** store is located at 402 Fifth Ave. (☎ 619/696-6709). Filling the whole block, the store sells clothing and housewares, along with vintage clothing in its boutique. It's open Monday through Friday from 8:30am to 6pm, Saturday from 10am to 6pm, Sunday from 10am to 5pm. For upscale second-hand selections, head for La Jolla and these three stores, where you're sure to find designer items: **Designer Consigner,** 834 Kline St. (☎ 619/459-1737); **Encore of La Jolla,** 7850 Herschel St. (☎ 619/454-7540); and **Second Act West,** 7449 Girard Ave. (☎ 619/454-6096). These are within walking distance of one another.

TOYS

You'll also find toys at the places listed under "Shopping Clusters" and "Crafts" earlier in this chapter.

Tienda California

2505 San Diego Ave., Old Town. ☎ **619/291-4699.** Bus: 4 or 5/105.

Most items sold here are diminutive: figurines, magnets, and striking Hagen-Renaker miniatures, made in California. The tiny animals will steal your heart: cats, dogs, horses, owls, wild animals, pandas, fish, unicorns, and carousel ponies. Most prices are diminutive, too, from $1.50 to $6.50, although the collectible pewter dragons and magicians are more expensive. Open daily from 9am to 9pm.

TRAVEL ACCESSORIES

You might try **Eddie Bauer** in Horton Plaza (☎ 619/233-0814) or **Traveler's Depot** (listed under "Books") for the travel gear.

Le Travel Store

745 Fourth Ave. ☎ **619/544-0005.** Bus: 2, 7, 9, 29, 34, or 35. Trolley: Civic Center.

In business since 1976, Le Travel Store has a nice selection of soft-sided luggage, travel books, language tapes, maps, and lots of travel accessories. A cafe on the premises serves beverages and snacks. The long hours and central location make this spot extra handy. Open Monday through Thursday from 8am to 10pm, Friday from 8am to midnight, Saturday from 10am to midnight, Sunday from 11am to 7pm.

10

San Diego After Dark

San Diego's rich and varied cultural scene includes more than a dozen theaters mounting classical and contemporary plays throughout the year; performances by the San Diego Symphony and the San Diego Opera; rock and pop concerts; and numerous movie houses and multiscreen complexes, including several that feature foreign and avant-garde films. Not all of the city streets pulsate with nightlife, but there are ever-growing pockets of late-night activity.

Half-price tickets to theater, music, and dance events are available at the **Times Arts Tix** booth, in Horton Plaza Park, at Broadway and Third Avenue. Park in the Horton Plaza parking garage and have your parking validated or pause at the curb nearby. The kiosk is open Tuesday through Saturday from 10am to 7pm. Half-price tickets for Sunday performances are sold on Saturday. Only cash payments are accepted. For a daily listing of half-price offerings, call 619/238-3810. Full-price advance tickets are also sold; the kiosk doubles as a Ticketmaster outlet, selling tickets to concerts throughout California.

For a rundown of the latest performances, gallery openings, and other events in the city, check the listings in "Night and Day," the Thursday entertainment section of the *San Diego Union-Tribune,* or *The Reader,* San Diego's free alternative newspaper, published weekly on Thursday. For what's happening at the gay clubs, get the weekly *San Diego Gay and Lesbian Times.* The *San Diego Performing Arts Guide,* produced, every two months by the San Diego Theatre Foundation, is also very helpful. You can pick one up at the Times Art Tix booth or write to 701 B St., Suite 225, San Diego, CA 92101-8101 (☎ 619/238-0700).

1 The Performing Arts

San Diego has many talented theater companies, so I've selected the ones that are best known. Don't hesitate, however, to try a lesser-known venue if the show appeals to you. Also, keep in mind that the **California Center for Performing Arts** in Escondido has its own schedule of productions; see Chapter 11 for details.

The **Gaslamp Quarter Theatre Company,** at 444 Fourth Ave. (☎ 619/232-9608 or 619/234-9583), stages contemporary productions in the 250-seat Hahn Cosmopolitan Theatre. The **San Diego Repertory Theatre** offers ethnically diverse productions, plus one bilingual (English/Spanish) production each year, at the Lyceum Theatre, 2 Broadway Circle, in Horton Plaza (☎ 619/235-8025 or 619/231-3586). In summer, the theaters—the 550-seat Lyceum Stage and the 250-seat Lyceum Space—host dance and musical programs, as well as other events. Situated at the entrance to Horton Plaza, the two-level subterranean theaters are tucked behind the tile obelisk.

Founded in 1948, the **San Diego Junior Theatre,** at Balboa Park's Casa del Prado Theatre (☎ 619/239-8355), is one of the country's oldest continuously producing children's theaters, providing training and performance opportunities for children and young adults 4 to 18. Students act and technically crew five main-stage shows each year.

In Coronado, **Lamb's Players Theatre,** at 1142 Orange Ave. (☎ 619/474-4542), is a professional repertory company whose season runs from February through December. Shows take place in their 340-seat theater in Coronado's historic Spreckels building, where no seat is more than seven rows from the stage.

MAJOR THEATER COMPANIES

La Jolla Playhouse

La Jolla Village Drive and Torrey Pines Road. ☎ **619/550-1010.** Tickets $19 to $37. Bus: 30, 34, or 34A.

Winner of the 1993 Tony Award for outstanding American regional theater, the playhouse stages six productions each year in its 500-seat Mandell Weiss Theater and 400-seat Mandell Weiss Forum on the campus of the University of California, San Diego. Performances are held May through November. Playhouse audiences cheered *The Who's Tommy*, and Matthew Broderick in *How to Succeed in Business without Really Trying* before they went on to Broadway fame and fortune. The original La Jolla Playhouse was founded by Gregory Peck, Dorothy McGuire, and Mel Ferrer in 1947 and closed in 1964; this stellar reincarnation emerged on the theatrical scene in 1983. The box office is open Monday from 11am to 6pm, Tuesday through Sunday from 10am to 8pm. Each show designates one Saturday matinee as a "pay what you can" performance. Reduced-price "Public Rush" tickets are available ten minutes before curtain, subject to availability.

Old Globe Theatre

Balboa Park. ☎ **619/239-2255** or 619/23-GLOBE for 24-hour hotline. Tickets $25–$36 (previews $20); Seniors and students $21 matinees, $26 weeknights. Bus: 7 or 25.

Near the entrance to Balboa Park and just behind the Museum of Man, this Tony Award–winning theater, fashioned after Shakespeare's, has produced world premieres of such Broadway hits as *Into the Woods,* plus the revival of *Damn Yankees,* and has billed such notable performers as Marsha Mason, Cliff Robertson, Jon Voight, and Christopher Walken. The 581-seat Old Globe is part of the Simon Edison Centre for the Performing Arts, which also includes the 245-seat Cassius Carter Centre Stage and the 620-seat open-air Lowell Davies Festival Theatre, and mounts a dozen plays a year on the three stages between January and October. Tours are offered Saturday and Sunday at 11am and cost $3 ($1 students, seniors, and military). The box office is open Tuesday through Sunday from noon to 8:30pm.

OPERA

San Diego Opera

Civic Theatre, 202 C St. ☎ **619/236-6510** (box office) or 619/232-7636 (for more information). Tickets $23 to $95; ask about standing room or discounts for students and seniors. Bus: 2, 7, 9, 29, 34, or 35. Trolley: Civic Center.

Founded in 1964, the opera showcases internationally renowned performers in operas and occasional special recitals. The season runs January through May. The 1996 season includes *Tosca* by Giacomo Puccini, January 20 to 31; *The Elixir of Love* by Gaetano Donizetti, February 10 to 21; *The Passion of Jonathan Wade* by Carlisle Floyd, March 2 to 10; *Cinderella* by Gioacchino Rossini, April 6 to 14; and *Aida* by Giuseppe Verdi, April 27 to May 8.

The box office is not in the Civic Theatre but on the outside of the adjacent Golden Hall. It's open Monday through Friday from 10am to 5:30pm; hours vary on weekends on the day of performance. Performances are Tuesday, Wednesday, and Saturday at 7pm, Friday 8pm, Sunday 2pm.

CLASSICAL MUSIC—ORCHESTRAL

San Diego Symphony

Copley Symphony Hall, 750 B St. (at Seventh Ave.). ☎ **619/699-4205.** Tickets from October to May $14 to $42; June to September (SummerPops concerts) $10 to $29. A discount "Tix at Six" for $7.50 available at the box office only between 6 and 6:30pm. Bus: 2, 7, 9, 29, 34, or 35. Trolley: Fifth Ave.

The 81-member symphony, led by Israeli-born Yoav Talmi, performs classical programs from October through May. Robert Shaw is the principal guest conductor. The symphony's SummerPops series is held from June through September at the southern end of Embarcadero Marina Park (get there via Eighth Avenue below Harbor Drive), food is available, and picnicking is allowed. In winter, the orchestra accompanies silent movies in its unique Nickelodeon Series—a clever use of the concert hall space. This is the only orchestra on the West Coast that owns its performing hall, the former Fox Theatre, built in 1929 and since 1989 topped by the 34-story Symphony Hall Towers. The 80-foot mural in the lobby, by Denver artist James Jackson, depicts the intense concentration of a symphony orchestra. Tours, by appointment, are free. Concerts are held Thursday through Saturday at 8pm, Sunday at 2pm; SummerPops concerts at Embarcadero Marina Park at 7:30pm (see "Only in San Diego" at the end of this chapter). The box office is open Monday through Friday from 10am to 6pm.

DANCE

San Diego–based dance companies include the **California Ballet,** a traditional ballet company, and other minor companies. San Diego's **International Dance Festival,** held annually in January, spotlights the city's ethnic dance groups and emerging artists; most performances are at the Lyceum Theatre, with free dance in public areas. Dance companies generally perform in San Diego from September through June. For specific information about time and place of performances or for a monthly calendar of events, call the **San Diego Area Dance Alliance Calendar** (☎ 619/239-9255).

2   The Club & Music Scene

San Diego has a good supply of popular discos, bars, and clubs. (The legal drinking age is 21.) Currently, the hottest ones are located in the Gaslamp Quarter. They include **Club 66,** at 901 Fifth Ave. (☎ 619/234-4166), which has a Route 66 motif and caters to an over-28 crowd; **E Street Alley**, on the north side of E Street between Fourth and Fifth avenues (☎ 619/231-9200), which is a dressier club; **Club 5th Avenue,** 835 Fifth Ave. (☎ 619/238-7191); **Ole Madrid,** 751 Fifth Ave. (☎ 619/557-0146), the destination of choice for Europhiles; and **Dick's Last Resort,** 345 Fourth Ave., with entrances on both Fourth and Fifth avenues (☎ 619/231-9100), popular with the college crowd; and **Buffalo Joe's Saloon,** 600 Fifth Ave. (☎ 619/236-1616), a country-western nightclub. The first four of these are underground discos, and their popularity rises and falls like the tide in the Pacific. I suggest you walk around the Gaslamp Quarter and check them out for yourself. Cover charges vary from nil to $10, depending on the group that is performing, the night of the week, and if it happens to be the "in spot" at the moment.

Fans of alternative music might enjoy the **Casbah,** 2501 Kettner Blvd. (☎ 619/232-4355), where breakthrough bands are the norm, or **Bodies,** 528 F St. (☎ 619/236-8988), where live original music is played nightly.

If you're under 21, **SOMA Live,** 5305 Metro St., Mission Bay (☎ 619/239-SOMA), is the place for you. This concert venue in a warehouselike building has hosted Courtney Love, Social Distortion, and Faith No More.

COMEDY CLUB

Comedy Store

916 Pearl St., La Jolla. ☎ **619/454-9176.** Cover Wed $6, Thurs and Sun $8, Fri–Sat $10. Two-drink minimum all shows.

If you can prove you're 21, you're in for a lot of laughs. Amateur night is Monday and Sunday is for nonsmokers. Sunday and Thursday shows start at 8:30pm, Monday to Wednesday 8pm, Friday and Saturday 8 and 10:30pm.

DISCOS

Cannibal Bar

3999 Mission Blvd. (in the Catamaran Hotel). ☎ **619/539-8650.** Cover Fri–Sun $3-$15. Bus: 34 or 34A.

Videos and live bands take center stage in this large, lively, and everpopular nightspot. Live entertainment Wednesday through Sunday features the best local entertainment and national recording artists.

A draft beer costs $1.50. Open Wednesday through Sunday from 7pm to 2am.

The Yacht Club

333 W. Harbor Dr. (in the San Diego Marriott Marina) ☎ **619/234-1500.** No cover. Bus: 2. Trolley: Convention Center.

The nautical theme and waterfront location, with a curving window wall looking onto the marina, make this a comfortable spot to park oneself. There's live dance music nightly, with appetizers and light fare available until 11pm, along with a dinner menu served from 5 to 11pm. It's open daily from 11am to 1am; a band plays five nights a week, a DJ two nights at 9pm. Prices range from $3 to $4.50; there's no drink minimum.

JAZZ & BLUES

Croce's

802 Fifth Ave. (at F Street). ☎ **619/233-4355.** No cover to either Croce's Jazz Bar or Croce's Top Hat with the purchase of dinner at Croce's Restaurant or Ingrid's Cantina. Cover for regional bands $3–$7, for national acts $10–$18. Minimum at both bars $5. Bus: 1, 3, or 25. Trolley: Gaslamp Quarter.

Groups and individuals perform traditional jazz every night in Croce's Jazz Bar and rhythm and blues at Croce's Top Hat, both named after the late musician Jim Croce and owned by his wife, Ingrid. Jim Croce's son, A. J., an accomplished musician in his own right, sometimes performs. Jazz holds sway in the Jazz Bar and drifts easily into the adjoining restaurant; it opens nightly at 5pm and music starts at 8:30pm. Next door, in Croce's Top Hat, balcony seating overlooks the stage, where rhythm 'n' blues is at its liveliest; it's open daily from 11am to 2am, with music starting at 9pm. Prices at either bar range from $2.25 to $6.

BIG BAND

Hotel del Coronado

1500 Orange Ave., Coronado. ☎ **619/435-6611.** Cover $10 without dinner. Bus: 901. Ferry: From Broadway Pier, then take taxi. Take the Coronado Bridge to Third Street, then left onto Orange Avenue.

The West Coast's most glorious Victorian hotel kicks up its heels on Sunday nights, when it's swing time in the Crown Room. Besides the music and dancing, the architecturally memorable room makes the trip here worthwhile. Prices are $24.95 with buffet dinner. Open Sunday from 6 to 9:30pm.

DINNER CRUISES WITH ENTERTAINMENT

Hornblower/Invader Cruises

1066 N. Harbor Dr. (at Broadway Pier). ☎ **619/234-8687.** Tickets Sunday through Friday $35, Saturday $40 adults and children; alcoholic beverages are extra. Bus: 2. Trolley: Embarcadero.

Aboard either the 151-foot schooner *Invader* or the 145-foot motorized vessel *Entertainer,* you'll be entertained—and encouraged to dance—by a DJ/host playing a variety of CDs, cassettes, and records.

The three-course meal includes a Caesar salad, chicken and beef main course, and double-fudge chocolate cake. Boarding is at 6:30pm, and the cruise runs from 7 to 9:30pm.

San Diego Harbor Excursion

1050 N. Harbor Dr. (at Broadway Pier). ☎ **619/234-4111.** Tickets $44 adults, $30 for kids ages 3 to 12. Bus: 2. Trolley: Embarcadero.

The company offers a dinner on board the 150-foot, 3-deck *Spirit of San Diego*, with not one but two main courses, dessert, and cocktails. A live band plays during the 2^1/$_2$-hour cruise, and you can dance all you like. Sometimes they add a country-western band or even a karaoke sing-along. Boarding is at 6:30pm, the cruise from 7 to 9:30pm.

ROCK AND POP CONCERTS

San Diego has become a popular performance destination for many major recording artists. In fact, there is a concert just about every week. *The Reader* is the best source of concert information. Tickets typically go on sale at least six weeks before the event and, depending on the popularity of a particular artist or group, last-minute seats are often available through the box office or Ticketmaster. Of course, you can always go through a ticket agency like **Advance Tickets** (☎ 619/ 581-1080) and pay a higher price for prime tickets at the last minute.

Main concert venues include the San Diego Sports Arena, a 15,000- to 18,000-seat indoor venue, where the acoustics are not the best but a majority of concerts are held here because of the seating capacity and plenty of paid parking; the San Diego Jack Murphy Stadium, a 50,000-seat outdoor stadium, which has okay acoustics and is only used for major concerts like The Who and the Rolling Stones; SDSU Open Air Amphitheater, a 4,000-seat outdoor amphitheater with great acoustics—if you are not able to get a ticket, you can stand outside and hear the entire show; Embarcadero Marina Park, a 4,400-seat outdoor setting on San Diego Bay with great acoustics; and Humphrey's Concerts by the Bay, a 900-seat outdoor venue on the water that has good acoustics but seats are close together and parking can be a challenge unless you arrive early.

3 The Bar & Coffeehouse Scene

POPULAR BARS

In downtown San Diego, the knowing crowd gravitates to the bars at **Athens Market** (sometimes there's a fire-eating belly dancer), **Dobson's,** and **La Gran Tapa.** For a quieter scene, try the **Palace Bar** in the Horton Grand hotel. Pubgoers head to the **Princess of Wales.** In Mission Bay, the **Cannibal Bar** in the Catamaran Resort Hotel is a popular spot. In La Jolla, favorites are the **Whaling Bar** in La Valencia hotel and nearby **George's Cafe.** The legal drinking age is 21.

Top O' The Cove

1216 Prospect St., La Jolla. ☎ **619/454-7779.**

In this intimate setting, the pianist plays favorites, but leans heavily toward Gershwin. Nab the corner table next to the piano. On nice evenings, the music is piped to the patio, another idyllic spot to sit and sip. Drinks run from $4 to $65 (that's for Louis XIII cognac; buy the last two drinks and you get to keep the Baccarat bottle). Open Wednesday through Sunday from 8pm to late (usually 1am).

GAY & LESBIAN BARS & CLUBS

Club Bombay

3175 India St. (at Spruce Street). ☎ **619/296-6789**. Cover Fri–Sat $2 after 9pm. Bus: 5/105.

This casual place for women has a patio bar in back, where barbecues with a keg of beer are hosted on Sunday beginning at 4pm. There's occasional live entertainment on Friday and Saturday nights, and karaoke on Wednesday nights. Prices range from $2 to $4.25. Open Monday through Thursday from 4pm to 2am, Friday through Saturday from 2pm to 2am, Sunday from 1pm to 2am.

The Flame

3780 Park Blvd. ☎ **619/295-4163**. Cover Sun–Fri $2, Sat $3. Bus: 7 or 7B.

For women, The Flame has a large dance floor and two bars, including a video bar open Tuesday through Saturday. Friday night is stand-up comedy night, and on Tuesday, when it's "Boys Night Out," don't be surprised to find a clientele of 95 percent men. The bar often hosts special events. Prices range from $2.25 to $4 (often with specials at $1.25). Open Monday through Thursday from 5pm to 2am, Friday from 4pm to 2am, Saturday and Sunday from 5pm to 2am.

Kickers/Hamburger Mary's

308 University Ave. (between 3rd and 4th avenues). ☎ **619/491-0400**. No cover.

Country-western fever arrived in San Diego in spring 1992 with Kickers, a foot-stomping gay-owned and operated bar with an adjacent outdoor restaurant, Hamburger Mary's. The atmosphere is relaxed and informal, and no western garb is expected (the waiters are likely to be in shorts). If you're unschooled in the art of country-western dancing (it's not square dancing), just show up on Monday and Friday for lessons from 7 to 8:30pm, then put what you've learned to the test for the rest of the evening. Beginner classes are taught Monday and Tuesday, tougher moves the rest of the week. There's line dancing, too. Before, during, or after an evening at Kickers, head outside to the patio and Hamburger Mary's for a burger or sandwich and a chance to catch your breath. This place, which is equally popular among men and women, is a definite kick. Prices range from $2.50 to $4.50. Open Monday through Saturday from 7pm to 2am, Sunday from 4pm to 2am.

Rich's

1051 University Ave. (between 10th and 11th avenues). ☎ **619/295-2195** or 619/497-4588 for upcoming events. Thurs–Sat $4–$5; Sun, no cover before 9pm, $3 afterward.

This popular club/dance space welcomes primarily gay men 21 and older. Sunday is popular for Tea and Me, when there is no cover between 7 and 9pm, and on Thursday for Club Hedonism, with techno

Pitcher This: San Diego's Microbreweries

A microbrewery revolution? Well, not exactly, but San Diego suds *have* come a long way in the last few years. It started in 1989 when Karl Strauss, a Bavarian brewmaster with 44 years of experience working for Pabst in Milwaukee, came to town. He opened **Karl Strauss' Old Columbia Brewery,** the first brewery here in more than 50 years. He named his brews after local attractions—Gaslamp Gold Ale, Red Trolley Ale, Black's Beach Extra Dark, Star of India Pale Ale—but he brought the recipes from the old world, and they adhere to the Bavarian Purity Laws of 1516.

Karl's crew makes 23 beers a year, on a rotational basis, with 8 available at any one time. Free brewery tours are conducted weekend afternoons. Want to try them all and be able to walk? You can order a Taster Series, 4 ounces of 8 brews for only $5.95. Old Columbia, at 1157 Columbia St. (☎ 619/234-BREW), serves great beer and hearty American fare. Happy hours run from 4 to 6pm Monday through Friday, and 10pm to 1am Thursday through Saturday.

While an upscale crowd of "suits" gathers at Karl's place, **R. J.'s Riptide Brewery,** at 5th and K in the Gaslamp Quarter (☎ 619/231-7700), attracts a sports-happy bunch who appreciate the pub's big-screen TV. Its location—277 steps from the Convention Center—also makes it popular with out-of-towners. The copper-clad brewing tanks take center stage here, with the large U-shaped bar curving around them. R. J.'s produces top-fermented English-, German-, Irish-, and Belgium-style ales, stouts, and porters (no lagers). These include Aztec Amber Ale, Padres Porter, and Riptide Red. In 1994, R. J.'s entered nine beers in a California blind tasting and won eight medals: three golds, two silver, and three bronze. This upbeat,

tunes and more. On Friday and Saturday nights, go-go dancers and high-energy music set the tone for the night. Always check the events hotline, since the schedules can change. Prices range from 50¢ to $3. Open Thursday through Saturday from 9pm to 2am, Sunday from 7pm to 2am.

West Coast Production Company

2028 Hancock St. ☎ **619/295-DRAG** (3724). Cover $3.

This state-of-the-art modern dance club with three floors of fun features a newly remodeled laser and light show as well as a smoke-free coffee bar. It attracts primarily gay men with lesbians and straight couples welcome. Pool tables, rooftop patio, and arcade games round out the largest dance club in San Diego for over 18 years. Wednesdays is the most popular night with 1970s and 1980s disco music and 50¢ well drinks. Fridays and Saturdays, dance all night with the latest and hottest sound from San Diego's best DJs. Open nightly from 9pm to 2am, Fridays and Saturdays after-hours till 4am.

lighthearted place adopted the slogan *Save the Ales.* During happy hour, daily from 4 to 7pm, a 60-ounce pitcher costs $6 and drinkers who stay to dine choose from the "best of the wurst platter," "not your mother's shepherds pie," and "wing ding fling." Seating is indoors and out.

In contrast, the **La Jolla Brewing Company,** at 7536 Fay Ave. (☎ 619/456-BREW), feels more like a neighborhood pub. The wood floor is appropriately worn, and pool and darts are played in the back room. The brewmaster here is John Atwater, graduate of La Jolla High, class of '76. During his years at UC Santa Barbara (where he earned a Ph.D. in biochemistry), John home-brewed in five-gallon bottles. During his postdoctoral fellowship at the Salk Institute, he opened this microbrewery. He makes his hand-crafted beers from his own recipes and names them after local spots: Windansea Wheat (an American-style wheat beer), Sealane Amber (similar to a California steam beer), Red Roost Ale (a red ale), and Pump House Porter (a dark, slightly sweet ale balanced with a bitter finish). John offers TVs for sports fans and serves meals such as Baja fish tacos, brewhouse pasta, and "cheeseburger in paradise." Oyster shooters are a local favorite. Happy hour is from 4 to 7pm Monday through Friday.

In total, San Diego, once strictly a white-wine or Perrier kind of place, now has nine brewpubs. Others you may want to try include **Hops Bistro and Brewery,** 4353 La Jolla Village Dr., in University Towne Centre (☎ 619-587-6677); **Pacific Beach Brew House,** 4475 Mission Blvd., in Pacific Beach (☎ 619/274-2537); and **San Diego Brewing Co.,** 10450 Friars Road at Mission Gorge, (☎ 619/284-BREW).

COFFEEHOUSES

For the inside scoop on where to go in La Jolla see "Coffeehouses with Character: Choices in La Jolla" in Chapter 7.

Quel Fromage

523 University Ave., Hillcrest. ☎ **619/295-1600.** Bus: 16 or 25.

This laid-back place looks as if people have been drinking lattes and espresso here for decades. The desserts are rich, and the art on the wall is the work of local artists. Prices range from $1.25 to $5. Open Sunday to Thursday 7:30am to 11pm, Friday and Saturday 7:30am to midnight.

Upstart Crow

Seaport Village (central plaza). ☎ **619/232-4855.** Bus: 7. Trolley: Seaport Village.

Where else but in a coffeehouse/bookstore can you mix cappuccino and Colette, where tables and chairs fill cozy spaces surrounded by books? The selection of books, coffees, and desserts is scrumptious. And coffee refills are only 25¢. Prices range from $1 to $5. Open Sunday through Thursday from 9am to 10pm (until 11pm in summer), Friday and Saturday from 9am to 11pm.

4　More Entertainment

MOVIES

Many multiscreen complexes around the city show first-release films. Avant-garde and foreign films are screened at the **Guild,** 3827 Fifth Ave., Hillcrest (☎ 619/295-2000); **Hillcrest,** 3965 Fifth Ave., Hillcrest, with three hours' free parking (☎ 619/299-2100); the **Ken Cinema,** 4061 Adams Ave., Kensington near Hillcrest (☎ 619/283-5909); and the **Cove,** 7730 Girard Ave., La Jolla (☎ 619/459-5404). The irrepressible *Rocky Horror Picture Show* is resurrected every Friday and Saturday at midnight at the Ken. The **OMNIMAX** theater at the Ruben H. Fleet Space Center features movies and three-dimensional laser shows projected onto the 76-foot tilted dome screen (☎ 619/238-1233).

LITERARY READINGS

The best way to find out if and when authors will be reading from their works is to check the daily *San Diego Union-Tribune* or *The Reader* and the *San Diego Gay and Lesbian Times,* which are published weekly. Authors sometimes read at the **Blue Door Bookstore,** 3823 Fifth Ave., in Hillcrest (☎ 619/298-8610); and in La Jolla at **Warwick's Books,** 7812 Girard Ave. (☎ 619/454-0347), and **D. G. Wills** bookstore, 7463 Girard Ave. (☎ 619/456-1800).

CASINOS

Native American tribes operate three **casinos** located in east county: **Barona Big Top Casino,** 1000 Barona Rd., Lakeside (☎ 619/443-2300); **Sycuan Casino,** 5469 Dehesa Rd., El Cajon, (☎ 619/445-6016); and **Viejas Casino and Turf Club,** 5000 Willows Rd., Alpine, (☎ 619/445-5400). All three offer full casino gambling à la Las Vegas, off-track betting, and bingo. To bet on the ponies, go to the **Del Mar Thoroughbred Club** during the local racing season (July through September). At anytime of the year bets can be placed on races being run far and wide at **Del Mar Satellite Wagering,** at the Del Mar Fair Grounds (☎ 619/755-1167). To place a wager on **greyhound racing** or **jai alai,** you have to cross the international border to Tijuana. It's only a 40-minute ride by car or trolley from San Diego; from the border you'll need a cab to get to the racetrack or jai alai palace (see "Tijuana: Going South of the Border" in Chapter 11). Bookmaker offices, where you can place a bet on just about any sport, are located throughout Tijuana.

POOL

If your image of a pool hall includes smoke and marginal characters, **Team Player's Billiard Club,** 379 Fourth Ave. at J St. (☎ 619/230-1968), will be a pleasant surprise, with 36 pool tables, 2 full bars, TVs, and pinball. Open daily from 11am to 2am.

5 Only in San Diego

During the summer the San Diego Symphony performs a series of outdoor **SummerPops** concerts at the southern end of Embarcadero Marina Park, with guest performers that have included Emmylou Harris, Tony Bennett, and Van Cliburn.

San Diego's Top three attractions—the San Diego Zoo, Wild Animal Park, and Sea World—all extend their hours into the evenings during summer. Sea World caps its **Summer Nights** off every night with a fireworks display.

Free summer concerts are held at the Spreckels Organ Pavilion in Balboa Park as part of **Twilight in the Park;** this musical entertainment can be enjoyed June through August, from 8 to 9:30pm. The **Festival Stage** in Balboa Park and the **Mt. Helix Amphitheater** in La Mesa are popular outdoor theater venues during the summer.

Another park event, **Christmas on the Prado,** has been a San Diego tradition since 1977. The weekend of evening events is held the first Friday and Saturday in December. The park's museums and walkways are decked out in holiday finery; the museums are free and open late from 5 to 9pm; and there is entertainment galore, from bell choruses to Renaissance and Baroque music to barbershop quartets. Crafts (including unusual Christmas ornaments), ethnic nibbles, hot cider, and sweets are for sale. A Christmas tree and nativity scene await you at the Spreckels Organ Pavilion.

Only-in-San-Diego movie venues include **Movies Before the Mast** aboard the *Star of India.* Here movies of the nautical genre (such as *Black Beard the Pirate* and *Hook*) are shown on a special "screensail" April through October (☎ 619/234-9153); at the **Sunset Cinema Film Festival** in August you can view a mix of classic and current films free of charge from a blanket or chair on the beach. Films are projected on screens mounted on a floating barges from San Diego to Imperial Beach (☎ 619/454-7373). **Dive-In Movies** are shown at the Plunge (☎ 619/488-3110), an indoor swimming pool in Mission Beach. Viewers float on rafts in 91° water and watch water-related movies projected onto the wall. *Jaws* is a perennial favorite. The San Diego Symphony, Copley Symphony Hall, 750 B St. (☎ 619/699-4205), accompanies **silent movies** during a film series in its winter concert season, October through May. Of course, you can always do as the locals do and walk on the beach, watch the sunset or go in-line skating year-round.

11

Easy Excursions
from San Diego

If you have time for a day trip away from San Diego, popular destinations include the beaches and inland towns of North County (what locals call the north part of San Diego County), as well as our south-of-the-border neighbor, Tijuana. You could also go relax at a spa or resort (see p. 219). All are no more than an hour away.

1 North County Beach Towns: Spots to Surf & Sun

Picturesque beach towns, each poised over their own stretch of sand, dot the coast of San Diego County from Del Mar to Oceanside. These make great day-trip destinations for sun worshippers and surfers. Getting there is easy: Del Mar is only 18 miles north of downtown San Diego; Carlsbad about 33; and Oceanside approximately 36. If you're driving, follow I-5 north: You'll find freeway exits for Del Mar, Solana Beach, Cardiff by the Sea, Encinitas, Leucadia, Carlsbad, and Oceanside. The furthest point, Oceanside, will take you about 45 minutes. The other choice by car is to wander up the coast road—known variously along the way as Camino del Mar, Pacific Coast Highway, Old Highway 101, and County Highway S21. Amtrak and the Coaster provide rail service to Carlsbad and Oceanside, and Amtrak also stops in Solana Beach, just a few minutes north of Del Mar. Check with Amtrak (☎ 800/USA-RAIL) or the local tourist information offices about schedules. The San Diego North County Convention and Visitors Bureau (☎ 800/848-3336) is also a good information source.

DEL MAR

Less than 20 miles up the coast lies Del Mar, a small community with just over 5,000 inhabitants in a 2-square-mile municipality. The town has adamantly maintained its independence, eschewing incorporation into the city of San Diego. Sometimes known as "the people's republic of Del Mar," this community was one of the nation's first to ban smoking. The upscale folks who live here grin and bear it during the summer racing season when the Del Mar Thoroughbred Club attracts droves of out-of-towners.

Del Mar Beach connects with Torrey Pines Beach, providing miles of sand for walking; swimmers congregate north of **Jake's** seaside restaurant, surfers go south. On the Del Mar Beach, **Powerhouse Park** has picnic tables and a children's playground. On the cliff above it overlooking the ocean is **Seagrove Park,** the scene of free concerts in July and August (☎ 619/755-9313).

A popular spot for **hot-air ballooning** (see Chapter 7), Del Mar is best known for its **racetrack,** founded in 1937 by Bing Crosby and Pat O'Brien. Thoroughbred racing still takes place here from late July to mid-September (see Chapter 7). The 243-room **Del Mar Hilton** (☎ 619/792-5200 or 800/445-8667) is conveniently located right across the road from the racetrack, and the boutique-filled Flower Hill Mall is nearby. The **Del Mar Fair,** one of the country's largest, occurs the last two weeks in June, culminating on the Fourth of July.

On Camino del Mar in the town center, the stylish **Del Mar Plaza** has shops and restaurants, as well as jazz concerts in summer. ✪ **Esmeralda Books and Coffee** on the upper level can provide food and food for thought. Parking is underneath the plaza.

For more information about Del Mar, contact or visit the **Del Mar Chamber of Commerce Visitor Information Center,** 1104 Camino del Mar, Del Mar, CA 92014 (☎ 619/793-5292).

WHERE TO STAY
Expensive
L'Auberge Del Mar Resort and Spa

1540 Camino del Mar (P.O. Box 2078), Del Mar, CA 92014. ☎ **619/259-1515** or 800/553-1336. Fax 619/755-4940. 120 rms, 8 suites. A/C MINIBAR TV TEL. $165–$300 single or double; from $400 suite. Packages available. AE, DC, MC. V. Parking $5, valet $8. Take Amtrak to Solana Beach and the hotel courtesy van will pick you up, or take I-5 to Del Mar Heights Road west, then turn right onto Camino del Mar Road; it's at 15th Street.

L'Auberge stands on the site of the old Del Mar Hotel—midway between the beach and the shops and dining spots in Del Mar Plaza. The resort, near Seagrove Park, retains the same exclusive air, and the lobby is reminiscent of the old hotel's, with a fireplace that is an exact replica. The rooms feature private balconies or terraces, sitting areas, marble baths and vanities, and traditional furnishings; about half have ocean views; some offer fireplaces; some have ceiling fans. Most rooms are nonsmoking.

Dining/Entertainment: The 15th Street Grille and Terrace serves three meals a day. There are three hours of free music and dancing in the lobby on Friday and Saturday nights, and you can pop into Durante's Pub most anytime.

Services: Room service (6:30am–10pm), complimentary newspaper, laundry/dry cleaning. In-room coffee service. VIK (Very Important Kids) program during summer months and holidays.

Facilities: Two tennis courts, pool, lap pool, Jacuzzi, full European-style spa (massage, hydrotherapy treatments, herbal wraps, steam room, sauna, spa cuisine, yoga on nearby beach), health club, nearby golf.

Moderate
Del Mar Motel on the Beach

1702 Coast Blvd. (at 17th Street), Del Mar, CA 92014. ☎ **619/755-1534** or 800/
223-8449 for reservations. 45 rms. TV TEL. Summer $95–$120, lower off-season rates;
sometimes higher weekends and holidays. Extra person $5. AE, CB, DC, DISC,
MC, V. Take I-5 to Via de la Valle exit; go west, then south on Highway 101 (Pacific
Coast Highway), veer west onto Coast Boulevard.

The only property in Del Mar right on the beach, this little white-
stucco motel with blue trim is clean and simply furnished and has been
here since 1946. Upstairs rooms have one king-size bed, while those
downstairs come with two double beds. All rooms have a refrigerator,
coffeemaker, and fan. Half are no-smoking rooms, and only those
rooms with ocean views have bathtubs (the rest have showers only).
This is a good choice for beach lovers, because you can walk from here
along the beach for miles, and the popular seaside restaurants Poseidon
and Jake's are right next door. The motel has a barbecue and picnic
table for guests' use.

Wave Crest

1400 Ocean Ave., Del Mar, CA 92014. ☎ **619/755-0100**. No fax. 31 bungalow/
condominiums. TV TEL. Late July–Sept 15, $175–$200 studio, $210–$240
one-bedroom, $300 two-bedroom; lower off-seasons rates; weekly rates available
year-round. MC, V. From I-5, exit Del Mar Heights Road west, turn right onto Camino
del Mar and drive to 15th Street, turn left and drive to Ocean Avenue; turn left.

On a bluff overlooking the Pacific, these gray-shingled bungalow/con-
dominiums containing studios and suites are beautifully maintained
and wonderfully private. For a honeymoon or romantic getaway, this
is tops. All the units surround a landscaped courtyard and have a
queen-size bed and sofa beds, artwork by local artists, VCR, stereo, full
bath, and fully equipped kitchen with dishwasher. The studios can
sleep one or two people, the one-bedroom suites up to four. Guests
enjoy a lounge with a fireplace, a TV, and newspapers; a pool and bubbling Jacuzzi overlooking the ocean; and the lush vegetation on the
grounds. It's only a five-minute walk to the beach from here, and shopping and dining spots are only a few blocks away. Irons, ironing boards,
and movies are available to guests at no charge. There is an extra fee
for maid service. Laundry facilities are on site.

Bed & Breakfasts
Gull's Nest

12930 Via Esperia, Del Mar, CA 92014. ☎ **619/259-4863**. 1 rm, 1 suite. TV. $75
rm; $95 suite (all with full breakfast). Extra person $10. No credit cards but personal
checks or traveler's checks accepted. From I-5, take the Carmel Valley Road exit west;
after a mile turn right onto Via Esperia; second house in second block.

A mile and a half south of downtown Del Mar, the Gull's Nest provides a tranquil getaway. Guests may enjoy two decks that overlook the
ocean and pine trees. The beach is only 2¹/₂ blocks away, the hiking
trails of Torrey Pines Reserve just a short drive away. Both accommodations have a full bath and a king-size bed, with a feather mattress and
down quilt. The smaller of the two, the Robin's Nest, has access to a
garden and coffee-making equipment, while the Gull Suite has a full

Northern San Diego County

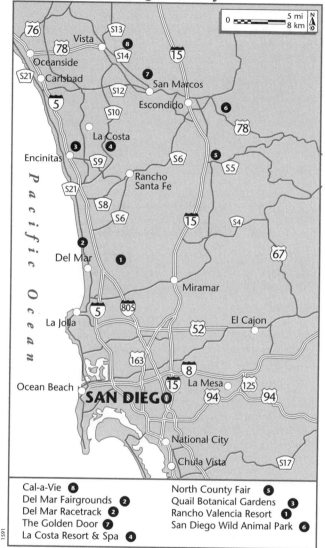

Cal-a-Vie **8**	North County Fair **5**
Del Mar Fairgrounds **2**	Quail Botanical Gardens **3**
Del Mar Racetrack **2**	Rancho Valencia Resort **1**
The Golden Door **7**	San Diego Wild Animal Park **6**
La Costa Resort & Spa **4**	

kitchen, a dining nook, a porch with a single bed, and a private cedar deck. Several eateries are within walking distance. Hosts Connie and Mike Segal are happy to supply guests with brochures and other information. Children are welcome.

✪ Rock Haus

410 15th St., Del Mar, CA 92014. ☎ **619/481-3764**. 10 rms. $90–$110 single or double without bath; $120–150 single or double with bath. Rates include continental breakfast. AE, MC, V. Take I-5 to Del Mar; exit Del Mar Heights Road west, turn right onto Camino del Mar and right again onto 15th Street; it's on north side of street.

In other incarnations, it has been a private home, a gambling hall, and a hotel. Now restored, the Rock Haus, run by innkeeper Doris Holmes, has 4 rooms with private baths and 6 sharing 3 baths; most rooms have ocean views. The Huntsman's Room has its own fireplace, as does the living room. Refreshments are served in the late afternoon. There is no smoking inside the house, and children under 13 are not permitted. Perched on a hill behind the Del Mar Plaza, overlooking the town, the Rock Haus is just a short stroll away from shopping, dining, and the beach. A two-night minimum stay is required on weekends and holidays from July through September.

WHERE TO DINE

Head to the upper level of the centrally located **Del Mar Plaza,** at Camino del Mar and 15th Street, and consider **Il Fornaio Cucina Italiana** for excellent Italian cuisine; **Epazote** for Mexican, Tex-Mex, and southwestern fare; or **Pacifica Del Mar** for outstanding seafood. Kids like to eat at **Johnny Rockets,** an old-fashioned diner on the lower level. Down on the beach, ✪ **Jake's** and **Poseidon** are both good for California cuisine and sunset views; Jake's has a Sunday champagne brunch, and Poseidon's club sandwich and grilled chicken salad are wonderful. The racetrack crowd congregates at **Bully's,** 1404 Camino del Mar, for Bully Burgers, prime rib, and crab legs.

CARLSBAD

Fifteen miles north of Del Mar and 33 miles from downtown San Diego (a 45-minute drive), the pretty beach community of Carlsbad provides many reasons to linger on the California coast: good swimming and surfing beaches; a mile-long, two-tiered beach walk that is accessible for travelers with disabilities; three lagoons perfect for walks or bird-watching; small-town atmosphere (the population is 63,000, but it actually feels smaller than Del Mar); landscaped streets; memorable restaurants; an abundance of antiques and gift shops; no high-rise buildings (and no plans for any); and a warm welcome to travelers in the town's recycled train depot (1887) that is now home to the **Visitors Information Center** (☎ 619/434-6093).

Carlsbad was named for Karlsbad, Bohemia, because of the similar mineral (some say curative) waters they both produced, but the town's once famous artesian well has long been plugged up. You can picnic in small **Florence Magee Park.** While there, peek into **St. Michael's by the Sea Episcopal Church** (1894) across the street; the original organ is to the right. In the spring, visit the 200 acres of cultivated **flower fields** that transform the hills south of town into a startling floral rainbow from mid-March to mid-May. Or see 3,000 varieties of flowers, plants, and trees year-round at the serene, 30-acre **Quail Botanical Gardens** in nearby **Encinitas** (☎ 619/436-3036), open daily from 8am to 5pm.

In March, the town hosts the Carlsbad 5000, the premier 5-km race in the United States; the men's and women's world records were attained here. **Legoland,** a Danish theme park made of the world-famous LEGO blocks, is scheduled to open here in 1999.

Note that **Palomar Airport** serves Carlsbad and nearby communities.

WHERE TO STAY

La Costa Resort and Spa

Costa del Mar Rd., Carlsbad, CA 92009. ☎ **619/438-9111** or 800/854-5000. Fax 619/931-7585. 478 rms and suites. A/C TV TEL. $225–$420 double; $395–$2,100 suites. AE, CB, DC, DISC, MC, V. Take I-5 to La Costa Avenue exit, go east to El Camino Real and turn left. Turn right into resort at sign.

La Costa resort boasts two championship 18-hole golf courses (home of the annual Mercedes Championships); a 21-court racquet club comprised of two grass, four clay, and 15 composite courts (home of the WTA Toshiba Tennis Classic); resident tennis pro Pancho Segura (who has coached Jimmy Connors and Andre Agassi); an extensive spa with a multitude of treatments available; and five restaurants. These amenities are spread over 450 landscaped acres. Attractive accommodations offer all the bells and whistles you'd expect at this price level. The big advantage here is that travel partners can do their own things during the day (golf, tennis, or the spa) and still rendezvous for dinner. This large resort, which has hosted many people over the years, isn't looking as fresh as it once did.

Beach Terrace Inn

2775 Ocean St., Carlsbad, CA 92003. ☎ **619/729-5951**, 800/622-3224 in California or 800/433-5415 elsewhere. Fax 619/729-1078. 41 rms, 5 suites. A/C TV TEL. Summer, $108–$219 double; from $139 suite. Winter $97–$177 double; from $117 suite. (Rates include continental breakfast.) Extra person $10. AE, CB, DC, DISC, ER, MC, V.

Carlsbad's only beach-side hostelry (others are across the road or a little farther away), this downtown Best Western property has a helpful staff, and rooms and an outdoor pool with ocean views. Rooms, although not elegant, are extra large, and some have balconies, fireplaces, and kitchenettes; suites have separate living rooms and bedrooms. VCRs and films are available at the front desk. It's good for families. You can walk everywhere from here, and there is street parking.

Pelican Cove Inn

320 Walnut Ave., Carlsbad, CA 92008. ☎ **619/434-5995**. 10 rms. $85–$175 double. (Rates include full breakfast.) Extra person $15. AE, MC, V. From downtown Carlsbad, follow Carlsbad Boulevard south to Walnut Avenue; turn left and drive 2¹/₂ blocks.

This Cape Cod–style hideaway near the beach combines romance with luxury—down to the bed covers, which resemble clouds more than comforters. All rooms have fireplaces, private entrances, and baths; some have spa tubs. You can lounge or have breakfast in the garden with a gazebo and a sundeck. Hosts Kris and Nancy Nayudu can provide you with beach towels and chairs or prepare a wonderful picnic basket (with 24 hours notice).

Tamarack Beach Resort

3200 Carlsbad Blvd., Carlsbad, CA 92008. ☎ **619/729-3500** or 800/334-2199. Fax 619/434-5942, 23 rms, 54 condominium suites. A/C TV TEL. $115–$135 double; from $155 suite. Children under 12 stay free in parents' room. AE (accepted for rooms, not suites), MC, V. Free parking.

This resort property's rooms, in the village and across the street from the beach, are restfully decorated in tropical colors and wicker furniture, with small refrigerators, coffeemaking facilities, and VCRs (movies are complimentary). The fully equipped suites (including washer and dryer) are available on a daily or weekly basis. The pretty Tamarack also has a pleasant lobby, a heated pool in a sunny courtyard setting, two Jacuzzis, exercise facilities, valet services, barbecue grills, and a good restaurant, Dini's by the Sea, that is popular with locals.

WHERE TO DINE

Branci's Caldo Pomodoro

2907 State St. ☎ **619/720-9998**. Reservations recommended Fri–Sat nights. Main courses $7.95–$18.95. AE, CB, DC, MC, V. Sun–Thurs 11am–9pm, Fri–Sat 11am–10:30pm, Sun 9:30am–2pm. ITALIAN.

The spotlight here is on sauces—13 to be exact—served on linguine, angel hair pasta, fettuccine, or mostaccioli. Brother and sister owners Francesco and Gina Branciforte (he's the chef, she's the maître d') have created a bistro ambience with black-and-white decor, and they have embellished their mom's family recipes impressively. Check out the daily specials. Beer and wine are available.

Neiman's

2978 Carlsbad Blvd. ☎ **619/729-4131**. Reservations not accepted. Main courses $9.95–$14.95. AE, MC, V. Cafe daily 11:30am–11pm. Dining room Mon–Thurs 5–9pm, Fri–Sat 5–10pm; Sun brunch 9:30am–2pm. CALIFORNIA.

Housed in the survivor of the town's historic Victorian twin inns (1887), Neiman's provides three-in-one: a casual cafe for lunch and dinner; a striking circular dining room open only in the evenings; and a congenial bar with dramatically displayed bottles. The food (primarily seafood, salads, and pasta, although the cafe also serves sandwiches and burgers) is fresh and well prepared; the desserts, enticing.

Tip Top Meats

6118 Paseo del Norte. ☎ **619/438-2620**. Menu items $2.25–$5. MC, V. Daily 7am–8pm. AMERICAN.

This cheerful, spacious deli/restaurant has the largest servings and lowest prices in town. Breakfast starts at just over $2 (for $1 more, you get unlimited smokehouse bacon, pork link, or sausage), and the prime-rib dinner special for $4.98 Friday through Sunday is hard to beat. Diners wander around with coffee pots serving refills to their friends.

OCEANSIDE

The most northerly town in San Diego County (actually it's a city of 150,000) and 36 miles from San Diego, Oceanside claims almost four miles of beaches and one of the West Coast's longest wooden piers, where a tram does nothing but transport people from the street to the end of the 1,954-foot-long pier and back for 25¢ one way. The restaurant at the end of the pier is a great place for lunch over the ocean. The wide, sandy beach, pier, and well-tended recreational area with playground equipment and an outdoor amphitheater are within easy walking distance of the train station.

Oceanside's world-famous surfing spots attract numerous competitions, including the **Longboard Surf Contest** and **World Bodysurfing Championships**, both in August. The small **California Surf Museum,** across the street from the pier, at 308 Pacific St. (☎ 619/721-6876), is open Monday, Thursday, and Friday from noon to 4pm, Saturday and Sunday from 10am to 4pm.

Four blocks west of the Surf Museum is the Moorish-style **Oceanside Civic Center**, at 300 N. Coast Hwy., designed by architect Charles Moore as a postmodern homage to renowned California architect Irving Gill.

A launch ramp, visitor boat slips, charter fishing, and a Cape Cod–style village of shops are found at **Oceanside Harbor**, about 1 mile north of the pier. Several excellent restaurants, including a Chart House, offer harbor-side dining. The **Marina Inn,** at 2008 Harbor Dr. North, Oceanside, CA 92054 (☎ 619/722-1561), has comfortable rooms and suites that offer harbor and ocean views. The **Harbor Days Festival** in mid-September typically attracts 100,000 visitors to enjoy a crafts fair, entertainment, and food booths.

The area's biggest attraction is **Mission San Luis Rey** (☎ 619/757-3651), which is a few miles inland. Founded in 1798, it is the largest of California's 21 missions. There is a small charge to tour the mission, its impressive church, exhibits, grounds, and cemetery. You might recognize it as the backdrop for several *Zorro* movies.

For an information packet about Oceanside and its attractions, send a check for $3 to the **Oceanside Chamber of Commerce,** P.O. Box 1578, Oceanside, CA 92051 (☎ 619/721-1101).

2 North County Inland: From Rancho Santa Fe to Palomar Mountain

The coastal and inland sections of North County are as different as night and day. Beaches and laid-back villages where work seems to be the curse of the surfing class characterize the coast, while inland you'll find beautiful barren hills, citrus groves, and conservative communities where agriculture plays an important role.

Rancho Santa Fe is located about 27 miles north of downtown San Diego, and from there the Del Dios Highway (S6) leads to Escondido, almost 32 miles from the city. San Marcos, Vista, and Fallbrook are even farther north. Nearly 70 miles away is Palomar Mountain in the Cleveland National Forest, which spills over the border into Riverside County. The **San Diego North County Convention and Visitors Bureau** (☎ 800/848-3336) can answer all your questions.

RANCHO SANTA FE

Certainly one of the county's loveliest communities, exclusive Rancho Santa Fe was once the property of the Santa Fe Railroad, and the eucalyptus trees they grew there create a stately atmosphere. To get to Rancho Santa Fe from San Diego, take Interstate 5 north to Via de la Valle east. The Del Dios Highway, which starts here, is the scenic route to Escondido and the Wild Animal Park. This road affords views of

Lake Hodges, as well as glimpses of expansive estates, some of the most expensive in the country.

WHERE TO STAY

✪ Rancho Valencia Resort

5921 Valencia Circle (Box 9126), Rancho Santa Fe, CA 92067. ☎ **619/756-1123** or 800/548-3664. Fax 619/756-0165. 43 suites in 21 casitas. MINIBAR TV TEL. $315–825 suite. Spa, tennis, golf, and romance packages available. AE, CB, DC, DISC, MC, V. Free parking. Take I-5 to Via de la Valle and travel east to El Camino Real (Mary's Tack Shop is on the corner); go south to San Dieguito Road and turn east; follow the signs for Rancho Valencia.

If you are in need of pampering and relaxation or a romantic getaway, read on. A member of Relais et Châteaux and Preferred Hotels, this sun-baked Spanish- and Mediterranean-style resort sits on 40 acres overlooking the San Dieguito Valley and the rolling hills of Rancho Santa Fe. Small and intimate, the resort is far removed from the fast pace of the real world, even though it's only a short way from I-5 and only 6 miles inland from Del Mar. Imagine having your own casita with cathedral ceilings, terra-cotta tiles, Berber carpets, wood-burning fireplace, ceiling fans, oversize tiled bath, walk-in closet, patio, and private terrace. To boot, spa treatments and massage can be given in the casita itself. Fresh-squeezed juice and a newspaper are left outside your door in the morning, and coffeemaking equipment is available. Those who actually do venture outside their casita will discover grounds filled with 2,000 citrus trees, bougainvillea, and air sweetened by flowers and birdsong.

There is a lap pool; a large, secluded pool; three Jacuzzis; and a fitness room. Those more athletically inclined can take advantage of the 18 tennis courts and tennis clinics with a four-to-one student/teacher ratio. You might check out the championship croquet lawn, or play a round of golf at private courses adjacent to the resort. Bikes for adults and kids are available at no extra charge, and there are plenty of hiking trails to enjoy. The Clintons dined here when they were in town, and Jessye Norman stayed while she was performing in San Diego. I highly recommend this place; I don't think you'll be disappointed.

Dining/Entertainment: The pretty dining room serves Mediterranean-California cuisine and three meals a day, with a cellist or guitarist on Friday and Saturday nights; there's dancing under the stars on Thursday nights in July and August. Tea and cocktails are served in La Sala, from which there is a great view of the hot-air balloons at sunset.

Services: 24-hour room service, daily turndown service, complimentary morning paper and fresh orange juice, airport transportation from San Diego's Lindbergh Field, valet parking.

Facilities: Two cable TVs and VCRs in each suite; video rentals; in-room safes; two pools; three Jacuzzis; unlimited use of 18 hard-turf tennis courts, tennis clinics, and match arranging; regulation croquet court; golf privileges at four nearby private golf clubs; fitness room; bicycles; massage rooms.

Select Spas

It's not too surprising that two premier spa retreats—the **Golden Door** and **Cal-a-Vie**—are discreetly tucked away in the hills of North County. After all, this is Southern California, where looking good is an art form and year-round outdoor rest and relaxation are possible. It seems only natural that those yearning to get into shape would find their way here. And they do, from all over the world.

Spa-goers receive unparalleled pampering, but they also work their buns off—or at least into shape. At the Golden Door, 39 guests follow their own personal schedule; everyone is encouraged to begin the day with an early morning hike, followed by exercise classes, healthy meals, "mocktail" parties, and—the best part—massages. You'll feel renewed by the diet, physical exertion, and the spa's peaceful atmosphere. "Everyone leaves here happy," I was told; about three-quarters of the guests return.

Women are the primary clientele; the spa only sets aside four weeks for men and designates two weeks as "co-ed." And paradise isn't cheap: the all-inclusive rate is $4,250 a week during the winter; $3,750 during the summer. But aren't you worth it? A three-to-one staff ratio means someone is always available to do your bidding. (Rooms are cleaned every two hours.) For more information, contact P.O. Box 463077, Escondido, CA 92046-3077 (☎ 619/744-5777 or 800/424-0777; fax 619/744-5007).

In the same price range, Cal-a-Vie caters to 24 guests a week. Most weeks are co-ed, although one or two a month are set aside for women only. Like the Golden Door, the spa emphasizes enacting lifestyle changes and de-stressing, but Cal-a-Vie focuses more on European spa treatments—real sybaritic stuff—and less on the spiritual side. This spot is popular with celebrities, such as Angelica Huston, Julia Roberts, and Kathleen Turner. Oprah found Rosie here! If you could handle 16 spa treatments a week (including outdoor massages on private decks) in absolutely gorgeous surroundings, contact 2249 Somerset Rd., Vista, CA 92084 (☎ 619/945-2055; fax 619/630-0074).

If the Golden Door and Cal-a-Vie are out of your price range, you might consider **Rancho La Puerta**, located in Tecate, Mexico, just over the border from San Diego County. It's under the same ownership as the Golden Door, but because it's less expensive; its local moniker is "The Back Door." It's not as exclusive, but offers similar programs. To request a brochure, call 619/744-4222 or 800/433-7565.

Several resorts in the San Diego area also offer extensive spa facilities: **L'Auberge Del Mar Resort and Spa** and **La Costa Resort and Spa** (both described above), and **Le Meridien** in Coronado (described in Chapter 5). If you're in town and want bodywork, I recommend my favorite massage therapist, Linda Lowe (☎ 619/454-6702).

ESCONDIDO

Best known as the home of the **Wild Animal Park** (described in Chapter 7), Escondido is also the site of the **California Center for the Arts**, an attractive 12-acre campus that includes two theaters, an art museum, a conference center, and a cafe. It's worth the 45-minute to 1-hour drive to Escondido, along Interstate 15 north to the Escondido exits, just to see the appealing post modern architecture of this facility, which opened its doors in 1994. (For what's-on and ticket information, call 619/738-4100.) This city of 125,000 is in the heart of a major agricultural area, so it's not surprising that the **Farmers Market** held here on Tuesday afternoons is one of the county's best. The nearby **Welk Resort Center**, at 8860 Lawrence Welk Drive (☎ 800/932-9355) offers lodging, golf, tennis, and live theatrical entertainment. In total, North County is home to 36 golf courses (some are described in Chapter 7). Orfila Vineyards is near the Wild Animal Park; for details, refer to "For Travelers Interested in Wine" in Chapter 7. For shopping, the **North County Fair**, at 272 E. Via Rancho Parkway (☎ 619/489-2332), is a three-story, fully-enclosed mall, with Nordstrom, The Broadway, and other department stores, plus a food court and nearly 100 smaller shops and boutiques.

WHERE TO DINE

✪150 Grand Cafe

150 West Grand Ave. ☎ **619/738-6868**. Reservations recommended, especially for weekend nights. Main courses $7.50–$17.50. AE, DC, MC, V. Mon–Thurs 11:30am–9pm; Fri–Sat 11:30am–9pm; Sun 4:30–9pm. MODERN MULTIETHNIC.

What a treat to discover this delightful cafe on the main drag in downtown Escondido—an area I hadn't associated with fine dining. However, now I keep finding excuses to go North County and 150 Grand Cafe, owned by English expatriates Cyril and Vicki Lucas. The bright, attractive decor feels like a cross between a conservatory and a library. Lunch-time favorites include grilled poblano chile (with Havarti cheese, roasted tomato vinaigrette, tomatillos, cilantro, and red and blue tortilla strips) and the flash-grilled tuna salad (Hawaiian ahi, orange basmati, mixed greens, rice noodles, sesame-ginger vinaigrette). Dinners include grilled filet mignon, forest mushroom pasta, sautéed salmon, and roast game hen. There's indoor and outdoor seating.

PALOMAR MOUNTAIN

Palomar Observatory and its mammoth telescope have kept a silent vigil over the heavens since 1949. To get there from San Diego, take I-15 north to Highway 76 east, and turn left onto County Highway S6. Even if you don't want to inch your way to the top, drive the 3 miles to the lookout or just beyond it to a campground, grocery store, restaurant, and post office. Palomar Observatory's impressive dome is 135 feet high and 137 feet in diameter. The telescope itself has a single 200-inch mirror and weighs 530 tons. Now completely computerized, it has an approximate light range of more than a billion light years. Start your visit in the museum, which is open daily 9am to 4:30pm (except December 24 and 25) and has a continuously running informative video that makes a walk up the hill to the observatory more meaningful. The observatory closes at 4pm, and you'll only be able to look at (not through) the mammoth telescope. Palomar is primarily a research facility. The museum and the observatory both have restrooms. Try to visit the observatory in the morning; late in the day, you'll have the sun in your eyes coming back down the mountain.

For a downhill thrill, take the **Palomar Plunge** on a 21-speed mountain bike. From the top of Palomar Mountain to its base, you'll experience, courtesy of gravity, a 5,000-foot vertical drop stretched out over 16 miles. **Gravity Activated Sports** (☎ 619/742-2294 or 800/985-4427) supplies the mountain bike, helmet, gloves, lunch, souvenir photo, and T-shirt. The plunge costs $75.

3 Tijuana: Going South of the Border

16 miles south of San Diego

Like many large cities in developing nations, Tijuana is a mixture of new and old, rich and poor, modern and traditional. With almost 2.5 million people, it's the second-largest city on the west coast of North America (only Los Angeles is larger). The Mexico you may be expecting—charming town squares and churches, women in colorful, embroidered skirts and blouses, and bougainvillea spilling out of every orifice—is to be found in southern Baja California and even more so in the interior of the country in places such as San Miguel de Allende and Guanajuato (but that's another trip and a different guidebook). What you'll find in Tijuana is poverty (begging in the streets is commonplace), sanitary conditions that may make you nervous, and, surprisingly, a local populace that seem no more or less happy than their north-of-the-border counterparts. If you're spending a few days or more in Baja, please refer to the "Baja California: Exploring More of Mexico" section in Chapter 12.

ESSENTIALS

GETTING THERE   If you plan to visit only Tijuana, I recommend leaving the car behind, as the traffic can be challenging. However, the tours only give you several hours in Tijuana in the afternoon, so you miss evening activities. Another alternative is walking across the border; you can either park your car in one of the safe, long-term parking lots on the San Diego side for about $8 a day, or take the San Diego trolley to the border. Once you're in Tijuana, it's easier to get around by taxi than to fight the local drivers. Cab fares from the border to downtown Tijuana run about $5. If you plan to visit the Baja Peninsula south of Tijuana, I suggest driving.

By Car   Take I-5 south to the Mexican border at San Ysidro. The drive takes about half an hour.

Many car-rental companies in San Diego now allow their cars to be driven into Baja California, at least as far as Ensenada. Avis (☎ 619/231-7155) and Courtesy (☎ 619/497-4800) cars may be driven as far as the 28th parallel and Guerrero Negro, the dividing line that separates Baja into two states, North and South; Bob Baker Ford

(☎ 619/297-5001) and Colonial (☎ 619/477-9344) allows their cars to be driven the entire 1,000-mile stretch of the Baja Peninsula.

Keep in mind that if you drive in, you'll need Mexican auto insurance in addition to your own. You can get it in San Ysidro, just north of the border at the San Ysidro exit, or from a car-rental agency in San Diego or from a AAA office if you're a member.

By Trolley In downtown San Diego, hop aboard the bright-red trolley headed for San Ysidro and get off at the last, or San Ysidro, stop (it's nicknamed the Tijuana Trolley for good reason). From here just follow the signs to walk across the border. It's simple, quick, and inexpensive; the one-way trolley fare is $1.75.

By Bus Mexicoach/Five Star Tours (☎ 619/232-5049) offers a $10 round-trip fare (less for seniors and children) between the San Diego train station and downtown Tijuana, with several departures a day; the new Mexicoach stop is at Revolución between Calles 6 and 7. **Gray Line** (☎ 619/491-0011) offers a tour to Tijuana for $26, with lunch $36, with a drop-off in the middle of town; you can spend a few hours or all day. **San Diego Mini Tours** (☎ 619/477-8687) also offers a tour to Tijuana for $26.

Visitor Information Prior to your visit, you can write for information, brochures, and maps from the **Tijuana Convention & Visitors Bureau,** P.O. Box 434523, San Diego, CA 92143-4523. Another good idea is to contact **Baja California Tourism Information** (☎ 619/298-4105, or in California, Arizona, or Nevada 800/522-1516, or rest of U.S. and Canada 800/225-2786). These capable folks dispense information and make bookings throughout Baja California. In Tijuana, visit the **Tourist Information Center,** at Avenida Revolución between Calles 3 and 4 (about four blocks from the border crossing, if you walk in). It's open daily from 9am to 7pm (☎ 83-14-05). If you call Tijuana from the United States, add 011-52-66 before the number for the international call.

The **State Tourism Assistance Office,** near the Tourist Information Office on Avenida Revolución, handles any complaints or problems that visitors might have, such as an auto accident or a theft (☎ 88-05-55). The number for the **U.S. Consulate** is 81-74-00.

Tijuana's climate is similar to San Diego's. Don't expect sweltering heat because you are south of the border, and remember that the Pacific waters are always cold in northern Baja, so you won't be swimming in tepid seas. The first beaches you'll get to are about 15 miles south of Tijuana.

The city does not take time for an afternoon siesta; you'll always find shops and restaurants open, as well as people in the streets, which are safe for walking. (Observe the same precautions you would in any large city.) Most people who deal with the traveling public speak English, often very well. To maneuver around someone on a crowded street or in a shop, say "con permiso" (with permission).

A taxi ride to most any destination in downtown Tijuana will cost about $5, but be sure to negotiate the price with the driver before you get in the cab. Local taxis, on the other hand, cost only 50¢ per

Tijuana

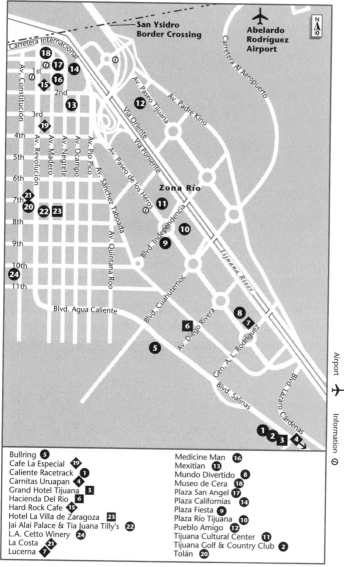

San Ysidro
Border Crossing

Abelardo
Rodríguez
Airport

N

Carretera Internacional

Av. Constitución

Av. Revolución
Av. Madero
Av. Negrete
Av. Ocampo
Av. Pío Pico
Av. Sánchez Taboada
Av. Quintana Roo

1st
2nd
3rd
4th
5th
6th
7th
8th
9th
10th
11th

Av. Paseo Tijuana
Av. Padre Kino
Via Oriente
Via Poniente
Av. Paseo de los Héros

Carretera Al Aeropuerto

Zona Río

Blvd. Independencia

Blvd. Cuauhtémoc

Blvd. Agua Caliente

Av. Diego Rivera

Gen. A. L. Rodríguez

Tijuana River

Blvd. Lázaro Cárdenas

Blvd. Salinas

Airport ✈

Information ⊙

person (American coins are accepted), which you pay when you disembark. The brown-and-white taxis parked on Calle 3 between Avenida Revolución and Avenida Constitución go to the Cultural Center; the black-and-red ones, parked on Calle 2 between Revolución and Constitución, go to the racetrack. You have to wait for the taxi to fill up, but that happens fairly quickly. The price can't be beat, and it's fun to get around the local way.

A sales tax of 10%, called an IVA, is added to most bills, including those in restaurants. This does not represent the tip; the bill will read "IVA incluído," but you should add about 15% for the tip if the service warrants.

You can visit Tijuana (or Ensenada, for that matter) without changing money because dollars are accepted everywhere and change is usually given in American currency and coins.

If you've come to Tijuana on the San Diego trolley or if you leave a car on the U.S. side of the border, you will walk through the border crossing. The first structure you'll see on your left is a **Visitor Information Center,** open daily from 9am to 7pm; ask for a copy of the *Baja Visitor* magazine and the *Baja Times*. From here, you can easily walk into the center of town or take a taxi.

EXPLORING TIJUANA

L. A. Cetto Winery

Calle Canon Johnson 2108 (at Avenida Constitución Sur). ☎ **85-30-31.** Admission $1 tour only, $2 for tour and tastings (for those 18 and older only; those 17 or younger are admitted free with an adult but cannot taste the wines), $3 with souvenir wine glass. Shop and tours, Tues–Sun 10am–6pm. Bus: Check if the shuttle bus from Revolución between Calles 4 and 5 is running. By foot: Take Revolución to Calle 10, turn right and continue one block, then turn left and proceed 1¹/₂ blocks. By car: Take Revolución to Calle 9, then an immediate left and continue for 2 blocks.

The striking building is shaped like a wine barrel, and the red-oak facade is actually made from old barrels in an inspired bit of recycling. In the entrance stand a couple of old wine presses that Don Angel Cetto used back in 1928 in the early days of production. His family still runs the winery, which opened this impressive visitor center in 1993. L. A. Cetto bottles both red and white wines, some of them award winners, including Petite Sirah, Nebbiolo, and Cabernet Sauvignon. The grapes come from the fertile Guadalupe Valley between Tecate and Ensenada. Visitors see a video that describes the 12 Cetto wines and the foods they complement. Most bottles cost about $5, the special reserves a little more than $10. The company also produces tequila, brandy, and olive oil, all for sale here.

Cultural Center

Avenida Paseo de los Héroes and Avenida Mina. ☎ **84-11-11.** Museum $1 adults, 50¢ children; OMNIMAX (including museum entry) $4.50 adults, $2.50 children 2 and over; children under 2 free. Daily 9am to 9pm.

Opened in 1982, Tijuana's busy Cultural Center is comprised of three entities: a museum with changing exhibits downstairs, primarily of contemporary Mexican artists, and a permanent exhibit upstairs, with clothing and artifacts from Mexican prehistory to its colonial era; a planetarium and OMNIMAX theater with regular showings of *Pueblo del Sol* (People of the Sun), an excellent film about the culture, beauty, and diversity of Mexico, with a daily show in English; and a performing arts center, where a large theater hosts international performers in drama, opera, dance, and symphony. The museum has a restaurant and a store selling books (in Spanish) at a discount. It's less than a mile from the border crossing.

Mexitlan

Ocampo and Calle 2. ☎ **38-41-01.** Admission $1.75, children under 12 free. Tues–Fri 9am–5pm, Sat–Sun 11am–7pm.

Here, in the space of a full city block, you can see exquisitely detailed models of Mexico's finest buildings, ruins, churches, plazas, and villages. From the pyramids of Tenochtitlán to the charming plazas of Taxco, all the models are built to scale, illuminated and animated. A favorite is Mexico City's University Stadium as it looked during the closing ceremonies of the 1968 Olympics, complete with spectators all doing "the wave." The park also includes shops, cafes, and restaurants, as well as free parking.

Mundo Divertido (Fun World)

2578 José M. Velasco (at Avenida Paseo de los Héroes). ☎ **34-32-14.** Admission free; prices vary for rides and other activities. Mon–Fri noon–9pm, Sat–Sun 11am–10pm. Follow Avenida Paseo de los Héroes to José M. Velasco; it's a block from the statue of Abraham Lincoln.

Kids will love an outing to Fun World, where they'll find everything from bumper boats and cars to miniature golf to a small roller coaster. Many attractions are outdoors.

Museo de Cera (Wax Museum)

8281 Calle 1 (at Calle Madero, a block from Avenida Revolución). ☎ **88-24-78.** Admission $1. Daily 10am–8pm.

One of Mexico's only wax museums, if not the only one, it opened in Tijuana in 1993; if you're walking across the border and into town, you'll pass it on your way to Avenida Revolución and the Visitor Information Center, which is a block away. Sixty figures, faithfully rendered, await you, many of them such key players from Mexican history as Moctezuma; Pancho Villa; Emilio Zapata; Father Hidalgo; the reviled Porfirio Díaz; and Lazaro Cardenas, who abolished gambling in Mexico in the 1920s and 1930s. Fr. Junípero Serra, João Cabrilho (Juan Cabrillo), and Father Kino, who played a large part in San Diego's history, are also included; Mahatma Gandhi, Marilyn Monroe, Michael Jackson, Whoopi Goldberg, and the infamous Freddy Krueger of Nightmare-on-Elm-Street fame have been thrown in for good measure. Texts are in Spanish and English.

SPECTATOR SPORTS & OUTDOOR ACTIVITIES

Tijuana is a major spectator sports center. At its **Jai Alai Palace,** at Avenida Revolución and Calle 7 (☎ 85-25-24), at least a dozen action-packed games are played daily except Wednesday, starting at 7:30pm. The ornate, colorful entrance has three arched doorways fronted by tall palms, a fountain, and a statue of a player atop a globe. During a game of jai alai, which is like high-speed racquetball, one opponent is pitted against another, and the ball travels faster than 100 miles per hour; you can bet on who you think will win, place, or show—or simply sit back and enjoy the fast-paced excitement.

Caliente Racetrack, on Bulevar Agua Caliente (☎ 619/231-1910 in San Diego, 81-78-11 in Tijuana), is the scene of greyhound races. The dogs run Monday to Friday at 7:45pm and on Saturday and Sunday at 2pm.

Bullfights are held in two rings from May through September, Sunday at 4pm. They feature matadors from Mexico and Spain, and tickets start at $7. The downtown ring is at 100 Bulevar Agua Caliente, not far from the twin towers of the Grant Hotel Tijuana. The Bullring by the Sea is located on the coast south of the city.

A fairly well-kept secret are Tijuana's fairways, at the **Tijuana Golf and Country Club,** also on Bulevar Agua Caliente even closer to the Grand Hotel Tijuana (☎ 81-78-55). Greens fees are $22 on weekdays and $27 on weekends, with cart and club rentals available. The course dates from the 1920s. There is a restaurant on the premises. Open daily from 7am to 8pm.

SHOPPING

Tijuana's biggest attraction is shopping—ask any of the 44 million people who cross the border each year to do it. They come to take advantage of the reasonable prices on liquor and other items, such as guayabera shirts, embroidered men's cotton shirts that are extremely cool and comfortable and so acceptable and attractive that Mexican businessmen often wear them to work.

American currency is fully accepted here and as far south as Ensenada. (If you plan to buy silver jewelry, wait and do it there.) You'll even get back nickels and dimes in change, and you can bring up to $400 in merchandise back across the border duty free.

Tijuana's shops are strung out along Avenida Revolución, the old downtown tourist strip with its perpetual carnival atmosphere; off this well-beaten but colorful track, there are fine, modern shopping centers, such as the Plaza Río Tijuana. Here, more than on Revolución, you can observe the "real" Tijuana, where the locals shop and stroll.

Avenida Revolución is lined with shops, stalls (where you can bargain), vendors hawking their wares, eateries, and burros festooned with garlands and sombreros, just waiting to be photographed with you. Many visitors think that this is all there is to Tijuana and they come away disappointed. But there's more than this.

Begin to browse, as most newcomers to Tijuana do, along Avenida Revolución. As you stroll down it, you'll notice a mixture of modern and traditional shops. **Le Drug Store,** with its sleek glass facade at Revolución and Calle 4, sells perfumes, cosmetics, and leather bags. It has a cafe and restrooms and accepts American Express and Visa.

Between Calles 4 and 5 stands the old **Hotel Caesar** (home of the original Caesar's salad), whose faded elegance recalls a bygone era. During the bullfight season, the matadors still headquarter here. In the lobby you can see, lovingly preserved, the "suits of lights" worn by some of Spain's and Mexico's most famous bullfighters, and along the stairwell, a photograph gallery commemorates their glory. Steps away from the commercial clatter of Avenida Revolución, this quiet oasis evokes one of Mexico's most romantic traditions.

To try your hand at bargaining, stroll through **Pasaje Sonia,** on Revolución between Calles 5 and 6. At 735 Revolución, **Hand Art** is an excellent source of hand-embroidered linens and clothing from the Mexican mainland.

At Revolución and Calle 7, across from the Jai Alai Palace, **Tolán** is the best place in Tijuana to shop for craft items. In six rooms you'll discover clothing, wall hangings, glassware, and tin work. My favorites are the clay-and-tin *arboles de la vida* (trees of life) from Metepec and Puebla; the blue glassware from Guadalajara; and the tin Christmas ornaments from Oaxaca. There's something here for every pocketbook.

A block from Tolán, at the corner of Calle 7 and Avenida Madero, is a little shopping center with a **Ralph Lauren** shop, a linen shop, and stores selling beachwear, sportswear, and evening wear. One block beyond Tolán, on the opposite side of Revolución, is **Sanborn's,** a Mexico City tradition expanded to Tijuana. Containing a modern pharmacy, restaurant, bookstore, and souvenir shop all under one roof, it is the one spot in town where you will find everything you need.

Shopping Centers There are excellent buys on French perfume, Italian leather, and liquor in the **Plaza Río Tijuana** shopping center, a cab ride away from Avenida Revolución, and across the street from the Cultural Center. Try **Importaciones Sara** for imported perfumes (they have another store on Revolución), and the huge **Comercial Mexicana** for an enormous variety of liquor at bargain prices. A cross between a modern supermarket and an open-air mercado, Comercial Mexicana delights the senses with displays of colorful chiles, exotic fruits, and fresh cheeses (which you're invited to sample). Next door, **Suzett** bakery makes irresistible pastries and breads. When your feet and your spirit need a rest, sip a free cup of their wonderful Mexican hot chocolate and munch on a fresh roll while watching couples, families, and young professionals stream by.

Catercorner to the Cultural Center, at Avenida Paseo de los Héroes and Avenida Independencia, **Plaza Fiesta** has many colorful cafes in colonial Mexican style featuring international cuisines, among them Spanish and Italian, and Harry's Bar for Mexican food. Next door is **Plaza del Zapato,** two levels of nothing but shoe stores. However, one renegade store squeaked in called **La Herradura de Oro,** which sells cowboy and horse gear, and it's fun for browsing or window shopping.

Just after you cross the border and take the pedestrian bridge over the now-dusty bed of the Tijuana River, there is a shopping center called **Plaza Californias,** with both shops and street vendors. As you make your way from here toward the Tourist Information Office, you'll see another little shopping center called **Plaza San Angel,** on Calle 1 between Avenidas Negrete and Madero, and opposite it is a helpful pharmacy called the **Medicine Man,** 613 Avenida Negrete and Calle 1.

TIJUANA AFTER DARK

Tijuana has several lively discos, and perhaps the most popular is **Baby Rock** (an obvious cousin to Acapulco's lively Baby O), which features everything from jungle rock to hard rock. It's located in the Zona Río, close to the Guadalajara Grill restaurant.

A recent addition to Tijuana's nightlife has been the proliferation of "sports bars," cheerful watering holes featuring satellite wagering from all over the United States, as well as from Tijuana's Caliente track. The most popular of these bars cluster in **Pueblo Amigo,** a new center designed to resemble a colonial Mexican village. Even if you don't bet on the horses, you can soak up the atmosphere. Two of the town's hottest discos, **Rodeo de Media Noche** and **Mr. Frogs,** are also in Pueblo Amigo, as well as **La Tablita de Tony,** an Argentinean restaurant. Pueblo Amigo is conveniently located less than 2 miles from the border: a short taxi ride or—during daylight hours—a pleasant walk.

WHERE TO STAY

Grand Hotel Tijuana

Agua Caliente 4500, Tijuana, Mexico. ☎ **81-70-00** in Tijuana, or 800/522-1516 in California, Arizona, and Nevada; 800/225-2786 elsewhere. 422 rms. A/C TV TEL. $80 single or double on weekdays; $90 single on weekends; $110 double on weekends; from $195 suite. AE, DC, MC, V. Free underground parking.

You can see the 22-story twin towers of the Grand Hotel Tijuana when you come into town (one tower contains offices; the other, this hotel). It's right beside the golf course and very near the racetrack.

Dining/Entertainment: Restaurant Las Torres offers Mexican food Monday through Saturday from noon to 5pm. For international fare, The Bistro, complete with piano music, is open for dinner from 6pm to midnight. The Plaza Café is open 24 hours. There's continuous music in the lobby bar from noon to 2am.

Services: 24-hour room service, laundry/dry cleaning, access to golf course, travel agency.

Facilities: Concierge level (called Fiesta Grand Club) on top four floors, heated pool, tennis courts, sauna, Jacuzzi, meeting rooms.

Hacienda Del Rio

Bl. General Sánchez Taboada 10606, Tijuana, Mexico. ☎ **84-86-44** in Tijuana, 619/298-4105 in California, or 800/522-1516 in California, Arizona, and Nevada; 800/225-2786 elsewhere. Fax 84-86-20. 130 rms, 4 suites. A/C TV TEL. $55–$65 single or double; $80 suite. Children under 12 stay free in parents' room. MC, V.

Just a block from Avenida Paseo de los Héroes, Hacienda del Río is a modern three-story property, which opened in August 1989. Rooms on the second and third floors have tubs in the baths; in the first-floor rooms, there are showers. Suites have separate living rooms and vanities and marble-tiled baths. Recliners, tables, and umbrellas surround the hotel pool. The restaurant is open for breakfast, lunch, and dinner. Facilities include a hotel shop and meeting room.

Hotel La Villa de Zaragoza

Av. Madero 1120, Tijuana, Mexico. ☎ **011-526-685-1832** from the U.S. or 85-18-32 in Tijuana. Fax 011-526-685-1832 from the U.S. or 85-18-37 in Tijuana. 66 rms. A/C TV TEL. $31.25–$35.70 single; $35.70–$45 double; $41.95–$59 suite. Extra person $5.35. Rates include tax. MC, V. Free parking.

Situated downtown behind the Jai Alai Palace, this is your best bet for convenience sake if you don't have a car and are on a budget. Rooms have furnishings that are worn but clean, tiled showers, and separate vanities. Courtyard rooms are the quietest, but other rooms are larger. There is no extra charge for local telephone calls. The hotel has a casual restaurant and a somewhat more formal bar. There is room service from 7am to 11pm, and laundry service is available. There's hotel security at night. Reserve two weeks in advance for weekends.

Lucerna

Av. Paseo de los Héroes 10902, Zona Río, Tijuana, Mexico. ☎ **34-20-00** in Tijuana, 619/298-4105 in California, or 800/522-1516 in California, Arizona, and Nevada; 800/225-2786 elsewhere. Fax 619/294-7366. 163 rms, 5 suites. TV TEL. $70 single; $75 double; $130 suite, AE, DC, MC, V.

This striking property, with a courtyard fountain, has a friendly, attentive staff. The pretty rooms have either balconies or brick patios. A French restaurant in the hotel serves dinner from 8 to 11pm, as well as Saturday and Sunday brunch; there are two bars, one of them featuring piano music nightly. In summer, there are cookouts around the pool, and room service is available 7am to 11pm. Car rental and laundry service are offered.

WHERE TO DINE
EXPENSIVE
La Costa

Calle 7, no. 150 (just off Av. Revolucion). ☎ **85-84-94.** Main courses $11–$22. MC, V. Daily 10am–midnight. SEAFOOD.

Fish gets top billing here, starting with the hearty seafood soup. There are combination platters of half a grilled lobster, stuffed shrimp, and baked shrimp; fish filet stuffed with seafood and cheese; and several abalone dishes.

Tour de France

Gobernador Ibarra 252 (on the old road to Ensenada between the Palacio Azteca Hotel and Motel La Sierra). ☎ **81-75-42.** Reservations recommended. Main courses (including soup and salad) $15; MC, V. Mon–Thurs 8am–10:30pm, Fri–Sat 8am–11:30pm. FRENCH.

Martín San Román, the chef and co-owner of Tour de France, was sous-chef at San Diego's famous Westgate hotel, and then went on to open the top-class Marius restaurant in the Meridian hotel in Coronado. His loyal clientele has followed him from San Diego, and he has acquired new devotees in Tijuana. It's worth a trip to Tijuana just to sample Martín's pâtés or his escargots; and the vegetables, prepared and presented with the flair of an artist, all come fresh from local Ensenada farms. The wine list is extensive and international, and the atmosphere is as fine as the food.

MODERATE
Hard Rock Cafe

520 Av. Revolución (between Calles 1 and 2). ☎ **85-02-06.** Menu items $3–$10. MC, V. Daily 11am–2am. AMERICAN/MEXICAN.

Here's proof of Tijuana's modernity: its own Hard Rock Cafe, complete with burgers and fries and, of course, the usual T-shirts and other merchandise. But this place, which is popular with families at lunchtime, also makes a bow to Mexico on its menu with fajitas, nachos, and guacamole. Daily specials include the catch of the day. There's live music on Thursday through Sunday evenings. It's conveniently located near the Tourist Information Office.

Tia Juana Tilly's

Av. Revolución 701 (at Calle 7). ☎ **85-60-24.** Main courses $8–$12. MC, V. Daily 11am–11pm. MEXICAN.

Centrally situated beside the Jai Alai Palace, this lively spot features all manner of Mexican fare, including chicken and beef dishes and combination plates. There is disco music and dancing on weekends, with a cover charge of $3 to $5.

INEXPENSIVE

Cafe La Especial

Av. Revolución 718 (at the foot of the stairway to Gómez Arcade). ☎ **85-66-54.** Menu items $3–$12. Daily 9am–10pm. MEXICAN.

For as many years as anyone can remember, La Especial has been a favorite refuge from the commotion of Avenida Revolución. The food is dependably fresh and well prepared, and the beer is always cold. Served with fresh, warm tortillas, the carne asada is particularly delicious; the cheese enchiladas are the best in town at any price. Traditional Mexican breakfasts are available all day.

Carnitas Uruapan

Bd. Díaz Ordáz 550 (across from Plaza Pacífica). ☎ **81-61-81.** Menu items $2.50–$8. No credit cards. Daily 7am–3am. MEXICAN.

Going to Carnitas Uruapan, 1½ blocks from the racetrack, is like attending a Mexican family celebration. You sit at brightly painted, long tables, often with other groups, while strolling mariachis and bustling waiters and waitresses contribute to a fiesta atmosphere. The only dish to order here is carnitas: succulent chunks of pork served family style with Mexican beans, hot sauce, and fresh cilantro, all of which gets rolled up in a warm tortilla to create an incomparable treat. Half a kilo (about 1 pound) of carnitas, plenty for two people, costs about $12 and comes with all the trimmings.

12

Excursions Farther Afield

If you have time for a longer trip outside of San Diego, you can choose to explore four very distinct areas, all of them within an hour or two of the city. They include the gold-mining town of Julian, now known for its apple pies, to the northeast of San Diego; the vast Anza-Borrego Desert, due east of Julian; the wine country of Temecula, due north of San Diego; and to the south of San Diego, just across the border, Baja California and a taste of Mexico. Whichever direction you choose, you're in for a treat.

1 Julian: Apple Pies and More

60 miles NE of San Diego

A trip to Julian (pop. 1,500) is a trip back in time. The old gold-mining town, now best known for its apples, has some good eateries and a handful of cute B&Bs, but its popularity is based on the fact that it provides a chance for city-weary folks to get away from it all. However, when it's sunny in San Diego, it may be snowing in Julian, perched at 4,235 feet above sea level.

People first ventured into these fertile hills in search of gold in the late 1860s; they discovered it in 1870 near where the Julian Hotel stands today, and 18 mines sprang up like mushrooms. During all the excitement, four cousins—all former Confederate soldiers from Georgia, two with the last name Julian—founded the town of Julian. The mines are estimated to have produced up to $13 million worth of gold in their day.

Before you leave, try Julian's apple pies; whether the best pies come from Mom's Pies or the Julian Pie Company is always a toss-up. It's fun to sample all of them and decide for yourself.

ESSENTIALS

GETTING THERE **By Car** The 90-minute drive can be made via Highway 78 or I-8 to Highway 79. I suggest taking one route going and the other coming back. Highway 79 winds through scenic Rancho Cuyamaca State Park, while Highway 78 traverses open country and farmland. If you come by Highway 78, you'll pass the **mission church of Santa Ysabel** (1812), where there is a tiny museum and a large Native American cemetery, on your right, as well as **Dudley's Bakery,** off to the left at the junction with Highway 79 and just 7 miles from

Julian. The bakery, here since 1963, is known for miles around for its breads, from raisin-date-nut to jalapeño, and on weekends 5,000 to 6,000 loaves come out of the ovens. Dudley's also makes pastries and cookies, and it's open from 8am to 5pm Wednesday through Sunday. Across the street from Dudley's is **Once Upon a Time**, a cute shop selling antiques and gifts.

By Public Transportation Getting to Julian by public transportation is a relatively slow, but inexpensive, process. You start by taking the trolley from San Diego to the El Cajon Station, then catch the Northeast Rural bus to Julian. The bus runs in the afternoon Monday through Saturday only, and the one-way trip costs $2.50, including the trolley. You have to pay the bus driver in exact change (show your trolley stub and you pay only an additional $1). Try to reserve your seat at least 24 hours in advance; call (☎ 619/765-0145) between 7 and noon and 2 and 5pm Monday through Saturday, or leave a message on the answering machine.

VISITOR INFORMATION Once in Julian, you'll need a car if you want to stay at one of the B&Bs that are located out of town. However, Main Street is only 6 blocks long, and some lodging, shops, and local cafes are on it or a block away. Town maps and flyers for accommodations are available from the Town Hall on Main Street at Washington Street; public restrooms are behind the Town Hall. There's no self-service laundry (so come prepared), but you'll find a post office, liquor store, and a few grocery stores. Shops are often closed on Monday and Tuesday. The town has a **24-hour hotline** (☎ 619/765-0707) to provide information on lodging, dining, shops, activities, upcoming events, weather, and road conditions. For a brochure on what to see and do in Julian, contact the **Julian Chamber of Commerce**, P.O. Box 413, Julian, CA 92036 (☎ 619/765-1857).

SPECIAL EVENTS Special events include Julian's popular **fall apple harvest** held the entire month of October (it used to be only one weekend, but the traffic in town got way out of hand); the **annual wildflower show** lasts for a week in early May, and the **annual weed show**, a tradition since 1961, is usually held the last few weeks in August or the beginning of September. There's a **craft show** on weekends in November. If you arrive on the **Fourth of July,** count on participating in a community barbecue and seeing a quilt exhibition and parade. It's also fun to visit in December when activities include caroling and a living nativity pageant. The first two weekends in December, the members of the **Julian Bed and Breakfast Guild** host open houses with complimentary refreshments.

TOURING THE TOWN

It's fun to learn about the town and surrounding area by visiting the **Julian Cider Mill,** which moved in about 20 years ago when a service station moved out. The father-and-son team of Turk and Fred Slaughter run the place, an actual mill where you can see cider being made; homemade peanut butter is ground on the premises too, and in the spring a glass-enclosed beehive bustles with activity. Because the town is relatively near to both desert and sea (either is within 1¹/₂ hours' drive away), Julian honey is particularly good. It's hard not to feel like a kid in this store filled with jawbreakers, nuts, preserves, trail mix, and easy conversation around a potbellied stove. Fred Slaughter calls it "a hobby that got a bit out of hand."

On the right as you come into town is the **Julian Pioneer Museum** (☎ 619/765-0227)**,** at 4th and Washington streets, housed in an old brewery and open Tuesday through Sunday from 10am to 4pm, April through November, weekends and holidays December through March. Here you can learn about some of the old-timers buried up the hill in the Haven of Rest Cemetery.

Near the museum, the **Julian Library** (☎ 619/765-0370), at Fourth and Washington streets, is housed in the old Witch Creek School (ca. 1888). The school closed in 1954, and in 1970 the building was cut in half and moved along a narrow two-lane road to this spot, as the photos in back by the stove attest. The library displays a model of the old school. It is open Tuesday through Saturday from 10am to 1pm and 2 to 5pm.

The **Eagle and High Peak Mines** (☎ 619/765-0036), 6 blocks from Main Street via C Street, still operate daily from 9am to 4pm, but only for educational reasons, since the gold is long gone.

SHOPPING   It's fun to dart in and out of the little shops in Julian. My favorites are the **Julian Farms Antiques Shop,** 2818 Washington St. (☎ 619/765-0250), for gifts and patio accessories, and **Warm Hearth,** 2125 Main St. (☎ 619/785-1022), for gifts, cassettes (a must since local radio stations don't come in well), and wood-burning stoves, if you're in the market for one. **Applewood,** next door to Julian Farms Antiques, is also very good for gifts and antiques.

EVENING FUN   You can mix culture with barbecue at the ✪ **Pine Hills Dinner Theater** on Friday and Saturday nights at **Pine Hills Lodge**, a few miles from Julian off Pine Hills Road (☎ 619/765-1100). The rustic lodge opened its doors on July 4, 1912; in 1980, Dave and Donna Goodman bought it and opened the 96-seat dinner theater, which has staged almost 70 productions, among them *I'm Not Rappaport*, and *Last of the Red-Hot Lovers*. The dinner buffet of delicious baby-back pork ribs or barbecue chicken starts promptly at 7pm; give them 24 hours notice and you can get a vegetarian plate. Show time is at 8pm, and the price for the dinner and the theater is $28.50; for the show alone, it's $14.50. The playhouse is boxing champ Jack Dempsey's former gym, built for Dempsey in 1926 when he was in training for his fight against Gene Tunney.

To hear some music—folk music or piano or maybe the strains of a hammered dulcimer—head out to the **Wynola Coffee Company,** in a big red barn just over 3 miles south of town on Highway 78; it'll be on the left. The musicians are on hand only on Saturday night from 7pm, and people of all ages come out to this local hangout with its mismatched tables and chairs to hear them and indulge in dessert and coffee. The cover is about $3 (☎ 619/765-2368).

EXPLORING THE COUNTRYSIDE   If there's something about being in the country that makes you want to hop in the car and drive down one rural road after another, Julian is an ideal starting point. You'll pass rolling hills, country stores, rambling houses, and fruit stands, and come upon towns with names like Ramona, Ballena, and Wynola.

One of my favorite short drives is along the road that leads to the **Menghini Winery,** owned and run by Toni and Michael Menghini; it's 2 miles out on Farmer's Road (follow it west out of town until you see the winery sign, and then bear to the left down the hill). The winery is usually open Monday, Friday, Saturday, and Sunday from 10am to 4pm, daily in October and December, or call for an appointment (☎ 619/765-2072). The grapes come from Ramona and Temecula (see later in this chapter), and the local favorite wine is Julian Blossom. The tanks are right in the tasting room, and the wines only are sold locally, for $7 to $10 per bottle. You may enjoy your purchase right away in the picnic area in the apple orchard.

If you don't make it to the desert this trip, at least take a moment to gaze out at it and the Salton Sea from **Inspiration Point,** just 1½ miles south of Julian on Highway 79 opposite Pinecroft Park. **Lake Cuyamaca** (pronounced kwee-yah-*MACK*-ah), 10 miles south on Highway 79, offers boating, fishing (bass, trout, and crappie), and recreational vehicle camping on a first-come, first-served basis. Its facilities are open from sunrise to sunset daily (☎ 619/765-0515 or 619/447-8123). There are motorboat and rowboat rentals, a 3½-mile hiking trail around the lake, and a charge for fishing ($4.50 for adults, $2.50 for children 8 to 15). A restaurant with a deck and adjoining store overlook the lake.

Back in Julian, **Country Carriages** (☎ 619/765-1471) will show you the sights and give you a spin down a country lane in a horse-drawn wagon for $20 per couple, or around the town for $5 per adult, $2 per child. It's a tradition for Julian locals to take a Christmas Eve carriage ride. Hop in front of, or catercorner to, the drugstore; the ride lasts a half hour. The **Julian Bicycle Company,** off Main Street at 1897 Porter Lane, is actively involved in the Julian Fat Tire Festival, held in mid- or late April, as well as several other biking-related events. Contact them for specific information and dates (☎ 619/765-2200) or drop by Wednesday through Saturday from 10am to 5pm. For a different way to tour, try **Llama Trek** (☎ 619/765-1890; fax 619/765-1512), P.O. Box 2363, Julian. You'll lead the llama, which carries packs, for trips to see rural neighborhoods, an historic gold mine, mountain and lake views, and apple orchards. Rates vary from $55 to $75 per person and include lunch.

WHERE TO STAY

⑤ Julian Farms Lodging

2818 Washington St. (P.O. Box 879), Julian, CA 92036. ☎ **619/765-0250.** 4 attached cottages and 1 cabin. TV. $69 single or double; $99 cabin. Extra person $5. AE, MC, V.

As you drive into town, it's easy to pass right by this little place on the left. That would be a shame because the yellow cottages with blue shutters and a grape arbor in front make the perfect secret hideaway. Three of the cottages have a double bed and a daybed in a single room; one has two double beds in two rooms and is perfect for families. All have small private baths with showers, hot pots, country antiques, goose-down comforters, and a split of Julian Blossom wine. A nearby cabin has a queen bed and a sitting area. You can pick all the grapes you want and eat them in the vine-covered gazebo. It's just down the hill from Main Street, and there is a wonderful gift shop on the premises. Reserve three to four months ahead for weekends. Smoking is permitted outside only. Breakfast isn't served here, but a few cafes in town open early. This is a good choice for visitors without cars.

Julian Hotel

Main St. and B St. (P.O. Box 1856), Julian, CA 92036. ☎ **619/765-0201**. 15 rms, 2 cottages. $72–$90 double without bath, $82–$110 double with bath; $125–$160 cottage. (Rates include full breakfast.) AE, MC, V.

The Julian Hotel has been putting a roof over travelers' heads since the days when the Butterfield stagecoach stopped across the street. A pot-bellied stove still sits in the parlor, along with an upright piano that arrived here from Philadelphia via Cape Horn. The hotel's original owners, Albert and Margaret Robinson, were former slaves; their photograph hangs on the parlor wall. There are a dozen rooms in the original part of the house—with "necessary rooms" at the end of the hall—and each room is decorated in a variation of a Victorian theme. Another three rooms added off the front porch in 1920 have private baths as do two cottages. One of them, the Honeymoon House, features a Franklin (freestanding) fireplace and an old-fashioned tub. The cottages book up to two months in advance. The hotel's generous breakfast menu includes apple-filled pancakes and omelets. Coffee, tea, cakes, and cookies are served in the parlor at 5pm. "O. J.," the resident parakeet, fills the lobby with happy chirps. This is a good choice for visitors who want to be in the thick of things on the main drag.

Orchard Hill Country Inn

2502 Washington St. at Second Street. (P.O. Box 425), Julian, CA 92036-0425. ☎ **619/765-1700**. Fax 714/765-2090. 22 suites and rooms. A/C MINIBAR TV TEL. $130–$155 single or double. Extra person $25. Two-night minimum stay if including Saturday. Deposit required. Midweek discounts available. Rates include full breakfast. AE, MC, V.

Hosts Darrell and Pat Straube offer the most upscale lodging in Julian—a two-story lodge and four 1928 California Craftsman-style cottages situated on a hill with a panoramic view that includes the historic townsite. Ten guest rooms, a guests-only dining room, and a "great room" with a massive stone fireplace are located in the lodge. Twelve suites are in cottages over three acres of grounds. All quarters feature attractive furnishings including plantation shutters and have private baths. Suite amenities include fireplaces, whirlpool tubs, wet bars, telephones, VCRs, books, videos, games, window seats and wrap-around porches. Breakfast can be delivered to suite occupants.

BED & BREAKFASTS

For a small place, Julian is blessed with some outstanding accommodations, including bed-and-breakfasts, even some for people who prefer not to share their breakfast with other guests or their hosts. For a list and a description of a dozen B&Bs, contact the **Julian Bed and Breakfast Guild**, P.O. Box 1711, Julian, CA 92036 (☎ 619/765-1555 daily from 9am to 9pm). All members are within a few miles of the town center. In the meantime, consider these quite different possibilities, all up in the Pine Hills, a few miles south of town.

Artists' Loft

4811 Pine Ridge Ave. (P.O. Box 2408), Julian, CA 92036. ☎ **619/765-0765.** 2 rms and 1 self-contained cabin. $105 Manzanita Room; $115 Gallery Room (including breakfast); $150 cabin (with breakfast ingredients). MC, V. Turn off Hwy. 78 one mile west of Julian, and follow Pine Hills Road to Pine Ridge Avenue; then drive .8 mile. Look for the "M*A*S*H" truck in the front yard.

This peaceful place, set on a hilltop under whispering pines, appeals to those with an interest in art, nature, and ideas. Owners Nanessence and Chuck Kimball are artists and have fashioned a most creative abode for themselves and others. Each room comes with tree limbs and trunks recycled in clever ways, a wood-burning stove, a comfortable queen-size bed, a coffeemaker, a private bath, pine tables, good reading lights, and original artwork (that's for sale). The cabin offers a screened-in porch, king bed, full kitchen, wood-burning stove, and CD player with a supply of classical and New Age CDs. This B&B best reflects the local environment—including fresh flowers. The natural decor is conducive to cocooning. You can easily go for walks from here. There is a Japanese-style teahouse on the 5-acre property and a wood deck overlooking the fabulous view that stretches across San Diego County to the ocean. The courtyard is filled with Adirondack chairs and a table, an apricot tree and a peach-nectarine tree, and even a Ho-Ti garden Buddha. A love for all living things is readily apparent. Breakfast is memorable at the Artists' Loft for two reasons: Chuck is a fabulous cook—he hands you a menu with almost 20 items to choose from— and the conversation is always lively and engaging and lasts two or three hours. This is a nonsmoking place, inside and out.

✪ Julian White House

3014 Blue Jay Dr. (P.O. Box 824), Julian, CA 92036. ☎ **619/765-1764** or 800/ WHT-HOUS. 4 rms. $90–$135 single or double (including breakfast and late-night sweets). MC, V. Turn off Hwy. 78 one mile south of Julian, and follow Pine Hills Road 2 miles, turn right onto Blue Jay, and right into their driveway.

This was the dream home of a contractor who put in a hand-worked curved staircase, molding, and woodwork; although it resembles an antebellum mansion, it was built in 1981. Mary and Alan Marvin, the helpful B&B hosts, are the second owners, and their family photographs, along with vintage clothing and Victorian furnishings, add a nice touch to the rooms. The old-fashioned small Blue Room, with a detached full bath, and the large honeymoon suite, with its four-poster queen-size bed and high-back bathtub, are especially popular. Three rooms (including these two) are upstairs; one is on the ground level. Guests love the peace and quiet here and can often be found lying in the double hammock under the towering pines in the backyard; communing with the deer that wander onto the property; star-gazing from the back porch; and reading, chatting, or playing backgammon and Trivial Pursuit by the sitting room's fireplace. It's a short walk from here through the woods to the Pine Hills Dinner Theatre, and Mary supplies flashlights for the walk back. William Hiese Park is 2 miles away. Smoking is allowed outside only.

Random Oaks

3742 Pine Hills Rd. (P.O. Box 454), Julian, CA 92036. ☎ **619/765-1094** or 800/BNB-4344. 2 cottages. $150–$160 Thurs–Sun, with full breakfast, $125–$135 Mon–Wed, with continental breakfast; $225 midweek special for two nights (Tues–Wed only), with a bottle of champagne on arrival, a one-hour carriage ride, and continental breakfast. MC, V. Turn off Highway 78 one mile west of Julian, and follow Pine Hills Road 1.4 miles; turn right at the white fence.

Definitely a choice for seclusion-seeking honeymooners or anniversary celebrants, Random Oaks offers two cottages, each elegantly decorated and equipped with a wet bar, a small refrigerator, a microwave, games, books on tape, snuggle blankets, robes, hairdryers, and a private deck or patio with a Jacuzzi (no TV or telephone, thankfully). The English Squire Cottage has Queen Anne furniture, a separate sitting area, bay windows, a marble fireplace with a mahogany mantle dating from 1898, and a lush green carpet. The Victorian Cottage has a period cherry bed, lovely bedside lamps, and a table beside a window. Breakfast is brought to each cottage. The owners, Shari and Gene Helsel, were in horse racing but now breed thoroughbreds. Random Oaks is set in 8 acres, with a small apple orchard in front.

Shadow Mountain Ranch

2771 Frisius Rd. (P.O. Box 791), Julian, CA 92036. ☎ **619/765-0323**. 2 rms in main house, 4 detached rooms, 1 cottage (all but one with bath). TV. $80–$90 single or double; $90–$100 cottage ($160 for 4 people). All rates include full breakfast and afternoon tea. MC, V. Turn off Hwy. 78 one mile south of Julian onto Pine Hills Road, follow it to Frisius and turn left; the ranch will be on the right.

This is one of the most unusual B&Bs I've ever seen, and owners Loretta and Jim Ketcherside have obviously had a lot of fun creating it. The Enchanted Cottage, the Gnome Home (a whimsical round room ideal for short people), and the Tree House (which lacks a tub or shower) all live up to their names. The western-theme Manzanita Cottage has two bedrooms, a full kitchen, living room, and a porch; and Grandma's Attic is a quaint choice. All rooms have coffee pots and TVs. Jim chalks up the creativity of the accommodations to the fact that he and Loretta grew up before TV. They have lived in the main house since 1970, and theirs was Julian's first B&B. Shadow Mountain Ranch, with eight head of cattle, is on 8 acres, with access to 20 more. Guests enjoy a great view over pine trees and pastures, as well as croquet, badminton, archery, horseshoes, an indoor 40-foot lap pool, and an outdoor Jacuzzi (they provide robes for the pool). The family style breakfast for a dozen people is so enormous you'll have to go into training to eat it all. The philosophy of the ranch, Loretta points out, is, "It's all yours—except my bed." Book six months ahead for weekends—while some folks might consider this place kitsch, others come back time and time again. No one under 18 is allowed, and there's no smoking in the rooms.

CAMPING

Cuyamaca Rancho State Park is only 11 miles from Julian, and a new camp store and interpretive center are located a mile from the entrance. It's another 2 miles to a little museum and park headquarters where you can stock up on maps, information, and even books to help you identify local flora and fauna. The park has more than 100 miles of trails, and you can see Mexico from Cuyamaca Peak (6,512 feet). Campsites are set in the midst of trees and scrubs; each one has a table and fire ring. Reserve a spot in **Paso Picacho** or **Green Valley Campground,** both with about 80 sites (☎ 800/444-PARK for reservations; 619/765-0755 for park information only). The camping fee is $14 in summer, $12 off-season, or $5 for day use only. They book up fast on weekends from Easter to Thanksgiving, so plan ahead. Park headquarters is open Monday through Friday from 8am to 5pm; the museum is open Monday through Friday from 8:30am to 4:30pm, Saturday, Sunday, and holidays from 10am to 4pm.

WHERE TO DINE

Julian Cafe

Main St. ☎ **619/765-2712.** Menu items $2.50–$13. MC, V. Mon–Fri 8am–7:30pm; Sat–Sun 7am–8pm. AMERICAN.

A tasty, filling chicken pie is the specialty here; buy it at lunch for $6.95 or pay $8.95 for the full dinner. Mashed potatoes come the old-fashioned way, smothered in country gravy. Other home-cooked offerings include fried chicken, liver and onions, meat loaf dinner, and a hot vegetable plate. This is a good place to bring kids; the waitresses are friendly and service is quick, even when it's packed. In the heart of town, this little place with welcoming lace curtains was built in 1882, burned in 1957, and was restored in 1978.

Julian Fondue and Cheesecake Company

1921 Main St. ☎ **619/765-2817.** Reservations advisable for dinner. Fondue $6.50 per serving. Cash only. Fri–Sat noon–9pm; Sun (and Monday holidays) noon–7pm; Mon and Thurs 6–8pm. SWISS.

You'll know you're in the right place when you see the red and white Swiss flag. Proprietor John Nyffenegger is proud of his heritage—and his grandfather, uncle, and cousins who were cheese-makers should be proud of him too. As one of California's few *authentic* fondue houses, this place is popular with Europeans and well-traveled Americans who have enjoyed this traditional Swiss dish overseas. John's fondue is made in the Bernese style with imported emmenthaler, Gruyère, and raclette cheese, as well as garlic, spices, and a blend of six Napa Valley wines. Chocolate fondue is available for dessert. There's no liquor license here, but you're welcome to bring your own wine and pay a small corkage fee. The local powers-that-be also won't let John wash dishes on the premises, so he unfortunately has to use disposable dishes and utensils. Couples who dine here will learn about the 600-year-old tradition that says if she drops her bread in the cheese he gets a kiss, if he drops his bread, he buys another bottle of wine for them to share. Either way, I figure he's going to get that kiss.

Julian Grille

2224 Main St. (at A Street). ☎ **619/765-0173.** Reservations required Fri–Sun. Main courses $10–$20. AE, MC, V. Mon 11am–3pm; Tues–Sun 11am–9pm. AMERICAN.

Julian's fanciest restaurant is in a cozy cottage with an enclosed porch. The dining room, complete with a fireplace, has lace, floral, and dusty-rose touches that look especially pretty by candlelight. The extensive lunch menu features hearty open-faced sandwiches. Dinner appetizers include prime tickler, Baja shrimp cocktail, and smoked fish. Main courses take down-home recipes and give them a creative twist; among the offerings are smoked pork chops in apple sauce (the local favorite), shrimp scampi, tenderloin, filet and prime rib, fisherman's stew, and vegetarian casserole. Dishes come with soup or salad and potatoes; children's selections are available. Beer and wine are served.

Kendall's Korner Cafe

3rd and B streets. ☎ **619/765-1560.** Menu items $4.25–$6. No credit cards. Daily 6am–5pm. AMERICAN.

This little hilltop cafe is the place to catch up on local goings-on, even if you're not local. At lunch there's a soup and half sandwich special for $4.25; they also have buffalo burgers, dinner specials, and take-out. It's a great place for early risers. Breakfast menu items include eggs, omelets, pancakes, ham, sausage, biscuits and gravy, doughnuts, and cereal. Sit inside or out on the porch.

Romano's Dodge House

2718 B St. (just south of Main). ☎ **619/765-1003.** Main courses $8.70–$14.60. No credit cards. Fri–Sat 11am–10pm (to 9pm in winter); Sun–Mon and Thurs 11am–9pm. ITALIAN.

In the historic Dodge House, this cozy place has a plank-and-beam ceiling, red-and-white tablecloths, artwork for sale, soft taped music, and a little saloon in the back. It serves individual pizzas at lunchtime only, for $5 to $6; otherwise, they're 13-inchers. All sandwiches are served with a side of pasta, and all full dinners (add a few more bucks to the main course prices) come with salad, vegetables, including great broccoli and unique candied red cabbage and carrots, and homemade bread. Sorry, no apple pie.

2 Anza-Borrego Desert State Park

90 miles NE of San Diego, 35 miles E of Julian

The sweeping 600,000-acre Anza-Borrego Desert State Park, one of the nation's largest state parks, lies mostly within San Diego County, and getting here is as much fun as being here. From Julian, the first 20 minutes of the winding hour-long drive feel as if you're going straight downhill; in fact, it's a 7-mile-long drop called Banner Grade, and it's better than the Big Dipper at Belmont Park—only you're inching along at 30 miles per hour. A famous scene from the 1954 movie *The Long, Long Trailer* with Lucille Ball and Desi Arnaz was shot on the Banner Grade, and countless westerns have been filmed in the Anza-Borrego Desert.

The desert is home to fossils and rocks dating from 540 million years ago; human beings arrived only 10,000 years ago. The terrain ranges in elevation from 15 feet above sea level to more than 6,000 feet and incorporates dry lake beds, sandstone canyons, granite mountains, palm groves fed by year-round springs, and more than 600 kinds of desert plants. After the spring rains, thousands of wildflowers burst into bloom, transforming the desert into a brilliant palette of pink, lavender, red, orange, and yellow. A sense of timelessness pervades this landscape; travelers tend to slow down and take a long look around.

When planning a trip here, keep in mind that temperatures rise to as high as 115° in summer.

ESSENTIALS

GETTING THERE   By Car   Anza-Borrego Desert State Park is about a two-hour drive from San Diego: take I-15 north to the Poway exit, then Hwy. 78 east at Ramona and continue to Julian and on to the desert. Hwy. 79 to county roads S2 and S22 will also get you there.

By Bus   The Northeast Rural bus connects Julian and Borrego Springs (☎ 619/765-0145). There is no bus service out of San Diego to Borrego Springs, but you can get the Northeast Rural bus (see telephone number above) in Escondido or El Cajon (the San Diego trolley connects with the El Cajon Station).

VISITOR INFORMATION   The **Anza-Borrego Desert State Park Visitor Center** lies just beyond the town of Borrego Springs; drive through the town and watch for signs on the right. It supplies information, maps, and a 15-minute audiovisual presentation on the desert's changing faces. You can contact park headquarters at 619/767-4205 (or 619/767-4684 for recorded information); it is open October through May daily from 9am to 5pm, June through September daily from 10am to 3pm. For information on lodging, including everything from budget and camping possibilities to resorts, as well as local eateries and activities, contact the **Borrego Springs Chamber of Commerce,** 622 Palm Canyon Dr., Borrego Springs, CA 92004 (☎ 619/767-5555).

SPECIAL EVENTS   From mid-March to the beginning of April, the desert wildflowers and cacti are in bloom, a hands-down, all-out natural special event that's not to be missed. It's so incredible there's a hot-line to let you know exactly when the blossoms burst forth (☎ 619/767-4684).

EXPLORING THE DESERT

Explore the desert's startling terrain via one of its trails or self-guided driving tours; the Visitors Center can supply maps. For starters, the **Borrego Palm Canyon self-guided hike** is beautiful, easy to get to, and easy to do, leading in half an hour to a waterfall and massive fan palms. It's grand for photos early in the morning. You can also take an organized tour of the desert, offered by **Big T's Desert Tours,** based in Julian. The company offers interpretive tours of—and hikes in—the desert for $30 for half a day and $60 for a full day (☎ 619/765-1309).

Golf and Bicycling   Golfers will be content on the 18-hole, par-72 championship golf course at **Ram's Hill Country Club**. The 6,886-yard course has seven artificial lakes (☎ 619/767-5124). For a thrilling 12-mile bicycle ride down Montezuma Valley Grade, try the **Desert Descent** offered by **Gravity Activated Sports** (☎ 619/742-2294 or 800/985-4427); see "Biking" in Chapter 7.

WHERE TO STAY & DINE

Borrego Springs is a small place, but there are enough accommodations to suit all travel styles and budgets. Camping in the desert is a meditative experience, to be sure, but if you truly want to splurge, you can do that too.

La Casa del Zorro Desert Resort

Borrego Springs, CA 92004. ☎ **619/767-5323** or 800/824-1884. Fax 619/767-4782. 4 rms, 54 suites, 19 casitas. A/C TV TEL. Nov 1–May 31, $110 single or double ($90 weekdays), from $180 suite ($135 weekdays), from $220 casita ($160 weekdays). June 1–Oct 31, $90 single or double ($65 weekdays), from $105 suite ($75 weekdays), from $125 casitas ($95 weekdays). Weekday rates do not apply on holidays. Extra person $10. Tennis, jazz, holiday, and other packages available. AE, CB, DC, DISC, MC, V.

This pocket of heaven on earth was built back in 1937, and the tamarind trees that were planted back then have grown up around it. Guests can choose standard hotel rooms; suites; or a one-, two-, or three-bedroom adobe casita with a tile roof. All the casitas have a full kitchen; some have a fireplace or pool; and each bedroom has a separate bath. If you come to this desert oasis during the week, you benefit from lowered room rates.

Dining/Entertainment: The Presidio and the Butterfield dining rooms serve breakfast, lunch, and dinner; a breakfast buffet is served poolside on Saturday and Sunday during summer, indoors the rest of the year. The Fox Den Lounge features live entertainment and dancing.

Services: Room service (9am–11pm), bicycle rentals, massage therapy, child care and holiday kids' camp, in-room movies, VCR and movie rentals, free transportation to golf and the airport.

Facilities: Three pools and Jacuzzis, beauty shop, six championship tennis courts, pro shop, nine-hole putting green, horseshoes, Ping-Pong, volleyball, jogging trails, basketball, shuffleboard, 27-hole championship golf course, shop, meeting rooms.

CAMPING

The park has two developed campgrounds: **Borrego Palm Canyon,** with 117 sites, is 2$^1/_2$ miles west of Borrego Springs and near the Visitors Center. Full hookups are available, and there's an easy hiking trail. **Tamarisk Grove,** at Highway 78 and county road S3, has 27 sites. Both have restrooms with showers and a campfire program; reservations are a good idea. The park allows open camping along many of the trail routes. For more information check with the Visitors Center (☎ 619/767-4205).

3 Temecula: Touring the Wineries

60 miles N of San Diego, 60 miles NW of Julian, 90 miles SE of Los Angeles

Located over the line in Riverside County, Temecula is known for its wineries and the excellent vintages they produce. The town's name (pronounced te-*MEC*-u-la) is a Native American word meaning "where the sun shines through the mist." If you gaze out over the vineyards early in the morning or in the middle of the afternoon, the name still holds true. It's California's only West Coast town that still goes by its aboriginal name. Helen Hunt Jackson used the region as the setting for her novel *Ramona*, first published in 1884.

Temecula has a couple of unique claims to fame. Granite from its quarries (most of which closed down in 1915, when reinforced concrete became popular) constitutes most of San Francisco's street curbs. The last person sentenced to death by hanging in California was Temecula's blacksmith, John McNeil, who killed his wife in 1936.

When you turn onto Rancho California Road, all you'll see at first is new construction, but soon the vineyards come into view and the countryside turns natural again—a relief after the onslaught of progress, something relatively new to this area. Back in 1968, one vintner recalls, "If you heard a car come down Rancho California Road, you'd go to the window to see who could possibly be lost way out here."

Temecula's microclimate, allowing grapes to flourish, is due to a notch in the coastal mountains called Rainbow Gap, which lets breezes blow through from the ocean, 22 miles away. They result both in temperatures that are 8° to 10° cooler than on the coast and in a longer growing season; this lets grapes ripen more slowly. Most vineyards here are more than 1,400 feet above sea level.

Temecula is not as well known for its wines as Napa or Sonoma because those wine-producing regions have been at it 100 years longer. Franciscan missionaries planted the first grapevines here in the early 1800s, but the land ended up being used primarily for cattle raising on the 87,000-acre Vail Ranch from 1904 until 1964, when the ranch was sold. Grapevines began to take root in the receptive soil again in 1968, and the first Temecula wines were produced in 1971.

ESSENTIALS

GETTING THERE   By Car   Drive north from San Diego on I-15 for 50 miles; when the Temecula Valley comes into view, it'll take your breath away. To reach the vineyards, head east on Rancho California Road.

VISITOR INFORMATION   For information on accommodations and maps and brochures on Old Town Temecula and the vineyards, contact the **Temecula Valley Chamber of Commerce,** 27450 Ynez Rd., Suite 104, Temecula, CA 92591 (☎ 909/676-5090) and the **Temecula Valley Vintners Association,** Box 1601, Temecula, CA 92593-1601 (☎ 909/699-3626). The telephone area code for Temecula is 909.

Temecula

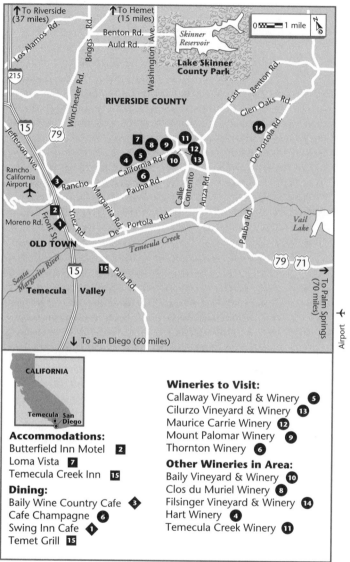

To Riverside (37 miles)

To Hemet (15 miles)

Benton Rd.
Auld Rd.

Los Alamos Rd.

Briggs Rd.

Washington Ave.

Skinner Reservoir

Lake Skinner County Park

215

Winchester Rd.

79

Jefferson Ave.

East Benton Rd.

Glen Oaks Rd.

RIVERSIDE COUNTY

De Portola Rd.

14

7
8 9 11
4 5 12
California Rd. 10 13
6

Rancho California Airport

3 Rancho

Margarita Rd.

Pauba Rd.

Calle Contento

Anza Rd.

2

Moreno Rd. 1

Front St.

Ynez Rd.

OLD TOWN

De Portola Rd.

Temecula Creek

Pauba Rd.

Vail Lake

Santa Margarita River

15

15 Pala Rd.

Temecula Valley

79 71

To Palm Springs (70 miles)

Airport

↓ To San Diego (60 miles)

1593

CALIFORNIA

Temecula San Diego

Accommodations:
Butterfield Inn Motel **2**
Loma Vista **7**
Temecula Creek Inn **15**

Dining:
Baily Wine Country Cafe **3**
Cafe Champagne **6**
Swing Inn Cafe **1**
Temet Grill **15**

Wineries to Visit:
Callaway Vineyard & Winery **5**
Cilurzo Vineyard & Winery **13**
Maurice Carrie Winery **12**
Mount Palomar Winery **9**
Thornton Winery **6**

Other Wineries in Area:
Baily Vineyard & Winery **10**
Clos du Muriel Winery **8**
Filsinger Vineyard & Winery **14**
Hart Winery **4**
Temecula Creek Winery **11**

TOURING THE WINERIES

Today the region has 11 wineries, most of them strung side by side for a few miles along Rancho California Road, producing white, red, and rosé wines. Most of them are not sold outside of California or the West, although some have made it as far as the White House. Since the wineries in Temecula are smaller than their counterparts in Northern

California, and are mostly family owned and operated, you're more likely to meet and talk with the owners when you come to their property. You're not likely to be there alone, however; 300 to 400 people can show up on the weekends.

Harvest time is usually mid-August through September, and visitors are welcome then and all the year through to tour, taste, and stock up. All the Temecula wineries welcome visitors and are well marked along the road. The wineries listed below are in the order you'll come to them as you drive along Rancho California Road.

In addition, a half-dozen local companies offer balloon rides over the vineyards, an unforgettable sight. Two that have been around for about 20 years are **DAE Flights** (☎ 909/676-3902) and **Sunrise Balloons** (☎ 800/548-9912).

Thornton Winery

32575 Rancho California Rd., Temecula. ☎ **909/699-0099.** Daily 10am–5pm (tours Sat–Sun).

The first wine-making establishment you come to along Rancho California Road is housed in a striking stone building with a waterfall and sloping lawn in front and an herb garden in back. Today Thornton produces Culbertson sparkling wine, à la méthode champenoise, as well as Brindiamo premium varietal wines. The wines, sold nationwide, have been poured at the White House for after-dinner toasts. The gift shop sells a nice range of wine-related items. There is a champagne bar with a jukebox where drinks are about $5 a glass, or you can pay $6 to taste two champagnes and two still wines. The bar opens daily at noon. Café Champagne, the vineyard's award-winning restaurant, is open for lunch and dinner and serves California cuisine (see "Where to Dine," below). The winery hosts jazz concerts from April through October.

Callaway

32720 Rancho California Rd. ☎ **909/676-4001.** Daily 10:30am–5pm; free tours at 11am, 1pm, and 3pm (11am–4pm on the hour weekends). Closed New Year's Day, Easter, Thanksgiving, Christmas.

Across the road from Thornton, in a long, low white building with brown trim, set in grounds lush with 2,500 rose bushes and orange trees, the winery is the area's oldest and now, at 720 acres, its largest. Producing wine here since 1974—nine labels in all, mostly whites— it offers the most in-depth tour. Each year 75,000 visitors look down on the operations from a raised, enclosed walkway. There's a $3 charge to sample four different wines; you get to keep the glass. The large gift shop features not only the Callaway Vintages, but also gift baskets, books on wine, aprons, cups, and T-shirts. A vine-covered picnic area overlooks the vineyards (if you didn't come prepared to dine alfresco, there's a market 4 miles down the road). Although the winery has foreign owners, its operation remains pure California.

Mount Palomar Winery

33820 Rancho California Rd. ☎ **909/676-5047.** Daily 10am–5pm Oct–March; daily 10am–6pm Apr–Sept. Free tours 1:30 and 3:30pm weekdays; 11:30am, 1:30, and 3:30pm weekends.

Turn off the main road and follow the blacktop up and over the hill to this 105-acre vineyard and its visitor center. Mount Palomar's Riesling and Chardonnay are particularly popular, along with their port and cream sherry. The sherry is aged by the Spanish method, in old brandy barrels set out in the sun for 24 to 30 months. One of the region's first vineyards, Mount Palomar has continued its innovative style by introducing two new labels; the Castelletto label features classic Italian varieties Sangiovese and Cortese, the Rey Sol label has Mediterranean varietals like Syrah and Rhone style blends.

Ribbons won in wine competitions over the years are proudly displayed on the walls. Outside, 60 tables are available for picnicking, some on a spot overlooking the property belonging to the vineyard. A shop runs a full-service deli Friday through Sunday, and deli snacks are always available. Tastings of four wines of your choice cost $2, including the souvenir glass. From the winery, you can gaze out at Mount San Jacinto and, behind it, Mount San Gorgonio, Southern California's highest mountain. John Poole opened the winery in 1975, and his eldest son, Peter, runs it. Try to come before 1pm on weekends, when people may stand five deep for tastings, and be sure to heed the quotation in the tasting room: *"Donde el vino entra, la verdad sale,"* ("Where wine enters, truth departs").

Cilurzo Vineyard & Winery

41220 Calle Contento (just off Rancho California Road). ☎ **909/676-5250.** Daily 9:30am–4:45pm.

In some L.A. circles, Vince Cilurzo may be better known as the man who has lighted the TV game show *Jeopardy!* for many years (he still does a few days a week; he also lit the Lawrence Welk Show for many years), but out in Temecula he's known as a vintner who established his 52-acre vineyard in 1968 and started producing wines in 1978. One of the most popular Cilurzo labels is the Petite Syrah, which, Vince claims, can be served with anything from tomato sauce to curry. The winery also produces a nouveau and a late harvest version of the Petite Sirah, along with a number of other wines. Unlike many other Temecula wineries, this one has no bar for tastings; instead, visitors sit in chairs and Vince Cilurzo or his wife, Audrey, serves them. A tasting of five or six wines costs $1, refundable with a purchase. Photos on the tasting room's back wall capture moments from Vince's star-studded career. A picnic area overlooks the pond.

Maurice Carrie

34225 Rancho California Rd. ☎ **909/676-1711.** Daily 10am–5pm.

It's the last of the wineries on Rancho California Road, off to your right. You can't miss the large two-story pseudo-Southern building with veranda and gazebo—a "Victorian farmhouse," Maurice Van Roekel likes to call it. She and her husband, Budd, came here to retire, but soon were producing red and white wines instead. They've named four wines after their grandchildren. The property has a wine boutique, a resident cat called Butterscotch, and a lovely oak bar trimmed with black and white tiles that draws a good afternoon crowd. The boutique sells wine and champagne glasses and insulated wine coolers, among other items. A deli section carries juice, crackers, and cold wine. Tastings are available.

EXPLORING OLD TOWN TEMECULA

A wonderful, eccentric counterpoint to the vineyards is the old part of the city of Temecula, preserved as it was in the 1890s, Western storefronts and all. It lies 4 miles west of the vineyards off Rancho California Road, stretches along 6 short blocks, and has a reputation as an antique hunter's haven.

Park at the south end of town near the Swing Inn Café or Butterfield Plaza and walk north along Main Street to Sixth Street and back, going up one side of the street and back on the other; take time to read the plaques on the old buildings along the way. Be forewarned that Temecula has become a traffic-clogged town, and you will hear the drone of cars most everywhere, even on the golf course.

One of my favorite spots in town, partly for the name, is the **Swing Inn Café,** at 28676 Front St. (see "Where to Dine," below), where a sign on the door announces *No Checks or Credit Cards.* Another sign claims that the cafe's been in existence since 1927. I asked my waitress if that was true. "Look around," she said. "Some of our customers have been here that long."

Continue along the same side of Front Street as the Swing Inn Café one block to Main Street to visit the **Temecula Valley Museum,** at 41950 Main St. On the right, the museum houses local Native American artifacts that are more than 1,000 years old, along with memorabilia from 1846 to the 1940s, and a model of the town from 1914. The museum, open Wednesday through Sunday from 11am to 4pm and by appointment, will eventually move into a new space three times larger a few blocks from here, at Sam Hicks Park, across from the post office on Moreno Drive (☎ 909/676-0021).

At 28532 Front St. (at Fifth Street), check out **Ronnie's House** for antiques. While a number of the town's "antiques" stores sell more of what I'd call "collectibles," Ronnie has the real thing—all more than 100 years old. She's originally from Brooklyn, New York, and has had her store here since 1980. Many items come from back East and beyond (☎ 909/676-4229).

At Front and Sixth streets, turn right and walk a short block to **Sam Hicks Park,** home to the "They Passed This Way" Monument and Old St. Catherine's Church, which dates from the early 1920s and is now part of the Temecula Valley Museum, which will relocate to the park.

Cross Front Street and walk back down the west side of the street. At Front and Sixth streets is the **Chaparral Antique Mall,** with more than 70 dealers under one roof (☎ 909/676-0070). Down at Front and Main streets stands the **First National Bank,** built in 1912, which managed to stay open during the Great Depression, gaining it the nickname the "Pawn Shop." The bank finally closed in 1941 and is now a Mexican restaurant. For many years, its second floor was the town's community center and dance hall.

Nearby are two plunderable antiques malls: **Morgan's Antiques,** in a brick building dating from 1891 that for 60 years was Burnham's

Store (☎ 909/676-2722), the mainstay of local ranchers, and beside it, the **Temecula Trading Post** (☎ 909/676-5759). Across the street stands the Old Welty/Temecula Hotel, built in 1882, the year the railroad came to Temecula; it burned and was rebuilt in 1891 and now is a private residence. Check out the store beside it, **Country Seller and Friends** (☎ 909/676-2322), which sells furniture and antiques.

At the southwest corner of Main and Front streets, the **Welty Building,** which dates from the 1880s, now houses a deli but it used to be a gym where Jack Dempsey worked out.

A Nature Reserve   For an outing in more than 3,000 acres of unspoiled terrain, take I-15 north to Clinton Keith Road and drive west on it for about 5 miles to the **Santa Rosa Plateau Ecological Reserve,** owned and maintained by the Nature Conservancy (☎ 909/677-6951). Here walking trails, coyotes, hawks, migrating birds, and maybe even an eagle or two await you.

Entertainment   On a spring or fall afternoon, head over to the **Thornton Winery** to hear jazz (there's an admission charge). Any time of year for a fun evening out in Old Town Temecula, indulge in a little bit of country-western dancing at **The Midnight Roundup,** 28721 Front St., opposite the Butterfield Inn (☎ 909/694-5686). This may be California's biggest saloon/dance hall, with 4,000 square feet incorporating dance areas for two-steppers, swing dancers, and line dancers. There's room left for eight pool tables; tables and chairs; and two impressive bars, one 110 feet long and the other 60 feet long. It's open Tuesday through Sunday from 6pm, with dance lessons given on Tuesday and Thursday nights; live bands are on hand from 8:30pm until 2am Thursday through Saturday nights, when there is a $5 cover; otherwise, there's a DJ. Devotees range in age from the minimum of 21 to 80-plus, most decked out in western garb; weekends are crowded. The entrance is at the back of the building.

WHERE TO STAY

Butterfield Inn Motel

28718 Front St., Temecula, CA 92390. ☎ **909/676-4833.** Fax 909/676-2019. 39 rms. A/C TV TEL. Weekdays, $35 single; $40–$43 double. Weekends $45 single; $45–$55 double. Extra person $5. AE, DISC, MC, V. Take I-15 north to Rancho California Road west to Front Street.

Within walking distance of Old Town Temecula shops, the motel (not really an inn) has an Old West facade, a small, unheated outdoor pool, and a Jacuzzi. There's complimentary coffee in the lobby in the morning. It's easy to imagine the Butterfield stagecoach pulling up any moment.

Loma Vista

33350 La Serena Way, Temecula, CA 92591. ☎ **909/676-7047.** 6 rms. A/C. $95–$125 single or double, $75–$95 mid-week (rates include full champagne breakfast). MC, V. Take I-15 to Rancho California Road east; inn is on left just beyond Callaway vineyard.

Betty and Dick Ryan came here from Los Angeles in 1988 and designed and built this tiled-roof mission-style house for their bed-and-breakfast inn. Perfectly named, it sits on a hill (*loma* in Spanish) overlooking the best vista around. From the living room, you can see the Callaway vineyard and the Santa Ana Mountains. All guest rooms have full private bath; four have private wisteria-covered balconies. Favorite balconied rooms are Sauvignon Blanc, with southwestern furnishings made of white pine and a four-poster queen-size bed; and Fumé Blanc, in California garden style with white wicker. Besides complimentary fruit and a decanter of sherry in each room, free wine and cheese are served by the fire at 6pm. A spa bubbles away on the back patio, while the front patio, a great place just to wile away the hours, has a fire pit. The property is a real oasis, with 85 rosebushes, ranunculus, daisies, Australian tea bushes, and 325 grapefruit trees. The Ryans—she actually runs the operation and does all the cooking—are both from Montana. The resident dog is a dalmatian named Casey. Old Town Temecula is 5 miles away.

✪ Temecula Creek Inn

44501 Rainbow Canyon Rd., Temecula, CA 92592. ☎ **909/694-1000** or 800/962-7335. Fax 714/676-3422. 70 rms (34 nonsmoking), 10 junior suites. A/C MINIBAR TV TEL. Sun–Thurs $115 single or double; from $135 junior suite. Fri–Sat $125 single or double; $150 junior suite. Golf and wine-country packages available. AE, DC, DISC, MC, V. From San Diego, take I-15 north to exit 79 (Indio); turn right off the exit ramp and proceed to Pala Road; turn right, go over a little bridge, then take an immediate right onto Rainbow Canyon Road; entrance to inn is ¹/₂ mile from here and well marked.

This small resort is more a country lodge than an inn, its inviting lobby replete with adobe walls, leather couch, Native American artifacts, and fireplace. Rooms in five two-story understated buildings all have restful views, as well as custom-designed Native American–inspired furnishings that creatively combine art, muted colors, and textures. Junior suites are oversize corner rooms with sitting areas, in-room safes, two balconies, and floor-to-ceiling windows. The TV is hidden away quite cleverly (under a piece of sculpture), and you'll luxuriate in down pillows, unless you're allergic. Magnolia trees line the walkway from the resort's lobby to the restaurant. There are no porters, but you can drive up close to many of the rooms.

Dining/Entertainment: The Temet Grill (see "Where to Dine," below) is outstanding; breakfast, lunch, dinner, and Sunday brunch are offered. There is live music nightly in the lounge adjoining the restaurant. Food and cocktail service is available poolside.

Services: Laundry/dry cleaning, complimentary newspaper in lobby.

Facilities: Hairdryer and magnifying mirror in baths, coffee and tea in room (including beans and a grinder), in-room safe, cribs. Outdoor pool, barbecue under live oaks, 27 holes of golf, driving range, volleyball, croquet, two tennis courts, golf and tennis pro shop, meeting rooms.

WHERE TO DINE

Baily Wine Country Cafe

27644 Ynez Rd. (in Miller's Outpost shopping center at Rancho California Road). ☎ **909/676-9567.** Reservations recommended, especially on weekends. Main courses $8.75–$19. AE, CB, DC, MC, V. Mon–Thurs and Sun 11:30am–9pm, Fri–Sat 11:30am–9:30pm. CALIFORNIA/CONTINENTAL.

If you aren't interested in winery tours and tastings, just come here. Baily's has the largest selection of Temecula Valley wines anywhere, including those from the Baily family's own winery on Rancho California Road. To show them off to best advantage, the cafe's chef has concocted some mouth-watering dishes, which change every few months. Consider such appetizers as crab cakes with roasted red-bell-pepper sauce and mixed greens, Caesar salad with shaved Parmesan cheese, and fresh mixed greens with balsamic shallot vinaigrette. At lunch, try the penne with roasted garlic, fresh vegetables, and tomato sauce made chunky with Italian sausage; southwestern-style grilled cheese sandwich with cilantro (a regional prize winner); and grilled chicken picata salad with mixed greens and lemon-caper vinaigrette. Dinner favorites include southwestern pork tenderloin with garlic mashed potatoes; salmon Wellington with cucumber and papaya relish and fresh vegetables, and chicken ravioli in a basil pesto. Finish off the meal with Carol Baily's white chocolate cheesecake, a top choice with local diners. If you're in luck, the Baily family, which is always in evidence at the cafe, will be hosting one of its celebrated Dinners in the Wine Cellar. Smoking is allowed on the patio but not inside the restaurant. They can provide picnics to go with 24 hours' notice. The restaurant is to your right and up the hill after you enter the shopping center.

✪ Cafe Champagne

Thornton Winery, 32575 Rancho California Rd. ☎ **909/699-0088.** Reservations recommended. Main courses $13–$21. AE, MC, V. Daily 11am–9pm. CALIFORNIA.

The toast of the Temecula wine country, this bistro and cafe features tasty dishes specially created to be served with nine Thornton champagnes. The wine list also features other Temecula and California labels. The lunch and dinner menus, California cuisine at its best, feature appetizers like soup du jour, warm brie en croûte with honey-walnut sauce, crab-and-shrimp strudel, and smoked salmon carpaccio. Among the entrées are angel-hair pasta primavera or angel-hair seafood pasta, mesquite-grilled tuna, and baked pecan chicken. The list of mesquite-grilled entrées expands at dinner, and at lunch tempting lighter fare includes hearty salads and sandwiches filled with mesquite-grilled hamburger, steak, or chicken. The setting, overlooking the vineyard, is sublime. It's a small place, so do reserve ahead. If you want really good food, you're going to like it here.

Temet Grill

In the Temecula Creek Inn, 44501 Rainbow Canyon Rd. ☎ **909/676-5631.** Reservations recommended. Main courses $15.50–$19.50. AE, DC, DISC, MC, V. Mon–Sat 6:30am–10pm, Sun 6am–10pm. CALIFORNIA/SOUTHWESTERN.

The Temet Grill is outstanding, from the service to the California wine country cuisine to the view beyond the dramatic window wall. The very attractive dining room has five striking chandeliers, Native American artifacts in glass cases, and floor-to-ceiling picture windows overlooking the golf course. The menu changes frequently, with house specialties like grilled tortilla pizza or grilled chiles rellenos with chipotle salsa. Main courses might include roasted sea bass in a five-spice crust, sautéed or grilled chicken breast with beer mustard and chipotle hollandaise, or grilled swordfish or steak. All the dishes are creatively presented. The wine list emphasizes California vintages, along with some from Oregon and Washington and a few French champagnes.

4 Baja California: Exploring More of Mexico

If you have a car or rent one, you can easily venture into Baja California for a getaway of a few days. Since 1991, American car-rental companies have allowed their cars to be driven into Baja. Avis (☎ 619/231-7155) and many other rental car companies let their cars go as far south as the 28th parallel, the dividing line between the states of Baja North and Baja South. Bob Baker Ford allows its cars to be driven the entire 1,000-mile stretch of the Baja peninsula (☎ 619/297-5001). Many other companies offer rentals to Baja, as well, so do a little comparison shopping before you sign a rental agreement. Whether you drive your own car or a rented one, you'll need Mexican auto insurance in addition to your own; it's available at the border in San Ysidro, or through the car-rental companies.

It takes relatively little time to cross the international border in Tijuana, but be prepared for a delay of an hour or more on your return to San Diego; if you take local buses down the Baja coast, which is possible, the delays come en route rather than at the border.

You can also visit Rosarito and Ensenada on a tour. Mexicoach (☎ 619/232-5049) makes daily trips.

VISITOR INFORMATION   The best source of information is **Baja California Tourism Information** (☎ 619/298-4105, or in California, Arizona, or Nevada 800/522-1516, or rest of U.S. and Canada 800/225-2786). This office provides advice and makes hotel reservations throughout Baja California.

A SUGGESTED ITINERARY   Begin your trip in Tijuana with an afternoon and maybe an overnight that includes watching some fast-paced jai alai (see "Tijuana" above for in-depth information), then head down the coast to the seaside town of Rosarito Beach, and then on to Puerto Nuevo and Ensenada.

Two roads run between the largest and third-largest cities in Baja: the scenic, coast-hugging toll road (marked "cuota") and the free but slower-going public road (marked "libre"). I strongly recommend starting out on the toll road, then following the free road along Rosarito Beach so that you can pull on and off easily to shop and look at the view. Pick up the toll road again at Puerto Nuevo for the remainder of the trip to Ensenada. Even if you don't plan to drive as far as Ensenada, at least go to an overlook called El Mirador, and slightly beyond it, because the drive is spectacular and shouldn't be missed.

ROSARITO BEACH

The main draw in Rosarito Beach, which is 36 miles south of San Diego and 20 miles south of Tijuana, is the **Rosarito Beach Hotel,** the Hotel del Coronado of Mexico. The hotel came first, and the town of

Baja California

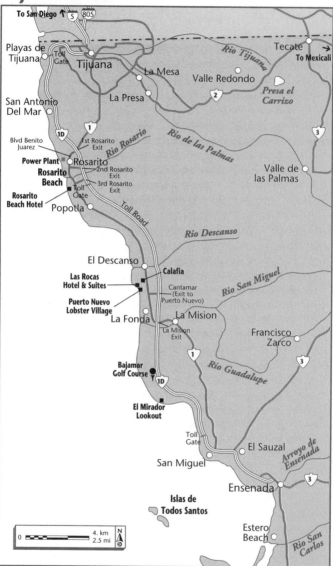

To San Diego ↑

Playas de Tijuana

Tecate

To Mexicali

Rio Tijuana

Toll Gate

Tijuana

La Mesa

Valle Redondo

Presa el Carrizo

San Antonio Del Mar

La Presa

Rio Rosario

Rio de las Palmas

Blvd Benito Juarez

1st Rosarito Exit

Rio Rosario

Valle de las Palmas

Power Plant

Rosarito

2nd Rosarito Exit

Rosarito Beach

3rd Rosarito Exit

Rosarito Beach Hotel

Toll Gate

Popotla

Toll Road

Rio Descanso

El Descanso

Calafia

Las Rocas Hotel & Suites

Cantamar (Exit to Puerto Nuevo)

Rio San Miguel

Puerto Nuevo Lobster Village

La Fonda

La Mision

Francisco Zarco

La Mision Exit

Bajamar Golf Course

Rio Guadalupe

El Mirador Lookout

Toll Gate

El Sauzal

San Miguel

Arroyo de Ensenada

Ensenada

Islas de Todos Santos

Estero Beach

Rio San Carlos

0   4. km   2.5 mi   N

Rosarito Beach, which now numbers 90,000 inhabitants, followed. And so did celebrities and heads of state. Paulette Goddard and Burgess Meredith were married here, and in 1955 Prince Ali Khan and actress Rita Hayworth brought an entourage of 24 and took over all the hotel's bungalows for several weeks. Telephone calls to Rosarito Beach from the United States are international calls and you need to add 011-52-661 before the number.

WHERE TO STAY

Rosarito Beach Hotel

P.O. Box 430145, San Diego, CA 92143. ☎ **619/498-8230** or 800/343-8582. Fax 011/52-661-21176. 275 rms, 80 suites. TV TEL. $59 in main building, $89 oceanfront rooms; from $99 suite ($10 less in winter). Two children under 12 stay free in parents' room. Packages available. AE, MC, V. Free parking.

Built in 1926 on the Baja coastline, the Rosarito Beach Hotel began as a small, 12-room inn with a big bar. The dream child of Los Angeles attorney Jacob Morris Danziger, who later became a vice president of Pan Am Petroleum in New York, it was part of the Baja scene that lured Americans, particularly Californians, with legal drinking and betting on the horses. All that would change soon enough with the repeal of Prohibition in the States in 1933 and the outlawing of gambling in Mexico in 1935. Of the three Baja resorts of that era, only the Rosarito Beach Hotel would survive as a hotel; Tijuana's Agua Caliente disappeared and Ensenada's Riviera del Pacífico became a community center.

The Rosarito Beach resort, on the other hand, expanded under the direction of Manuel Barbachano, a Mexican businessman credited with bringing electricity and television to Tijuana, Tecate, Ensenada, and Mexicali. In 1937 the present owner, Hugo Torres Chabert, took over, and the hotel was remodeled by a Belgian architect—tiles, murals, and painted rafters were added generously throughout. From 1937 to 1939 Mexican artist Matias Santoyo created the striking murals in the lobby. The old man with his dog depicted in the mural on the south wall was actually a mason who kept a vigilant eye on the progress of the artist, who decided to immortalize him in the finished work.

The original rooms, in colonial Mexican decor with white stucco walls and hand-painted trim, are most inviting. They have beamed, painted ceilings, two double beds (some rooms have queen- or king-size beds), tiled baths with showers, TVs, telephones, tables and chairs, and heaters. Only the rooms in the new tower have air-conditioning.

The hotel entry features a welcoming stained-glass depiction of a Latin beach beauty and a sign reading, *Por esta puerta pasan las mujeres mas hermosas del mundo* ("Through this doorway pass the most beautiful women in the world"). The hotel is now quite popular with families.

Dining/Entertainment: Chabert's Steakhouse serves steaks and international cuisine in a mansion built by the Torres-Chabert family in 1926. The Azteca Restaurant serves breakfast, lunch, dinner, and Sunday buffet brunch, and there's an oceanside bar. The striking Sala Mexicana, with tiles, murals, and painted ceiling, has live music on Friday, Saturday, and Sunday nights, as well as a Fiesta Mexicana dinner buffet on Friday and Saturday.

Services: Room service (7:30am–10pm).

Facilities: Fully equipped European-style spa in elegant mansion; sauna, Jacuzzi, gym, aerobics classes ($10 charge per day for them); pool with a slide; Olympic-size pool trimmed in tiles; minigolf, gym, racquetball and tennis courts, playground overlooking the beach; nonsmoking rooms, meeting rooms; shopping arcade on the property.

WHERE TO DINE

While in Rosarito Beach, you may want to try **Chabert's** or the more casual **Azteca Restaurant** in the Rosarito Beach Hotel, or outside the hotel, the nearby **Cazuela del Mole** for chicken enchiladas with mole sauce and caldo de pollo (chicken broth), **Ortega's** for lobster (unless you plan to drive south to Puerto Nuevo, see below) and, across the street from it, the tiny **Tacos Meno** for delicious fish tacos. All of these places are conveniently located on the main street, Avenida Benito Juárez.

Bibi's Bakery, in Plaza Quinta, has good pastries and bread. In front of the plaza, you'll find the **tourist information kiosk,** open weekdays from 10am to 4pm, weekends from 10am to 5pm; English is spoken (☎ 2-03-96).

SHOPPING

Interiores Los Ríos, is in Rosarito Beach at Avenida Benito Juárez 25500. Owned by transplanted Californian David Lugo, who has made this his home since 1954, the shop is filled with colonial Mexican furniture and folk art. The furniture is mainly of pine, stained or hand-painted, and it can be custom-made and delivered anyplace in the United States. Pieces include chests, tables, chairs, stools, cradles, hutches, and headboards. Prices tend to be high, but the quality is excellent and you're likely to find folk art from Michoacán, Oaxaca, or Puebla on the sale rack. There are also some paintings, prints, and photographs. The shop accepts personal checks (with identification) and traveler's checks, but no credit cards. It is open daily from 10am to 6pm (☎ 2-16-51, or write 416 W. San Ysidro Blvd., Ste. L-714, San Ysidro, CA 92173).

If you love colorful Mexican fabrics and designs, drop by Nelda Stoke's fun shop, **El Último Tango,** south of Interiores Los Ríos on Avenida Benito Juárez, open Monday through Saturday from 9:30am to 5:30pm; cash is accepted, credit cards aren't (no telephone).

EVENING ENTERTAINMENT

Because the legal drinking age in Baja is 18, the under-21 crowd from Southern California tends to flock across the border on Friday and Saturday nights. The most popular spot in town is **Papas and Beer,** a relaxed come-as-you-are type club on the beach a block north of the Rosarito Beach Hotel. Even for those young in spirit only, it's great fun, with open-air tables and a bar surrounding a sand volleyball court. Music, dancing, and volleyball games all go on simultaneously, and the camaraderie is contagious. Cover charge varies depending upon the season, the crowd, and the mood of the staff. The **Salon Méxican** in the Rosarito Beach Hotel itself attracts a slightly more mature crowd, with live music on Friday, Saturday, and Sunday nights.

EN ROUTE FROM ROSARITO TO ENSENADA

The toll-free road south from Rosarito Beach passes numerous stands selling pottery, as well as new homes, beach-front condos, and resort hotels. About 6 miles south, at km 35.5, on the right, stands **Calafia,** a restaurant/bar on Descanso Bay. Here tables rest on terraces created from the cliff overlooking the sea, and the breathtaking view is not to be missed. About a mile further south, also on the right, an arched entryway will come into view, inviting you to **Puerto Nuevo**, a real treat if you're a lobster lover. That's all the dozens of eateries in this tiny seacoast community serve. About 40 years ago the local fishermen's wives began to serve lobster in their kitchens, and a tradition was born. Baja lobster is available year-round (fresh from September to March); a filling meal of lobster with beans, rice, tortillas, and fresh limes and salsa costs about $10 or more, depending on the size of the lobster. Of the many dining choices in this "colonia" my friends and I always eat ✪ at the place right across from the tiny chapel. There isn't a name on the outside, but the last time I was there it was painted blue. Don't expect to be handed a menu; everyone has the same thing. Do watch Maria and her helpers make the tortillas. Be prepared to wait for a table on weekends. Telephone calls to Ensenada from the United States are international calls and you need to add 011-52-617 before the number.

WHERE TO STAY

Hotel Las Rocas

Km 37.5 Free Road, (P.O. Box 8851, Chula Vista, CA 91912-8851). ☎ and fax **011-52-661-2-21-40,** 619/425-2682, or 800/733-6394 in the U.S. 48 rms, 26 suites. TV TEL. June–Sept, from $70 single or double; from $90 suite. Oct–May, from $49 single or double; from $83 suite. Senior discounts; packages available. AE, DC, MC, V. Take the second Rosarito exit off the toll road, then drive 6 miles south; or follow the free road south from Rosarito; it'll be on the right.

Six miles south of Rosarito, on the free road, stands the striking Las Rocas, designed by the internationally known architect José Orozco. The lagoonlike swimming pool, poolside bar, and two Jacuzzis carved into rocks emphasize the hotel's dramatic setting on a cliff overlooking the Pacific Ocean. The suites and rooms all have ocean views and private terraces. The suites also feature an enormous sunken tiled shower, fireplace, wet bar, refrigerator, microwave, and coffeemaker. Add a tennis court, restaurant, cozy piano bar, and nearby tide pools to explore, and you have one of Baja's most romantic hideaways.

Dining/Entertainment: Colorful Café Carnaval is open for breakfast and lunch from 7:30am to 3pm and has a terrace for outdoor dining. Pretty Restaurante El Meson serves Mexican and European cuisine from 3 to 10pm; Bar Olé, off the main lobby, often has piano music. Under a thatched roof, Bar La Palapa serves drinks during the day overlooking the pool and the Pacific.

Services: Room service, *Los Angeles Times* and *San Diego Union-Tribune* for sale in lobby; satellite TV.

Facilities: Outdoor pool and two Jacuzzis are open from 8am to 10pm, tennis court, gift shop.

FARTHER SOUTH

Continuing south on the free road, you will soon come to a Moorish-looking building set back from the road, at km 51, which is actually **Café Americana,** run by the Piazza family from Los Angeles, who after years of vacationing here decided to put down roots. Popular for its 21 gourmet pizzas, including traditional cheese and vegetarian, the restaurant, beautifully decorated inside, also serves meatless (and meaty) pasta dishes, lobster or chicken Alfredo, lasagne al forno, eggplant parmesan, chicken marsala, and salads at moderate prices.

Just down the free road, at km 59, is a nostalgic favorite with authentic Mexican ambience, **La Fonda,** both a restaurant and an ocean-front hotel clinging to a cliff about 25 miles north of Ensenada. It's been here since 1936 and is the perfect place for a secret getaway or a leisurely lunch or supper on the bougainvillea-covered terrace overlooking the Pacific. House specialties include black-bean soup, homemade tortillas, scalloped potatoes, spit-roasted suckling wild piglet, and fresh spring lamb. Sunday brunch, from 10am to 3:30pm, is particularly popular, and San Diegans sometimes drive south just to enjoy it and go for a stroll on the beach, accessible via a cliff-side walkway, afterward. The rooms at La Fonda are basic, with few amenities, but the location is terrific; if you stay, request a new room.

At La Fonda, you can pick up the toll road once more to drive the remaining 28 miles along the coast to Ensenada—or at least 10 or so more miles to a fantastic lookout or a beach-side campground. The free road also continues to Ensenada, but it heads inland, winding through vineyards, citrus groves, and farmland; an occasional roadside stand sells cold drinks, snacks, and homemade local cheeses—and it circumvents the dramatic view.

Eight miles along this stretch of the toll road, you pass **Bajamar Golf Course and Resort.** About a mile beyond it, you'll find **El Mirador,** a lookout over the dramatic sweep of Todos Santos Bay and the graceful curve of the Baja coastline. It was said the lookout, which has a restaurant and bar, shops, and a little playground for children, was built to keep Americans from running their cars off the cliff here to collect the insurance.

A few miles farther south on the toll road, you'll come to a sign for **Salsipuedes Bay** (the name means "leave if you can"); the dramatic scenery along the drive ends here, so you can take the exit if you want to turn around and head north again, or if you plan to do some camping, head down the near mile-long, rutted road to **Salsipuedes Campground,** set under olive trees on a cliff. Each campsite has a fire ring and costs $5 a day (day use is also $5). There's a natural rock tub with hot-spring water at the campground and some basic cottages that rent for $30 a day. There is no easy access to the beach, known for its good surfing, from the campground.

Ensenada, with its shops, restaurants, and winery, is another 15 miles away.

ENSENADA

Ensenada, 84 miles south of San Diego and 68 miles south of Tijuana is a pretty town surrounded by sheltering mountains; and it's the kind of place that loves a celebration. Most any time you choose to visit, the city is festive—be it for a bicycle race or a seafood festival.

There are a couple of **tourist information** offices in Ensenada. The one at the northern entrance to town, on your right at the beginning of the Paseo Costera, is open Monday through Saturday from 9am to 7pm, on Sunday from 9am to 2pm in winter, from 9am to 4:30pm in summer. The one at Avenida López Mateos 138, at the southern end of the tourist strip, is open Monday through Friday from 9am to 7pm, Saturday from 9am to 3pm, and Sunday from 10am to 2pm. **Taxis** park along López Mateos.

WHAT TO SEE & DO

Compared to Tijuana's Avenida Revolución, with its jumble of activity and street vendors constantly hawking their merchandise, Ensenada's main drag, **Avenida López Mateos,** is cool, calm, and collected. No bargaining goes on in the stores, but the merchandise, which is of good quality and variety, is reasonably priced. You'll find leather goods, textiles, fashions, and hand-crafted Mexican jewelry.

Among the outstanding shops in town are **Galería Sterling,** López Mateos 851, for crafts and silver jewelry; **Tesoros del Mar,** López Mateos 871, for shells galore and shell jewelry; **Artesanias Castillo,** López Mateos 656, for leather and high-quality designs in silver jewelry for which Mexico—and more specifically the town of Taxco and the Castillo name—is justifiably known; and **Tannery South,** López Mateos 675, for leather products. From the shopping street, it's easy to stroll down to the **pier** where the fishing boats go out; munch on some fish tacos sold at the stands. You can also arrange fishing trips here.

You won't be in town long before you hear the name **"Houssong."** It's the local honky-tonk cantina, at the northern end of town off López Mateos at Avenida Ruiz 113, and it's been around since 1892. Sawdust covers the floor, and local musicians are liable to be serenading anyone who sits at a table instead of at the bar. Don't expect glamour, or even doors on the stalls in the women's room. The place is open daily from 10am to 2am.

If you linger too long at Houssong's, you might need to pay a visit to the **Medicine Man** pharmacy, on López Mateos at Castillo, conveniently open daily from 9am to 9pm (☎ 8-31-54). A block away, at López Mateos and Blancarte, is one of the best restaurants in Mexico, **El Rey Sol,** which features French cuisine. It was founded in 1947 by Baja-born, Cordon Bleu–trained Virginia Geffroy (see "Where to Dine," below).

A local Ensenada attraction, **La Bufadora,** a blowhole, sends water spouting 75 feet into the air. The name means "the snort," and if you go at high tide, you'll see why. It's 16 miles south of town on Route 1 at the tip of Punta Banda.

Wine lovers may tour **Santo Tomas Winery,** Baja's oldest, established in 1888, now with a production of about 100,000 cases a year. It offers daily bilingual tours and wine tastings with cheese and bread daily. The cost is $2 per person.

There is now a restaurant, La Embotelladora Vieja, in one of the aging rooms; it serves Mediterranean-style cuisine, with an emphasis on local ingredients, and wines from Baja, Chile, and Europe (☎ 4-08-07 for restaurant). The winery is centrally located at the northern end of town, at Avenida Miramar 666 between Calle 6 and Calle 7 (☎ 8-25-09 for general information).

WHERE TO STAY

While most visitors to this part of Baja tend to stay at the large waterfront properties along Rosarito Beach, some do stay in town. The following hotels in downtown Ensenada are within easy walking distance of the shops and restaurants along López Mateos.

Remember that in Mexico a single- or double-room rate has nothing to do with people, just beds: a single room has one bed, a double has two, and you pay accordingly.

San Nicolas Resort Hotel

Avenidas López Mateos and Guadalupe, P.O. Box 437060, San Ysidro, CA 92073-7060, Ensenada. ☎ **52/617-61901** in Mexico, 619/298-4105 in California, or 800/522-1516 in California; 800/225-2786 elsewhere. Fax 52-667/64-930. 143 rms, 7 suites. AC TV TEL. $48–$68 single; $58–$88 double; from $130 suite. Extra person $10. AE, MC, V. Free parking.

This cheerful place glows with color, from the green trim of its roof to the bright green, red, and blue of the carpeting in its hallways. Rooms have balconies, most facing the Olympic-size pool lined with palms and beach chairs. Courtyard rooms, with high, wood-beamed ceilings, are particularly quiet, except for the relaxing sounds of a waterfall wafting in the window. Hallways on the second and third floors are unique and Spanish in style. Suites are large, lovely, and made for romance, with dimmer switches and large mirrors everywhere; the split-level La Condesa suite has a huge raised Jacuzzi and two living rooms.

Dining/Entertainment: Choose from a restaurant, cocktail lounge, and discotheque.

Services: Welcome margarita at the bar, room service (7am–11pm).

Facilities: Two pools, Jacuzzi, beauty salon, gift shop, travel agency.

Villa Fontana Hotel—Days Inn

Av. López Mateos 1050, Ensenada, Mexico. ☎ **52/617-83434** or 800/422-8204 in California, Nevada, and Arizona. 63 rms, 2 suites. Winter, $36 single or double, $70 suite; summer, $41 single or double, $80 suite (higher holidays). All rates include continental breakfast but do not include tax. AE, MC, V. Free parking.

This pretty downtown hotel is peach-colored, with gray-and-white trim and gabled roofs. Rooms continue the color theme; baths, usually with showers, rather than tubs, are on the small side. Some second-story rooms have balconies and A-frame ceilings with rafters. Since the hotel is right on the main street, rooms in the back tend to be quieter. There's a patio on the second story and a small pool.

WHERE TO DINE

El Charro

Av. López Mateos 475 (between Ruiz and Gastellum). ☎ **8-38-81**. Menu items $3–$12; $18 for lobster. No credit cards. Daily 11am–2am. MEXICAN.

You'll recognize El Charro by its front windows: Whole chickens rotate slowly on the rotisserie in one, while a woman makes tortillas in the other. This little place has been here since 1956 and looks it, with charred walls and ceiling made of split logs. The simple fare consists of such dishes as half a roasted chicken with fries and tortillas, or carne asada (grilled steak) with soup, guacamole, and tortillas. Giant piñatas hang from the walls above the concrete floor. Kids are welcome; they'll think they're on a picnic. Wine and beer are served, and beer is cheaper than soda.

El Rey Sol

Av. Loópez Mateos 1000 (at Blancarte). ☎ **8-17-33.** Reservations recommended for weekends. Main courses $12–$32. AE, MC, V. Daily 7:30am–10:30pm. FRENCH/MEXICAN.

Its name means the "Sun King," and the restaurant is housed in a building that is red, white, and blue on the outside and country French on the inside. Waiters wear white jackets, and tables are covered with white-and-blue linen cloths. All the ingredients in the dishes served here are fresh, many of them grown on the family farm of the restaurant's founder, Virginia "Pepita" Geffroy. Her family carries on the tradition of fine food, service, and ambience that she began in 1947. Appetizers include escargots and house pâté, and main courses feature fish and seafood—seafood puff pastry; butterfly shrimp; médaillons topped with capers and a white-wine sauce; trout amandine; and baby clams steamed in butter, white wine, and cilantro. There are some meat and Mexican dishes, such as chicken chipotle (half a chicken cooked with brandy, port wine, chipotle chiles, and cream). Lunch is a good value; along with your main course, you get homemade soup or green salad, vegetables, bread and butter, plus sorbet to clear the palate. You can choose from a French, American, or Mexican breakfast. Or enjoy cappuccino and pastries in its pretty, European-style tearoom.

Index

Now Save Money on All Your Travels by Joining

Frommer's
TRAVEL BOOK CLUB

The Advantages of Membership:

1. Your choice of any **TWO FREE BOOKS.**

2. Your own subscription to the **TRIPS & TRAVEL** quarterly newsletter, where you'll discover the best buys in travel, the hottest vacation spots, the latest travel trends, world-class events and festivals, and much more.

3. A **30% DISCOUNT** on any additional books you order through the club.

4. **DOMESTIC TRIP-ROUTING KITS** (available for a small additional fee). We'll send you a detailed map highlighting the most direct or scenic route to your destination, anywhere in North America.

Here's all you have to do to join:

Send in your annual membership fee of $25.00 ($35.00 Canada/Foreign) with your name, address, and selections on the form below. Or call 815/734-1104 to use your credit card.

Send all orders to:

FROMMER'S TRAVEL BOOK CLUB
P.O. Box 473 • Mt. Morris, IL 61054-0473 • ☎ 815/734-1104

YES! I want to take advantage of this opportunity to join Frommer's Travel Book Club.

[ ] My check for $25.00 ($35.00 for Canadian or foreign orders) is enclosed.
  All orders must be prepaid in U.S. funds only. Please make checks payable to Frommer's Travel Book Club.

[ ] Please charge my credit card: [ ] Visa or [ ] Mastercard

  Credit card number: _____

  Expiration date: ___ / ___ / ___

  Signature: _____

  Or call 815/734-1104 to use your credit card by phone.

Name: _____

Address: _____

City: _____ State: _____ Zip code: _____

Phone number (in case we have a question regarding your order): _____

Please indicate your choices for TWO FREE books (*see following pages*):

  Book 1 - Code: _____ Title: _____

  Book 2 - Code: _____ Title: _____

For information on ordering additional titles, see your first issue of the *Trips & Travel* newsletter.

Allow 4–6 weeks for delivery for all items. Prices of books, membership fee, and publication dates are subject to change without notice. All orders are subject to acceptance and availability.   AC1

The following Frommer's guides are available from your favorite
bookstore, or you can use the order form on the preceding page
to request them as part of your membership in
Frommer's Travel Book Club.

FROMMER'S COMPLETE TRAVEL GUIDES

*(Comprehensive guides to sightseeing, dining and accommodations,
with selections in all price ranges—from deluxe to budget)*

FROMMER'S $-A-DAY GUIDES

(Dream Vacations at Down-to-Earth Prices)

FROMMER'S COMPLETE CITY GUIDES

(Comprehensive guides to sightseeing, dining, and accommodations in all price ranges)

Amsterdam, 8th Ed.	S176	Miami '95-'96	S149
Athens, 10th Ed.	S174	Minneapolis/St. Paul, 4th Ed.	S159
Atlanta & the Summer Olympic		Montréal/Québec City '95	S166
Games '96 (avail. 11/95)	S181	Nashville/Memphis, 1st Ed.	S141
Atlantic City/Cape May,		New Orleans '96 (avail. 10/95)	S182
5th Ed.	S130	New York City '96 (avail. 11/95)	S183
Bangkok, 2nd Ed.	S147	Paris '96 (avail. 9/95)	S180
Barcelona '93-'94	S115	Philadelphia, 8th Ed.	S167
Berlin, 3rd Ed.	S162	Prague, 1st Ed.	S143
Boston '95	S160	Rome, 10th Ed.	S168
Budapest, 1st Ed.	S139	St. Louis/Kansas City, 2nd Ed.	S127
Chicago '95	S169	San Antonio/Austin, 1st Ed.	S177
Denver/Boulder/		San Diego '95	S158
Colorado Springs, 3rd Ed.	S154	San Francisco '96 (avail. 10/95)	S184
Disney World/Orlando '96		Santa Fe/Taos/	
(avail. 9/95)	S178	Albuquerque '95	S172
Dublin, 2nd Ed.	S157	Seattle/Portland '94-'95	S137
Hong Kong '94-'95	S140	Sydney, 4th Ed.	S171
Las Vegas '95	S163	Tampa/St. Petersburg, 3rd Ed.	S146
London '96 (avail. 9/95)	S179	Tokyo '94-'95	S144
Los Angeles '95	S164	Toronto, 3rd Ed.	S173
Madrid/Costa del Sol, 2nd Ed.	S165	Vancouver/Victoria '94-'95	S142
Mexico City, 1st Ed.	S175	Washington, D.C. '95	S153

FROMMER'S FAMILY GUIDES

(Guides to family-friendly hotels, restaurants, activities, and attractions)

California with Kids	F105	San Francisco with Kids	F104
Los Angeles with Kids	F103	Washington, D.C. with Kids	F102
New York City with Kids	F101		

FROMMER'S WALKING TOURS

(Memorable strolls through colorful and historic neighborhoods, accompanied by detailed directions and maps)

Berlin	W100	San Francisco, 2nd Ed.	W115
Chicago	W107	Spain's Favorite Cities	
England's Favorite Cities	W108	(avail. 9/95)	W116
London, 2nd Ed.	W111	Tokyo	W109
Montréal/Québec City	W106	Venice	W110
New York, 2nd Ed.	W113	Washington, D.C., 2nd Ed.	W114
Paris, 2nd Ed.	W112		

FROMMER'S AMERICA ON WHEELS

(Guides for travelers who are exploring the U.S.A. by car, featuring a brand-new rating system for accommodations and full-color road maps)

Arizona/New Mexico	A100	Florida	A102
California/Nevada	A101	Mid-Atlantic	A103

FROMMER'S SPECIAL-INTEREST TITLES

Arthur Frommer's Branson!	P107	Frommer's Where to	
Arthur Frommer's New World		Stay U.S.A., 11th Ed.	P102
of Travel (avail. 11/95)	P112	National Park Guide, 29th Ed.	P106
Frommer's Caribbean		USA Today Golf	
Hideaways (avail. 9/95)	P110	Tournament Guide	P113
Frommer's America's 100		USA Today Minor League	
Best-Loved State Parks	P109	Baseball Book	P111

FROMMER'S BEST BEACH VACATIONS
(The top places to sun, stroll, shop, stay, play, party, and swim—with each beach rated for beauty, swimming, sand, and amenities)

California (avail. 10/95)	G100	Hawaii (avail. 10/95)	G102
Florida (avail. 10/95)	G101		

FROMMER'S BED & BREAKFAST GUIDES
(Selective guides with four-color photos and full descriptions of the best inns in each region)

California	B100	Hawaii	B105
Caribbean	B101	Pacific Northwest	B106
East Coast	B102	Rockies	B107
Eastern United States	B103	Southwest	B108
Great American Cities	B104		

FROMMER'S IRREVERENT GUIDES
(Wickedly honest guides for sophisticated travelers and those who want to be)

Chicago (avail. 11/95)	I100	New Orleans (avail. 11/95)	I103
London (avail. 11/95)	I101	San Francisco (avail. 11/95)	I104
Manhattan (avail. 11/95)	I102	Virgin Islands (avail. 11/95)	I105

FROMMER'S DRIVING TOURS
(Four-color photos and detailed maps outlining spectacular scenic driving routes)

Australia	Y100	Italy	Y108
Austria	Y101	Mexico	Y109
Britain	Y102	Scandinavia	Y110
Canada	Y103	Scotland	Y111
Florida	Y104	Spain	Y112
France	Y105	Switzerland	Y113
Germany	Y106	U.S.A.	Y114
Ireland	Y107		

FROMMER'S BORN TO SHOP
(The ultimate travel guides for discriminating shoppers—from cut-rate to couture)

Hong Kong (avail. 11/95)	Z100	London (avail. 11/95)	Z101